DATA
MINING

VIKRAM PUDI
Assistant Professor
International Institute of Information Technology
Hyderabad

P. RADHA KRISHNA
Principal Researcher, SET Labs
Infosys Technologies Limited
Hyderabad

OXFORD
UNIVERSITY PRESS

OXFORD
UNIVERSITY PRESS

Oxford University Press is a department of the University of Oxford.
It furthers the University's objective of excellence in research, scholarship,
and education by publishing worldwide. Oxford is a registered trademark of
Oxford University Press in the UK and in certain other countries

Published in India by
Oxford University Press
22 Workspace, 2nd Floor, 1/22 Asaf Ali Road, New Delhi 110 002

First Edition published in 2009
15th impression 2023

ISBN-13: 978-0-19-568628-9
ISBN-10: 0-19-568628-4

Typeset in Baskerville
by Text-o-Graphics, Noida 201301
Printed in India by Rakmo Press, New Delhi 110 020

For product information and current price, please visit www.india.oup.com

PREFACE

Data mining and warehousing are recent technologies that enable the discovery of interesting patterns from large collections of data. Pattern discovery had earlier been the domain of Artificial Intelligence (AI). The failure of AI to achieve its grandiose objectives had spawned several branches of independent study including machine learning, pattern recognition, and data mining. While there is a large amount of overlap in these subjects, data mining emphasizes *human understandability* of the discovered patterns, and *scalability* of its techniques to huge stores of data such as the World Wide Web.

Researchers have been attracted towards data mining and warehousing due to the presence of practically relevant problems that are simple to state, and the possibility of very elegant, efficient, generic, and scalable solutions. Industrialists, on the other hand, have profited by the application of these techniques to decision support in complex scenarios where manual analysis alone is impractical. Today, these decision support technologies form a multi-billion dollar industry.

ABOUT THE BOOK

Data Mining covers both the foundational concepts and recent trends of the subject in a manner that is easily understood. It discusses algorithm design issues, not restricting itself to the mechanics of their working. We hope this would motivate students to pursue research in these or related areas. Towards this end, we have at several places included historical contexts and reasons that had stimulated the field to develop in different directions.

To make the book an easy read, we have avoided scholastic terms, making a deliberate effort to use sentences that are brief, to the point, and easily understood. All the basic algorithms have been illustrated with example runs on toy datasets. Concepts and techniques that had been earlier described in diverse ways have been brought to a common format. Abiding by these guidelines, we hope we have been successful in bringing out a concise book without sacrificing on comprehensiveness.

Owing to its lucid presentation and style, the book will be useful to a wide audience. It can be used as a textbook for graduate and postgraduate students of engineering (BE/BTech/MTech) and computer applications (BCA/MCA). We have tried our best to ensure coverage of topics listed in most of the engineering curricula. It can also be used as a textbook for business students (MBA) because of a clear demarcation between the sections containing technical topics such as the design and working of algorithms and other sections discussing managerial and decision-making aspects.

CONTENT AND STRUCTURE

Chapter 1 provides an introduction to data mining and warehousing from the viewpoint of its end-users. It describes the context in which these technologies are useful and the manner in which a non-technical user should use them.

Chapters 2, 3, and 4 discuss the three major data mining technologies of frequent pattern mining, classification, and clustering, respectively, along with their applications.

Chapter 5 discusses the application of pattern discovery techniques to various kinds of real-world data, such as relational, spatial, time-series, text, web, and multimedia data.

Chapter 6 and 7 cover data warehousing. Chapter 6 discusses modeling of the data warehouse, whereas Chapter 7 discusses query processing on it.

Chapter 8 describes several case studies that enable the reader to appreciate the role of pattern discovery in large applications.

Chapter 9 concludes the book by describing the future directions of these pattern discovery technologies.

There is not much dependency between chapters and they can be read in any order, with a few exceptions: Chapter 7 must follow Chapter 6. Also, it is useful to read Chapter 9 last, and Chapter 5 after Chapters 2, 3, and 4.

VIKRAM PUDI
P. RADHA KRISHNA

ACKNOWLEDGEMENTS

Writing a book is a collective effort that requires a great deal of perseverance. It would have not been possible without the implicit and explicit support of our affiliated institutes, colleagues, students, and family. They encouraged and allowed us to take this task that eats upon time which would have otherwise been spent with them. We express our sincere acknowledgement to them.

IIIT Hyderabad and SET Labs provided us a congenial environment to write and produce this book. We would like to thank our colleagues, particularly Dr Rajeev Sangal and Dr Kamal Karlapalem for providing such a constructive atmosphere.

We are grateful to those who refined our skills of analytical ability, research capability, and clear writing. For this, we would like to express our gratitude to Prof. Jayant Haritsa and Prof. Adeel Ahmad.

We are also thankful to the editorial staff of Oxford University Press for their interest and support, wealth of good ideas and suggestions, forceful requests and sweet reminders, without which this book would not have happened.

VIKRAM PUDI
P. RADHA KRISHNA

CONTENTS

1

INTRODUCTION

Pattern discovery is the prime prerequisite to intelligent behaviour.

Arguably, one of the main reasons behind maintaining any database is to enable human users to find interesting patterns and trends in it. While *data warehousing* is a technology that enables users to manually explore data in search of patterns and trends, *data mining* is a technology that automates the process of pattern discovery.

In this chapter, a user's perspective of these pattern discovery technologies is given. The chapter discusses various kinds of patterns that can be discovered and gives examples of their application. It also explores the relationships between these technologies and other fields such as artificial intelligence, statistics, and database systems. In addition, an introduction to various general issues relating to pattern discovery, including the interestingness of the discoverd patterns, the discovery of patterns from changing data, and people's privacy, is also given. Finally, the chapter throws some light on the major challenges related to research in this field.

1.1 MOTIVATION

Imagine that you own a chain of supermarkets in a city. You have digitized data of every sale in the past several years available with you (thanks to computers and bar-code technology!). How can this data be used optimally?

Until recently, when the pattern discovery technologies were not available, the enormous data collected was used mainly by the accounts and inventory departments. These departments used this data to monitor inventory and finances only. The supermarket would generate megabytes of data everyday that would eventually fill the available hard disk space and be transferred to larger back-up disks or tapes. These tertiary storage spaces also would eventually be filled and the historical data collected (sometimes along with the tertiary storage devices) would be destroyed, as illustrated in Fig. 1.1.

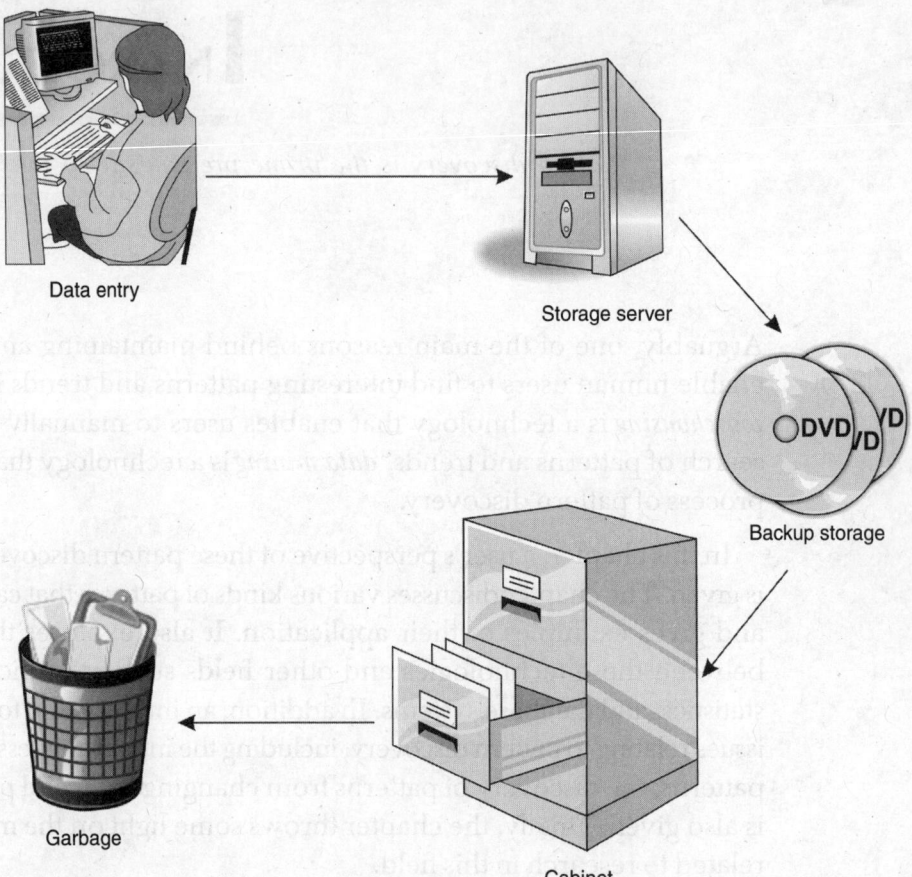

Data entry

Storage server

DVD/D

Backup storage

Garbage

Cabinet

Fig. 1.1 Typical data life cycle before the birth of pattern discovery technologies

The aforementioned scenario did not make optimal use of data. So the question that arises is: Can the obsolete historical data be put to better use? The answer, we now know, is 'yes'—there is gold in the data waiting to be mined. This gold is in the form of useful patterns waiting to be discovered. Today, the worldwide market for pattern discovery technologies exceeds four billion rupees (*source*: www.olapreport.com).

Patterns are considered useful if they are *actionable*, i.e. they suggest decisions that could improve some utility. For business applications, such as the one pictured above, utility may be measured in terms of total sales or profit. Examples of patterns that the supermarket chain owner can discover are shown in Fig. 1.2.

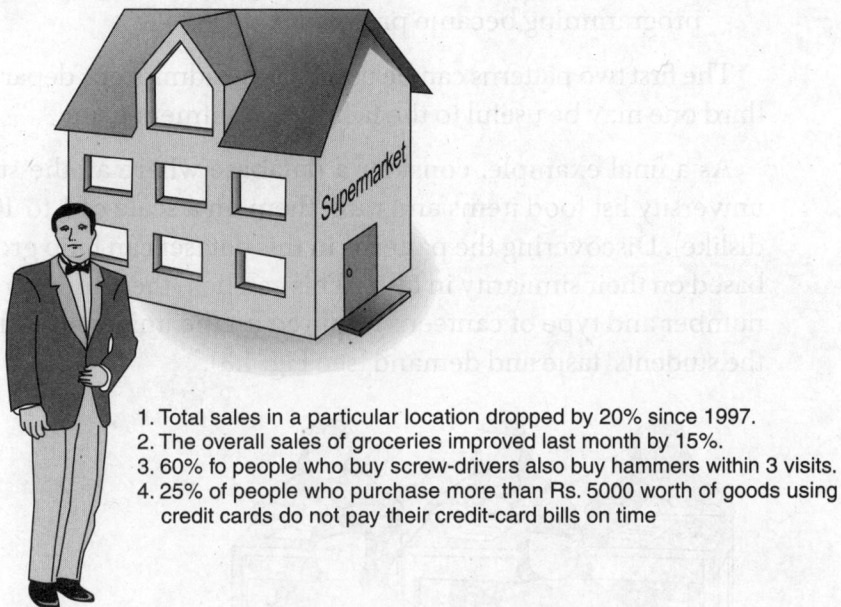

1. Total sales in a particular location dropped by 20% since 1997.
2. The overall sales of groceries improved last month by 15%.
3. 60% fo people who buy screw-drivers also buy hammers within 3 visits.
4. 25% of people who purchase more than Rs. 5000 worth of goods using credit cards do not pay their credit-card bills on time

Fig. 1.2   Supermarket patterns

Consider the first pattern (see point 1 in Fig. 1.2) that says that the total sales in a particular location dropped significantly since 1997. Upon investigation, it could turn out that in 1997 a competing supermarket opened up nearby. This additional information could suggest several strategies such as negotiating with the competitor, launching an aggressive advertisement campaign, or cutting down prices.

As another example, imagine that you are the director of one of the leading computer science universities. Your university receives applications from students all over the world. These applications provide the applicant's qualifications, motivation, marks in various subjects, other achievements, and contact information. You also have historical data regarding the performance of your students in previous years such as their programming skills, research publications, marks in various subjects, and their jobs after graduation. By integrating this information, you might be able to discover patterns such as given below:

• 70% of students who scored high in mathematics also scored high in C programming.

- 90% of students from region X did not do well even though they had high marks in their various subjects.

- 80% of students who scored high in mathematics and low in C programming became professors.

The first two patterns can be useful to the admissions department, while the third one may be useful to the faculty recruitment team.

As a final example, consider a database where all the students in some university list food items and rank them on a scale of 1 to 10 (1 = like, 10 = dislike). Discovering the patterns in this dataset can help group the students based on their similarity in taste. This can help the administration decide the number and type of canteens required on the university campus to cater to the students' taste and demand (see Fig. 1.3).

Food preferences

There are three clusters of students based on food preferences. It is recommended to set up three canteens serving the following menus: ...

Fig. 1.3 Deciding on canteens in a university campus

1.2 DATA WAREHOUSING AND DATA MINING TECHNOLOGIES

The aforementioned scenarios are just a few simple examples of finding useful patterns. During the past several years, huge amounts of data concerning various fields have been stored, and lots more are being generated and stored in digital form. This has been made possible by the widespread use of computers and the ease with which data can be easily collected using technologies such as bar codes, radio frequency identification (RFID) tags, scanned text, digital cameras, and satellite remote sensing systems. Also, the World Wide Web offers an ever-increasing collection of data and information, most of which is known to be useful. It is humanly impossible to digest and interpret all this data without the help of automated tools.

Data warehousing is a technology that allows one to gather, store, and present data in a form suitable for human exploration. This involves *data cleaning* (removing noise and inconsistent data) and *data integration* (bringing data from multiple sources to a single location and into a common format). *On-line analytical processing* (OLAP) tools then enable us to explore the stored data along multiple dimensions, at any level of granularity, and manually discover patterns. Although this is possible using the standard relational database technology, data warehouses make the process more effective and efficient.

Knowledge discovery in databases (KDD) is the 'automatic' extraction of novel, understandable, and useful patterns from large stores of data. It is a multi-disciplinary field involving artificial intelligence, statistics, information retrieval, database technology, high-performance computing, and data visualization. Data mining, in which intelligent methods are applied to extract patterns, is an essential step in the KDD process. Other steps in the process include pre-mining tasks such as data cleaning and data integration, as well as post-mining tasks such as *pattern evaluation* (identifying the truly interesting patterns representing the knowledge) and *knowledge presentation* (presenting the discovered patterns using visualization and knowledge representation techniques).

As illustrated in Fig. 1.4, a huge amount of data is generated and stored digitally from various domains such as businesses, government organizations, research labs, and the internet. This data contains many rich patterns, which may be discovered using the pattern discovery technologies—data warehousing and data mining. The discovered patterns can be used for decision-making in businesses and the government, or for generating and testing hypotheses while conducting research. The decisions that are implemented may ultimately have an impact on the data source; for example, it could improve sales in a business. Pattern discovery is thus an iterative feedback process.

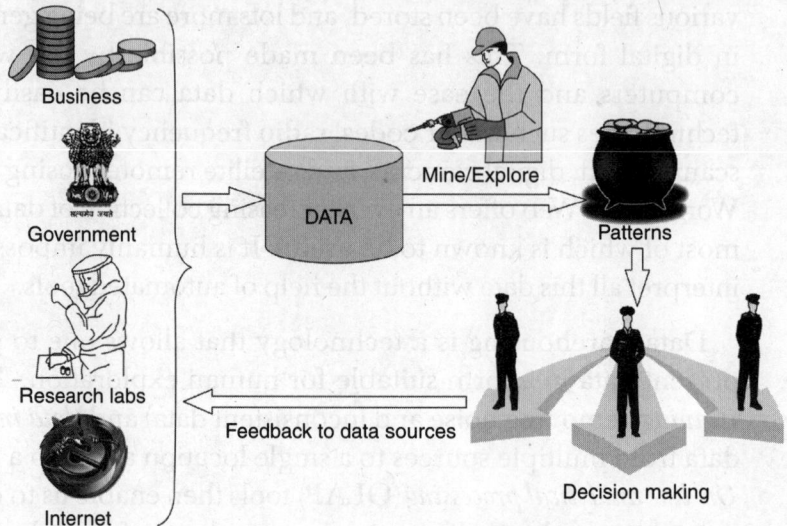

Fig. 1.4 Pattern discovery

1.3 DATA MODELS

A data model is a description of the organization or the structure of data in an information system. The structure of data can be observed at different levels of abstraction––conceptual, logical, and physical—as described below.

Conceptual data model   The manner in which users view the overall structure of the data is denoted as a conceptual data model. Entity relationship models and ontologies are examples of conceptual data models.

Logical data model   The way in which a database system views the overall structure of the data is denoted as a logical data model. Examples of logical data models include relational, object-oriented, and object-relational models.

Physical data model   The way the data is actually stored in a disk (in terms of cylinders and tracks) or in other storage media is denoted as a physical data model.

Real world data is often *unstructured* (e.g., plain text, video data, etc.) or *semistructured* (e.g., web data). Such data may need to be structured according to a specific data model to facilitate data warehousing and mining tasks. Even structured data may need to be restructured in different ways to bring out implicit patterns that may not be apparent otherwise. Data models are discussed in detail in Chapter 2.

1.4 DATA WAREHOUSING AND OLAP: USER'S PERSPECTIVE

A data warehouse is a repository of data *integrated* from multiple data sources. Each data source is a collection of data pertaining to some aspect of day-to-day operations in an enterprise. Data sources may be *volatile*, i.e. their accumulated data is removed periodically. But, the data werehouse is relatively *non-volatile* and accumulates data over several years (*time-variant*).

Data warehouse users are analysts who explore data to find useful patterns. They study how certain attributes of data elements (called *measures*) are related to other attributes (called *dimensions*). It is the user's job to initially specify which attributes of the original data to treat as measures and which to treat as dimensions. The data warehouse is then structured in terms of these *subjects*, i.e., measures and dimensions, to facilitate exploration. The data is conceptually organized as a multi-dimensional array, where each dimension corresponds to a dimension of the warehouse, and the values stored in each cell of the array correspond to the measures of the warehouse. This way of organizing data is referred to as a *multi-dimensional model* and the data repository is said to be *subject-oriented.*

The above description of a data warehouse is summed up in the following definition, originally proposed in 1990 by W.H. Inmon (known as the founder of data warehousing).

Data warehousing   A data warehouse is a subject-oriented, integrated, time-variant, and non-volatile collection of data to support the decision-making process of an enterprise.

Example 1.1   The owner of a supermarket chain is interested in identifying the factors that affect the sales of items.

There are three broad classes of operations to be carried out for the owner to make this study.

Data integration   Each supermarket location maintains its own data. This data needs to be collected and stored in a central repository for analysis. This is not a one-time task. As the data in each location changes, the central repository needs to be updated regularly. Integration may be tedious due to two reasons: (a) different locations may use different codes for the same product; (b) the same product may be sold at different prices at different locations.

Data cleaning   The use of bar code technology has made it possible for operators to enter data without errors. However, errors and inconsistencies may occasionally creep in. For example, when a new product is introduced in the supermarket, its code may not be registered in the data entry program. So whenever the product is sold, the operator may manually enter its code and price.

Aggregation   The data stored at each location is very detailed; it contains the repetitive details of items in each transaction. The supermarket owner is not interested in such fine-grained data, but instead he wants to obtain a bird's eye view of the data, looking for anything that might necessitate new policies. The data needs to be aggregated (e.g., averaged or totalled) for this purpose. Common aggregation operators include average, total, count, max, and min.

The owner suspects that the supermarket location and product category are the factors that affect the sales. Further, the overall sales seem to be changing year by year. Pondering in this manner, the owner decides that for the multi-dimensional model, the measure should be total sales and the dimensions should be *supermarket location*, *product category*, and *year*.

Once the data warehouse has been built, the owner proceeds to explore several *views* of the data. Some possible views are shown in Fig. 1.5. Here, the dimension *store* represents the specific supermarket location and the dimension *product* represents the product category. *Sales* is the measure that represents the total number of sales. In Fig. 1.5(d) the total sales for each store and each product are given, whereas in Fig. 1.5(a) the overall sales of products (across all stores) are given. In Figs 1.5(b, c), sales are aggregated over the store and product dimensions, respectively. Note that several views including the most detailed view—sales totalled separately over stores, products, and years, have not been shown in this figure. Starting from the most detailed view, the owner can explore any of these views by using OLAP operations. While viewing a particular view, the owner may be interested in more details and may request for a more detailed view; this operation is called *drilling down.* Alternatively, the owner may be interested in further aggregating along some dimension; this operation is called *rolling up.*

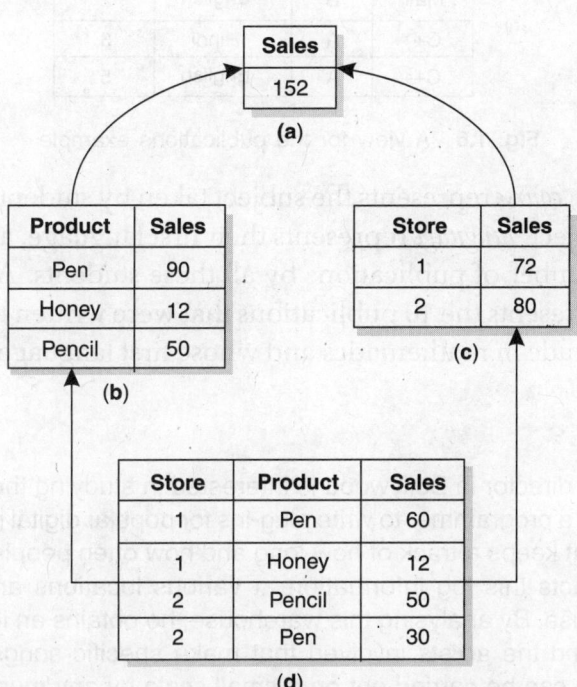

Fig. 1.5 Some possible views of the sales data

Concept hierarchies may be defined over each dimension. For example, product categories may be defined in terms of a specific model (e.g., Parker pen model 75), or an item type (e.g., all pens), or an item category (e.g., all stationary items). The term 'granularity' defines the hierarchy level at which a dimension is specified; more granularity means more detail. The owner can view the data at any level of granularity and may interactively ask to roll up to a lower level of granularity or drill down to a higher level.

The user may also specify an interest in some particular value(s) of specific dimensions. For example, the sales tables should show the total sales of items for the years 2003 and 2005 only. Computing such views is called a *slice and dice* operation. By exploring all of these views, the owner obtains a good understanding of the overall working of his supermarket chain.

Example 1.2   A university director is interested in studying how the number of publications of students is related to their grades in various subjects and their first language.

One view for this example is shown in Fig. 1.6.

Course	Grade	Language	Papers
Math	A	English	10
Math	B	English	2
C++	A	Hindi	3
C++	A	English	5

Fig. 1.6 A view for the publications example

Here, *course* represents the subject taken by students, *grade* is their grade in that subject, *language* represents their first language, and *papers* represent the total number of publications by all these students. As an example, the first row represents the 10 publications that were written by students who scored an 'A' grade in mathematics and whose first language is English.

Example 1.3 A music director in Bollywood is interested in studying the music tastes of people. He hires a programmer to write plug-ins for popular digital media players to maintain a log that keeps a track of how long and how often people listen to specific songs. He collects this log information at various locations and integrates it into one warehouse. By analysing this warehouse, he obtains an idea of the features of the music and the artists involved that make specific songs popular. Note that this exercise can be carried out on a small scale by any music enthusiast on his own data of listening patterns (data warehousing is not for only the rich and famous!). Any sufficiently large collection of data should be probed for its potential in containing interesting patterns.

Example 1.4 An organization wants a web application that can download data from the website of Indian Railways and keep track of the number of available seats in trains going to different destinations. Here the measure is the number of available seats and the dimensions could be the class of the coach (AC-2 tier, sleeper, etc.), the destination, the type of train (express, passenger, etc.), and so on. By exploring this warehouse, users can detect patterns such as 'Express trains travelling from Chennai to New Delhi typically have more vacancies in the sleeper class than the AC classes'.

Traditionally, data warehousing has been prescribed for use in business applications; however, as seen from these examples, these concepts are applicable in more general scenarios as well. In most of these examples, each record (even in the most detailed view) is actually the aggregated sum over several records in the original data sources. Hence, trying to compute views in a naïve manner directly from the original data would consume a lot of time. The original data may be scattered across several locations, in different formats, constantly updated, partly inaccurate, and incomplete. The technical challenge in data warehousing is to overcome these hurdles and enable the user to have an *interactive* response time in obtaining multi-dimensional views.

1.5 DATA MINING: USER'S PERSPECTIVE

Human beings are adept at identifying patterns, and data warehousing depends on them for this task. Data mining, on the other hand, is a tougher job since it seeks to *automatically* discover patterns in data. To do this, first the notion of 'pattern' must be precisely defined. Unfortunately, the notion of what constitutes a pattern is unclear and hence many kinds of patterns have been defined in the context of data mining. These are described in the following.

1.5.1 CLASSIFICATION MODELS

The input data for classification consists of objects each of which belongs to a specific 'class'. For example, customers who have applied for loans from a bank could be classified into three classes: *good* (repay loan on time), *ugly* (repay loan late), and *bad* (do not repay loan). Each object in the input data is defined by a number of features or attributes, which could be numeric (such as the age and annual income) or categorical (such as the gender and occupation).

The classification system is provided with the class labels of some objects known as *exemplars* and these are said to be *labelled*. The data mining task is to compute a model from the labelled objects and use this model to predict the classes of unlabelled objects.

An implicit assumption is that the class value depends, at least to a large extent, only on the features that are actually used in the input data model. If the class value depends heavily on features that are not part of the data model, then the classification model built will not be accurate even when the finest classification techniques are used. Thus the task of selecting the right features for a particular application is important.

1.5.2 REGRESSION MODELS

In classification, the field being predicted consists of discrete-valued classes. Regression is similar to classification except that the field being predicted comes from a real-valued domain. For instance, we can use regression in the earlier loan example to predict the *time* when customers will repay loans instead of merely predicting the class of customers.

Regression has numerous applications. In businesses it is commonly used to determine how the volume of sales of products can be affected if one modifies other parameters such as the cost price, quality, etc. Regression is also used to determine how different physical parameters are related (e.g., the temperature and the pressure of a liquid).

Like in classification, regression techniques also assume that the predicted field depends only on the features that are actually used in the input data model. Most regression techniques further assume some specific form for this dependency. For instance, *linear regression* assumes that the predicted field can be described as a weighted sum of the features.

1.5.3   TIME-SERIES PATTERNS

In time-series patterns, the input data consists of values of attributes as they change over time. Examples include stock market data, traces of scientific experiments, medical treatments, etc. The goal of mining such data is to form a model that can be used to predict the time series for future values of time. While this can be considered as a special case of regression, it is often considered separately because it is an important case and techniques have been developed that are suitable only for time-series prediction. There are also other studies that take a sequence as a query and retrieve similar sequences or sub-sequences from a large database of sequences.

Classification, regression, and time-series models are used for prediction and hence, designated as *predictive* models. The other kinds of patterns, described hereafter, are primarily meant to describe the input data in a succinct way and are called *descriptive* models.

1.5.4   CLUSTERS

The input data model for clustering is similar to that in classification, except that there are no class labels for objects. The task here is to cluster or group the data objects in such a manner that the objects in a cluster are very similar to each other (maximize intra-cluster similarity) and the objects that are not in the same cluster are significantly different from each other (minimize inter-cluster similarity).

Defining the exact notion of similarity between two data objects is a non-trivial task. Several similarity measures have been proposed in the research literature for various types of data objects. Applications of clustering include market segmentation for identifying the target groups of people requiring similar promotion strategies, discovering types of stars in datasets of stellar objects, and so on.

1.5.5   SUMMARIES

The input data model for summarization is typically a relational model. A summary of a dataset is a succinct representation showing data at a low level of granularity. It is obtained by identifying attributes such as the customer name, address, etc., that have too many distinct values and either removing them or performing a roll-up operation identical to that in data warehousing. Summarization is also known as *characterization* or *generalization.*

Alternatively, standard statistics (such as the mean or some other measure of central tendency) can be derived from the data to represent its summary.

1.5.6   FREQUENT PATTERNS

In frequent pattern mining, the input data consists of records, each of which contains a set (or sequence) of items. Examples include customers buying sets of items from a supermarket or users visiting a sequence of web pages. The task in this case is to find subsets (or sub-sequences) that occur more frequently than some user-specified threshold.

If X and Y are sets of items, then an association rule $X \to Y$ is a statement of the form: 'Among the records that contain set X, c% also contain set Y'. Sequential rules are similar except that X and Y are sequences instead of sets. These rules can be easily calculated once the frequent patterns have been mined.

Frequent patterns can be considered as a succinct summary of set- and sequence-valued attributes. They have been found to be useful for classification and clustering tasks especially on large datasets. These broad application areas indicate that frequent pattern mining is an important area of study. Table 1.1 sums up the above discussion on pattern types.

Table 1.1 Pattern types

Pattern Type	Input Data Model	Description	Example Applications
Classification	Data objects consisting of numeric or categorical features. Each object belongs to one among a finite set of classes.	A model learnt from input data that can be used to predict class labels of objects whose class is unknown.	Detecting e-mail spam, computer intrusion, fraud. Speech recognition. OCR.
Regression	Data objects consisting of numeric or categorical features. One real-valued feature is designated as a response variable.	A model learnt from input data that can be used to predict the value of the response variable when it is unknown.	Variation of sales with cost-price (in business). Variation of temperature with pressure (in science)
Time series	Values of attributes as they change over time.	A model learnt from input data to predict the time series for future values of time.	Stock market data, Scientific experiments, Medical prognosis
Clusters	Data objects consisting of numeric or categorical features.	Clusters of objects such that objects in a cluster are similar and objects not in the same cluster are significantly different.	Market segmentation, Spatial data segmentation
Summaries	Relational database table	Table obtained by removing or summarizing attributes with too many distinct values.	Any application having large relational tables
Frequent patterns	Records consisting of sets or sequences of items.	All sets or sequences that frequently occur within records as subsets or sub-sequences	E-commerce, census analysis, sports, Medical diagnosis, Web search

1.6 RELATED DISCIPLINES

Data mining is a multi-disciplinary area and draws upon resources from many subjects. We will discuss these subject areas one by one in the following sections.

1.6.1 ARTIFICIAL INTELLIGENCE

The task of automatically discovering patterns in data has so far been the domain of artificial intelligence (AI). Two aspects differentiate data mining techniques from those in AI. First, data mining emphasizes the human understandability of discovered patterns; whereas in AI, the discovered patterns are meant to be used by the machine itself. Second, data mining techniques are meant to be scalable to huge stores of data such as the World Wide Web. In contrast, the traditional AI approaches have mostly been researched using small 'toy' datasets that fit in the main memory.

Data mining has borrowed a good deal from AI, especially from the field of *machine learning* which concerns itself with constructing programs that automatically improve with experience. Almost all classification techniques of machine learning have been used in data mining, either directly or adapted to scale to huge datasets. Only those classification models that are not easily understandable by human users, such as some neural network techniques, have been omitted.

1.6.2 STATISTICS

Research in statistics has produced sophisticated techniques to analyse collections of data. Most of these techniques can be considered as also belonging to data warehousing and mining. Data distributions, measures of central tendency, histograms, and samples are summaries of data and hence can be viewed as descriptive patterns. Warehousing and mining can be viewed as computer-assisted, simplified statistical exploration of data.

1.6.3 INFORMATION RETRIEVAL

Information retrieval involves retrieving information from textual data such as web data or digital libraries. Many classification and clustering approaches have had their origins in this field. Notions of information content (entropy) in a collection of data, information gain of an attribute, maximum entropy models, concept hierarchies, and similarity measures have been borrowed from the field of information retrieval.

1.6.4 DATA COMPRESSION

Data compression is the computing of a concise version of data for the purpose of later retrieval of original data by decompression. In a sense, data warehousing and mining tasks strive to show the human user a concise version of the original data. This concise version is supposed to represent the patterns that the entire data follows. Due to this common goal, there is much scope for these fields to interact closely.

1.6.5   DATABASE TECHNOLOGY

Data warehousing and mining are considered to be a part of the database technology by most researchers. However, traditional database technology is generally associated with on-line transaction processing (OLTP), which is concerned with providing efficient and concurrent read/write access to the data stored in relational form. Queries in OLTP systems are ordinarily simple views of small parts of the data. These systems are highly optimized to support efficient updates to the data. Data warehouse technology on the other hand is more concerned with OLAP, where complex queries with multiple aggregations over large parts of the data are involved. Data mining also involves complex algorithms that call for the data to be read in non-traditional ways. Efficient updates are not as much an issue with OLAP systems. In spite of these differences, both data warehousing and mining technologies have the option of using relational databases for storing data.

1.6.6   HIGH-PERFORMANCE COMPUTING

Both data warehousing and mining are *highly computation intensive* because they require operating on huge quantities of data in complex ways. Hence researchers have been studying the option of using additional hardware and designing parallel algorithms to simplify these tasks. Often, several machines are required to store the huge amount of raw data itself. In such cases, it would be an added benefit to make use of all these machines for parallel processing of warehousing and mining tasks.

1.6.7   DATA VISUALIZATION

Since both warehousing and mining are user-driven tasks, the end product should be visually appealing and semantically rich in describing the discovered patterns. Various kinds of diagrams, charts, and graphs have been designed to display the output. However, sometimes neatly formatted text may be desirable. In either case, care needs to taken to ensure that the output shows all the important patterns without burdening the user with too much information. After all, the purpose of warehousing and mining is to enable humans to digest vast amounts of the available information. This is made possible by organizing the output well. Also each visual element on screen can be decorated in different ways to convey additional information. For example, if the output consists of a tree of nodes, each node can be coloured differently to indicate its type.

1.7 OTHER ISSUES

In this section, we will discuss some other issues having some bearing on the understanding, study, and simplification of data mining and warehousing concepts and techniques.

1.7.1 INTERESTINGNESS OF DISCOVERED PATTERNS

The notion of what constitutes an interesting pattern is important in the context of data mining. Because, if computer programs are to automatically discover interesting patterns, they need to know the meaning of interestingness. Even in data warehousing, the notion of interestingness is important because if it is well defined, then the interesting parts from the whole data can be highlighted to enable better exploration by human users.

Different metrics of interestingness have been developed for different kinds of patterns such as classification models, clusters, and frequent patterns. These will be explored in detail in later chapters. Here we list some generic characteristics of interesting patterns.

Stability   The stability of a pattern is a measure of the invariance of the pattern throughout the entire data collection. Patterns that hold in just some parts of the data are not so stable. Several objective metrics exist to determine stability.

Novelty   A pattern is novel if it was not known previously. Novelty is a subjective measure. Measuring novelty is possible if the users' knowledge of the data is extracted and modelled in some way.

Actionability   A pattern is actionable if its existence leads to some profitable decision. This measure is generally application dependent.

1.7.2 INCREMENTAL PATTERN DISCOVERY

In most organizations, the historical dataset is dynamic in that it is periodically updated with fresh data. For such environments, pattern discovery is not a one-time operation; it is a recurring activity, especially if the dataset has been significantly updated. Pattern discovery may need to be repeated over and over in order to evaluate the effects of the strategies that have been implemented based on previously discovered patterns. For example, a supermarket owner may decide to package soaps and shampoos together for a discount, based on a discovered pattern that showed that many people purchase soaps and shampoos together. After the strategy is implemented, the owner will want to mine new sales data to see whether or not people are availing this discount. The strategy will need to be revised, reviewed, and/or repeated in light of the conclusions drawn from the data.

In an overall sense, pattern discovery is essentially an exploratory activity and therefore, by its very nature, operates as a *feedback* process where new discoveries are guided by previous discoveries. In this context, it is worthwhile to consider using previously discovered patterns in order to discover new ones instead of processing the updated dataset from scratch. Depending on the context, it may be necessary to mine patterns from the entire updated dataset, or just from the increment, or from both.

In this context, as illustrated in Fig. 1.7, it is worthwhile to consider the possibility of incremental mining—that is, to use the previously mined patterns

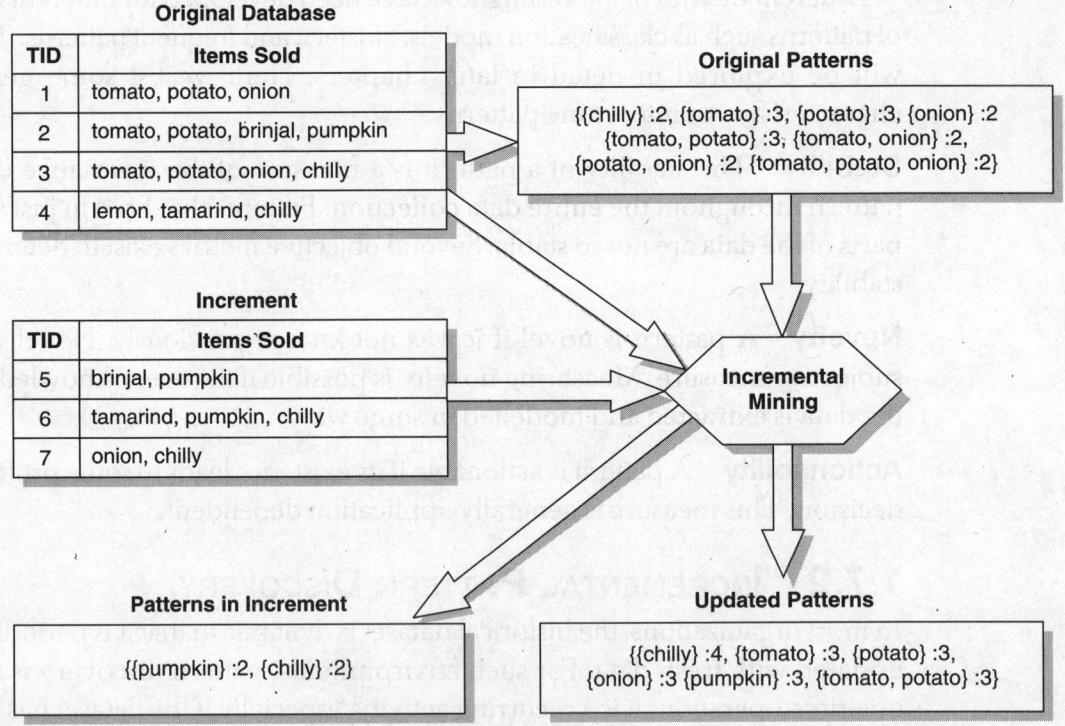

Fig. 1.7   Incremental mining

in order to perform the new mining operation more efficiently. Ideally, it is desirable if we can get away by mining only the freshly added data in order to get the updated patterns. Unfortunately, it is not always possible. Studies have shown that it is sometimes necessary to access the original data in order to mine the updated patterns. However, the incremental mining algorithms are usually able to process the original data very quickly. These techniques can result in substantial benefits, especially as the dataset grows (the original dataset will eventually be many orders of magnitude larger than the fresh data).

1.7.3 PRIVACY

The prospect of striking gold from data has led many organizations to collect additional information from the people they deal with. For example, a music website may lure you into revealing your music preferences and contact information by promising to deliver a free T-shirt. The intention may be honourable because the purpose is to discover patterns that help make decisions that ultimately benefit everyone concerned. In this case, the data you provide can be used by the website maintainers to deliver a more popular content.

However, some data could be personal (e.g., music preferences) or sensitive (e.g., medical profiles). Sometimes, revealing simple contact information could make a person victim to numerous calls from sales people. This problem is worsened by the fact that some organizations sell their data to third parties—for instance, hotels in a particular city will be interested in luring potential customers who have recently booked a flight to that city. In a futuristic scenario (perhaps not too far in the future), some web mail servers and search engines may monitor your actions and automatically decide that you are potentially interested in some product, and then alert some vendors with your contact information!

Most people are concerned about protecting their privacy. They do not reveal any data about themselves, unless necessary. Often they provide inaccurate data. Consequently, most data collected by ad hoc sales people or filled out on web forms is inaccurate.

What most people view as a problem, researchers view as an opportunity! They have been studying the privacy problem from different angles as follows:

1. How can patterns be discovered from inaccurate data?

2. How can data be modified to ensure privacy without tempering with the inherent patterns?

3. How can data be modified minimally to hide sensitive patterns?

4. Can discovered patterns be used to retrieve the original data records?

The last question can be answered affirmatively for patterns that are very specific. For example, a pattern such as 'men in ABC company who wear red hats also grow beards' would compromise privacy if there are just a few men who wear red hats.

1.8 FUTURE TRENDS

Data warehousing and mining technologies have been well researched and deployed in many real-world scenarios. Though research to develop more efficient algorithms for specific components continues, the major focus should be on integrating all warehousing and mining components together with database backends into a *simple unified framework*.

In the context of algorithms for specific components, almost all of them need the user to provide various parameters based on prior experience. Selecting values for these parameters is currently a 'black art', so techniques will be developed to obtain them automatically. Along a similar thread, research is expected to proceed to design algorithms that do not require any parameters at all. A true integration of pattern discovery technologies into database backends should be seamless. In the final scenario, the user will not have to even initiate the process of pattern discovery. Instead, the system will show the patterns as and when they emerge in the data—a technology that can well be called 'proactive data mining'.

SUMMARY

One of the main reasons behind maintaining any database is to enable the users to find interesting patterns and trends in the data. Interesting patterns must be stable, novel, and actionable. Pattern discovery is a multi-disciplinary field, drawing work from artificial intelligence, statistics, information retrieval, database systems, high-performance computing, and data visualization.

Data warehousing is a technology that enables users to explore data in search of patterns. Data warehouse users are analysts who explore the data represented using a multi-dimensional model, in search of useful patterns.

Their exploration involves complex multiple aggregation queries over the data.

Data mining automates the process of pattern discovery. Various kinds of patterns can be discovered such as classification and regression models, clusters, frequent patterns, time-series patterns, and summaries. The algorithms used to discover these patterns typically require several parameters to be input from the user. One future research direction is to automate the process of setting values to these parameters. The integration of data warehousing and mining components with the database backends into a simple unified framework is another major area open for research.

EXERCISES

Test Your Understanding

1. Differentiate between the following:

   (a) Data warehousing and Data mining

   (b) Classification and Clustering

   (c) Classification and Regression

   (d) Data mining and Statistics

2. What is incremental pattern discovery? How is it done?

3. What is frequent pattern mining? What is it useful for?

4. What is the relationship between data compression and data mining?

5. What are the various privacy related issues in pattern discovery technologies?

Improve Your Research Skills

1. In our daily life, we discover patterns in the world around us. We constantly apply classification, regression, clustering, frequent pattern mining, time-series mining, and summarization. Mention one instance in your daily life where you (perhaps subconsciously) apply each of these mining tasks.

2. Explore journals, technical magazines, and the Internet, and write a survey on the applications of pattern discovery technologies. Categorize these applications and mention what you feel is the most successful application in each category.

Improve the Field

1. Several kinds of patterns have been suggested in the research literature. Explore these and come up with the most elementary kinds of patterns from which all other kinds of patterns can be derived?

2. Describe how proactive mining software should look and behave if it is to be used by non-technical users and yet supports the discovery of complex patterns.

CHAPTER 2

FREQUENT PATTERN MINING

That which is infrequent is not worth worrying about.

INTRODUCTION

In comparison to other data mining fields, frequent pattern mining is a relatively recent development. In 1993, Rakesh Agrawal *et al* introduced this field in a paper published in the proceedings of the prestigious ACM SIGMOD international conference. This paper mentioned the task of mining *association rules*. In the subsequent year's VLDB conference, Rakesh Agrawal and Ramakrishnan Srikant published a paper on the classical algorithm named *Apriori* to solve this task. Henceforth, this field became immensely popular among researchers owing to the fact that the problem is simple to state, but difficult to solve. Several efficient and elegant algorithms have been discovered since then.

Frequent pattern mining is the most important step in mining association rules, i.e. patterns showing that some items in a dataset frequently occur along with other items. Most researchers subsequently focused only on this step as it was technically challenging. It soon became clear that frequent pattern mining was a fundamental problem in data mining, which has many more applications than just mining association rules. In this chapter it shall be illustrated that many kinds of rules can be mined from a dataset after its frequent itemsets have been discovered.

There are two types of frequent patterns—frequent sets (also known as frequent itemsets) and frequent sequences. The basic difference between them is that frequent sets are unordered collections of items, whereas the frequent sequences are ordered collections. When sets are stored in a computer, some ordering must be imposed on their items. Hence, most algorithms used to mine frequent itemsets can be slightly modified to mine frequent sequences as well. This chapter will mainly focus on frequent items. However, later in Section 2.8, the same techniques will be illustrated to be used effectively for frequent sequences.

The notion of sets and sequences is very fundamental and almost any data pertaining to real-world applications can be modelled to contain set-valued and sequence-valued attributes. It is for this reason that frequent patterns have applications in diverse areas such as marketing, medicine, sports, and agriculture. More importantly, frequent patterns have been shown to be useful in classification and clustering tasks, which by themselves have numerous applications. Further, they can be considered a good summary of set-valued and sequence-valued attributes. These broad application areas indicate that frequent pattern mining is an important area of study.

This chapter will explain frequent patterns, their efficient discovery methods from large datasets, their variations, and popular applications of all these kinds of patterns. Also the techniques to make the output of frequent itemset-mining algorithms concise, which can otherwise be very large, will be explained. You will also study how to mine frequent patterns incrementally from changing datasets.

2.1 BASIC PROBLEM DEFINITION

The input data for frequent itemset mining consists of records, each of which contains a set of items. Examples include customers buying sets of items from a supermarket, or users submitting sets of words as queries to a search engine. The task is to find all the subsets (also known as itemsets) that occur more frequently than some user-specified threshold.

Example 2.1 Consider the dataset given in Fig. 2.1 that details the transactions of a grocery store.

Transaction ID	Items Sold
1	tomato, potato, onion
2	tomato, potato, brinjal, pumpkin
3	tomato, potato, onion, chilly
4	lemon, tamarind, chilly

Fig. 2.1 Sample market-basket dataset

Here the itemset {tomato, potato, onion} has a frequency of 50% since it is present in 2 of the 4 records. The frequency of an itemset is a measure of its probability and is also known as its *support*. Typically, the user provides a minimum support threshold (denoted *minsup*) indicating that the itemsets having a support less than the minsup are not interesting. Itemsets having a support more than (or equal to) the minsup are known as frequent itemsets. Given the frequent itemsets, it is possible to discover rules such as the one given below:

Rule *R* tomato, potato → onion (confidence: 66%, support: 50%)

This rule states that 66% of records that contain tomato and potato also contain onion. The confidence of this rule is 66% because two of the three records that contain tomato and potato also contain onion. The support of a rule is the support of the union of its Left Hand Side (LHS) and Right Hand Side (RHS). In this case, it is 50% because two of the four records contain {tomato, potato, onion}.

The problem of frequent itemset mining is formally described below.

Itemset   An itemset is a set of items where each item is an element drawn from a finite set of possible items. An itemset having k items is said to have length k and is often denoted as a k-itemset.

Count   The count of an itemset X in a database D is the number of records of D that contain X as a subset.

Support   The support of an itemset X in a database D is the fraction of records of D that contain X as a subset, i.e.,

$$support(X) = \frac{count(X)}{|D|}$$

Minimum support   The minimum support (or minsup) is a user-defined threshold indicating that the itemsets whose support is less than this threshold are not interesting.

Frequent itemset   An itemset X is frequent if support(X) $\geq$ minsup.

Association rule   Given two itemsets X, Y such that $X \cap Y = \emptyset$ (empty set), an association rule is of the form $X \rightarrow Y$, and it semantically means that the presence of X is a good indicator of the presence of Y.

Confidence   Given an association rule $X \rightarrow Y$, its confidence is defined as

$$confidence\ (X \rightarrow Y) = \frac{support(X \cup Y)}{support(X)}$$

Support of rule   Given an association rule $X \rightarrow Y$, its support is defined as

$$support\ (X \rightarrow Y) = support(X \cup Y)$$

Minimum confidence   Minimum confidence (or minconf) is a user-defined threshold indicating that the association rules with confidence less than this threshold are not interesting.

Interesting association rule   An interesting association rule is one whose support and confidence is not less than the minsup and the minconf, respectively.

Example 2.2   For the table shown in Fig. 2.1 of Example 2.1, the count of the itemset {tomato, potato} is 3, whereas its support is ¾ = 0.75. If the minimum support is 0.5, then the set of all frequent itemsets is {{chilly}, {tomato}, {potato}, {onion}, {tomato, potato}, {tomato, onion}, {potato, onion}, {tomato, potato, onion}}.

The problem statement of association rule mining is to mine all the interesting association rules. As shown in the next section, this problem can be effectively reduced to the mining of all frequent itemsets.

2.2 MINING ASSOCIATION RULES

Association rules are typically mined by following a two-phase strategy as follows:

Phase 1   Frequent itemset mining (FIM) algorithms are applied on the dataset to retrieve all the frequent itemsets along with their supports. FIM algorithms are further discussed in Section 2.5.

Phase 2   In this phase, the information output by phase 1 is used to form interesting association rules. Phase 2 does not need to access the dataset and therefore, it is relatively straightforward.

Example 2.3   For the table shown in Fig. 2.1 of Example 2.1, the phases involved in mining association rules are illustrated in Fig. 2.2.

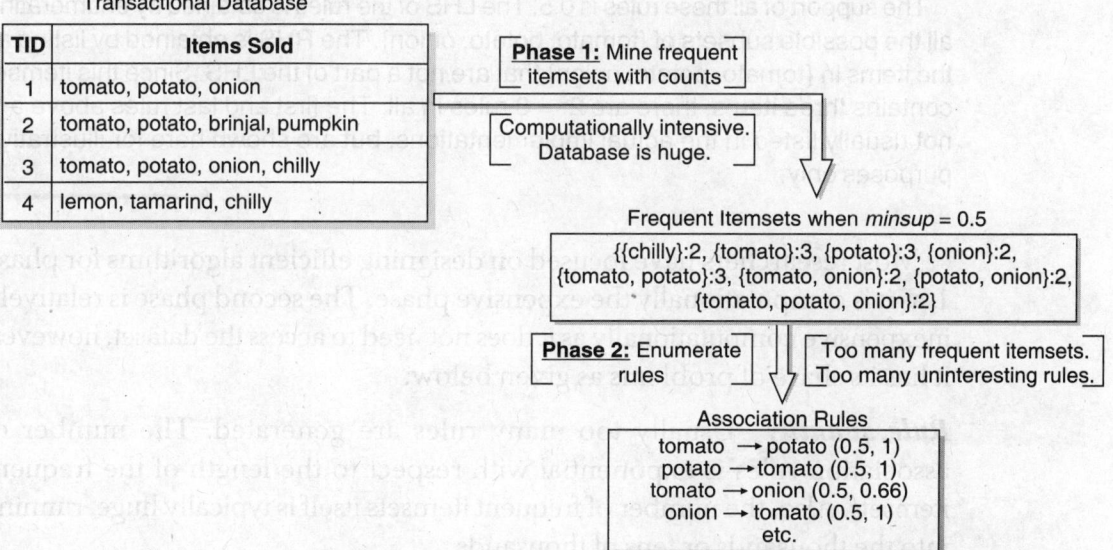

Fig. 2.2   Association rule mining phases

Lemma 2.1   The information obtained at the end of phase 1 is sufficient to output interesting association rules without further access to the dataset.

Proof   In phase 2, for each frequent itemset W obtained at the end of phase 1, enumerate all its subsets. For each subset X, output an association rule by treating X as its LHS and $W-X$ as its RHS. Since X is a subset of W, it must be present in every record that contains W and hence, must be frequent. Therefore, its support must be available after phase 1. The confidence of this rule can thus be calculated from the definition in Section 2.1 as support(W)/support(X).

Example 2.4   In case of Fig. 2.1 of Example 2.1, several rules will be enumerated from the frequent itemset {tomato, potato, onion} as shown below.

1. $\varnothing \rightarrow$ tomato, potato, onion   (confidence = support = 2/4 = 0.5)

2. tomato $\rightarrow$ potato, onion   (confidence = 2/3 = 0.66)

3. potato $\rightarrow$ tomato, onion   (confidence = 2/3 = 0.66)

4. onion $\rightarrow$ tomato, potato   (confidence = 2/2 = 1)

5. tomato, potato $\rightarrow$ onion   (confidence = 2/3 = 0.66)

6. tomato, onion $\rightarrow$ potato   (confidence = 2/2 = 1)

7. potato, onion $\rightarrow$ tomato   (confidence = 2/2 = 1)

8. tomato, potato, onion $\rightarrow \varnothing$ (confidence = 2/2 = 1)

The support of all these rules is 0.5. The LHS of the rules is obtained by enumerating all the possible subsets of {tomato, potato, onion}. The RHS is obtained by listing all the items in {tomato, potato, onion} that are not a part of the LHS. Since this itemset contains three items, there are $2^3 = 8$ rules in all. The first and last rules above are not usually listed in the actual implementations, but are shown here for illustrative purposes only.

Most researchers have focused on designing efficient algorithms for phase 1, as it is computationally the expensive phase. The second phase is relatively inexpensive computationally as it does not need to access the dataset, however, it has its share of problems as given below:

Rule quantity   Usually too many rules are generated. The number of association rules is exponential with respect to the length of the frequent itemsets. Also, the number of frequent itemsets itself is typically huge, running into the thousands or tens of thousands.

Rule quality Not all rules are actually interesting. This problem arises because most of the rules are actually redundant—they can be anticipated by a user who is aware of merely a small fraction of the rules.

Elegant solutions to these difficult problems have been proposed by a number of researchers. However, to better appreciate the importance of designing efficient alogrithms for mining frequent itemsets, their applications and related patterns types should be studied.

2.3 APPLICATIONS

The notion of a set is perhaps the most fundamental concept in modern mathematics. The real world is full of set-valued data. In general, frequent itemset mining can be applied whenever a dataset contains set-valued attributes. Frequent itemsets can be considered as a good summary of set-valued attributes because they represent the frequent (and hence significant) part of the dataset. By being a good summary, frequent itemsets can effectively replace the original dataset for most pattern discovery tasks.

Owing to this, frequent itemset mining has applications in diverse areas such as marketing, medicine, sports, and agriculture. More importantly, it has also been shown to be useful in classification and clustering tasks, especially on large datasets. These tasks by themselves have an impressive range of applications.

2.3.1 MARKETING

Marketing is a branch of business management dealing with the techniques that attract and persuade customers through such means as advertising and promotional offers. The ability to identify sets of items that the customers would want to purchase together is useful in many marketing situations, as described below:

Cross-marketing In cross-marketing, customers are given suggestions to buy additional products based on those that they have already purchased (see Fig. 2.3). For example, when a person buys the book 'Sundarakandam' from an online bookstore, 'Srimad Bhagavatham' could also be recommended. Such suggestions can automatically be provided by mining the association rules from past book-sale transactions.

Fig. 2.3 Cross-marketing

Attached mailing Promotional offers are attached to mails sent on a direct-marketing campaign of some particular product. As an example, if you receive a text message from a new mobile phone service provider to purchase their services, you are more likely to respond if they give additional exciting offers.

Catalogue design Catalogue pages that contain description of a particular product could, in addition, contain information regarding other products that are frequently purchased along with it. For example, flight tickets and hotel rooms could be advertised on the same pages.

Add-on sales Multiple products are sold together at discounted rates. By selling multiple products that are related such as dinner sets, home-theatre systems, holiday packages, etc., both the customer and the seller are likely to benefit (see Fig. 2.4).

Fig. 2.4 Add-on sales

Store layout   Items that are frequently purchased together could be placed near each other in a store so that the customers would tend not to overlook them. Alternatively, they may be placed far away from each other, so that the customers may pick up other items on the way.

2.3.2   MEDICINE

In order to help diagnose conditions in patients, modern medicine employs several imaging techniques such as X-ray, CT scans, MRI scans, computed tomography-angiography imaging, retinal imaging, etc. Expert physicians and radiologists study these images in search of the regions of interest that indicate abnormal conditions. This process is often tedious and sometimes error-prone. Subtle signs present at the very early stages of a disease are often missed. This is unfortunate as most diseases can be easily treated in their early stages.

Computer-aided detection (CAD) systems are tools designed to help physicians detect these regions of interest in medical diagnostic images. While this field has until now, largely been an academic activity of computer scientists, it is begining to be well utilized in robust commercial systems used by physicians in their clinical practice. CAD systems in combination with recent diagnostic techniques such as virtual colonoscopy have been immensely successful.

A study by Alexandru Coman *et al* in which association rules were used to detect signs of cancer from mammograms, was published in 2001 during the proceedings of the workshop on Multimedia Data Mining (MDM–2001). This study showed promising results.

Besides CAD systems, we can envisage other scenarios in which frequent itemset mining can benefit medicine, as described in the following examples:

Example 2.5   In web-based telemedicine systems, patients submit their symptoms online and receive candidate diagnoses from doctors. They may also be required to undertake several diagnostic tests such as blood tests or radiological imaging studies. These tests are often expensive.

In this context, frequent itemset mining can be used to correlate various symptoms and medical conditions of the patients over a period of time. The resulting patterns can be used to compute the risk of a specific patient having a particular condition. A risk/cost analysis can then be undertaken to decide whether this patient needs to undergo a specific test.

Example 2.6   In immunology, it is often required to test a patient for sensitivity to various allergens. These tests are expensive. The immunologist asks a detailed set of questions to the patient to decide the candidate allergens that the patient could be allergic to. The sensitivity tests are then carried out on the patient to confirm the diagnosis. This procedure is error-prone because the patients often mistakenly believe that they are allergic to certain substances and misguide the immunologist during consultation.

In this context, association rules mined from the immunological data can be very valuable. An example rule that could be obtained is 'people having allergy to latex rubber usually have allergies to banana and tomato as well'. Such rules can be used to first select a small battery of tests to conduct on the patient. The results of these tests can then be used to decide what other tests can be conducted. Such a procedure ensures that a wide variety of allergens that the patient has perhaps never heard of, are tested for.

2.3.3 Sports

Association analysis has successfully been used in basketball games using an IBM data mining product known as the 'Advanced Scout'. Raw data is collected from basketball games and fed into the Advanced Scout system. This data includes the name of the player who took a shot, the type of shot, the outcome, any rebounds, etc. Each action is associated with a time code. The software uses a technique known as Attribute Focusing. However, it is possible to use the association rule mining techniques to achieve the same purpose.

This data is mined for attributes that are significantly associated with each other. Example rules could be of the form 'When player *A* was at position *X*, player *B* missed 0% of his goal attempts. Generally, player *B* misses 50% of his goal attempts'. The rules obtained can be used by the coaches to devise strategies for better game. The system has been very successful and teams using it have reported significant improvements in their game.

An example workflow of the Advanced Scout system is shown in Fig. 2.5. It consists of data collection, pre-processing the data into a form consisting of sets of events that occur together, and finally, mining rules from the pre-processed data. The generic nature of the workflow suggests that it can be applied for any sport—hockey, cricket, chess, etc. Sports enthusiasts and coaches of every sport have collected an immense amount of data related to their sport and much of this data is available on the web to download.

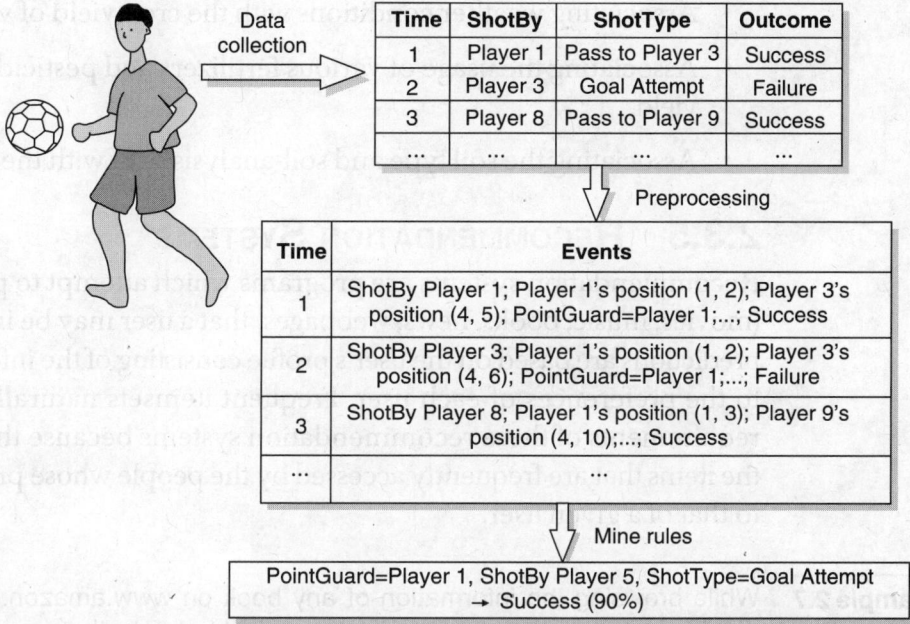

Time	ShotBy	ShotType	Outcome
1	Player 1	Pass to Player 3	Success
2	Player 3	Goal Attempt	Failure
3	Player 8	Pass to Player 9	Success
...	...	...	...

Data collection

Preprocessing

Time	Events
1	ShotBy Player 1; Player 1's position (1, 2); Player 3's position (4, 5); PointGuard=Player 1;...; Success
2	ShotBy Player 3; Player 1's position (1, 2); Player 3's position (4, 6); PointGuard=Player 1;...; Failure
3	ShotBy Player 8; Player 1's position (1, 3); Player 9's position (4, 10);...; Success
...	...

Mine rules

PointGuard=Player 1, ShotBy Player 5, ShotType=Goal Attempt → Success (90%)

Fig. 2.5   Mining rules from the basketball data

2.3.4 AGRICULTURE

In a work published in the proceedings of the ACM Symposium on Applied Computing in 2000, Jingkai Zhou *et al* mined association rules from *remotely sensed imagery data* of fields to determine the associations between the attributes of particular locations in the image and the crop yield at those locations. The resulting rules can be used to predict whether the crop yield at new locations will be good or otherwise.

Association rule mining has also been used successfully for predicting pest attacks. This is important as it alerts farmers to purchase appropriate pesticides in a timely manner, thereby avoiding crop damage. Generally, the development of small pests, such as insects, is hastened under certain climatic conditions. By finding rules that associate climatic conditions with the previous pest attacks, it becomes possible to predict new attacks. Such a system was developed by P.K. Reddy *et al*, and this work was published in the ICDM–2003. The system was originally built using neural networks, but was later enhanced to use association rules.

We can visualize several useful applications of frequent itemset mining in the domain of agriculture, limited only by the availability of data. Following are some sample applications:

- Associating weather conditions with the crop yield of various crops.

- Associating the usage of various fertilizers and pesticides with the crop yield.

- Associating the soil type and soil-analysis data with the crop yield.

2.3.5   RECOMMENDATION SYSTEMS

Recommendation systems are programs which attempt to predict the items (movies, music, books, news, webpages) that a user may be interested in. The predictions are based on the user's profile consisting of the information related to the preferences of each user. Frequent itemsets naturally fit in with the requirements of these recommendation systems because they help identify the items that are frequently accessed by the people whose profiles are similar to that of a given user.

Example 2.7   While browsing the information of any book on www.amazon.com, the website provides you with the recommendations of other books that you may be interested in. It does this based on its past history of the sales of that book—of the other books that customers have purchased along with it.

Example 2.8   Simple plug-ins can be written for popular digital media players such as iTunes, Winamp, etc. to maintain a log that keeps track of how long and how often people listen to specific songs. Each song can be modelled by a set of features—composer, artist, genre, music type, number of beats, etc.

By extracting the frequent itemsets from the logs of different users, we can obtain a profile for each user. Then for a specific user (say user X), we can identify other users with similar profiles by searching for logs that mostly contain the same frequent itemsets. If any of these other users with the similar profiles frequently listen to a song that has not yet been played by the user X, then that song can be recommended to the user X. It is quite likely that the user X will also like that song.

2.3.6   CLASSIFICATION

Researchers have recently begun to study the utility of frequent itemsets for classification tasks, starting with a seminal paper by Bing Liu *et al* published in the KDD–1998 conference. These studies have shown promising results– the resulting algorithms were highly efficient and scalable, while being as accurate as traditional approaches. Classification, by itself, has an impressive range of applications in areas such as machine learning, fraud detection, natural language understanding, etc. This makes the frequent itemset mining a very high-impact area of study.

As seen in the first chapter, the input for classification consists of data objects each of which belongs to a specific class. The task is to then construct a model from these objects such that this model can be used to predict the classes of unlabelled objects. In many classification problems, the input data objects can be represented as sets of *binary* features wherein, a feature is either present or absent for a given object. In such cases, the input data objects of each class can be mined for frequent itemsets. The frequent itemsets so obtained constitute a good summary of the features of that class. This is valuable for classification—given a new object to classify, it can be verified if its features match significantly with the frequent features of a particular class. If so, the new object can be assigned the label of that class.

Note that the above methodology is applicable even when the input data objects are represented as numeric or categorical features. As will be shown in Section 2.5.1, these features can always be converted to binary features. The reason why this classification approach is effective boils down to the highly efficient and scalable nature of modern frequent itemset-mining algorithms – they are capable of handling thousands of features and billions of objects.

Example 2.9   The above approach for classification based on frequent itemsets is illustrated in Fig. 2.6. The figure shows sample training data from the bank loan example of section 1.5.1 of chapter 1. In this example, customers apply for loans from the bank and fall into one of the three classes—good (repays the loan on time), ugly (repays the loan late) and bad (does not repay the loan). In Fig. 2.6, for ease of understanding, we have considered only two classes, good and bad. Each object in the input data is defined by a number of features or attributes, which could be numeric (such as age and annual income) or categorical (such as gender and occupation).

As shown in the figure, the training data, after removing irrelevant features such as customer identity (CID) and customer name, is converted into binary-featured data that is separated for each class. Next, the frequent itemsets are extracted from each class and they constitute the model of that class. Data of new customers, who apply for loans, is compared to the model of each class to decide which class they are likely to fall into.

2.3.7 CLUSTERING

As in classification, the input for clustering also consists of objects containing numeric or categorical features. In situations where each object can be described by a set of binary features, it becomes possible to apply frequent itemset mining. As mentioned in Section 2.3.6, the numeric or categorical features of data objects can always be converted into binary features. Hence, this methodology is always applicable.

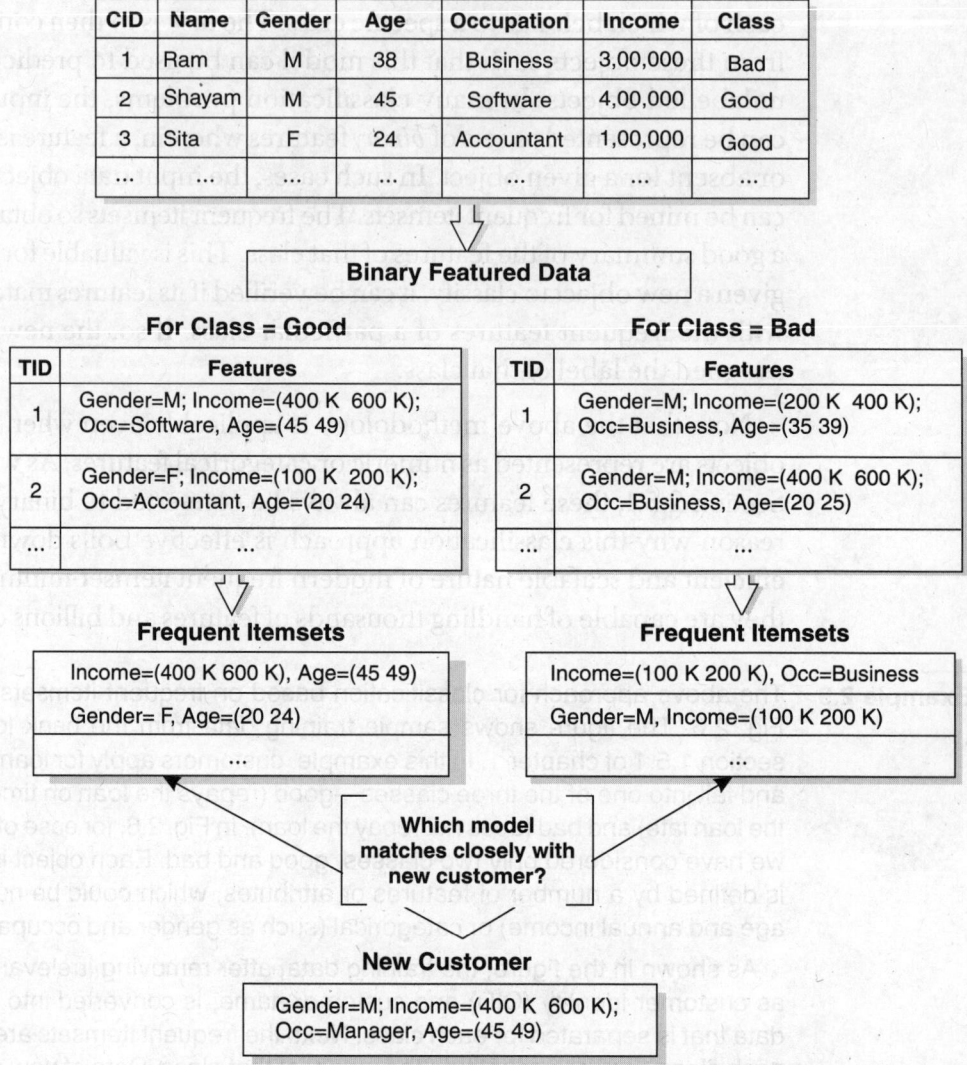

Training Data

CID	Name	Gender	Age	Occupation	Income	Class
1	Ram	M	38	Business	3,00,000	Bad
2	Shayam	M	45	Software	4,00,000	Good
3	Sita	F	24	Accountant	1,00,000	Good
...	...	...	...	...	...	...

Binary Featured Data

For Class = Good

TID	Features
1	Gender=M; Income=(400 K 600 K); Occ=Software, Age=(45 49)
2	Gender=F; Income=(100 K 200 K); Occ=Accountant, Age=(20 24)
...	...

For Class = Bad

TID	Features
1	Gender=M; Income=(200 K 400 K); Occ=Business, Age=(35 39)
2	Gender=M; Income=(400 K 600 K); Occ=Business, Age=(20 25)
...	...

Frequent Itemsets

Income=(400 K 600 K), Age=(45 49)
Gender= F, Age=(20 24)
...

Frequent Itemsets

Income=(100 K 200 K), Occ=Business
Gender=M, Income=(100 K 200 K)
...

Which model matches closely with new customer?

New Customer

Gender=M; Income=(400 K 600 K); Occ=Manager, Age=(45 49)

Fig. 2.6 Frequent itemset-based classification

The frequent itemsets mined from the data can be used to define clusters–all objects that contain a frequent itemset can be grouped together to form a cluster. The frequent itemsets chosen to form such clusters should be selected carefully to ensure that data objects across clusters do not share too many frequent itemsets. Finally, the superset-subset relationships between frequent itemsets can be used to organize these clusters into a hierarchy.

The above approach has been found to be effective for clustering text documents in a study in 2003 by Benjamin Fung *et al* published in the proceedings of the SIAM International Conference on Data Mining. In this study, each document was represented using a set of words present in the document—a set of binary features. The large data size can pose a problem for many clustering approaches—the total vocabulary of words can run into thousands and the number of documents can also be very large. In this approach, however, due to the scalability of frequent itemset mining, the clustering problem is made easily tractable.

2.4 VARIATIONS

The basic notion of frequent itemsets and association rules described so far has been extended in a variety of ways to provide more complex patterns that might be useful in real-world applications. Fortunately, all these variations can be reduced to the original problem of frequent itemset mining, with some pre-processing and/or post-processing.

2.4.1 QUANTITATIVE AND CATEGORICAL RULES

The basic problem of frequent itemset mining has been defined in terms of items, which are binary attributes, i.e., an item is either present in a record or absent. As a rule, real-world data has richer attribute types. Attributes in relational database tables can be quantitative (for example, age, income, etc.) or categorical (for example, postal code, day of the week, etc.).

The basic strategy to mine rules from such a data is to first convert these quantitative and categorical attributes into binary attributes, then apply the standard frequent itemset-mining algorithms. For quantitative attributes, this is accomplished by dividing the possible values of each attribute into *ranges* and treating each range as a binary attribute—the value of the attribute for a given record lies either within the range or outside it.

Equi-depth partitioning   Splitting an attribute into ranges is typically done using equi-depth partitioning, wherein the values of an attribute, say age, are first sorted without removing any duplicates. This results in a large list of numbers, which is equal to the number of records in the table. This list is then broken into k equal parts where k is the desired number of ranges.

For categorical attributes, a binary attribute is created for each possible value of the attribute, indicating whether that value is present in a given record. Additional optimizations are usually performed by taking advantage of the fact that only one binary attribute can be set to *true* for each quantitative or categorical attribute.

Example 2.10   Given the table shown in Fig. 2.7, a rule that could be generated is,

Name	Age	Married?	Income	NumCellPhones
Ram	25	N	1.2 lakh	1
Shyam	28	Y	2.8 lakh	2
Mohan	33	Y	4.2 lakh	2
Chandra	26	N	2.3 lakh	1
...	...	...	...	...

Fig. 2.7   Sample table with quantitative attributes

(Age: 30 ... 39), (Married: Yes), (Income: > 400K) → (NumCellphones: 2)

The quantitative attributes in this table are age, income, and the number of cell phones. Since the number of cell phones owned is a small number (say, between 0–4), it can be treated as a categorical attribute.

The attributes age and income have a large range therefore they need to be broken into smaller ranges. Suppose there are 12 records in the above table with the following values for the age attribute (25, 28, 33, 26, 35, 32, 39, 40, 25, 32, 41, 24). Then after sorting, the records will be as follows:

(24, 25, 25, 26, 28, 32, 32, 33, 35, 39, 40, 41)

If four ranges are required for the age attribute, this list will be divided into four parts of size near 3, as follows:

(24, 25, 25), (26, 28, 32, 32), (33, 35, 39), (40, 41)

As a result the ranges obtained for the age attribute are as follows:

(24–25), (26–32), (33–39), (40–41)

The quantitative and categorical rules have also been referred to as *multiple-dimensional* rules in the research literature in order to contrast them against the more basic rules that deal with a single dimension such as *buys*(bread) → *buys*(milk). All the items in such rules deal with the single dimension *buys*.

2.4.2   HIERARCHICAL RULES

In many applications, *is-a hierarchy* (or ontology) of items exists. A familiar example of ontology is the biological classification tree that classifies the entire animal and plant kingdom into classes and subclasses. Ontology is a tree structure where each node indicates a concept and the children of that node indicate specific instances of that concept.

Is-a Hierarchy   Is-a hierarchy is a tree where each node is labelled by a predicate of first-order logic, and, for any parent-child pair in the tree, if $P(x)$ and $Q(x)$ are the predicates of the parent and child, respectively, then $\forall x\ Q(x) \to P(x)$.

The actual data objects or records in any application contain very specific data, i.e., they contain elements present only at the leaves of the hierarchy. An ordinary frequent item set-mining algorithm would only use these items to form patterns. In the presence of such hierarchies, the problem is to mine patterns that include the internal nodes as well.

Hierarchical rules   Association rules where the LHS or RHS include items corresponding to the internal nodes of an is-a hierarchy are known as hierarchical rules.

Sometimes hierarchical rules are also known as *multi-level* association rules. Mining hierarchical rules is useful in applications where there are too many leaf-level items. In such applications, typically each leaf item is present in only a few records. This means that for reasonable values of the minsup threshold, most leaf-level items would not qualify as frequent. However, many internal nodes may still be frequent. Hence, it is important to mine patterns involving the internal nodes.

The basic strategy to mine hierarchical rules is to modify each data record to contain all the ancestors of the items present in the record. Following this, any ordinary frequent item set-mining algorithm can be applied. Typical implementations include extra optimizations to avoid enumerating rules that contain both an item and its ancestor, such rules are considered obvious.

Example 2.11   Consider a store that sells several hundreds of items including different types of clothing. This store maintains a database of sale transactions containing information about the items sold, the customer information, the bill date, and the payment type (cash, credit card, etc.). An example of the hierarchy of clothes is shown in Fig. 2.8.

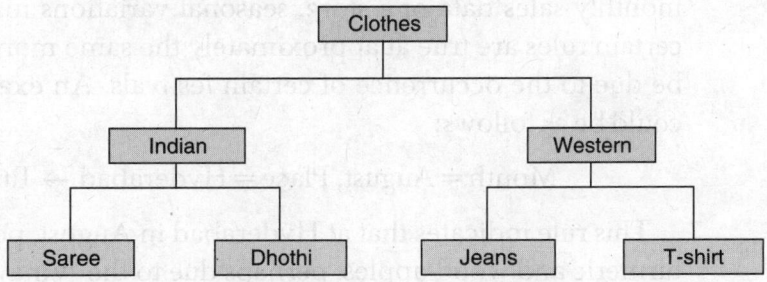

Fig. 2.8   A hierarchy of clothes

Note that the actual data records will only contain the items present at the leaves of the above hierarchy. However, the presence of a leaf in a record implies the presence of all ancestors of that leaf. As an example, if a person buys a saree, she has bought an item in the 'Indian' category, which itself is in the 'Clothes' category.

By mining for hierarchical rules, the owner of the store gets to discover rules such as,

Saree, Western → Credit Card Payment

This rule has items across various levels in the hierarchy—both at the leaf and the internal nodes. To mine hierarchical rules, each input data record is modified to explicitly include all the ancestors of items contained in it. Typical implementations include extra optimizations to avoid enumerating redundant and obvious rules that contain an item and its ancestor (for example, {Jeans → Western}).

Multiple minsup thresholds The above notion uses a single minsup threshold to mine frequent patterns across various levels in the hierarchy. However, items at the interior levels in the hierarchy have higher supports than the items near the leaves. This suggests that different minsup thresholds should be used for items at different levels in the hierarchy. This would be an extension of the notion of the hierarchical rules explained earlier. The algorithms to mine such patterns using multiple minsup thresholds were suggested by Jiawei Han in a CIKM–1995 publication. In this approach, patterns across various levels in the hierarchy need to be dealt with carefully because it is not clear which minsup threshold should be used for them.

2.4.3 CYCLIC/PERIODIC RULES

Cyclic or periodic rules are the association rules that display regular cyclic variations over time. For instance, on computing the association rules for monthly sales data of a store, seasonal variations may be observed where certain rules are true at approximately the same month each year, this may be due to the occurrence of certain festivals. An example rule of this kind could be as follows:

Month = August, Place = Hyderabad → Turmeric, Wood-apple

This rule indicates that at Hyderabad in August, people usually purchase turmeric and wood-apples, perhaps due to the 'Vinayaka Chavithi' festival. Discovering such rules and their periodicities may reveal interesting information that can be used to predict sales and make decisions accordingly.

The basic approach to mine periodic rules is to modify each data record in a pre-processing phase to include date and time-related attributes at various levels of granularity such as 'month', 'year', 'day of the week', 'day of the month', 'week of the month', etc. By following this, any standard frequent item set-mining algorithm can be applied.

2.4.4 CONSTRAINED RULES

In several situations, users may not be interested in all the association rules or frequent itemsets. They may have certain constraints that need to be satisfied by the LHS or RHS of the rules.

Example 2.12 A user may want to find associations from the itemsets whose total price is under Rs 1,000 to the itemsets whose total price is at least Rs 10,000. Such rules are interesting because they indicate combinations of the low-cost items that will trigger customers into buying high-cost items.

Another example of the constraints on rules is that the user may specify that some particular item should appear in the RHS.

One approach to mine such constrained rules is to first mine all the rules as usual and then post-process them to output only those that satisfy the user-given constraints. Additional optimizations could be applied on this basic approach by pushing the constraints into the mining process itself so that the space of the candidate itemsets is reduced.

2.5 INTERESTINGNESS

The algorithms used to mine frequent itemsets and related patterns typically generate a huge amount of output running into thousands or tens of thousands of patterns. Usually, most of the patterns generated are not interesting. These uninteresting patterns are mostly of two types: (1) obvious patterns that are implicitly known to most people and hence, are not novel; recall that novelty was one of the generic interestingness measures listed in Section 1.7.1 of Chapter 1; (2) redundant patterns that are not obvious in the beginning, but they become obvious by looking at the other patterns that have been generated.

It may seem that this problem of generating a huge amount of uninteresting patterns is easily solvable—simply decrease the values of minsup and minconf. By doing this, we should be able to obtain only a few highly interesting patterns. Unfortunately, this simple approach has drawbacks that are made evident in

Section 2.5.1 below. Therefore, to solve this problem, researchers have proposed several objective measures of interestingness that can be applied to separate out the gold from the rock. Sections 2.5.2–2.5.5 describe these measures.

2.5.1   DEFECTS OF SUPPORT AND CONFIDENCE

The traditional measure of interestingness of an itemset is its support and for association rules, it is both support and confidence. Both these measures have been shown to be defective. The defects in these measures can be clearly seen from the following simple example.

Example 2.13   Consider a population of 100 people in which there are 50 researchers and 50 non-researchers. 80 out of the 100 people are coffee drinkers and 20 are coffee abstainers. Suppose 35 researchers drink coffee and the remaining 15 do not. It follows that 45 non-researchers drink coffee and the remaining 5 do not.

From this data, we know that compared to the non-researchers, the researchers are more likely to be coffee abstainers. But, the support of the itemset {researcher, coffee drinker} is 35% whereas the support of {researcher, coffee abstainer} is only 15%. Also, the confidence of the rule 'researcher → coffee-drinker' is 70% whereas the confidence of 'researcher → coffee-abstainer' is only 30%. This is counter-intuitive.

The above example shows that support and confidence, by themselves, fail as measures of interestingness. Alternative measures of interestingness have been proposed and are discussed below.

2.5.2   INTEREST

Interest, also referred to as *correlation*, is a measure of the dependence between two sets of items. If X and Y are two itemsets, which occur independently of each other, then we would expect from the probability theory that,

$$P(X \cup Y) = P(X)\, P(Y)$$

Hence, to measure the dependence between X and Y, the interest measure I, is mathematically defined as follows:

$$I(X, Y) = P(X \cup Y)/P(X)\, P(Y)$$

If the interest value is close to 1, it means that X and Y are independent of each other; if it is significantly greater than 1, it means that they are positively correlated; and if it is significantly less than 1, it means that they are negatively correlated.

In practice, the probability of an itemset is measured by its support. In the above form, the interest function is analogous to confidence, where it measures the relationship between two sets of items. To measure the interestingness of a single itemset $X = \{x_1, x_2, \ldots x_k\}$, the following form could be used:

$$I(X) = P(X)/P(\{x_1\})\, P(\{x_2\})\ldots P(\{x_k\})$$

Example 2.14   From the data distribution in Example 2.13,

I(researcher, coffee drinker) = P(researcher, coffee drinker)/P (researcher) P(coffee drinker)

$$= (35/100)/(50/100)\,(80/100)$$

$$= 0.875$$

This clearly shows that being a researcher and being a coffee drinker are negatively correlated.

While this interest measure overcomes the drawbacks of support and confidence, it has two disadvantages; (1) it does not advise whether the correlation computed is statistically significant or not. In other words, it does not advise if the data is strongly indicative of a relationship between the researchers and the coffee drinkers, or if the computed correlation is possibly obtained by random chance, and (2) interest is a symmetric function and hence it cannot be used to form rules of the kind 'X (statistically) implies Y'. This is because implication is not a symmetric relation–'X may imply Y, but Y may not imply X'.

2.5.3 χ^2 (Chi-squared) Measure

The χ^2 test is a statistical test that can be used to determine if the items in an itemset $X = \{x_1, x_2, \ldots x_k\}$ are correlated. To do this, X_i is defined which represents several events that occur when items in X are present or absent in a record. There will be 2^k such events since there are k items in X that could either be present or absent in a record. The probabilities of these 2^k events can be measured from the data and the observed probabilities can be denoted as $O(X_i)$. These probabilities can also be estimated (assuming independence) by multiplying the probabilities of occurrence or absence of items in X. The estimated probabilities are denoted as $E(X_i)$. The χ^2 value of X can then be calculated as follows:

$$\chi^2(X) = \sum \frac{\left(O(X_i - E(X_i)\right)^2}{E(X_i)}$$

If the items in X are really independent, the value computed by this formula would be near zero. If the value computed is more than a cut-off value (3.84 at the 95% significance level), then the items are assumed not to be independent and X is output as an interesting itemset. Cut-off values for the various significant levels can be obtained from widely available tables for the χ^2 distribution.

Example 2.15   For the data distribution given in Example 2.13, Fig. 2.9 shows the required probabilities when $X =$ {researcher, coffee drinker}.

Event (X_i)		$O(X_i)$	$E(X_i)$
Researcher	Coffee		
No	No	5%	50% × 20%
No	Yes	45%	50% × 80%
Yes	No	15%	50% × 20%
Yes	Yes	35%	50% × 80%

Fig. 2.9   Required probabilities for {researcher, coffee drinker}.

From this table, we can calculate c^2 ({researcher, coffee drinker}) as

$$\frac{(0.05 - 0.1)^2}{0.1} + \frac{(0.45 - 0.4)^2}{0.4} + \frac{(0.15 - 0.1)^2}{0.1} + \frac{(0.35 - 0.4)^2}{0.4} = 0.0625$$

This value is close to zero, indicating that the observed negative correlation between the researchers and the coffee is probably due to a random chance, than any actual relationship between the two.

The χ^2 measure is a good measure of the interestingness of an itemset and it overcomes the first drawback of the interest measure described above. Unfortunately, like the interest measure, it is still not directly useful for measuring the interestingness of rules.

2.5.4 CONVICTION

A rule of the form $X \rightarrow Y$ intuitively conveys the meaning that X (statistically) implies Y. In other words, if X has occurred, then Y is certain to occur. Conviction is a measure of the interestingness that satisfies this meaning. It is computed by the following formula,

$$\text{conviction}(X \rightarrow Y) = \text{P}(X)\,\text{P}(\neg Y)/\text{P}(X, \neg Y)$$

The basis for this formula is that in logic, a conditional implication $X \rightarrow Y$ can be rewritten as $\neg(X \wedge \neg Y)$. Hence, a measure of the dependence between X and $\neg Y$ could be useful to measure the implication strength. A conviction value of 1 indicates that X and Y are independent. If conviction is 0, then X implies the absence of Y. If conviction is infinity, then X implies the presence of Y.

Example 2.16   For the data distribution given in Example 2.13,

$$\text{conviction(researcher} \rightarrow \text{coffee drinker)} = 0.5 \times 0.2/0.15 = 0.67$$

This reinforces the intuition provided by previous interestingness measures that being a researcher mildly implies being a coffee abstainer.

2.5.5   SURPRISE

If the support of an itemset does not change much over time, then it is quite likely that the user would already have a good idea of the itemset and its support. It is therefore unlikely to be interesting. To quantify the amount that the support of an itemset X changes over time, the following approach was used by Byron Dom *et al* in a work published in VLDB–1998 as follows:

First remove all the items in the dataset that are not in X. Then encode the resulting dataset according to some good compression scheme. If the compressed dataset is very small, then it indicates that there is not much variation in the dataset, and so the support of X does not change much with time. Hence, the size of the compressed dataset is used to represent the *surprise* measure.

Even if X changes to a great extent with time, it may still be uninteresting if its support can be estimated based on the supports of its subsets. To take care of this, the encoding scheme used above is enhanced to use the information about the subsets of X to make a tighter encoding.

2.6   FREQUENT ITEMSET MINING (FIM) ALGORITHMS

The previous section argues that the support of itemsets is not a good measure of their interestingness. However, the notion of support is still important because itemsets with too little support are unlikely to be interesting according to any other measure of interestingness. The notion of a minimum support that the itemsets should satisfy is still valid. The arguments in the previous section only indicate that it is incorrect to assume that itemsets with larger support will be more interesting than those with smaller supports.

It is important to apply a minimum support threshold and extract frequent itemsets because once this is accomplished, other interestingness measures can be applied during the post-processing phase to remove the obvious or redundant itemsets. Attempting to extract interesting itemsets according to these other measures, without first extracting the frequent itemsets, is likely to be exceptionally intensive computationally—usually it is intractable. Some research efforts in this direction have however been made (the surprise measure in the Section 2.5.5 is one such example).

In this section, several frequent itemset mining (FIM) algorithms will be explored. These algorithms are used to mine all itemsets whose supports are not less than a user-provided minimum support or minsup from a given dataset. Along with the frequent itemsets, their supports are also output. These algorithms lie at the centre of the discovery process of all the patterns discussed in this chapter. Over thirty FIM algorithms have been developed so far in the research literature. Here a representative subset of these algorithms will be studied.

2.6.1   THE CHALLENGE

In the previous sections, we have seen that frequent itemset mining is a very high-impact problem and is worthy of study. Before exploring FIM algorithms *per se*, it is important to know why designing good algorithms for mining frequent itemsets is a challenging problem. The following are the primary reasons why the task of mining frequent itemsets is difficult:

Input/Output(I/O) cost   FIM algorithms often need to work with huge databases. The sales transaction data of large companies could contain millions or billions of records. It is infeasible to read the entire dataset into the main memory and then contemplate fancy processing to extract the frequent itemsets. This means that the FIM algorithms must work with the records on disk reading them whenever required.

Itemset lattice size   From the space of all the possible itemsets, the FIM algorithms must extract the frequent itemsets. The space of itemsets can be organized in the form of a lattice as illustrated in Fig. 2.10. For this figure, there are four items in the dataset labelled A, B, C, and D. This results in $2^4 = 16$ possible itemsets. It is clear that the size of the itemset lattice is usually exponential with respect to the number of distinct items in the dataset. This is a huge number since most stores sell hundreds of distinct items, at least.

Central processing unit (CPU) cost   FIM algorithms work by intelligently guessing what itemsets could be frequent–these itemsets are known as *candidates* since they may or may not be frequent. The counts of these candidates are determined by scanning the database to verify if they are actually frequent. The number of candidates is usually huge; it could run into thousands or tens of thousands. Thus determining the counts of these candidates is a highly intensive task computationally.

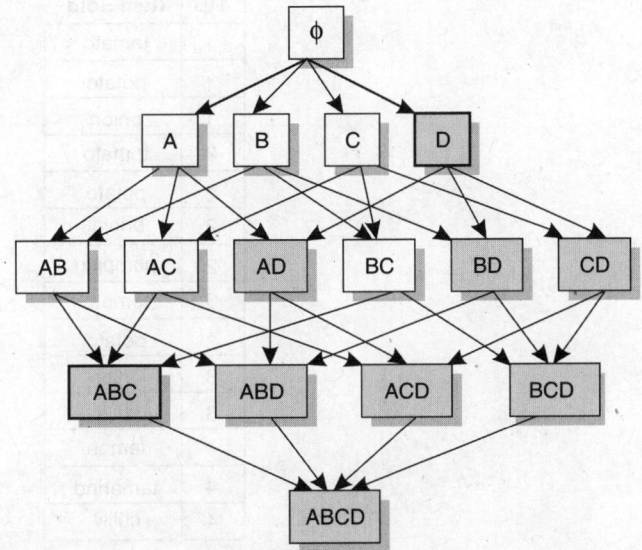

Fig. 2.10   Itemset lattice

Since its inception in 1993, researchers have strived to design efficient FIM algorithms. Dozens of algorithms exist today. The first two difficulties mentioned above have largely been mitigated. Current state-of-the-art algorithms require only one or two scans of data on the disk. This overcomes the I/O cost problem. The second problem regarding the huge size of the itemset lattice has also been overcome–current algorithms utilize intelligent pruning techniques to eliminate most of the lattice from consideration. The third problem, the CPU cost of counting is perhaps the most significant problem among the three. The time required for counting is an order-of-magnitude longer than that required for the disk I/O. It still remains the primary bottleneck of FIM algorithms.

2.6.2   DATASET FORMAT

Conceptually, the input data for frequent itemset mining consists of records containing sets of items as shown in Fig. 2.1. Such data might come in many forms. In most applications, the data is either stored in text files or in relational databases. Packaging the data in a form suitable for frequent itemset mining may itself require a lot of forethought and effort.

Companies that store their sales transactions digitally usually use relational database software. This data is normalized in the form of a relational table as shown in Fig. 2.11, using the sample data in Fig. 2.1.

TID	Item Sold
1	tomato
1	potato
1	onion
2	tomato
2	potato
2	brinjal
2	pumpkin
3	tomato
3	potato
3	onion
3	chilly
4	lemon
4	tamarind
4	chilly

Fig. 2.11 Normalized (relational) representation of transactional data

Irrespective of the original data format, the FIM algorithms typically expect their input to adhere to one of the four logical formats, as outlined below. If the original dataset is not already in the required format, it needs to be converted before the FIM algorithms can be applied.

Horizontal list format

This is the most common input format for FIM algorithms. For the sample dataset in Fig. 2.1, the horizontal list format is shown in Fig. 2.12. The data consists of records or transactions, where each record has a unique identity, referred to as a transaction identity (TID). The items in the record are listed one after the other. Most algorithms expect the items to be listed in a consistent order for all the records. For example, if *tomato* occurs before *potato* in some record, then in all the records containing *tomato* and *potato*, *tomato* should occur before *potato*.

TID	Items Sold
1	tomato, potato, onion
2	tomato, potato, brinjal, pumpkin
3	tomato, potato, onion, chilly
4	lemon, tamarind, chilly

Fig. 2.12 Horizontal list format

Horizontal vector format

In this logical format, each record is represented by a vector of bits of length m, where m is the number of distinct items in the dataset. The kth bit is set to 1 if the kth item is present in the record and 0, if it is absent. For the sample dataset in the horizontal vector format is shown in Fig. 2.13.

Tid	Tomato	Potato	Onion	Brinjal	Pumpkin	Chilly	Lemon	Tamarind
1	1	1	1	0	0	0	0	0
2	1	1	0	1	1	0	0	0
3	1	1	1	0	0	1	0	0
4	0	0	0	0	0	1	1	1

Fig. 2.13 Horizontal vector format

Vertical list format

The vertical list format, for the sample dataset in Fig. 2.1, is shown in Fig. 2.14. In this format, for each item, a list of TIDs of records containing that item is stored; this is also referred to as the *tidlist* of that item.

Tidlist   The tidlist of an itemset X is the list of TIDs of records that contain X as a subset.

The tidlist of an itemset can be computed by intersecting the tidlists of the items contained in it.

Tomato	Potato	Onion	Brinjal	Pumpkin	Chilly	Lemon	Tamarind
1	1	1	2	2	3	4	4
2	2	3			4		
3	3						

Fig. 2.14 Vertical list format

Vertical vector format

In this format, for each item, a vector of bits having length n is stored, where n is the number of records in the database. For a given item x, the corresponding vector has its kth bit set to 1 if the kth record contains x or else, the bit is set to 0. These vectors are known as *tid-vectors*.

> **Tid-vector**   The tid-vector of an itemset X is a vector of bits of length n, where n is the number of records in the database, and the kth bit is set to 1 if the kth record contains X, else it is set to 0.

The tid-vector of an itemset can be computed efficiently by doing a bit-wise AND operation on the tid-vectors of the items contained in it. The vertical vector format is shown below in Fig. 2.15 for the sample dataset in Fig. 2.1.

tomato	potato	onion	brinjal	pumpkin	chilly	lemon	tamarind
1	1	1	0	0	0	0	0
1	1	0	1	1	0	0	0
1	1	1	0	0	1	0	0
0	0	0	0	0	1	1	1

Fig. 2.15   Vertical vector format

Comparison of formats

While the horizontal list format is the most commonly used format for input to the FIM algorithms, the other formats are also useful. Some algorithms convert the dataset or a part of it from one format to another, when required. The conversion is efficient and can be done dynamically for parts of the dataset without having to store multiple formats on disk. For the FIM algorithms covered in this chapter, we shall assume the horizontal list format for input.

The horizontal vector format is used when it is necessary to check for the presence of items in records very often. In this format, the operation can be done continuously. The vertical list format is useful to efficiently determine the count of items and itemsets. The count of an item or itemset is simply the length of its tidlist. The tidlist of an itemset is computed as the intersection of the tidlists of its items. This is a simple operation for which efficient algorithms can be easily designed. For the vertical vector format, this is even more efficient because the bit-wise AND operation required for it can be implemented in the hardware itself.

2.6.3 OVERALL STRATEGY

FIM algorithms work by intelligently guessing what itemsets could be frequent; these itemsets are known as candidates since they may or may not be frequent. The counts of these candidates are determined by scanning the database to verify if they are actually frequent. As will be seen, some algorithms convert the dataset into a more suitable representation and then perform counting on this representation rather than on the actual dataset.

> **Candidate itemset** A candidate itemset is one whose count is being determined during the execution of a FIM algorithm, to evaluate if it is a frequent itemset or not.

In order to effectively eliminate most of the itemset lattice from consideration, FIM algorithms depend heavily on two very useful lemmas as given below:

Lemma 2.2 Every subset X of a frequent itemset W is also frequent.

Proof Every record that contains W also contains X. Hence the support of X must be at least as much as W. Since W is frequent, X must also be frequent.

Lemma 2.3 Every superset W of an infrequent itemset X is also infrequent.

Proof Only those records that contain (all the items in) X can contain W. Hence the support of W cannot exceed that of X. Since X is infrequent, W must also be infrequent.

Due to Lemma 2.3, huge portions of the itemset lattice can be pruned during mining because once an itemset is known to be infrequent, none of its supersets need to be considered.

2.6.4 THE APRIORI ALGORITHM

The Apriori algorithm has been the most influential FIM algorithm. It was the first algorithm to effectively make use of Lemma 2.3. It follows the strategy of first evaluating the support of short itemsets before proceeding to the longer itemsets. This way, if an itemset is found to be infrequent, its supersets can be eliminated from further consideration.

The algorithm

Apriori starts with itemsets of length 1 (also known as 1-itemsets or singletons) as candidates, and determines their support by making a scan of the dataset D. Candidates that are infrequent are discarded, while the frequent ones are output. The frequent itemsets are then used to form candidate itemsets of length 2 (known as 2-itemsets). This process repeats for longer itemsets until there are no more candidates to count. The pseudo-code for this algorithm is shown in Fig. 2.16.

```
Appriori (D, minsup):
C = {all 1-itemsets} //candidates
While (|C| > 0):
    Scan D to find counts of C
    F = sets in C with count ≥ minsup × |D|
    Output F
    C = AprioriGen(F) //gen.candidates
```

Fig. 2.16 The Apriori algorithm

The procedure to form the candidates is shown in Fig. 2.17 as function AprioriGen. It takes the set of frequent itemsets of length k during the kth iteration of Apriori, as input. Note: Item sets of length k are also denoted as k-itemsets.

```
AprioriGen (F):
for each pair of itemsets X, Y in F:
    if X and Y share all items, except last
        Z = X ∪ Y  //generate candidate
    if any immediate. Subset of Z is not in F:
        prune Z    // gen. candidates
```

Fig. 2.17 The AprioriGen function

The AprioriGen function requires that items within the itemsets be ordered in some way. In the examples given below, a lexicographic ordering of items within the itemsets is assumed. The function consists of two parts—*generate* and *prune* steps. During the generate step, it forms candidates of length $k+1$. To do this, it enumerates all the pairs of the itemsets X and Y that share all the items except the last (according to the lexicographic ordering).

Example 2.17 If A, B, C, and D are items and $k = 3$, then the AprioriGen function enumerates the pairs of 3-itemsets, (X, Y) that share all the items except the last. For instance, X and Y could be {A, B, C} and {A, B, D}, respectively, because these two itemsets are identical except for the last item. By taking the union of these two itemsets, an itemset of length 4, i.e. {A, B, C, D} is obtained This 4-itemset is formed during the generate step of AprioriGen.

The itemsets formed during the generate step could be frequent because each of them has two subsets that are known to be frequent. Whether they are actually frequent can be confirmed by counting their support during the next database scan. Unfortunately, counting the supports of the itemsets during the database scans turns out to be the most time-consuming part of the FIM algorithms. Therefore, care should be taken not to count any itemsets that could be infrequent by other means. This is where the prune step of the AprioriGen comes into picture.

For each itemset Z of length $k+1$ formed during the generate step, the prune step makes additional checks to see if all the subsets of Z are frequent or not. Even if one subset of Z turns out to be infrequent, we can conclude from lemma 2 that Z is infrequent. This step is possible for the reason that during the formation of the candidates of length $k+1$, Apriori would have already processed the itemsets having lengths k and less. As a result it can be checked if any subset of Z of length k and less is found to be infrequent.

The prune step does this checking in a clever way—it just checks the immediate subsets of Z, the subsets of length k. This is sufficient because if an immediate subset is frequent, all its subsets are known to be frequent (by Lemma 2), and do not need to be checked separately. On the other hand, if it is infrequent, it can be concluded that Z is infrequent.

Example 2.18 For the situation in Example 2.17, the following 3-itemsets will be verified for being frequent by the prune step of AprioriGen: {A, B, C}, {A, B, D}, {A, C, D} and {B, C, D}. If any of these itemsets are not frequent during the previous scan, {A, B, C, D} will be pruned from the list of candidates. An efficient implementation of Apriori would avoid verifying {A, B, C} and {A, B, D} as these have already been confirmed to be frequent during the generate step.

Proof of Correctness
Theorem 2.1 demonstrates that the Apriori algorithm works correctly.

Theorem 2.1 The Apriori algorithm outputs all frequent itemsets.

Proof It is trivial to show that Apriori outputs all the frequent itemsets of length 1. By mathematical induction, assume that Apriori outputs all the frequent itemsets of length k. We now show that it also generates all frequent itemsets of length $k+1$. To do this, it is sufficient to show that 'the generate step of the AprioriGen function called from Apriori at the end of the kth database scan, will generate all frequent itemsets of length $k+1$'.

Consider any frequent itemset $x = \{X_1, X_2, \ldots, X_k, X_{k+1}\}$ of length $k+1$. This itemset will have two subsets $x_1 = \{X_1, X_2, \ldots, X_k\}$ and $x_2 = \{X_1, X_2, \ldots, X_{k-1}, X_{k+1}\}$

obtained by removing the last two items, respectively, from x. Since x is frequent, from Lemma 2, both x_1 and x_2 are also frequent. Hence, x_1 and x_2 must have been discovered as frequent items during the kth database scan. Consequently, x_1 and x_2 would be enumerated by the AprioriGen function and x will be formed as a candidate. Hence, the theorem is proved.

Data structures and counting

Now, the data structures used to store counts of the candidate itemsets during the execution of Apriori will be described. The third line in the pseudo-code of the Apriori algorithm, in Fig. 2.16, is the most critical and time-consuming step of the algorithm. It involves determining the counts of all the candidates by scanning the database. The data structures must be designed in such a way as to allow this step to be implemented as efficiently as possible.

Efficient implementations of Apriori use two different data structures for efficient counting of candidates: a simple array-based data structure for candidates of lengths 1 and 2; and a more complex tree-based data structure for longer candidates.

For candidates of lengths 1 and 2   For 1-itemsets or singletons, counts are stored in a 1-dimensional array; whereas for 2-itemsets, counts are stored in a triangular 2-dimensional array as illustrated in Fig. 2.18.

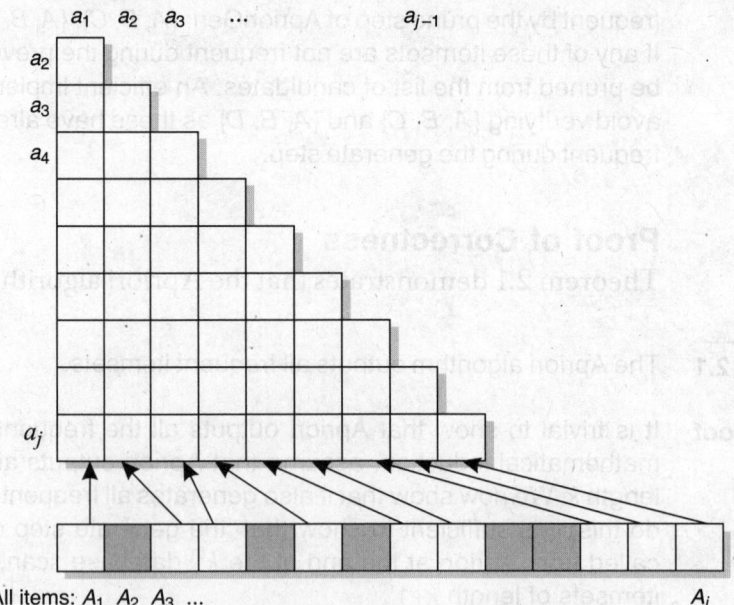

Fig. 2.18   Data structures for 1- and 2-itemsets

In the figure, the counters for singletons (in the bottom array) are black if the corresponding item is infrequent. The triangular array stores counters for 2-itemsets and its indices correspond to the frequent singletons; the reason being that for each candidate 2-itemset, both subsets must be frequent. This is illustrated in the figure using arrows that map from the frequent singletons to the indices on the triangular array.

In the first scan of Apriori, the singletons array is allocated and the counts of the 1-itemsets are obtained. After determining the frequent 1-itemsets, the space for the triangular array is allocated and a mapping between the frequent 1-itemsets and the indices of the triangular array is chosen. The counters of the triangular array are initialized to zero and incremented during the second scan of Apriori in the manner shown in Fig. 2.19.

Increment count(t):
$t' = \{\}$
for each x in t
   if $\{x\}$ is frequent: $t' = t' \cup \{x\}$
     for x in $1...|t'|$
       for y in $(x + 1)...|t'|$
         counter (x, y) ++

Fig. 2.19   Counting 2-itemsets in Apriori

The increment_count function, shown in Fig. 2.19, takes as input a record t and increments the counters of all the candidates of length 2 that are present in t. To do this, it first builds a set t' that consists of all the frequent items in t, then it enumerates all the pairs of items in t' and increments the corresponding counter.

For longer candidates   For longer candidates, Apriori uses a tree-based data structure to store the counters. The Apriori algorithm, described in the original SIGMOD–93 paper, utilizes a data structure known as *hash-tree*. Here, a simpler data structure known as *set-enumeration tree*, which became popular with the later algorithms is introduced. The data structure is illustrated in Fig. 2.20 for four items A, B, C, and D. The root node consisting of the null set is not shown in the figure.

The nodes in the data structure storing counters of the itemsets are mentioned as labels in each node. In the kth database scan of Apriori, the tree only contains nodes up to the level k and the counters are maintained only at the leaves. The nodes are organized in such a way that the prefixes of itemsets in any node are present in the ancestors of that node, i.e. if a node n corresponds to an itemset X, then the descendents of n will correspond only to the supersets of X.

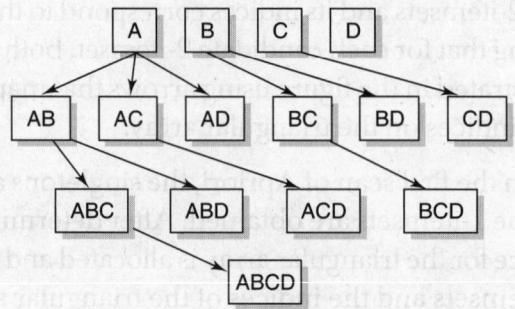

Fig. 2.20   Data structure for the candidates of length greater than 2

While processing a particular record r of the database, the above data structure enables an efficient search of the candidates that are contained in r. If the itemset corresponding to a node n is not a part of r, then any descendent of n cannot be a part of r. Therefore, the sub-tree rooted at n can be eliminated from the search.

Example 2.19   During a database scan, if Apriori reaches a record that contains the items: A, C, and D, then the counters for A, C, and D in Fig. 2.20 are first incremented. The sub-trees rooted at these three nodes then traverse to search for the other candidates that are present in the record. However, the sub-tree rooted at B is entirely eliminated from the search because it is not present in the record.

In order to efficiently check whether a given item is present in a record r, efficient implementations of Apriori convert r into a horizontal vector format (see Section 2.6.2). In this format, checking for the presence of an item in r is as easy as a single array lookup.

Illustration 2.1   To illustrate the mechanism of the Apriori algorithm, the sample dataset shown in Fig. 2.21 is used, which has hypothetical items labelled using the letters A–P. Apriori

TID	Items
1	A, C, D F, G, I, M, P,
2	A, B, C, F, L, M, O
3	B, F, H, J, O
4	B, C, K, P
5	A, C, E, F, L, M, N, P.

Fig. 2.21   Sample dataset

assumes that the items within each record are sorted in a consistent order—in this case, lexicographically. If the records are not sorted, they need to be sorted on the fly while reading them from disk. The minsup threshold is set to 60%, which means that all the itemsets whose count is not less than 3 should be output.

The algorithm starts with all 1-itemsets as candidates and determines their counts by making a scan over the dataset. The counts so determined, are shown in the array in Fig. 2.22. The shaded cells of the array indicate the itemsets that were found to be infrequent.

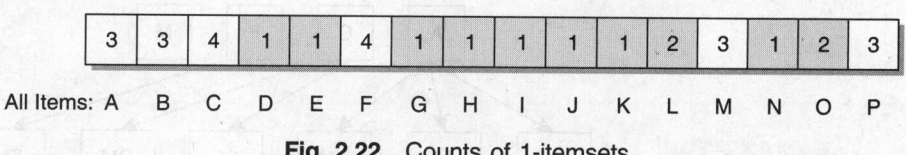

| 3 | 3 | 4 | 1 | 1 | 4 | 1 | 1 | 1 | 1 | 1 | 2 | 3 | 1 | 2 | 3 |

All Items: A B C D E F G H I J K L M N O P

Fig. 2.22 Counts of 1-itemsets

Next, the AprioriGen function is called to generate candidates of length 2. All combinations of frequent 1-itemsets will be formed. None of them can be pruned because all their subsets are frequent. A triangular array is set up to store the counts of the candidate 2-itemsets and these counts are obtained by making a second scan over the dataset. The triangular array and the resulting counts are shown in Fig. 2.23. The shaded cells of the array indicate the itemsets that were found to be infrequent.

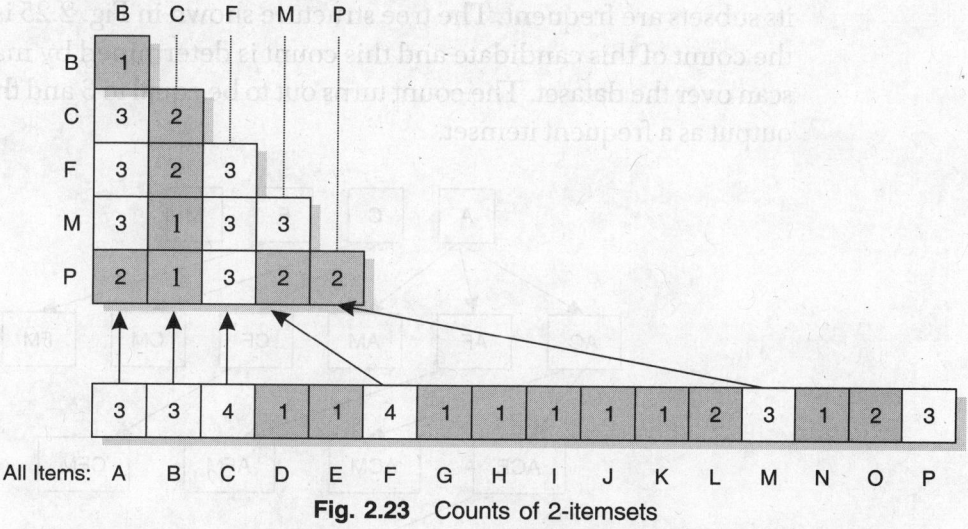

Fig. 2.23 Counts of 2-itemsets

Next, the AprioriGen function is called to generate candidates of length 3. All the pairs of the frequent 2-itemsets, that share the same first item, will be combined. These pairs are (AC, AF), (AC, AM), (AF, AM), (CF, CM), (CF, CP), (CM, CP). When combined they form {ACF, ACM, AFM, CFM, CFP,

CMP}. The prune step of AprioriGen is then applied on these itemsets. CFP and CMP get pruned during this step because they have subsets that are not frequent, FP and MP, respectively. A tree structure is used to store the counts of the candidate 3-itemsets and these counts are obtained by making a third scan over the dataset. The tree structure and the resulting counts are shown in Fig. 2.24. In this case, it turns out that all the 4 candidates have count = 3 and are frequent.

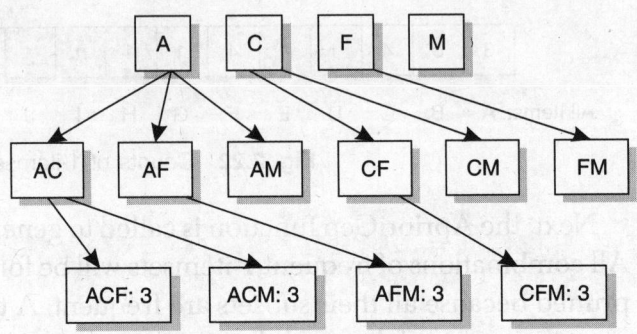

Fig. 2.24 Counts of 3-itemsets

Next, the AprioriGen function is used to generate candidates of length 4. Only one candidate is generated this time, ACFM. It cannot be pruned as all its subsets are frequent. The tree structure shown in Fig. 2.25 is used to store the count of this candidate and this count is determined by making a fourth scan over the dataset. The count turns out to be equal to 3 and the candidate is output as a frequent itemset.

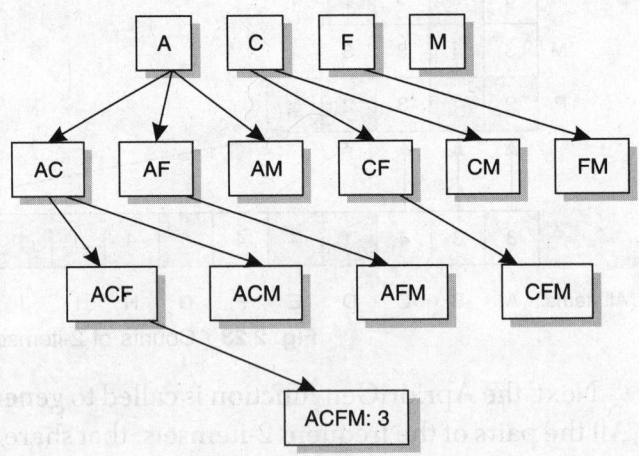

Fig. 2.25 Counts of 4-itemsets

When the AprioriGen function is called again to generate candidates of length 5, it produces no candidates. Hence, the algorithm ends at this point.

Analysis The candidate itemsets counted in the Apriori algorithm constitute unerringly, the frequent itemsets and their negative border. Although difficult to prove, it is well acknowledged that any FIM algorithm must count at least these many candidates. The Apriori algorithm is superior to most other algorithms in this respect.

One drawback in the Apriori algorithm is that it is I/O intensive; there are as many scans of the dataset as the length of the longest frequent itemset. An even bigger drawback is the CPU usage during counting; for each record, the counting technique traverses huge data structures to enumerate all the candidates present in that record. Most candidates enumerated do not actually turn out to be present in the record.

2.6.5 THE PARTITION ALGORITHM

The partition algorithm, published by Navathe *et al* in VLDB–1995, was a very elegant algorithm designed to alleviate the first bottleneck of Apriori; it requires only two disk-based scans of the data to perform mining. This algorithm first partitions the dataset horizontally. Each partition is then chosen to be small enough to fit well into main memory. Note that this partitioning is only logical; the data on the disk is not touched during this process.

The Algorithm
The algorithm proceeds in the following manner:

Scan 1 During the first scan of the dataset, each partition is loaded into the main memory and an Apriori-type mining (in the main memory) is carried out on it. The frequent itemsets local to each partition are pooled together to form a global candidate itemset collection.

Scan 2 Finally, the candidates pooled in the scan 1 are counted over the entire dataset during a second scan and then the globally frequent itemsets are output.

The key observation that makes the partition algorithm possible is discussed in Theorem 2.2.

Theorem 2.2 An itemset can be globally frequent only if it is locally frequent in at least one partition.

Proof   Let X be an itemset that is infrequent locally in all the partitions. It will be shown that X cannot be globally frequent. Let P_i be the ith partition and its size be $|P_i|$ records. Let c_i be the count of X in P_i and c be its count over the entire dataset D. Because X is infrequent in P_i,

$$c_i < minsup \times |P_i|$$

Summing this over all partitions, we get,

$$c < minsup \times |D|$$

Hence X is globally infrequent.

Illustration 2.2   In order to illustrate the partition algorithm, sample dataset from Fig. 2.26 is used. The minsup threshold is set to 60%. This dataset has been divided logically into two partitions. The first part is identical to the sample dataset used to illustrate Apriori in Fig. 2.21. Its local frequent itemsets are therefore the same as what were obtained in Illustration 2.1.

TID	Items
1	A, C, D, F, G, I, M, P
2	A, B, C, F, L, M, O
3	B, F, H, J, O
4	B, C, K, P
5	A, C, E, F, L, M, N, P
6	D, E, F, K, L, M, P
7	A, C, F, L, M, P
8	A, C, F, J, M, P
9	B, G, J, K, O
10	C, E, F, L, M, N, P

Fig. 2.26   Sample dataset

By applying Apriori over the two partitions separately, we obtain the local frequent itemsets for each partition. These itemsets are combined to form the global candidate set. The counts of the global candidates are obtained by making one more scan of the entire dataset.

The local frequent itemsets over each partition and the global candidate set, along with their counts are shown in Fig. 2.27. The global candidates, whose count ≥ 6, are output as being globally frequent. These itemsets are: C, F, M, P, CF, CM, CP, FM, FP, MP, and CFM. The remaining itemsets are infrequent and their counts have been shown in the shaded boxes.

Local Frequent Itemsets in Partition 1		Local Frequent Itemsets in Partition 2		Global Candidates	
Itemset	Count	Itemset	Count	Itemset	Count
A	3	C	3	A	5
B	3	F	4	B	4
C	4	L	3	C	7
F	4	M	4	F	8
M	3	P	4	L	5
P	3	CF	3	M	7
AC	3	CM	3	P	6
AF	3	CP	3	AC	5
AM	3	FL	3	AF	5
CF	3	FM	3	AM	5
CM	3	FP	4	CF	6
CP	3	LM	3	CM	6
FM	3	LP	3	CP	6
ACF	3	MP	4	FL	5
ACM	3	CFM	3	FM	7
AFM	3	CFP	3	FP	6
CFM	3	CMP	3	LM	5
ACFM	3	FLM	3	LP	4
		FMP	4	MP	6
		FLP	3	ACF	5
		LMP	3	ACM	5
		CFMP	3	AFM	5
		FLMP	3	CFM	6
				CFP	5
				CMP	4
				FLM	5
				FMP	5
				FLP	4
				LMP	4
				ACFM	5
				CFMP	4
				FLMP	4

Fig. 2.27 Local frequent itemsets and global candidates

Analysis Although the partition algorithm alleviates the I/O bottleneck of Apriori, it actually fares poorly due to the following reasons:

The number of candidates counted in each scan of partition is similar to that of the entire number of candidates counted in Apriori. So, if the counting technique used is similar to that of Apriori, then the total work of the CPU double that of Apriori.

The partition algorithm starts a fresh Apriori over each partition instead of using the results of the previous partition.

The partition algorithm could be sensitive to a distotion in the data distribution across partitions—some partitions could be very dissimilar and could contribute some spurious candidate itemsets.

2.6.6   THE SAMPLING ALGORITHM

Statistical analysis over a small random sample of a dataset is often considered to be as good as the statistical analysis over the entire dataset. The same holds true for frequent itemset mining. A random sample S of size m is obtained by selecting m records randomly (i.e., with a uniform distribution) from the original dataset.

The frequent itemsets F_S (and their supports) mined from the sample are a good representative of the frequent itemsets F mined from the entire dataset D. Unfortunately, there is always a small chance that important frequent itemsets are missed out in the sample or their supports are grossly misrepresented. The user may therefore, be interested in the exact mining results.

Scan 1   Fortunately, it turns out that the sampling approach is useful even if the user is interested in the exact mining results. The frequent itemsets F_S obtained over a sample are counted by making a scan of the entire dataset D to obtain their actual supports. At the end of this scan, it may turn out that some itemsets in F_S are not frequent over D. These itemsets can easily be discarded as being infrequent.

Unfortunately, there may be other (as yet unknown) itemsets that are frequent in D, but not present in F_S. To identify such itemsets, the *negative border technique* described below is employed.

Candidate generation—The negative border technique   The negative border of a set of frequent itemsets consists of all infrequent itemsets that do not have any infrequent subsets. Intuitively, the negative border of a set of frequent itemsets consists of itemsets that are *minimally infrequent.*

Negative Border   The negative border of a set S of itemsets consists of those itemsets, which do not belong to S, but all of whose subsets belong to S. This is expressed as

$$x \in NegativeBorder(S) \Leftrightarrow x \notin S \wedge \forall y (y \subset x \rightarrow y \in S)$$

Example 2.20   In the lattice shown in Fig. 2.27, if the itemsets, which are not shaded, are frequent, and the shaded itemsets are infrequent, then the itemsets shown in the shaded boxes with thick borders (i.e., D and ABC) form the negative border. Notice that for these negative border itemsets, all their subsets are frequent, but they themselves are not frequent. For instance, {A, B, C} is not frequent, but all its subsets are frequent.

Let N_S be the negative border of F_S. In this context, the technique is as follows: During scan 1, while counting F_S over D, itemsets in N_S are also counted. At the end of the scan 1, some itemsets in N_S may turn out to be frequent in D, known as *promoted borders.* An important observation concerning the negative border technique is discussed in Theorem 2.3.

Theorem 2.3   The (as yet unknown) itemsets that are frequent in D, but not present in F$_S$ must be promoted as borders, or supersets of promoted borders.

Proof   Itemsets in N_S that continue to be infrequent in D, i.e., the 'unpromoted' borders cannot have frequent supersets (Lemma 3, Section 2.6.3). Therefore, itemsets that are frequent in D, but not present in F_S must be promoted borders, or supersets of promoted borders.

If the sample is good, the number of promoted borders is likely to be small and therefore, all their supersets can be generated. However, care should be taken to avoid generating supersets that have infrequent subsets (i.e., itemsets identified to be infrequent in D at the end of the first scan). The resulting supersets form the set of candidates that are to be counted during a second scan of D.

Scan 2   The technique ends with a second scan of the dataset D during which, the supports of the generated candidates are counted to determine those that are frequent.

Illustration 2.3   In order to illustrate the Sampling algorithm, we use the same dataset shown in Fig. 2.26 in Illustration 2.21. The minsup threshold is set to 60%. The first partition of this dataset (TIDs 1–5) is used as a sample of the dataset. Note that in a realistic scenario, the sample will be much smaller than the entire dataset, and it will be a random sample. In this case, for illustration, we have just taken the first five records as a sample.

The sample is identical to the dataset used to illustrate Apriori in Fig. 2.21. The frequent itemsets of the sample (F_S) are therefore identical to the sets that were obtained in Illustration 2.1. The negative border of the sample (F_S) consists of those item sets, which were discarded as being infrequent during the execution of Apriori in Illustration 2.1. The frequent itemsets and the negative border of the sample with their counts are shown in Fig. 2.28. These itemsets are recounted over the entire database; the updated counts are also shown.

F_S: Local Frequent Itemsets in Sample				N_S: Local Negative Border in Sample		
Itemset	Count in Sample	Updated Count		Itemset	Count in Sample	Updated Count
A	3	5		D	1	2
B	3	4		E	1	3
C	4	7		G	1	2
F	4	8		H	1	1
M	3	7		I	1	1
P	3	6		J	1	3
AC	3	5		K	1	3
AF	3	5		L	2	5
AM	3	5		N	1	2
CF	3	6		O	2	3
CM	3	6		AP	2	4
CP	3	6		BC	2	2
FM	3	7		BF	2	2
ACF	3	5		BM	1	1
ACM	3	5		BP	1	1
AFM	3	5		FP	2	6
CFM	3	6		MP	2	6
ACFM	3	5				

Fig. 2.28   Frequent itemsets and negative border of the sample

The shaded boxes in Fig. 2.28 represent the counts that do not satisfy the minsup threshold. The itemsets in F_S that do not satisfy the minsup, when counted over the entire database, are discarded as being infrequent in general. However, the itemsets in N_S that satisfy the minsup (in this case, FP and MP) are promoted borders and they are output as being frequent in general. Their supersets need to be generated and checked for being generally frequent.

To generate supersets of the promoted borders, the itemsets, which are known to be frequent, are combined in a manner similar to that in the AprioriGen function of Fig. 2.17. In this case, only FP can combine with FM to form a candidate FMP. This candidate is not pruned because all its subsets FM, FP, and MP are frequent. No other candidates can be formed.

A second scan of the entire database is conducted to determine the count of the new candidate FMP. The count turns out to be 5 and therefore, it is rejected as an infrequent itemset.

Analysis The sampling approach is at its best when a random sample is already available and the user is satisfied with approximate results. This is usually the case in most applications. If a random sample is not available, then it needs to be created. This can involve a scan of the dataset if there is no random-access data structure to retrieve the random records efficiently.

If the user is not satisfied with the approximate results, then the entire processing described in the previous subsection needs to be carried out. However, this might actually turn out to be costlier than running Apriori; (1) the first dataset scan itself has CPU cost similar to Apriori because the number of candidates counted ($|F_S \cup N_S|$) is similar to the total number of candidates in Apriori, and (2) the second scan results in an additional CPU cost.

2.6.7 THE FP-GROWTH ALGORITHM

The Frequent Pattern Growth (or FP-Growth) algorithm, published by Jiawei Han *et al* in SIGMOD-2000, is a dramatically different algorithm than its predecessors. Rather than making several scans of the dataset, it makes just a single scan of the dataset and represents it using a *prefix-tree* data structure known as the FP-tree. Subsequently, it only uses this FP-tree to mine frequent itemsets and does not need to access the dataset. Prefix-trees are classical data structures that are used to compactly store multiple sequences of items (see Fig. 2.29).

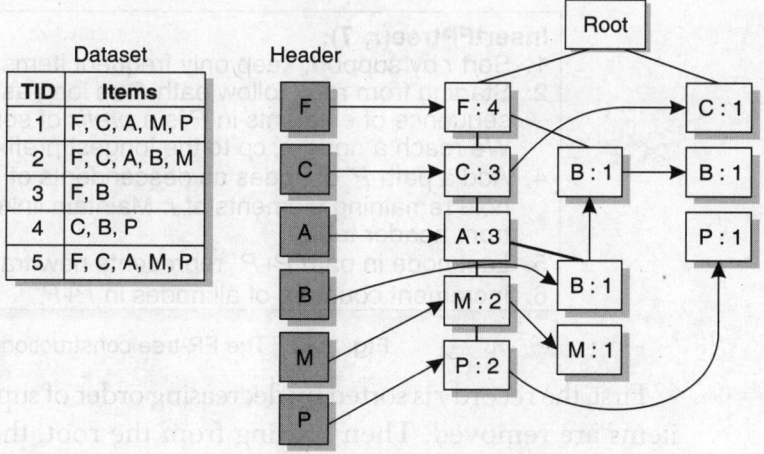

Fig. 2.29 The FP-Tree

Prefix trees store sequences of items and sequences are ordered entities. Since dataset records contain sets of items and sets are unordered entities, an ordering is first imposed upon the items; the items are ordered in the decreasing order of their supports. Obtaining these supports may require a (pre-processing) scan of the dataset.

FP-tree description

As an illustration, a small dataset and its corresponding FP-tree are shown in Fig. 2.29. The records in this dataset have been pre-processed. During this pre-processing stage, the supports of single items are obtained, the items in each record are sorted by their support, and the infrequent items are removed.

The nodes, which are not shaded, constitute the FP-tree. The shaded nodes constitute the header of the FP-tree. For each frequent item, a node is maintained in the header. From each node in the header, a linked list is formed to keep track of all occurrences of the item in that header node. The links of these linked lists are shown with arrowheads in the figure.

Each node in the FP-tree is shown with a numeric count field. This count represents number of records in the data set, which contain a prefix having the sequence of the items in the path from the root till that node. For example, the path (F, C, A, M) has a count of 2 because there are exactly two records (the first and the last) in the dataset that contain FCAM as a prefix.

FP-tree construction

The FP-tree is constructed by inserting records from the dataset sequentially into an initially empty FP-tree. Each record r is inserted into the FP-tree T, according to the algorithm shown in Fig. 2.30 (which takes r and T as inputs), as described below.

InsertFPtree(r, T):
1. Sort r by support, keep only frequent items
2. Starting from root, follow path P as long as sequence of elements in P is a *prefix* of sorted record r. We reach a node n, cp to the longest prefix of r in T.
4. Add a path P' of nodes as descendents of n to hold remaining elements of r. Maintain linked lists from header table
5. Last node in path $P+P'$ represents new transaction
6. Increment counters of all nodes in $P+P'$

Fig. 2.30   The FP-tree construction

First, the record r is sorted by decreasing order of support and the infrequent items are removed. Then starting from the root, the longest prefix of the record is traced such that, a path exists from the root having the items in that prefix. Items beyond the longest prefix in the record are stored as descendents along the same path.

Example 2.21   In Fig. 2.29, while inserting the first record FCAMP into the initially empty FP-tree, the left-most path shown in the tree is created containing the nodes labelled F, C, A, M, and P. Next, when the record FCABM is inserted, its longest prefix that exists as a path from the root is F, C, A. Next, new descendents are created for the node A to contain the remainder of the record, which is B, M.

While creating the prefix tree, the above algorithm also builds linked lists for each item to keep track of all the nodes that contain that item. A header table of all these linked lists is maintained. These lists are illustrated using grey arrows in Fig. 2.29.

Mining the FP-tree

The FP-tree T is mined using a recursive algorithm. Initially, items in the header table are enumerated and for each item i, its linked list is traversed. The support of the singleton itemset containing i can be computed by totalling the counters of nodes during this traversal. If this singleton is frequent, then we need to evaluate the supports of its supersets. To do this, the records in the dataset that contain the item i will have to be identified, and an FP-tree will have to be constructed on them. This FP-tree is recursively mined in a similar fashion.

The portion of the dataset that contains item i can be compactly represented by the *conditional-pattern base* of item i. This is obtained as given: Consider the paths from the nodes containing i to the root. Each such path P represents an itemset that is present in the records that contain i. The count of this itemset would be equal to the minimum counter value in path P. For example, the conditional-pattern base of the item B in Fig. 2.29 is {FCA: 1, F: 1, C: 1} corresponding to the three paths that lead from the root to the nodes containing B.

The above ideas materialize in the following pseudo-code (Fig. 2.31) for mining an FP-tree T. It is initially called with a null set as the second argument.

Analysis   The FP-growth algorithm is very efficient on dense datasets—datasets that have long frequent itemsets. It effectively reuses the work done while processing the records that share a common prefix. The counting technique is very different from that of Apriori—there is no explicit data structure traversal for each record. Unfortunately, the FP-growth algorithm is not effective for sparse datasets—datasets that have only short frequent itemsets. This is due to the following reasons; (1) if a sequence of items appears

---

FP-Growth (*T*, α):

if T contains a single path P
  for each combination β of nodes in P
    generate pattern β ∪ α with
      minimum support among nodes in β
  else for each a_i in header table of T
    generate pattern β = a_i ∪ α with $a_i \cdot$ support
    construct β's conditional pattern base
    construct β's conditional fp-tree T′
    if T′ is non-empty
      FP-Growth (T′, β)

Fig. 2.31   FP-growth algorithm

in even one record, it will still be represented in the FP-tree, (2) for a large random sparse dataset, each sequence of items is likely to appear in at least one record, and (3) the FP-tree grows linearly with dataset size and eventually runs out of main memory.

2.7 CURRENT STATUS OF FIM ALGORITHM COMPARISON

Since 1993, in addition to the above algorithms, over 30 FIM algorithms have been proposed by researchers. All these algorithms are required to output frequent itemsets; therefore, there is no question of comparing the outputs to decide which ones are better. Instead, the primary metric of comparison is the response time required by the algorithms to output all the frequent itemsets. As each new FIM algorithm is designed, its inventors empirically compare its response time performance against its predecessors on a set of standard databases, and thereby demonstrate their algorithm to outperform its predecessors.

In a study by Jochen Hipp *et al*, published in SIGKDD Explorations in the year 2000, a general survey and comparison of FIM algorithms was undertaken. The result of this study startled researchers. It showed that the response time behaviour of all the algorithms is rather similar and that there is no single algorithm that fundamentally beats the others. Their results showed that the simple classical Apriori algorithm was nearly as good as the more state-of-the-art approaches. In fact, there are many instances where it even outperformed the more modern algorithms.

The above study created a ripple in the FIM algorithm research community. The basic approach of comparing the FIM algorithms by their empirical response times was criticized by some researchers who (correctly) argued that the algorithms are complex and can be implemented in a variety of ways. Some implementations may be significantly more efficient than the others. Hence, all the studies so far have only been comparing the performance of FIM implementations and not the algorithms *per se*.

In order to concentrate on the above criticism, a series of international workshops on FIM Implementations (FIMI) took place since 2003. In these workshops, FIM algorithm inventors were required to submit the source code of their implementations, which were then evaluated over a set of standard databases. FIM algorithm inventors thus had another chance to implement their algorithms more efficiently in order to compete with the best.

Other metrics of comparison of the FIM algorithms are the maximum main memory used and the additional disk space they require, if any. These are usually treated as secondary measures because modern computers have sufficiently large main memories and disk spaces. Algorithm designers must, however, ensure that the main memory consumed is not dependent on the number of records in the data set; this could be huge, and at some point, the main memory of the machine will run out.

It is generally acceptable that the main memory consumed by an algorithm is dependent on the number of patterns that will be output. Unfortunately, sometimes this can be huge; for some values of minsup, FIM algorithms could generate hundreds of thousands of patterns. Researchers have recently started designing new algorithms that require a constant amount of main memory irrespective of the size of the dataset or the number of patterns output.

2.8 OPTIMAL FIM ALGORITHMS

Ever since the FIM problem was formulated in 1993, a large number of novel and elegant algorithms have been proposed. Each effort has shown itself to outperform its predecessors on a set of standard databases. A natural question that arises is whether there is an *end* to such efforts. In a poster paper in ICDE 2002, V. Pudi and J. Haritsa approached this problem by quantifying algorithmic performance with regard to an idealized, but practically infeasible, 'Oracle'.

Oracle 'magically' knows the identities of all frequent itemsets in the database and only needs to gather their actual supports to complete the mining process. Clearly, any practical FIM algorithm must at least do this much work. This approach permits to clearly demarcate the maximal space available for performance improvement over currently available algorithms. Moreover, it also enables to construct new FIM algorithms from a completely different perspective, e.g., as *minimally-altered derivatives* of Oracle.

While the notion of Oracle is conceptually simple, its *construction* is not equally straightforward. In particular, it is critically dependent on the choice of data structures used during the counting process. A carefully engineered implementation of Oracle was presented that makes the best choices for these design parameters at each stage of the counting process.

2.8.1 THE MECHANICS OF ORACLE

Oracle takes as input the database, D in item-list format (which is organized as a set of rows with each row storing an ordered list of item-identifiers (IID), representing the items purchased in the transaction), the set of frequent itemsets, F, and its corresponding negative border, N, and outputs the supports of these itemsets by making *one scan* over the database.

For ease of exposition, we first present the manner in which Oracle computes the supports of 1-itemsets and 2-itemsets and then move on to longer itemsets. Note, however, that the algorithm actually performs all these computations *concurrently* in one scan over the database.

Counting Singletons and Pairs

Data-structure description The counters of singletons (1-itemsets) are maintained in a 1-dimensional lookup array, A_1, and that of pairs (2-itemsets), in a lower triangular 2-dimensional lookup array, A_2. (Similar arrays are also used in Apriori for its first two passes.) The kth entry in the array A_1 contains two fields: (1) *count*, the counter for the itemset X corresponding to the kth item, and (2) *index*, the number of frequent itemsets prior to X in A_1, if X is frequent; null, otherwise.

Algorithm description The `ArrayCount` function shown in Fig. 2.32 takes as inputs, a transaction T along with A_1 and A_2, and updates the counters of these arrays over T. In the `ArrayCount` function, the individual items in the transaction T are enumerated (lines 2–5) and for each item, its corresponding count in A_1 is incremented (line 3). During this process, the frequent items in

T are stored in a separate itemset T^f (line 5). ArrayCount then enumerates all pairs of items contained in T^f (lines 6–10) and increments the counters of the corresponding 2-itemsets in A_2 (lines 8–10).

ArrayCount (T, A_1, A_2)

Input: Transaction T, Array for 1-itemsets A_1, Array for 2-itemsets A_2
Output: Arrays A_1 and A_2 with their counts updated over T

```
1.      Itemset T f = null; // to store frequent items from T in Item-List format
2.      for each item i in transaction T
3.          A1[i.id].count ++;
4.          if A1[i.id].index ≠ null
5.              append i to T f
6.      for j = 1 to |T f| // enumerate 2-itemsets
7.          for k = j + 1 to |T f|
8.              index1 = A1[T f[j].id].index // row index
9.              index2 = A1[T f[k].id].index // column index
10.             A2[index1, index2] ++;
```

Fig. 2.32 Counting singletons and pairs in oracle

Counting *k*-itemsets, *k* > 2

Data-Structure Description   Itemsets in $F \cup N$ of length greater than 2 and their related information (counters, etc.) are stored in a DAG structure G, which is pictorially shown in Fig. 2.33 for a database with items $\{A, B, C, D\}$. Although singletons and pairs are stored in lookup arrays, as mentioned before, for expository ease, let us assume that they too are stored in G in the remainder of this discussion.

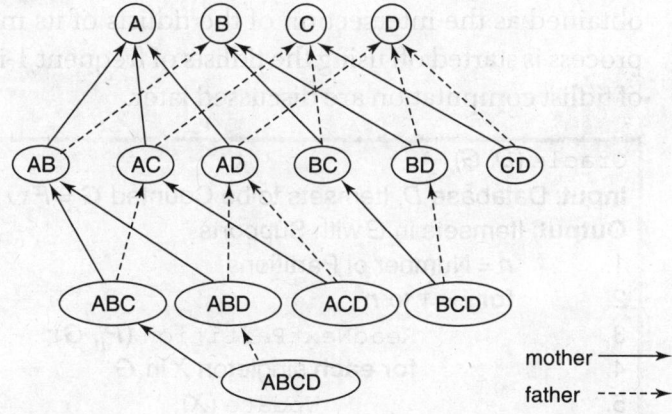

Fig. 2.33   DAG structure containing power set of {A,B,C,D}

Each itemset is stored in a separate node of G and is linked to the first two (in a lexicographic ordering) of its subsets. The terms 'mother' and 'father' of an itemset are used to refer to the (lexicographically) first and second subsets, respectively. For example, {A, B} and {A, C} are the mother and father respectively of {A, B, C}. For each itemset X in G, links to supersets of X (for which X is a mother) are stored. This list of links is called as *childset*. For example, {BC, BD} is the childset of B.

Since each itemset is stored in a separate node in the DAG, the terms 'itemset' and 'node' are used interchangeably in the remainder of this discussion. Also, G denotes the set of itemsets that are stored in the DAG structure G.

Algorithm description   Oracle uses a *partitioning scheme* wherein the database is logically divided into n disjoint horizontal partitions $P_1, P_2, \ldots, P_n$. In this scheme, itemsets being counted are enumerated only at the *end of each partition* and not after every tuple. Each partition is as large as can fit in available main memory. For ease of exposition, let us assume that the partitions are equi-sized. However, the technique is easily extendible to arbitrary partition sizes.

The pseudo-code of Oracle is shown in Fig. 2.34 and operates as follows: The `Read-NextPartition` function (line 3) reads tuples from the next partition and simultaneously creates tid-lists (within that partition) of singleton itemsets in G. Recall that a tid-list of an itemset X is an ordered list of TIDs of transactions that contain X. The `Update` function (line 5) is then applied on each singleton in G. This function takes a node M in G as input and updates the counts of all descendants of M to reject their counts over the current partition. The count of any itemset within a partition is equal to the length of its corresponding tidlist (within that partition). The tidlist of an itemset can be obtained as the intersection of the tidlists of its mother and father and this process is started off using the tidlists of frequent 1-itemsets. The exact details of tidlist computation are discussed later.

```
Oracle (D, G)
Input: Database D, Itemsets to be Counted G = F ∪ N
Output: Itemsets in G with Supports
1.        n = Number of Partitions
2.        for i = 1 to n
3.               ReadNextPartition (Pᵢ, G);
4.               for each singleton X in G
5.                      Update (X);
```

Fig. 2.34   The oracle algorithm

We now describe the manner in which the itemsets in G are enumerated after reading in a new partition. The set of links, $\cup_{M \in g} M.childset$, induce a spanning tree of G (e.g. consider only the solid edges in Fig. 2.33. Oracle performs a *depth first search* on this spanning tree to enumerate all its itemsets. When a node in the tree is visited, Oracle computes the tidlists of all its children. This ensures that when an itemset is visited, the tidlists of its mother and father have already been computed.

The above processing is captured in the function `Update` whose pseudo-code is shown in Fig. 2.35. Here, the tidlist of a given node M is first converted to a tidvector format (line 1). Recall that a tid-vector of an itemset X is a bit-vector of 1's and 0's to represent the presence or absence respectively, of X in the set of customer transactions. Then, tidlists of all children of M are computed (lines 2–4) after which the same children are visited in a depth first search (lines 5–6).

```
Update (M)
Input: DAG Node M
Output: M and its Descendents with Counts Updated
1.          B = convert M.tidlist to Tid-vector format // B is statically allocated
2.     for each node X in M.childset
3.          X.tidlist = Intersect(B, X.father.tidlist);
4.               X.count + = |X.tidlist|
5.     for each node X in M.childset
6.          Update(X);
```

Fig. 2.35   Updating Itemset counts

The mechanics of tidlist computation, as promised earlier, are given in Fig. 2.36. The `Intersect` function shown here takes as input a tid-vector B and a tid-list T. Each *tid* in T is added to the result if $B[offset]$ is 1 (lines 2–5) where *offset* is defined in line 3 and represents the position of the transaction T relative to the current partition.

```
Intersect (B, T)
Input: Tid-vector B, Tid-list T
Output: B ∩ T
1.          Tid-list result = φ
2.     for each tid in T
3.          offset = tid +1— (tid of first transaction in current partition)
4.     if B[offset] =1 then
5.               result = result ∪ tid
6.     return result
```

Fig. 2.36   Tid-vector and Tid-list Intersection

2.8.2   OPTIMALITY OF ORACLE

Oracle is optimal in two respects: (i) it enumerates only those itemsets in G that need to be enumerated, and (ii) the enumeration is performed in the most efficient way possible. These results are based on the Theorems 2.4 and 2.5.

Theorem 2.4   If the size of each partition is large enough that every itemset in $F \cup N$ of length greater than 2 is present at least once in it, then the only itemsets being enumerated in the Oracle algorithm are those whose counts need to be incremented in that partition.

Proof   The first observation is that *all* 1-itemsets must be in either F or N. Hence every occurance of a 1-itemset in the entire database needs to be accounted for in the final output. Oracle does no more than this, as it enumerates each singleton in every transaction only once (lines 2–5 in Fig. 2.32).

The 2-itemsets that are enumerated (lines 6–10 in Fig. 2.32) are all guaranteed to be either in F or in N, since only combinations of frequent 1-itemsets are considered. Hence, there is no wasted work in enumerating them.

If each partition is large enough that every itemset in $F \cup N$ of length greater than 2 is present at least once in it, then it is *necessary* to increment the counts of all these itemsets over that partition. This is precisely what is done in Oracle. Also, note that by the definition of depth first search, each node in the DAG is visited *only once*. Hence, it follows that there is no wasted enumeration of itemsets in Oracle.

The assumption in Theorem 2.4 that every itemset in $F \cup N$ of length greater than 2 is present *at least once* in each partition would typically hold on large partitions. Even if this does not strictly hold, the Oracle algorithm degrades gracefully in that: If there are m itemsets that are not present in some partition, then the amount of wasted enumeration is only *m*.

The next theorem shows that the data-structures used in the Oracle algorithm are the most efficient for the range of operations required in Oracle.

Theorem 2.5   The cost of enumerating each itemset in Oracle is $\Theta(1)$ with a tight constant factor.

Proof   Since the counts of singletons and pairs are stored in direct lookup arrays, the cost of finding the counters of an arbitrary singleton or pair is $\Theta(1)$.

For an itemset X such that $|X| \geq 2$, the cost of enumerating its children is $\Theta(|X.childset|)$ since links to all nodes in $X.childset$ are available in the node containing X. Amortizing this cost over all the children results in $\Theta(1)$ cost per child. Also, X has direct pointers to its mother and father. Hence, the cost of finding them in order to compute the tidlist of X is $\Theta(1)$.

Since the only operations done in Oracle in each visit to a node during the depth-first search are to compute the tidlists of each of its children, the amortized cost incurred for enumerating each node is $\Theta(1)$.

While Oracle is optimal in these respects, there may remain some scope for improvement in the details of *tidlist computation*. That is, the Intersect function (Fig. 2.36) which computes the intersection of a tid-vector B and a tid-list T requires $\Theta(T)$ operations. B itself was originally constructed from a tidlist, although this cost is amortized over many calls to the Intersect function.

Advantages of partitioning schemes   Oracle, as discussed above, uses a partitioning scheme. An alternative common in Apriori-like algorithms is to use a tuple-by-tuple approach. A problem with the tuple-by-tuple approach, however, is that there is considerable wasted enumeration of itemsets. The core operation in these algorithms is to determine all candidates that are subsets of the current transaction. Given that a frequent itemset X is present in the current transaction, we need to determine all candidates that are immediate supersets of X and are also present in the current transaction. In order to achieve this, it is often necessary to enumerate and check for the presence of many more candidates than those that are actually present in the current transaction.

2.8.3 THE ARMOR ALGORITHM

Once an optimal counting technique has been designed for constructing an Oracle, the same technique can be used in FIM algorithms also. A study of the ARMOR algorithm (Association Rule Mining based on Oracle) shows how this can be done.

The guiding principle in the design of ARMOR is to consciously make an attempt to determine the *minimal amount of change* to Oracle required to result in a real FIM algorithm. This is in marked contrast to the earlier approaches which designed new algorithms by trying to address the limitations of *previous* FIM algorithms.

In ARMOR, as in Oracle, the database is conceptually partitioned into n disjoint blocks $P_1, P_2, \ldots, P_n$. At most *two* passes are made over the database. In the first pass, ARMOR forms a set of candidate itemsets, G, that is guaranteed to be a superset of the set of frequent itemsets. During the first pass, the counts of candidates in G are determined over each partition in exactly the same way as in Oracle by maintaining the candidates in a DAG structure. The 1-itemsets and 2-itemsets are stored in lookup arrays as in Oracle. But unlike in Oracle, candidates are inserted and removed from G at the end of each partition. Generation and removal of candidates is done *simultaneously* while computing counts. For ease of exposition, we assume in the remainder of this section that all candidates (including 1-itemsets and 2-itemsets) are stored in the DAG.

Along with each candidate X, the following three integers are stored:

(i)   *X.count*: the number of occurrences of X *since* X was last inserted in G.

(ii) *X.firstPartition*: the index of the partition *at* which X was inserted in G.

(iii) *X.maxMissed*: upper bound on the number of occurrences of X *before* X was inserted in G.

If the database scanned so far is d, then the support of any candidate X in G will lie in the range $[X.count/|d|, (X.maxMissed + X.count)/|d|]$. These bounds are denoted by $\text{minSupport}(X)$ and $\text{maxSupport}(X)$, respectively.

> **d-frequent itemset**   An itemset X is defined to be d-frequent if $\text{minSupport}(X) \geq minsup$.

Intuitively, these d-frequent itemsets are the itemsets that are frequent within d. In addition to the d-frequent itemsets, the DAG structure in ARMOR also stores their *negative border* to ensure efficient candidate generation.

At the end of the first pass, the candidate set G is pruned to include only d-frequent itemsets and their negative border. The counts of itemsets in G over the entire database are determined during the second pass. The counting process is again identical to that of Oracle. No new candidates are generated during the second pass. However, candidates may be removed.

The pseudo-code of ARMOR is shown in Fig. 2.37 and is explained below.

First pass   At the beginning of the first pass, the set of candidate itemsets G is initialized to the set of singleton itemsets (line 2). The `ReadNextPartition` function (line 4) reads tuples from the next partition and simultaneously creates tid-lists of singleton itemsets in G.

After reading in the entire partition, the `Update1` function is applied on each singleton in G (lines 5–7). It increments the counts of existing candidates by their corresponding counts in the current partition. It is also responsible for generation and removal of candidates.

```
ARMOR (D, I, minsup)
Input: Database D, Set of Items I, Minimum Support minsup
Output: F ∪ N with Supports
1.          n = Number of Partitions

            // —— First Pass ——
2.          G = I    // candidate set (in a DAG)
3.          for i = 1 to n
4.                    ReadNextPartition(Pᵢ, G);
5.                    for each singleton X in G
6.                              X.count+ = |X.tidlist|
7.                              Update1(X, minsup);
            //—— Second Pass ——
8.          RemoveSmall(G, minsup);
9.          OutputFinished(G, minsup);
10.         for i = 1 to n
11.                   if (all candidates in G have been output)
12.                             exit
13.                   ReadNextPartition(Pᵢ, G);
14.                   for each singleton X in G
15.                             Update2(X, minsup);
```

Fig. 2.37 The ARMOR algorithm

At the end of the first pass, G contains a superset of the set of frequent itemsets. For a candidate in G that has been inserted at partition P_j, its count over the partitions $P_j, \ldots, P_n$ will be available.

Second pass   At the beginning of the second pass, candidates in G that are neither d-frequent nor part of the current negative border are removed from G (line 8). For candidates that have been inserted in G at the first partition, their counts over the entire database will be available. These itemsets with their counts are output (line 9). The OutputFinished function also performs the following task: If it outputs an itemset X and X has no supersets left in G, X is removed from G.

During the second pass, the ReadNextPartition function (line 13) reads tuples from the next partition and creates tid-lists of singleton itemsets in G. After reading in the entire partition, the Update2 function is applied on each singleton in G (lines 14–15). Finally, before reading in the next partition function checks to see if there are any more candidates. If not, the mining process terminates.

2.8.4 MEMORY UTILIZATION IN ARMOR

The main memory consumption of ARMOR comes from the following sources: (i) the 1-d and 2-d arrays for storing counters of singletons and pairs, respectively; (ii) the DAG structure for storing counters of longer itemsets, including tidlists of those itemsets; and (iii) the current partition.

The total number of entries in the 1-d and 2-d arrays and in the DAG structure corresponds to the number of candidates in ARMOR, which is only marginally more than $|F \cup N|$. For the moment, if we disregard the space occupied by tidlists of itemsets, then the amortized amount of space taken by each candidate is a small constant (about 10 integers for the DAG and 1 integer for the arrays). For example, if there are 1 million candidates in the DAG and 10 million in the array, the space required is about 80MB. In environments where the pattern lengths are small, the number of candidates will typically be comparable to or well within the available main memory.

Regarding the space occupied by tidlists of itemsets, note that ARMOR only needs to store tidlists of d-frequent itemsets. The number of d-frequent itemsets is of the same order as the number of frequent itemsets, $|F|$. The total space occupied by tidlists while processing partition P_i is then bounded by $|F|$ $|P_i|$integers. For example, if $|F| = 5K$ and $|P_i| = 20K$, then the space occupied by tidlists is bounded by about 400MB. Note that the above bound is very pessimistic. Typically, the lengths of tidlists are much smaller than the partition size, especially as the itemset length increases.

Main memory consumed by the current partition is small compared to the above two factors. For example, if each transaction occupies 1KB, a partition of size 20K would require only 20MB of memory. Even in these extreme examples, the total memory consumption of ARMOR is 500MB, which is acceptable on current machines.

Therefore, *in general, we do not expect memory to be an issue* for mining market-basket databases using ARMOR. Further, even if it does happen to be an issue, it is easy to modify ARMOR to free space allocated to tidlists at the expense of time: *M.tidlist* can be freed after line 3 in the Update function shown in Fig. 2.35.

A final observation to be made from the above discussion is that the main memory consumption of ARMOR is proportional to the size of the *output* and does not 'explode' as the input problem size increases.

2.9 INCREMENTAL MINING

In Section 2.6, we have seen a few algorithms that mine frequent itemsets from a dataset. As the dataset changes owing to updates, it will eventually need to be mined again. Repeated discovery may also be required to evaluate the effects of the strategies that have been implemented based on the previously discovered patterns. This means that frequent itemsets in the increment as well as the entire updated database are required to be computed.

Algorithms that make use of the results of the previous mining exercise for re-mining are referred to as incremental mining algorithms. Fig. 2.38 illustrates the possibility of efficient incremental mining.

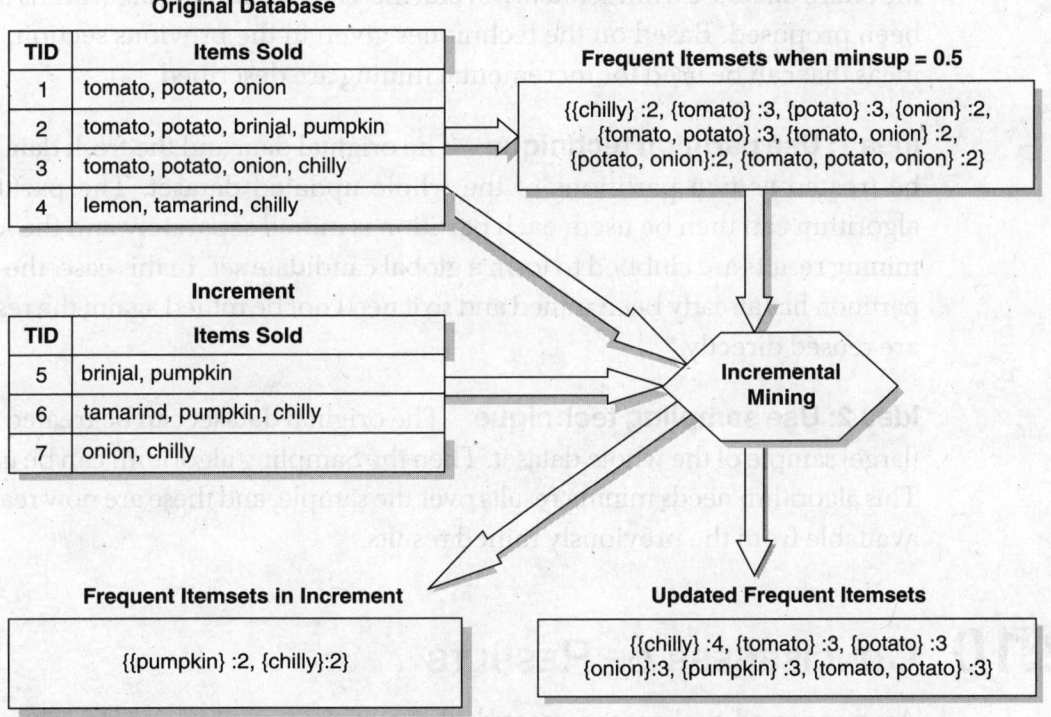

Fig. 2.38 Incremental mining

Example 2.22 In the sample data shown in Fig. 2.38, the frequent itemsets in the increment (shown in the left bottom box) are mined by processing just the increment, without touching the original database. To get the updated frequent itemsets, the following procedure will work:

Consider each frequent itemset mined from the original database. Check how many times it occurs in the increment and update its count. If it remains frequent, retain it in the updated frequent itemsets. For instance, {tomato} is in the frequent itemsets of the original database; although it does not appear in the increment, its count is sufficient to retain it in the list of updated frequent itemsets.

So far, the original database has not been accessed for incremental mining. Next, consider each frequent itemset in the increment. If it is not already a part of the list of updated frequent itemsets, check how many times it occurs in the original database. If it remains frequent, it is retained in the list of the updated frequent itemsets.

Although the original database is required to be accessed in Example 2.22, it is clear that incremental mining is much less time consuming than re-mining the entire database from scratch. Several incremental mining algorithms have been proposed. Based on the techniques given in the previous section, key ideas that can be used for incremental mining are described.

Idea 1: Use partition technique The original data and the fresh data can be treated as two partitions of the whole updated dataset. The partition algorithm can then be used; each partition is mined separately and the local mining results are clubbed to form a global candidate set. In this case, the first partition has already been mined and so it need not be mined again; the results are reused directly.

Idea 2: Use sampling technique The original dataset can be treated as a (large) sample of the whole dataset. Then the Sampling algorithm can be used. This algorithm needs mining results over the sample, and these are now readily available from the previously mined results.

2.10 CONCISENESS OF RESULTS

As mentioned earlier, the second phase of the association rule mining is relatively inexpensive computationally; but it has its share of problems as follows:

Rule quantity Too many rules are usually generated–typically in the tens of thousands.

Rule quality Not all rules are actually interesting. Most are redundant.

The second problem can be partially addressed by using the additional interestingness measures discussed in Section 2.4. The problem of redundancy of rules still remains. To remedy these problems, several solutions have been proposed and are outlined below.

2.10.1   POST-MINING RULE-PRUNING SCHEMES

Several solutions require applying some rule-pruning techniques after the frequent itemsets have been mined. One example is to output only those rules that satisfy a user-given *minimum improvement*.

Improvement   It is defined as the minimum difference between the confidence of a rule and any of its sub-rules with the same RHS.

Intuitively, a sub-rule with the same RHS is more valuable because the same RHS is deduced from less information on the LHS. Therefore, unless a rule has significantly more confidence than its sub-rule, it is not useful.

The problem with these schemes that are applied after mining frequent itemsets is that the number of the frequent itemsets itself may be so huge that it may be impractical to mine all of them.

2.10.2   CONSTRAINED ASSOCIATION RULES

Here, the problem of too many rules is solved by users specifying constraints on the rules that they are interested in. Constrained association rules have been discussed in Section 2.3.4. The problem with this approach is that since mining is an exploratory activity, the user may not have any realistic constraints in mind. It would be artificial, if the user is asked to provide constraints just for the sake of reducing the number of rules.

2.10.3   MAXIMAL FREQUENT ITEMSETS

Another approach to solve the problem of too many redundant rules is to mine only the maximal frequent itemsets.

Maximal frequent itemset   A maximal frequent itemset is one that has no frequent supersets.

Such itemsets are said to constitute the *positive border* of the frequent itemsets and are typically, only a small fraction of it. The idea is that by Lemma 2.2, every subset of a frequent itemset is also frequent. Hence, they need not be output separately.

This approach too has its share of problems as follows:

- Given the maximal frequent itemsets, the identity of their subsets, but not their supports, can be deduced.
- Their subsets may have unexpected supports and thus be interesting on their own.
- The maximal frequent itemsets cannot be used to form rules since the supports of their subsets are necessary for this.

2.10.4 FREQUENT CLOSED ITEMSETS

Frequent closed itemsets form another approach designed to alleviate the problem of redundant patterns.

Closed itemset   An itemset is said to be closed if it has no superset with the same support.

If an itemset X has a superset Y with the same support, then any superset Z of Y can be considered redundant because its support can be deduced to be equal to the support of $Z - (Y - X)$. Most FIM algorithms can be modified to generate frequent closed itemsets by repeatedly applying the following principle during mining: If an itemset has a subset with the same support, it does not generate any of its supersets as candidates. For example, in Apriori, such itemsets can be removed from the frequent itemsets before applying the AprioriGen function.

The closed itemset scheme has desirable properties; (1) the itemsets that are discarded are truly redundant—they can be regenerated along with their supports, and (2) on dense datasets the closed frequent itemsets are only a small fraction of all frequent itemsets. This property does not hold true for sparse datasets. However, on sparse datasets the problem of 'too many rules' is not so severe.

2.11 SEQUENTIAL RULES

While association rule mining is applied on the records containing sets of items, sequential rule mining is applied when the records contain sequences of items. Examples include customers buying items on successive visits to a store, or users visiting a sequence of webpages. Frequent sequences of webpage visits could be used to decide if new links should be provided on some of the webpages pointing to other pages frequently visited after them.

A frequent sequence $< page_1, page_2, ..., page_k>$ indicates that the number of sessions in which all these pages have been visited, in that *relative order*, is more than a user-specified threshold. By relative order, it is meant that as an example, $page_2$ need not be visited immediately after $page_1$. Instead, there could be other pages visited after $page_1$ and before $page_2$.

If X and Y are sequences, then X is said to be a sub-sequence of Y if all the items in X are present in Y, and in the same relative order. Y is said to be a super-sequence of X. The techniques used to mine frequent itemsets can be modified suitably to mine frequent sequences as well because the space of all sequences shares similar properties as the itemset lattice shown in Fig. 2.10. In particular, Lemmas 2.2 and 2.3 of Section 2.6.3 have their correspondences in the sequential world.

Lemma 2.4 Every sub-sequence X of a frequent sequence W is also frequent.

Proof Every record that contains W also contains X. Hence, the support of X must be at least as much as W. Since W is frequent, X must also be frequent.

Lemma 2.5 Every super-sequence W of an infrequent sequence X is also infrequent.

Proof Only those records that contain (all items in) X in the same relative order, can contain W. Hence, the support of W cannot exceed that of X. Since X is infrequent, W must also be infrequent.

It is clear that in an overall sense, the problem of frequent sequence mining shares the same basic structure as that of frequent itemset mining. Hence, the same FIM algorithms, albeit modified slightly, will apply here.

SUMMARY

Frequent patterns have applications in diverse areas such as marketing, medicine, sports, and agriculture. They have also been useful in classification and clustering tasks, especially on large datasets. Further, they can be considered a good summary of set-valued and sequence-valued attributes. These broad application areas indicate that frequent pattern mining is an important area of study.

Several variations of frequent patterns have been proposed such as hierarchical, quantitative, categorical, and cyclic patterns. Fortunately, mining these variations can be reduced to the problem of mining frequent patterns. In addition, several interestingness measures have been proposed for frequent patterns other than the traditional measures of support and confidence. These include conviction, interest, surprise, and the X^2 measure. Fortunately, it turns out that most of these measures can be applied as a post-processing step after the frequent patterns are mined with respect to some minimum support.

The above observations imply that efficient frequent pattern mining algorithms are very of immense importance. Dozens of such algorithms have been proposed over the past decade and a few important ones have been discussed.

The counting of the candidates is a major bottleneck in the FIM algorithms. Algorithms that count lesser number of candidates are, therefore, better. It is a well-acknowledged fact that the number of candidates counted in Apriori is very small and cannot be improved significantly. The Apriori algorithm is superior to most other algorithms in terms of the total number of candidates counted. One major drawback with the Apriori algorithm is that it is I/O intensive; there are as many scans of the dataset as the length of the longest frequent itemset. An even bigger drawback is the CPU usage during the counting–for each record, the counting technique traverses huge data structures to enumerate all the candidates present in that record. Most candidates enumerated do not actually turn out to be present in the record.

The partition algorithm alleviates the I/O bottleneck of Apriori since it requires only two disk-based scans of the dataset. Yet, it actually fares poorly due to various reasons; (1) the number of the candidates counted in each scan of the partition is similar to that of the entire number of candidates counted in Apriori. Hence, if the counting technique used is similar to that in Apriori, then the total work done by the CPU is double that of Apriori, (2) the partition algorithm starts a fresh Apriori over each partition instead of using the results of the previous partition, and (3) the partition algorithm could be sensitive to a distortion in the data distribution across partitions–some partitions could be very different and could contribute spurious candidate itemsets.

The sampling approach is at its best when a random sample is already available and the user is satisfied with the approximate results. This is usually the case in many applications. Unfortunately, if a random sample is not available, then it needs to be created. This can involve scanning the dataset if there is no random-access data structure to retrieve random records efficiently. If the user is not satisfied with the approximate results, then two full scans of the Sampling algorithm needs to be carried out. Scanning might actually turn out to be costlier than running Apriori because of two reasons; (1) the first dataset scan itself has a similar CPU cost as Apriori because the number of candidates counted ($|F_S \cup N_S|$) is similar to the total number of candidates in Apriori, and (2) the second scan results in additional CPU cost.

The FP-growth algorithm is very efficient on dense datasets—datasets that have long frequent itemsets. It effectively reuses the work done while processing the records that share a common prefix. The counting technique is very different from that of Apriori— there is no explicit data structure traversal for each record. Unfortunately, the FP-growth algorithm is ineffective for sparse datasets—datasets that have only short frequent itemsets. This is due to the following reasons: (1) if a sequence of items appears in even one record, it will still be represented in the FP-tree, (2) for a large random sparse dataset, each sequence of items is likely to appear in at least one record, and (3) the FP-tree grows linearly with the dataset size and eventually runs out of main memory.

The output of frequent item set mining algorithms is usually very large. Methods such as mining constrained, maximal, or closed frequent patterns alleviate this problem.

Future work in this area includes integrating the ideas used in various frequent pattern mining algorithms to result in a grand algorithm that imbibes the best of the all the algorithms. There is also a requirement to be able to automatically determine good values of parameters such as minimum support and confidence.

EXERCISES

Test Your Understanding

1. What are the difficulties associated with each of the two phases of association rule mining?

2. How can frequent itemset mining be used for classification?

3. How can frequent itemset mining be applied on data that contains numeric attributes such as age, height, etc.?

4. What is the X^2 measure of interestingness of frequent itemsets? How is it measured?

5. What is the intuition behind conviction as a measure of interestingness of association rules?

6. Show the steps of Apriori on the following dataset with mincount = 3. Show candidate and frequent itemsets of each length. Dataset: deflmkp, mpfalc, cpmjfa, jkogb, lefcnpm.

7. Prove that the partition algorithm is correct.

8. Define negative border. How is it used in the sampling algorithm?

9. The Apriori algorithm obtains supports for all frequent itemsets and their negative border. For how many itemsets does the FP-growth algorithm obtain supports?

10. How can sampling algorithm be used for incremental mining? Write a pseudo-code illustrating the steps involved.

　Prove that an itemset that was infrequent in the original database can become frequent only if it has a subset that is in the promoted border.

11. What are closed frequent itemsets and maximal frequent itemsets? How do they help in solving the problem of 'too many rules' output by association rule mining algorithms?

　Mention drawbacks in each approach, if any. How can closed frequent itemsets be mined efficiently?

Projects

1. Implement two of the FIM algorithms discussed in the chapter and compare their response times over a sample dataset.

2. Implement one of the incremental mining techniques and compare its response time with the option of re-mining the entire dataset from scratch.

3. Implement a toolkit that makes it easy for the FIM algorithm developers to evaluate their algorithms.

　The toolkit should automatically implement the new algorithm on standard datasets for a good range of minsup thresholds.

　The toolkit should also plot the response time results on a graph and show the results.

Improve Your Research Skills

1. Many FIM algorithms have been designed based on FP-growth. Write a survey paper summarizing these algorithms.

2. Design an efficient algorithm that takes as input, the set of frequent itemsets and their supports and outputs association rules, satisfying minsup and minconf.

Improve the Field

1. How can the minimum support and confidence thresholds for association rule mining be selected automatically?

　Redundant rules should not be output; take into consideration closed itemset concepts to remove redundancy. Analyze the efficiency of your algorithm.

3. Think of a new application for frequent itemset mining and describe it in detail.

2. Write a software to visualize frequent closed itemsets graphically in a lattice structure. Use edge weights to represent the confidence of rules.

Users should be able to dynamically change the minimum support or confidence. The software should proactively point users to the interesting areas in the lattice.

3. Integrate the ideas used in the various frequent item set mining algorithms to result in a grand algorithm that imbibes the best of the other algorithms.

CHAPTER 3

CLASSIFICATION

To be or not to be: That is the question.
—WILLIAM SHAKESPEARE

INTRODUCTION

Humans have always aspired to predict the future based on the past and the nature of the unknown based on the qualities of the known. It can be said that 'knowledge is power' only to the extent that it is useful in making such predictions as accurately as possible. The phenomenal success of fields such as astrology and palmistry to which people flock, despite the fact that their scientific value is under debate, attests to the importance of making accurate predictions.

Machine learning is a branch of artificial intelligence whose goal is to write programs that automatically learn from experience. This field started in the 1950s, but went out of fashion in the 1960s when limitations in the explored methods became evident. It re-emerged in the 1970s and today it is a reasonably mature field.

Classification techniques were developed as an important component of machine learning algorithms in order to extract rules and patterns from data that could be used for prediction. Classification techniques are used to classify data records into one among a set of predefined classes. They work by constructing a model of a *training dataset* consisting of example records with known class labels.

Many classification techniques developed in machine learning have been used in data mining applications. Unlike machine learning, where the extracted patterns are meant to be used by programs to make better predictions, in data mining the emphasis is on the human understandability of the extracted patterns. Many data mining applications also require that the techniques be scalable to a huge amount of data. Classification techniques have been used in numerous applications ranging from *spam* detection in electronic mails (*e-mails*), credit-card fraud detection, speech recognition, and computer vision.

In this chapter, the various classification algorithms (or classifiers), their applications, and evaluation will be studied. Other issues that will be touched upon include the selection of features for good classification, the methods used to handle missing data, and the ways in which classifiers can be combined to yield better classification.

3.1 BASIC PROBLEM DEFINITION

Consider the following example that can be used to grasp the abstract definitions provided later in this section.

Example 3.1 A customer who applies for a loan from a bank may fall into one of three classes—good (repays the loan on time), ugly (repays the loan late) and bad (does not repay the loan). The bank, of course, wants all its customers to be good.

In order to maximize the chance that all its customers are good, the bank normally screens each customer for their potential to repay the loan. Each customer is expected to fill detailed forms about themselves, their family, existing property, and occupation. Each customer is thus defined by a number of properties, which could be numeric (such as age and annual income) or categorical (such as gender and occupation).

Over a period of time, the bank obtains sufficient data about the customers of each class. This data can be analyzed by a classification program to determine the properties of the customers of each class. Subsequently, when new customers apply for loans, their properties can be verified to check the class to which they are likely to belong. If they are likely to be ugly or bad, then more stringent measures can be applied to ensure that they have the potential to repay the loan.

The problem of classification is formally defined below.

Instance An instance is an object that is represented by a vector of numeric or categorical attributes.

The input data model for classification consists of instances (also known as samples, cases, objects, or records) each of which belongs to a specific 'class'. In Example 3.1, the objects are customers and the classes are 'good', 'ugly', and 'bad'. Each object is defined by a number of attributes (also known as features or variables), which could be numeric (such as age and annual income) or categorical (such as gender and occupation).

Labelled instance   An instance is said to be labelled if the class that it belongs to is known.

The classification system is provided with the class labels of some objects, such objects are said to be labelled and are also referred to as exemplars. Classification is also known as supervised learning because it uses available examples to supervise the learning process.

Classification   Given a set of n labelled instances $x_1,...,x_n$ represented by vectors $v_1,...,v_n$, and corresponding classes $C_1,...,C_n$, the classification problem is to determine a function f such that $f(x_i) = C_i$.

In the above definition, f is usually not a closed-form function, but an algorithm that takes as input, an instance x_i, and outputs a class. In practice, different types of algorithms have been devised in the research literature and each type takes the set of labelled examples as input and computes a 'classification model'. This model is then used to predict the classes of unlabelled objects. Thus, classification is a two-phase approach as follows:

Phase 1: Model Construction   During this phase, the labelled examples are analyzed and a model is built and stored on disk.

Phase 2: Classification   During this phase, the model stored on the disk is loaded into the main memory and used to classify new unlabelled instances.

For most applications, however, it is not possible to determine a function that exactly solves the classification problems in the manner described in the above definition. Instead, most approaches settle with an approximate solution that produces some error during classification, i.e. for some of the instances x_i, $f(x_i)$ may not be equal to C_i. It is desirable to have classifiers that are as accurate as possible. The different ways of measuring accuracy will be described in Section 3.3.

An implicit assumption in classification is that the class value, to a large extent, depends only on features that are actually used in the input data model. If the class value depends heavily on the features that are not part of the data model, then the classification model built will not be accurate even when the best classification techniques are used. Hence, the task of selecting good features for a particular application is important.

3.2 APPLICATIONS

Classification has a wide spectrum of applications including detecting *spam* in *e-mails*, medical diagnosis, detecting credit-card fraud, stock market analysis, classifying DNA sequences, speech and handwriting recognition, game playing, and robot locomotion. In fact, the entire scientific knowledge can be viewed as a means to predict the future in terms of the past. This is precisely the goal of classification.

3.2.1 TEXT CLASSIFICATION

If we are to identify a single application that has made computers and the Internet popular, it would probably be *e-mail*. Applications, such as *e-mail*, which are responsible for making technology popular, are sometimes known as 'killer applications'. Unfortunately, the existence of numerous *spam* (or unwanted) *e-mails* makes it quite painful for the users to use this technology.

The task of automatically separating out *spam e-mails* is a form of text classification—the objects to be classified consist of text documents or their parts (such as words, sentences, and paragraphs). Text classification is also useful on the web for classifying webpages into a Yahoo!-type directory hierarchy. Several natural language processing (NLP) applications involve classification. These include tagging (classifying words into their part of speech) and word-sense disambiguation (when words have multiple meanings, they have to be classified into one of those meanings).

3.2.2 FRAUD DETECTION

Fraudsters have been exploiting businesses for their own financial gain ever since the beginning of commerce. The problem is worse today due to technological advances, which make fraud relatively easy to commit and difficult to detect. From cheque fraud and credit card fraud to computer intrusion and identity theft, fraud is a crime to which every business is vulnerable. This is particularly true of banks that trade money digitally rather than using paper.

Given the properties of a transaction (such as items purchased, amount, location, customer profile, etc.), classification techniques can be used to determine if it is likely to be a fraud or not. Any classification technique cannot be fully accurate in all situations. Therefore, it is imperative to treat the results of a classification as indicative only and to cross-check the same using other stringent methods.

3.2.3 PATTERN RECOGNITION

Pattern recognition applications such as optical character recognition (OCR), handwriting recognition, and speech recognition rely on classification techniques. The different characters of handwriting (or phonemes of speech) can be treated as classes and modelled using available examples. These models can then be used to classify other characters (or phonemes) to aid in recognising them. The difficulty in the pattern recognition applications usually lies in selecting the attributes of the objects (characters, phonemes, etc.) that are relevant for classification, a problem known as *feature selection*.

3.3 EVALUATION OF CLASSIFIERS

As described in Section 3.1, it is rarely possible to build fully accurate classifiers. It is desirable to build classifiers that make as few mistakes as possible in deciding the classes of instances. In this section, popular approaches that are used to measure the accuracy of a classifier are described.

3.3.1 HOLDOUT METHOD

In general, all the available labelled examples are not used for building the classification model. Instead, the labelled examples are randomly divided into two parts, the *training dataset* and the *test dataset*. Only the training dataset is used to construct the classification model.

Training dataset   The training dataset is that portion of the available labelled examples that is used to build the classification model.

The reason for keeping aside some of the labelled examples for a test dataset is to test the performance of the constructed classification model. It would be a gross error if we do not keep aside a test dataset and instead use the same examples for building the model and testing it. The accuracy values reported by such a method would make even some very naïve classifiers seem highly accurate.

Test dataset   The test dataset is that portion of the available labelled examples that is used to test the performance of the classification model.

In order to use the test dataset to evaluate the classifier, each record in the test dataset is entered as input to the classifier and the class predicted by the classifier, for that record, is noted. During this classification, the available class label of the record being classified is ignored. Once the predicted class is obtained, it is compared to the actual class of the record. If they are the same, then the classifier has been successful, else it has failed.

In order to obtain a good measure of the performance of a classifier, it is necessary that the test dataset has approximately the same class distribution as the training dataset, as illustrated in the following example.

Example 3.2 Consider that 5% of the records in a training dataset belong to a class C and 60% of the records in a test dataset belong to class C. The test dataset and the training dataset differ significantly in their class distribution.

From the training dataset, the classifier may incorrectly assume that only a minority of all the records actually belong to class C. It may use this incorrect assumption and decide not to classify a majority of the test data records into class C. Doing this would lead to many errors in the classification.

In order to rectify this situation, it is necessary that both the training data and the test data have similar distribution of classes.

Stratified test dataset A stratified test dataset is one that has the same distribution of classes as the training dataset.

If we focus on any particular class C, there are four possibilities obtained by comparing the actual class labels with those output by the classifier. These possibilities are shown in the matrix, in Fig. 3.1, which shows that the fraction of records those were not actually in class C, but classified as C, is b. Such a matrix is known as a *confusion matrix* because it shows the percentage of records of a class that were confused as belonging to other classes.

		Actual Class	
		C	Not C
Predicted Class	C	a	b
	Not C	c	d

Fig. 3.1 Normalized confusion matrix (2 classes)

The most popular metric to evaluate the merit of a classifier is the accuracy with which it classifies new records.

> **Accuracy**   The accuracy of a classifier is the probability of it correctly classifying records in the test dataset.

In practice, accuracy is measured as the percentage of records in the test dataset that are correctly classified by a classifier. If there are only two classes (C and not C) then accuracy is computed as

$$accuracy = a + d$$

where a and d are defined in the matrix in Fig. 3.1.

Other popular metrics include *precision, recall,* and *F-score,* which are defined below.

> **Precision**   The precision of a classifier is the probability of records actually being in a class C if they are classified as being in class C.

For the two class situation of Fig. 3.1, precision is computed as $a/(a+b)$.

> **Recall**   The recall of a classifier is the probability that a record is classified as being in a class C if it actually belongs to class C.

Recall may seem similar to *precision,* but it is quite different. For the two class situation of Fig. 3.1, it is computed as $a/(a+c)$.

> **F-score**   F-score is the harmonic mean of precision and recall.

It is computed as $2 \times recall \times precision/(recall + precision)$ and is intended to exhibit the merits of both precision and recall.

3.3.2   CROSS-VALIDATION

The holdout technique described above is the basic technique used most commonly for evaluating the performance of a classifier. Sometimes, to obtain a better measure of the performance, the holdout technique is repeated several times over different training and test datasets and the average accuracy is reported.

One practical problem that is usually faced in the basic holdout method is that the available labelled examples are few in number. Some of these examples are used for the training dataset and some for the test dataset. The test data records are not used for training and thus, are wasted, in a sense. To make the best use of all available examples for training, the following scheme known as *cross-validation* is employed.

Cross-validation technique First the labelled examples are randomly divided into k partitions $S_1, S_2, \ldots, S_k$, where k is user-defined (usually about 10). Then each S_i, in turn, is treated as a test dataset, and the remaining partitions are clubbed together as the training dataset, and the classification performance is measured via the holdout method. After repeating this for each S_i, i.e. k times, the accuracy of the classifier is output as the percentage of the correctly classified records with respect to the total number of the examples. This strategy ensures that every example is used for training as well as testing.

3.3.3 CONFUSION MATRIX

Often, popular measures of accuracy are misleading. For example, if only 1% people in the entire population have cancer, then a classifier that classifies all people as having no cancer would be 99% accurate!

Therefore, it is often best to output a confusion matrix to the user showing the classification statistics for each class, as shown in Fig. 3.2. Here, for example, there are 8% records of class C_3 that were classified as C_1. If the classifier is perfect, then the diagonal entries would all be 100% and the remaining entries would be zero. Notice that the entries in each column add up to 100%—this is because the records of that class is classified into some class or the other.

		Actual Class		
		C_1	C_2	C_3
Predicted Class	C_1	90%	2%	8%
	C_2	5%	91%	3%
	C_3	5%	7%	89%

Fig. 3.2 Normalized confusion matrix (3 classes)

3.3.4 OTHER PERFORMANCE METRICS

While predictive accuracy is the most important metric, classifier performance can be measured in other ways as follows:

Classification time   This is the amount of time taken to classify a new record. In several applications, classification needs to be done online and in real time. Hence, it is imperative that the classification time is as small as possible.

Training time   This is the amount of time taken to build a classification model from the training data. In most applications, this metric is not very critical, however, the training time should be within practical limits, i.e. at most a few hours or days.

Main memory usage   This is the amount of main memory required during the classification. Again this is not critical, but the usage should be within practical limits, so as to work on current machines.

Scalability   It is important that the classification algorithm be scalable to handle the training datasets that contain a huge number of instances and/or attributes.

3.4   OTHER ISSUES

3.4.1   DATA PREPROCESSING

Most pattern discovery technologies require that the input data be passed through a preprocessing stage in order to prepare it for pattern discovery. Preprocessing includes *data cleaning* and *data transformation* as described below. The terms data preprocessing, cleaning, and transformation conjure up mental images of the manual labour involved in these tasks. Therefore, most students and even researchers shy away from this area. This is unfortunate since it is a very important field. Many automated techniques could be built to ease the task of data preprocessing, and the discovery of such techniques is an interesting part of research.

Data cleaning

Data cleaning involves handling noise, inconsistency, and missing values in the input data. Techniques for pattern discovery are normally designed to detect general trends that are persistent throughout the data. Such strong trends are unlikely to be affected by a small amount of noise, inconsistency, or missing values in the data. However, in situations where these undesirable characteristics are present in more than a negligible amount, they must be reduced by using special techniques.

Noise is the presence of inaccuracies in data. This may be caused due to manual or experimental error in measuring some attributes. Several 'smoothing' approaches are available to reduce noise such as the following:

Binning   In this method, the values of an attribute are first sorted and then partitioned into ranges or 'bins'. All values within a bin are then replaced by a single value such as the mean or median of that bin.

Regression   Smoothing can be achieved by fitting the data into a function such as a linear or non-linear regression. Data values can then be replaced by their smoothed values.

Outliers   A special class of data mining algorithms are available to detect outliers. Outliers are the isolated data objects that do not follow the general trends in the data. They are most likely to be noise. These algorithms will be discussed in Chapter 4 along with clustering techniques.

Inconsistencies in data arise due to errors in data entry. An example of an inconsistency is the pin code of a town being wrongly typed while entering the addresses of customers. This kind of error is not noise, it is an inconsistency. The presence of inconsistencies can be prevented to a large extent by following a good database design and explicitly specifying integrity constraints. Nevertheless, even in the most rigorous scenarios, some inconsistency eventually seeps in and may need manual correction.

Both noise and inconsistency are problems in most pattern discovery techniques and can be solved by using generic techniques such as good database design or statistical techniques. For the problem of missing values in data, however, special techniques have been evolved in classification, and these are described in Section 3.4.4.

Data transformation

Data transformation involves handling data format issues, discretization, normalization, generalization, and feature construction.

Data format conversion   Data format issues typically arise when data in different formats, from multiple sources, need to be combined into one data repository. Also, different implementations of algorithms may require different input formats and the available data needs to be converted into that format.

Discretization   Many algorithms require their input data to consist of only categorical attributes. In such cases, discretization is indispensable. Discretization is the process of converting a numeric attribute into a categorical one. Basic discretization techniques involve sorting the values of an attribute and then dividing these sorted values into ranges. An example of this is equi-depth partitioning (Section 2.4.1, Chapter 2). More complex methods have been evolved in the research literature. Some of these techniques utilize the clustering algorithms to divide the attribute values into groups. Others use measures such as information gain (described in Section 3.1) to determine the best points at which an attribute can be split to form ranges.

Normalization Numeric attributes are usually scaled to lie within a small range, such as between −1.0 to +1.0. An example of this is the calculation of z-score of an attribute (Section 4.3.2, Chapter 4). Normalization is required to avoid giving undue significance to the attributes having large ranges.

Generalization Some categorical attributes may contain too many values and thereby becoming highly detailed. For example, in a census database, there may be a 'location' attribute whose value could be one amongst hundreds of towns and villages. Generalization involves transforming such attributes into 'higher-level' concepts. In this case, the location attribute could be modified to contain the name of the district in which a town or village is present, instead of the actual town or village.

Feature construction In this process, new features are constructed from the original features and added to the classification problem to help in the mining process. For example, in a spatial dataset that contains, among other things, the widths and lengths of several rectangles, a new attribute could be constructed to store the area of the rectangles as well.

3.4.2 Feature Selection

In many applications, the objects to be classified could be described by a large number of attributes. Some of these attributes may be directly relevant to the classification problem, some attributes may be relevant after some kind of transformation, and some attributes may not be relevant at all.

For example, in classifying *e-mails* as *spam* or *non-spam*, binary attributes indicating the presence or absence of certain words would be relevant. The presence of certain combinations of words might also be very relevant, while there may be some words whose presence would not be helpful in classifying the *e-mail* as *spam* or *non-spam*.

It is desirable that the classifiers automatically decide which attributes are relevant for the problem. However, most classifiers cannot do this and hence, depend on a pre-processing stage where the relevant features are selected. Often, this stage requires input from the users or experts who are well acquainted with the domain under study.

3.4.3 OVER-FITTING

The general trends in the training dataset are likely to persist in the future data records. It would be unwise to make similar assumptions about details that are too specific to the training dataset and are supported by only a few records. These details may or may not persist in future.

Therefore, classifiers should be built based on the general trends inherent in the training data and not on specific details. When a classifier begins to depend on specific details, it is said to over-fit the training data. Most classifiers have input parameters that decide the level of detail required to depend on the training data. Some classifiers have post-processing stages where the effects' of over-fitting are rectified.

3.4.4 MISSING DATA

Both training data and test data may contain records with missing or incorrect attribute values. Classifiers that can correctly learn and classify even such data are said to be robust. Several approaches exist to deal with missing data and some are listed below. The example shown in Fig. 3.3 is used to demonstrate these techniques. Each record represents the weather condition and the class attribute represents whether people generally play sports in that weather condition, or not. Notice that, in this table, the first row where 'Outlook' is 'overcast' has its 'Windy' attribute as a missing value.

Outlook	Temperature (Farenheit)	Humidity (%)	Windy	Class
Sunny	75	70	true	play
Sunny	80	90	true	don't play
Sunny	85	85	false	don't play
Sunny	72	95	false	don't play
Sunny	69	70	false	play
Overcast	72	90		play
Overcast	83	78	false	play
Overcast	64	65	true	play
Overcast	81	75	false	play
Rain	71	80	true	don't play
Rain	65	70	true	don't play
Rain	75	80	false	play
Rain	68	80	false	play
Rain	70	96	false	play

Fig. 3.3 Dataset with a missing value

Approaches

Ignore missing values   This method just ignores the records that contain missing values. This is the simplest method of all and yields good results if just a few values are missing. After all, data mining techniques are designed to detect general trends that are persistent throughout the data. These strong trends are unlikely to be affected by a few missing values or errors.

Most common value   In this method, the attribute value that occurs most often is selected for all the unknown values of that attribute. In the example table above, the missing value is taken as false because this is the most common value of the Windy attribute.

When the number of missing values is more than 'just a few', it becomes necessary to employ special techniques to handle them. By selecting the most common value, this method is actually making a good guess for each missing value, as to what might have been the actual value in its place. If most of the guesses turn out to be right, the model built from the resulting data is more accurate. By selecting the most frequent value for each attribute, it is likely that most of the guesses are right.

Concept most common value   In this method, the attribute value that occurs most often within the records of a class is selected for the unknown values of that attribute in the records of that class. In the given example table, this method would again use the value of false for the missing value. This is because the record with the missing value belongs to the 'play' class. In this class, there are more records whose 'Windy' attribute is 'false'.

Essentially, this method makes a more sophisticated guess than the previous approach by making use of the class information of the records having missing values. This method is therefore likely to make fewer errors in rectifying the missing values. However, it requires more time to compute this guess.

All possible values   In this method, a record with a missing attribute value is replaced by several records, in which the missing value is replaced by all possible values of that attribute. In the current example, a new record will be inserted into the table that is identical to the record with the missing value. Then, for the two records with missing values, one will be given a value of 'true' for the 'Windy' attribute, while the other will be given a value of 'false'.

This approach is meant to be used when the number of distinct values of an attribute is few. Although not as sophisticated as the previous two 'guessing' techniques, this technique is likely to be better than the first technique above. The reason being, instead of entirely ignoring a record with missing values, the values of other attributes (without missing values) that occurred together, are used.

Missing values as special values   In this technique, missing values are treated as special values labelled 'unknown'. The advantage of this approach is that if there are any patterns relating missing values to class labels, they might be detected. However, in general applications, where there may be missing values at random, this approach is not useful.

Use classification techniques   This is a very thorough technique, but it requires much more computation than any of the previous techniques described. In this approach, the classification techniques are themselves used to predict the entries of the missing values.

For an attribute A with missing values, this approach first considers set S of the training records for which the value of attribute A is known. The set S is used as a training dataset of another classification problem where the distinct values of attribute A are considered as classes, and the class labels of the original problem are treated as another attribute. By solving this classification problem, it becomes possible to predict the values of the attribute A in those records where it is missing.

3.4.5 COMBINING CLASSIFIERS

One interesting question that may arise to the reader is whether it is possible to design a classification algorithm that is inherently superior to the others in terms of accuracy. The infamous 'no-free-lunch' theorem states that this is impossible. Given any classifier, it is always feasible to artificially construct an equal number of test datasets in which it performs well and the ones in which it performs poorly. It follows that any classifier that is good for some applications may not be suitable for others. It is therefore desirable to consider using more than one classifier to solve a given problem because at least some of classifiers considered may be good for that particular task. Hence, some techniques are required to combine classifiers. There two broad techniques to combine classifiers in the research literature are as follows:

Bagging

This technique was published in 1996 by Leo Breiman in the *Machine Learning Journal*. In this technique, first each classifier is applied separately for a given test data record, selecting a class label for that record. This is like a democracy, where each classifier 'votes' for some class. Then, the class, which was selected the maximum number of times, is chosen as the class for that record.

Boosting

This technique was published in 1990 by R.E. Schapire in the *Machine Learning Journal*. It is similar to bagging except that the vote of each classifier is weighted according to its performance on the training dataset.

Both bagging and boosting techniques were originally intended to combine the classification models built by a single classification algorithm on different random samples of the training dataset. In fact, bagging is an acronym for 'bootstrap aggregating', which is a technique used to produce multiple random samples of the training dataset. In this technique, m records from the training dataset are selected at random (using uniform distribution) with replacement in order to produce a bootstrap sample, which is used to build a base classifier. Many such classifiers are built and combined using the bagging technique described above.

In boosting, the generation of random samples of the training dataset is achieved in a slightly different way. In 1995, an improvement to the basic boosting algorithm, known as *AdaBoost* (adaptive boosting), was proposed by R.E. Schapire *et al* and published in the proceedings of the European Conference on Computational Learning Theory. In AdaBoost, rather than selecting records from the training dataset at random with uniform distribution, each record is given weightage based on whether it is correctly classified by the classifiers built so far. Records that are difficult to classify are given a higher weightage so that they are more likely to be selected. In a sense, this approach tries harder to tackle difficult records.

An important context, in which combining multiple classifiers is really useful, is in multi-class problems. In some applications, although there may be many classes, it would be easy to create classifiers that discriminate well between just two classes. An example of such an application is OCR where it is required to recognize images of letters of the alphabet of some language. In this problem, there are as many classes as there are the letters of the alphabet.

Usually, it is quite easy to create a classifier that can discriminate well between any two of these classes. Since the classification problem actually contains more than two classes, several of these two-class classifiers can be combined to determine the actual class.

3.5 CLASSIFICATION TECHNIQUES

In this section, several classification techniques are described. Most of these techniques have their origins in the field of machine learning. The emphasis on data mining is that the approaches should result in classification models that are easy to understand by humans. Another requirement is that the techniques be scalable to large datasets.

Some approaches, such as support vector machines (SVM) and most neural networks, are typically not considered as data mining solutions because they do not satisfy the criteria of understandability and scalability. Hence, these approaches will not be discussed here.

3.5.1 DECISION TREES

Decision trees are one of the most popular classification models in current use in data mining.

Decision tree

A decision tree is a labelled tree where,

- Each interior node is labelled with an attribute.
- Each leaf node is labelled with a class.
- Each edge directed from an internal node *n* is labelled with a value or range of values of the attribute at node *n*.

Example 3.3   Consider the following dataset shown in Fig. 3.4 where each record represents the weather condition and the class attribute shows whether people generally play sports in that weather condition, or not.

Outlook	Temperature (Farenheit)	Humidity (%)	Windy	Class
Sunny	75	70	true	play
Sunny	80	90	true	don't play
Sunny	85	85	false	don't play
Sunny	72	95	false	don't play
Sunny	69	70	false	play
Overcast	72	90	true	play
Overcast	83	78	false	play
Overcast	64	65	true	play
Overcast	81	75	false	play
Rain	71	80	true	don't play
Rain	65	70	true	don't play
Rain	75	80	false	play
Rain	68	80	false	play
Rain	70	96	false	play

Fig. 3.4 Play outside?

An example decision tree constructed from this dataset is shown in Fig. 3.5. The root node represents the entire dataset of 14 records, 9 of which are classified as 'play' and 5 as 'DP' (do not play). Interior nodes are shown with rounded rectangles whereas the leaf nodes are shown with normal rectangles. Node labels are shown in bold.

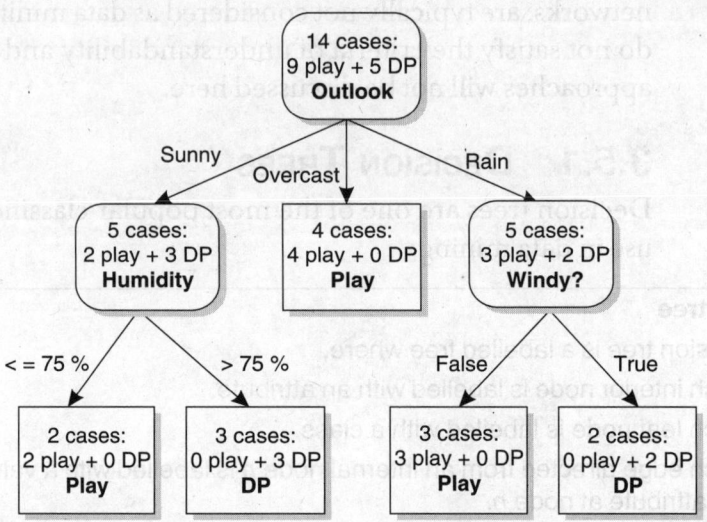

Fig. 3.5   A decision tree

The records at the root node are divided into three nodes at the next level, corresponding to the three possible values of the 'Outlook' attribute—sunny, overcast, and rain. There are five records in the first node representing 'sunny' as indicated in the dataset. Two of these are classified as 'play' and three as 'DP'. These records are further divided into two nodes, corresponding to the 'Humidity' attribute being greater than 75%, or not.

Classification using decision trees

A decision tree is a model of the dataset and can be used to predict the class label for new records. For any new record, it starts at the root node and at each edge a decision is taken whether to follow that edge or not, depending on its state. When a leaf node is reached, the class labelled at the leaf is output.

Example 3.4   Consider the situation, in Example 3.3, where a new unlabelled record has to be classified. For the left-most edge in Fig. 3.4, a question arises whether the 'outlook' attribute of this new record is equal to 'sunny'. If so, that edge is followed and the next node is reached. If not, the question moves on to the next edge. Eventually, a leaf node is reached. Notice that at the leaf nodes, all the records belong to simply one class. For instance, in the left-most leaf node, all the records are classified as 'play'.

In each leaf node of any decision tree, there will always be one such class that will dominate and be used as the label for that node. The remaining classes will either be absent in that leaf node, or their presence will be negligible.

Hence, when we reach the leaf node during classification, we choose the dominant or 'winning' class of that leaf node as the class of the new record being classified. As seen in this example, decision trees are very easy to interpret and use for classification. This has made them very popular in data mining applications.

Decision tree construction

Decision tree construction algorithms initially start with a root node that represents all the records in the training dataset. Next, they recursively partition the records into each node of the tree and for each partition, they create a child to represent it. The split into partitions is determined by the values of some attribute, known as the *splitting attribute*, which is chosen based on various criteria. This recursive splitting terminates at nodes that are pure, i.e. all the records in these nodes belong to only one class. This recursive procedure is shown in the pseudo-code in Fig 3.6.

Partition (Data _D_):

1. *If* all records in _D_ are of same class: return
2. Evaluate splits for each attribute _A_
3. Use best split found to partition _D_ into $D_1, D_2, ..., D_n$
4. *For each* D_i : Partition (D_i)

Fig. 3.6   Decision tree construction

Several criteria have been devised to determine the best split to partition a dataset. Two popular criteria are described in the following two subsections.

Information gain

The *entropy* H(_D_) of a dataset _D_ is a measure of the disorder/variation/information in it. If all the records in the dataset belong to the same class, then the entropy would be zero. If the records are uniformly distributed among the different classes, the entropy would be maximized. In general, entropy is computed and defined as follows:

Entropy The entropy H(_D_) of a dataset _D_ whose records are divided into _m_ classes with probabilities $p_1, p_2, ..., p_m$ is defined as

$$H(D) = -\sum_{i=1...m} p_i \log p_i$$

For the purpose of this calculation, 0 log 0 is taken to be zero.

The ID3 algorithm is a decision tree construction algorithm that follows the overall approach described in Fig. 3.6. The best split for each node is chosen based on a criterion known as *information gain*. Given that a dataset D is split into $D_1, D_2, \ldots, D_n$, the information gain of the split is computed as,

$$\text{gain} = H(D) - \sum_{i=1}^{n} P(D_i) H(D_i) \qquad (3.1)$$

In this equation, the first part is the entropy of the dataset before the split, whereas the second part is the average or expected entropy of the collection of the datasets after the split. Since entropy is a measure of the information content, the difference computed in Equation (3.1) represents the gain in the information content due to the split.

The ID3 algorithm selects the split with maximum information gain. The principle behind this choice is that such a split would result in a collection of the datasets whose average information content (the second part in Equation (3.1)) is the least. This is desirable because each dataset in this collection would contain records belonging mostly to one class. Hence, classification becomes possible.

In order to select the split with maximum information gain, the ID3 algorithm enumerates all the possible splits for each attribute value. That is, for each attribute A, and each value v of A, the records are split based on whether they contain v or not. To make this approach feasible, the ID3 algorithm only considers categorical attributes because the number of distinct values is small and hence, can be enumerated.

Example 3.5　For the sample data shown in Fig. 3.3, the entropy of the data D is calculated as

$$H(D) = H(p_{\text{play}}, p_{\text{don't play}}) = - p_{\text{play}} \log p_{\text{play}} - p_{\text{don't play}} \log p_{\text{don't play}}$$

Since the number of instances of 'play' in the D is 9 and that of 'do not play' is 5,

$$H(D) = - (9/14) \log (9/14) - (5/14) \log (5/14) = 0.94$$

Note, that the log function here is calculated to the base 2. The ID3 algorithm requires us to calculate the information gain for each possible split.

Let us calculate the gain for the split based on the 'Outlook' attribute. This attribute has three values—'sunny', 'overcast', and 'rain'. The original dataset is therefore split into three parts based on these values. Let us call these three parts as D_{sunny}, D_{overcast}, and D_{rain}. The entropy for these three datasets is as follows:

$$H(D_{\text{sunny}}) = -(2/5) \log (2/5) - (3/5) \log (3/5) = 0.97$$
$$H(D_{\text{overcast}}) = -(4/4) \log (4/4) - (0/4) \log (0/4) = 0$$
$$H(D_{\text{rain}}) = -(3/5) \log (3/5) - (2/5) \log (2/5) = 0.97$$

The probabilities of the outlook attribute being 'sunny', 'overcast', and 'rain' are 5/14, 4/14, and 5/14, respectively, based on their relative frequencies in the data. Thus, the information gain of this split can be computed as follows:

$$\text{gain} = H(D) - \sum_{i=1}^{n} P(D_i) H(D_i)$$

$$= 0.94 - [(5/14) \times 0.97 + (4/14) \times 0 + (5/14) \times 0.97]$$

$$= 0.25$$

Similarly, other splits can be enumerated and their information gain computed. The ID3 algorithm will then select the split with the maximum information gain to form a level of the decision tree.

Gini value

The gini value of a dataset D is computed as

$$\text{gini}(D) = 1 - \sum_{i=1}^{m} p_i^2$$

In the above expression p_i is the probability of the ith class in D. In this context, the goodness of a split of D into $D_1, D_2, \ldots, D_n$ is computed as

$$\text{gini}_{\text{split}}(D) = \sum P(D_i) \text{gini}(D_i)$$

This measure is used in a classification algorithm known as SPRINT (Scalable PaRallelizable INduction of decision Trees). The principle behind this measure is similar to that of the information gain.

Example 3.6 For the sample data shown in Fig. 3.3, the gini value of the dataset D is calculated as follows:

$$\text{gini}(D) = 1 - \sum_{i=1}^{m} p_i^2$$

$$= 1 - [(9/14)^2 + (5/14)^2]$$

$$= 0.46$$

Let us calculate the goodness of the split based on the 'Outlook' attribute. This attribute has three values—'sunny', 'overcast', and 'rain'. The original dataset is therefore split into three parts based on these values. Let us call these three parts as D_{sunny}, D_{overcast}, and D_{rain}. The gini values for these three datasets are as follows:

$$\text{gini}(D_{\text{sunny}}) = 1 - (2/5)^2 - (3/5)^2 = 0.48$$

$$\text{gini}(D_{\text{overcast}}) = 1 - (4/4)^2 - (0/4)^2 = 0$$

$$\text{gini}(D_{\text{rain}}) = 1 - (3/5)^2 - (2/5)^2 = 0.48$$

The probabilities of the outlook attribute being 'sunny', 'overcast', and 'rain' are 5/14, 4/14, and 5/14, respectively, based on their relative frequencies in the data. Thus, the goodness of this split can be computed as follows:

$$\text{gini}_{\text{split}} = \sum_{i=1}^{n} P(D_i) \, \text{gini}(D_i)$$

$$= (5/14) \times 0.48 + (4/14) \times 0 + (5/14) \times 0.48$$

$$= 0.343$$

Similarly, other splits can be enumerated and their gini values computed. Then the split with the maximum gini value is to be used to form a level of the decision tree.

Other decision tree approaches

C4.5 is a popular classification algorithm that is based on the ID3 algorithm and provides several enhancements over it.

Handling missing data   During the tree construction, the C4.5 algorithm ignores the missing data values. Next, at the time of classification, it predicts the values of missing data based on the attribute values of other records, using the techniques described in Section 3.4.4.

Continuous data   Unlike the ID3 algorithm, the C4.5 algorithm also handles attributes having numeric values such as age, temperature, etc. This is done by dividing the domain into ranges based on attribute values that actually exist in the training data.

Pruning   Conventionally, decision tree construction is stopped at nodes that are 'pure', i.e. all the examples present in these nodes belong to a single class. However, it could also be stopped at nodes that are almost pure, i.e. the examples mostly belong to a single class. This approach is known as *pre-pruning*. Alternatively, the tree could be grown fully and then *post-pruning* can be applied–in this method, a sub-tree is replaced by a leaf if the misclassification on the test data does not change much.

Gain ratio   ID 3 uses gain to measure the goodness of a split. One problem with gain is that it favours the attributes with many values. This leads to over-fitting. To avoid this, in C4.5, the goodness of a split is measured in terms of *gain ratio* which is computed as $\text{gain}/H(P(D_1), P(D_2), \ldots, P(D_n))$.

Decision rules   Instead of a outputting a decision tree, C4.5 has the option to output decision rules of the form such as 'if these attributes have these values, then the record belongs to this class'.

C5.0 is a commercial version of C4.5 that includes other enhancements including boosting. In all these algorithms, computing the goodness of a split on a dataset D involves a scan of all the records in D. This could be costly if there are many attributes having numerous distinct values. SLIQ and SPRINT are scalable algorithms that overcome this problem by computing the goodness of all the possible splits of a node in a single scan of the dataset. These algorithms are discussed in Chapter 8.

3.5.2 NAÏVE BAYES

Naïve Bayes is one of the simplest classifiers and works surprisingly well for many applications especially those involving text classification. Given a record X to classify, the general approach is to output that class C_i whose probability of occurrence $P(C_i | X)$ is maximum. To estimate the value of $P(C_i | X)$, this classifier naively assumes that the attributes of X are independent of each other, therefore it is known as Naïve Bayes. Once independence has been assumed, the derivation is used to compute $P(C_i | X)$ as follows:

$$P(C_i|X) = P(X \wedge C_i)/P(X)$$
$$= P(X|C_i)\ P(C_i)/P(X)$$
$$\propto P(X|C_i)\ P(C_i)$$
$$\propto P(A_1{=}x_1|C_i)\ P(A_2{=}x_2|C_i)...P(A_k{=}x_k|C_i)\ P(C_i)$$

Here, the record X contains attributes A_j with values x_j. The denominator $P(X)$ is ignored because it is common for all the classes. The last line of the derivation is obtained by assuming independence between the attributes.

For classification, the values of $P(A_j{=}x_j|C_i)$ are *pre-computed* and stored for all possible attribute values and classes. At the time of classification, these probability values are used to estimate $P(C_i/X)$ as per the above derivation and the class with the maximum probability of occurrence is output.

Example 3.7   Consider an *e-mail* dataset as a training dataset, where some *e-mails* are classified as *spam* and some as *non-spam*. Consider three keywords 'sell', 'buy', and 'soap'. These three keywords have different probabilities of occurrence in the *spam* *e-mails* and *non-spam e-mails*. Their presence and absence can be treated as three binary attributes of *e-mails*. Assuming that the presence of any one of these keywords in an *e-mail* does not affect the probability of any of the other two keywords, the attributes are mutually independent.

For the sake of efficiency, the probabilities of these binary attributes in the *spam* and *non-spam* classes are *pre-computed*. In other words, from the entire training data, P('sell' = present | *spam*), P('sell' = absent | *spam*), etc. for each keyword and class, is computed. These are simply the relative frequencies of the presence and absence of the keywords in each class.

Now, given a new *e-mail* X to be classified as *spam* or *non-spam*, it needs to be checked whether each of the three keywords is present or absent in this *e-mail*. Assume that the new *e-mail* contains 'sell' and 'soap', but not 'buy'. Then, by the Naïve Bayes formula,

P(*spam* | X) ∝ P('sell'= present | *spam*) × P('buy'= absent | *spam*) ×

P('soap'= present | *spam*) × P(*spam*)

The values of the probabilities on the RHS have already been *pre-computed*, therefore, this computation is a fast operation. Similarly, the indication for P(*non-spam* | X) is computed. Finally, for X, the class is output as *spam* or *non-spam*, depending on whether P(spam | X) or P(non-spam | X) is higher.

3.5.3   BAYESIAN BELIEF NETWORKS

Naïve Bayes assumes independence between the attributes and hence, is computationally efficient and conceptually simple. Unfortunately, the independence assumption does not hold in many applications. If we remove the independence assumption completely, the problem of estimating $P(C_i/X)$ becomes exponentially complex because every attribute can be dependent on every other attribute.

Luckily, in practice, most attributes do not depend on the other attributes directly. An attribute A_1 may directly affect an attribute A_2 which in turn may directly affect another attribute A_3. But it could be that A_1 does not directly affect A_3. This means that given the value of A_2, the value of A_1 does not have to be known in order to predict the value of A_3. Put another way, A_3 is *conditionally independent* of A_1. Mathematically, this is defined as

$$P(A_3 = x \mid A_2 = y, A_1 = z) = P(A_3 = x \mid A_2 = y)$$

Example 3.8   Both heredity and environment may cause people to have an allergy to peanuts and thereby cause them to test positive during a skin-prick test. The result of a skin-prick test does depend on heredity and environment, but not directly.

If we know that a person has peanut allergy, then the probability that he will test positive no longer depends on heredity or environment. In short, heredity and environment affect whether a person gets peanut allergy, which in turn, causes a positive result during a skin-prick test.

A Bayesian Belief network (or simply bayesian network) is a data structure that represents the direct dependencies between the attributes in a dataset.

Bayesian belief network   A Bayesian Belief network is a directed acyclic graph whose nodes represent attributes and an edge exists from a node A_1 to A_2 if A_2 is directly dependent on A_1.

Thus, if there is no path between two nodes in a Bayesian Belief network, then the corresponding attributes are conditionally independent. Since Naïve Bayes can be applied whenever the attributes are independent, here computations can be used which are similar to those in Naïve Bayes. In general, the probability $P(X|\ C_i)$ can be computed as

$$P(X|\ C_i) = \Pi_{j=1\ldots k}\ P(A_j = x_j |\ \text{Parents}(A_j),\ C_i)$$

Here, the record X contains attributes A_j with values x_j. Parents(A_j) represent the nodes that are connected by edges pointing towards A_j, since these are the nodes that directly affect the value of A_j.

Example 3.9   Consider a training dataset of text documents, some of which are related to astronomy and the others are not. We thus have two classes—astronomy and general. Consider four binary attributes corresponding to the four keywords 'science', 'technology', 'physics', and 'chemistry'. Unlike in Example 3.7, these attributes are not independent of each other, but are related by the Bayesian network shown in Fig. 3.7.

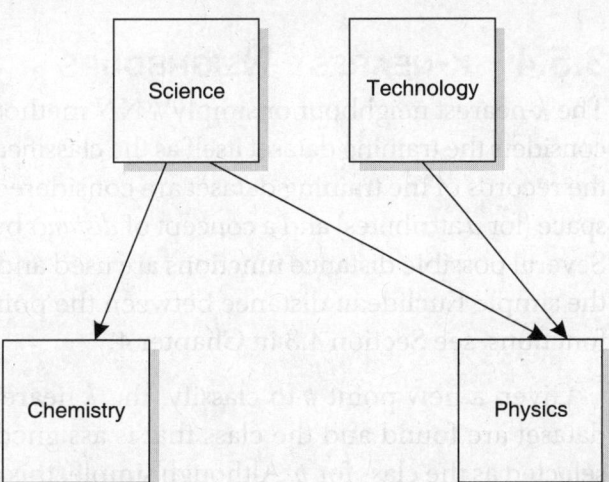

Fig. 3.7 A Bayesian Belief network

From this *Bayesian network*, we can understand relationships between the presences of these keywords. For example, the presence of the keyword 'Science' directly affects the presence of the keywords 'Chemistry' and 'Physics'. But the presence of 'Chemistry' does not directly affect the presence of 'Physics' and vice versa.

Suppose a document X is found, which contains the keywords 'Chemistry', 'Science' and 'Technology', but no 'Physics'. Based on this information, to evaluate whether the document is related to astronomy or not, the following is computed,

$$P(astronomy \mid X) \propto P('Chemistry'=present \mid 'Science', astronomy) \times$$

$$P('Physics'= absent \mid 'Science', astronomy) \times$$

$$P('Physics'= absent \mid 'Technology', astronomy) \times$$

$$P('Science'= present \mid astronomy) \times$$

$$P('Technology'= present \mid astronomy) \times$$

$$P(astronomy)$$

The values of the probabilities on the RHS could be computed in the pre-processing phase making this computation a fast one. The precomputation of these probabilities is simply a matter of determining the relative frequencies of the presence and absence of various keywords in the astronomy documents. For example, in order to compute P('Physics' = absent | 'Science', astronomy), the relative frequency of the documents, which do not contain the keyword 'Physics' among the astronomy documents that contain the keyword 'Science' in the training dataset, is measured.

The same process is repeated, to compute P(general | X). Finally, the class for X is output as astronomy or general depending on whether P(astronomy | X) or P(general | X) is higher.

3.5.4   K-NEAREST NEIGHBOURS

The k-nearest neighbour or simply k-NN method is a simple technique which considers the training dataset itself as the classification model. In this approach, the records of the training dataset are considered as points in a d-dimensional space (for d attributes) and a concept of *distance* between the records is defined. Several possible distance functions are used and the most popular function is the simple Euclidean distance between the points. For more about distance functions, see Section 4.3 in Chapter 4.

Given a new point p to classify, the k nearest points of p in the training dataset are found and the class that is assigned to most of these k points is selected as the class for p. Although simple, this approach could be very slow during classification because it needs to search for the k nearest points among the entire training dataset, which could be huge. This search can be speeded up considerably by precomputing spatial indices or voronoi diagrams. However, the resulting speed is still likely to be slower than other approaches.

Example 3.10 Consider the 2-class data of heights and weights of students studying in class 7 and class 8 given in Fig. 3.8.

In order to determine the class of the student with roll no. 6 in the table, the k-NN method finds the nearest neighbours of this student. When $k = 1$, only one nearest neighbour of this student is found. Evidently the student with roll no. 3 has exactly the same height and weight as the student with roll no. 6. Hence, the roll no. 3 student is the nearest neighbour and belongs to class 7. Therefore, the student with roll no. 6 is also assigned to class 7 by the k-NN algorithm when $k = 1$.

Roll No	Height	Weight	Class
1	4'7"	50 kg	7
2	4'9"	52 kg	7
3	5'2"	55 kg	7
4	5'3"	54 kg	8
5	5'2"	56 kg	8
6	5'2"	55 kg	?

Fig. 3.8 Heights and weights of students

However, when $k = 3$, three nearest neighbours need to be determined. In this case, it turns out to be the students with the roll nos 3, 4, and 5. These three students belong to classes 7, 8, and 8, respectively. Since the majority of these neighbouring students belong to class 8, the student with roll no. 6 is assigned to class 8.

Example 3.10 demonstrates that the value of k in the k-NN method is critical. If it is too small, then the method may occasionally be affected by some exceptional records. If it is too large, then unrelated records will be used to decide the class of a given instance.

3.5.5 NEURAL NETWORKS

Neural networks use a technology that attempts to produce intelligent behaviour by trying to mimic the structure and function of our nervous system. This nervous system is usually abstracted as a weighted directed graph where the nodes are neurons (nerve cells) and the edges between them are the connections between the neurons. The weight on each edge indicates the type (inhibiting or stimulating) and strength of interaction between the adjacent neurons.

Perceptrons

The simplest kind of neural network is a *perceptron* that consists of a single neuron having several real-valued or binary inputs and a binary output. The inputs come via weighted edges and are multiplied by the weights on those edges. The net input to the neuron at any time is the sum of all the weighted inputs. If this net input exceeds a threshold, then the neuron will trigger and produce an output of '1', or else, the output will be '0'. The perceptron is shown in Fig 3.9.

Ideally, this perceptron is trained to respond to certain inputs with certain desired outputs. Initially, the weights of the perceptron are assigned arbitrarily. Next, during the training period, a series of inputs are presented to the perceptron—each of the form $(x_1, x_2,...,x_n)$. For each such input, there is a desired output, either 0 or 1. The actual output is determined by the net input which is

$$\text{Net input} = w_1 x_1 + w_2 x_2 +...+ w_n x_n \qquad (3.2)$$

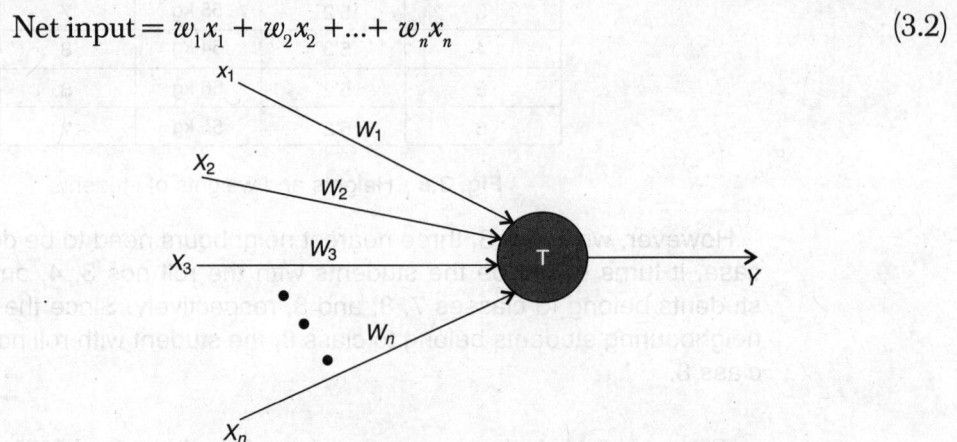

Fig. 3.9   A perceptron

If the net input is less than the threshold then the output is 0, or else the output is 1. If the perceptron gives a wrong (undesirable) output, then the following situations could have taken place.

The desired output is 0, but the net input is above threshold. Hence, the actual output becomes 1. As a result the net input should decrease.

In such a case the weights should be decreased. The decrease in weights is determined using the *perceptron learning algorithm* according to which, the decrease in the weight of an edge should be directly proportional to the input through that edge. Therefore,

New weight of an edge $i =$ old weight $- c x_i$

There are several algorithms depending on what c is. At present it is assumed to be a constant.

The idea here is that if the input through some edge was very high, then that edge must have mostly contributed to the error. Hence, the weight of that edge is reduced more (proportional to the input along that edge).

The other case of the perceptron making a mistake is when the desired output is 1, but the net input is below threshold. Hence, the net input should increase.

In this case the weights should be increased. Using the same intuition as above, the increase in the weight of an edge should be proportional to the input through that edge. Hence,

New weight of an edge i = old weight + cx_i

What about c? If c is actually a constant, then the algorithm is known as the 'fixed increment rule'. Note that in this case, the perceptron may not correct its mistake immediately. Even though the weights are changed because of a mistake, the new weights do not guarantee that the same mistake will not be repeated. This could happen if c is very small. However, by repeated application of the same input, the weights will change slowly each time, until that mistake is avoided.

c could also be chosen in such a way to definitely avoid the most recent mistake the next time it is presented the same input. This is known as the 'absolute correction rule'. The problem with this approach is that by learning one input, it might 'forget' a previously learnt input. For example, if one input leads to an increase in some weight and then, if the next input decreases it, then such a problem might arise.

Example 3.11 Consider the data shown in Example 3.10, reproduced below for convenience.

Roll No	Height	Weight	Class
1	4'7"	50 kg	7
2	4'9"	52 kg	7
3	5'2"	55 kg	7
4	5'3"	54 kg	8
5	5'2"	56 kg	8
6	5'2"	55 kg	?

Fig. 3.10 Heights and weights of students

A perceptron can be built that takes two inputs, the height and the weight of students, and produce an output of 0 if the input record is of a student of class 7 and an output of 1 if the input record is of a student of class 8. The perceptron being built is shown in Fig 3.11. The height and weight are treated as variables x_1 and x_2, respectively.

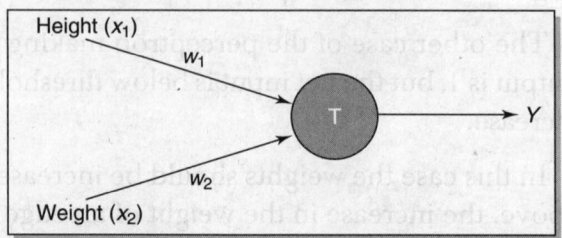

Fig 3.11   Perceptron predicting the classes of students

Step 1   Assume that initially, both weights w_1 and w_2 are equal to 1. Now, consider the first record, i.e. the student with roll no. 1. The height and weight of this student is 55 inches and 50 kg, respectively. The net input, therefore, is equal to $55 \times 1 + 50 \times 1 = 105$. For this input, the desirable output is 0 because the student belongs to class 7. Hence, the initial threshold should be set to something beyond 105. Assume it to be set to 110.

Step 2   Next, consider the second record, i.e. the student with roll no. 2, whose height and weight is 57" and 52 kg, respectively. The net input is $57 \times 1 + 52 \times 1 = 109$. Since the threshold was set at 110 in Step 1, the net input is less than the threshold. As a result, the output will be 0 corresponding to class 7; this is the desirable result.

Step 3   Next, consider the third record, i.e., the student with roll no. 3, whose height and weight is 62" and 55 kg, respectively. The net input is $62 \times 1 + 55 \times 1 = 117$. Since the existing threshold is 110, the net input is more than the threshold. Hence, the output will be 1 corresponding to class 8; this is undesirable since, the student with roll no. 3 actually belongs to class 7.

Hence, the net input has to be reduced, and as a result the weights will also have to be reduced (or increase the threshold). According to the perceptron learning algorithm,

New weight of an edge i = old weight $- cx_i$

Thus,

$$w_1 = 1 - 62c$$

$$w_2 = 1 - 55c$$

By using the 'absolute correction rule', c will have to be set to the minimum possible real number that will result in a correct output for the current record.

The desired expression is

$$w_1 x_1 + w_2 x_2 \leq T$$

The desired output will be

$$(1 - 62c) \times 62 + (1 - 55c) \times 55 \leq 110$$

Solving this,

$$c = 0.00102$$

With this value,

$$w_1 = 1 - 62c = 0.93676$$

$$w_2 = 1 - 55c = 0.9439$$

With these new weights, the net input becomes

$$w_1 x_1 + w_2 x_2 = 0.93676 \times 62 + 0.9439 \times 55 = 109.99362$$

This input is less than the threshold, thus the output class is the desired class. This procedure continues for all the available input records in the training data. The final weights are used as the weights of the model and the new records such as that of the student with roll no. 6, is fed to the perceptron, to estimate their class.

Beyond Perceptrons

Perceptrons cannot learn to successfully classify all kinds of data. If data records are represented as points in a high-dimensional space, then the points corresponding to different classes should be *linearly separable*, i.e. there should be a *hyperplane* that separates them. This is because the net input is computed by an equation that represents a *hyperplane*.

For the data that is not linearly separable, a single perceptron is not useful. However, it has been shown that by using multiple perceptrons connected into a network, it is possible to learn any training data. In particular, neurons organized into three layers, such that the neurons in one layer are only connected to the neurons in the next layer, are sufficient for any training data. Such networks are known as *feed-forward back-propagation networks* because the input records are fed from the first layer of neurons to the next, whereas the classification error is propagated from the last layer to the previous layers.

Back propagation networks and other neural network architectures are popular in pattern recognition and machine learning applications. However, in data mining, where the models should be easily interpretable by humans, they have not been very successful.

3.5.6 ASSOCIATIVE CLASSIFIERS

Approaches based on association rule mining – called *associative classifiers* have been devised for classification. These approaches assume that each record contains only *boolean* attributes and a *categorical* class label. Since categorical and quantitative attributes can ultimately be converted to boolean attributes, this assumption is not restrictive.

Once all attributes (including the class label) are made boolean, the dataset becomes a transactional dataset and association rule mining can be applied. Any standard association rule mining algorithm can be used for this purpose. For classification purposes, it is only necessary to mine rules where the RHS consists of a class label. Such rules are called *class association rules*.

Intuitively, a class association rule: $X \rightarrow C_i$ indicates that when X is present in a given test record, its class is likely to be C_i. Typically, a given test record would match several such rules and some of them may conflict. Different associative classifiers resolve these conflicts in different ways. For example, one may select the rule with best confidence, or select some k most-confident rules and take their majority vote.

Associative classifiers have several advantages:

1. Frequent itemsets capture all *dominant relationships* between items in a dataset.

2. Efficient linear-time algorithms exist for mining frequent itemsets.

3. These classifiers naturally handle *missing values* and *outliers* as they only deal with *statistically significant* associations.

4. Extensive performance studies have shown associative classifiers to be as accurate, or even better, than previous approaches.

3.5.7 OTHER APPROACHES

Other classification approaches based on the Naïve Bayes model, but bypassing the independence assumption, have been developed. The general approach is to estimate the distribution of records in each class $P(X|C)$ and use this for classification.

Approaches based on the *maximum entropy principle* have been devised by considering the characteristics of the training data as constraints on the distribution of records. This principle states that the distribution $P(X|C)$ will have the maximum entropy among all the distributions that satisfy the constraints observed from the training data. It is based on the intuition that if there is no evidence of any particular order in a system, then no such order exists and hence, entropy (or disorder) should be maximized.

Approaches based on association rule mining, known as *associative classifiers*, have been devised for classification. First rules are mined where the LHS contains attributes and the RHS consists of a class label. Such rules indicate that when the attributes in the LHS are observed in a record, the class label of the RHS should be output. There may be several rules which conflict for a given record and the conflict is resolved using the support and confidence of those rules.

Frequent itemset mining has also been combined with the maximum entropy approach described above by treating the frequent itemsets (with their supports) as constraints on the distribution of records in each class. Several studies have shown associative classifiers to be as good as other approaches in terms of classification accuracy. Since very efficient algorithms exist for frequent itemset mining, these associative classifiers are also efficient. Finally, they are also robust to noise and missing values in the data as they are based on the statistically significant relationships between attributes.

3.6 OPTIMAL CLASSIFICATION ALGORITHMS

Classification is such an important problem with diverse applications, that the discovery of an optimal solution would be a landmark in the history of technology. This objective is impeded by the infamous *no-free-lunch* theorem as discussed below.

3.6.1 NO-FREE-LUNCH THEOREM

Intuitively, this theorem indicates that it is impossible to obtain an optimal classifier that has the best accuracy on all datasets. In fact, this theorem makes a stronger statement:

Theorem (No-Free-Lunch) Represent a classifier as a function $h(X)$ that takes an input record and outputs a class label. Let $f(X)$ be an idealistic function that always outputs the correct class label. Then, for any given training dataset d, the expected misclassification rate of any two classifiers A and B on unseen records, when averaged over all possible f, is equal.

Before abandoning the pursuit for an optimal classifier, one should look at this theorem more closely. It not only claims that there is no best classifier, it claims that *all classifiers are equally good.* But experimentation with real-life datasets reveals that some classifiers do perform better than others in specific domains.

The problem in the above theorem arises from the fact that the misclassification rate is *averaged over every possible real world scenario f.* If we are given no information about the real-world, this makes sense because any scenario *f* must be considered equally likely. However, if we *do* have specific information about the real-world domain then we should be able to do better.

3.6.2 MAX-ENTROPY BASED CLASSIFIERS

In many applications, specific information about the real-world domain may be available in terms of *constraints* on the function $f(X)$ that maps input records to class labels. For example, we might know that if X contains a particular attribute-value combination, then the class-label will definitely be C_1.

If such real-world constraints are available, the no-free-lunch theorem above doesn't hold strictly. In the theorem statement above, the misclassification rate must be averaged over only those *f* which satisfy the real-world constraints. It may then be possible to design a classifier that performs better than others.

Max-entropy classifiers make use of such input constraints on the distribution of records in classes, $P(X|C)$. There could be many ways of distributing records in classes such that they satisfy the given constraints. Max-entropy classifiers follow the *maximum entropy principle* to decide on the correct distribution. This principle states that the distribution is *as random as possible while satisfying the given constraints.*

The intuition behind this principle is that if we do not have evidence for any particular *order* in a system, we should assume that no such order exists and hence entropy (or disorder or randomness) should be maximized. Technically, the entropy of a distribution is computed using the formula:

$$H = -\sum P(X) \, log \, P(X)$$

where the summation is over each possible record X.

Another way to look at max-entropy classifiers is as a refinement of Naïve Bayes, which assumes *independence* between attributes to calculate $P(X|C)$. The real-world constraints that are input to a max-entropy classifier represent *dependencies* that need to be considered while calculating $P(X|C)$.

Example 3.12 Consider the application of detecting spam emails. Assume that each email is represented as a set of keywords. Then the training data consists of records each of which is a set of keywords and has a class label in {*spam, nonspam*}. For simplicity assume that the total domain of keywords consists of only 3 keywords: {A, B, C}.

Suppose, from real-world domain knowledge, we know the following constraints regarding records in the *spam* class:

1. $P(A) = 0.2$
2. $P(B) = 0.3$
3. $P(C) = 0.1$
4. $P(AB) = 0.1$

Our task is to determine the distribution $P(X|spam)$ given these constraints. These constraints form constraints on the distribution of records. For example, from the first constraint, we get:

$$P(A) = P(A\overline{B}\overline{C}) + P(A\overline{B}C) + P(AB\overline{C}) + P(ABC) = 0.2$$

We get 4 such equations using the above constraints. In addition, one more constraint can be added to ensure that the sum of probabilities of all records must be 1. There are 8 possible records in this domain and 5 equations. Hence, there would be multiple solutions.

Using the maximum entropy principle, we should select from these distributions the one with maximum entropy. We can enumerate possible solutions, or use other analytical means to arrive at this distribution.

3.6.3   GIS Algorithm

In simple cases, it may be possible to enumerate possible distributions, or otherwise analytically arrive at the maximum entropy distribution. In realistic cases with more than a few variables, this is not possible. Fortunately, there exist simple iterative techniques to compute the max-entropy distribution. One such technique is the Generalized Iterative Scaling (GIS) algorithm.

The GIS algorithm relies on a result which states that the max-entropy distribution $P(X|C)$ will always be of the form:

$$P(X/C) = \mu_0 \prod \mu_i^{f_i(X)}$$

where, $f_i(X)$ is an indicator function whose value is 1 if record X satisfies the ith constraint, 0 otherwise; and μ_i is a real-valued coefficient, or weight of the ith constraint and μ_0 is a normalization parameter to ensure that the distribution sums up to 1.

The algorithm starts with a uniform distribution for $P(X|C)$ and the values for all weights as 1. It then iteratively proceeds to compute the required max-entropy distribution that satisfies known constraints. Each iteration consists of 3 steps:

$$Ef_i = \sum_X P(X/C)f_i(X)$$

$$\mu_i = \mu_i \frac{\tilde{E}f_i}{Ef_i}$$

$$P(X/C) = \mu_0 \prod \mu_i^{f_i(X)}$$

In the second step, the denominator Ef_i is the expected value of f_i computed over all possible records in the domain, where as the numerator is the observed value of f_i and is computed over the training data. The iterations continue until there is not much change in the value of the weights, or until all constraints are satisfied by the distribution.

Although theoretically robust, one drawback in the GIS algorithm is that it can be computationally expensive, being linear in both the number of constraints and the number of possible records in the domain.

3.6.4   ACME ALGORITHM

Max-entropy classifiers yield accurate results if the given constraints reflect all the dependencies of the real-world domain. Extracting the right set of constraints for a domain has been more of an art than a science. The ACME algorithm (Associative Classifier based on Maximum Entropy) is a recent max-entropy classifier that uses frequent itemsets (and their supports) as the constraints.

The motivation is that frequent itemsets capture all *dominant relationships* between items in a dataset. Hence, the combination is potent – it combines the theoretical robustness of max-entropy models with the exhaustiveness of frequent patterns. The drawback of computational expense remains and more research is needed for more efficient algorithms for computing max-entropy models.

3.7 REGRESSION

The techniques discussed in Section 3.6 are useful for estimating or predicting unknown class labels of data records. A class attribute is essentially a categorical attribute having discrete values. In many applications, it is necessary to estimate or predict the values of a *numeric* attribute that has a continuous range. Techniques that are used for this purpose are called as regression techniques.

The numeric attribute to be estimated (often called as the *dependent variable*) may depend on a single input attribute (called as univariate regression) or on multiple attributes (called multivariate regression). Broadly, regression techniques are classified as *linear* or *non-linear* depending on whether the numeric attribute to be estimated has a linear or a non-linear relationship with the input variables.

3.7.1 LINEAR REGRESSION

Regression problems are usually solved by assuming some form of an equation that relates the input variables to the dependent variable. In linear regression, the equation takes the form of a line (in 2 dimensions) and a (hyper) plane in higher dimensions. If y is the dependent variable and $x_1, x_2, \ldots, x_n$ are the input variables, then the relation between them is of the form:

$$y = w_1 x_1 + w_2 x_2 + \ldots + w_n x_n$$

The training data contains multiple records giving the values of y for specific values of the input variables. The problem thus reduces to computing the values of $w_1, w_2, \ldots, w_n$ that *best fits* the data. The best fit is obtained by the equation that minimizes some error function. An example of an error function is the standard mean square error:

$$E = (1/n) \sum (y_i - y_i')^2$$

where, y_i is the actual value of the dependent variable and y_i' is its estimated value using the linear equation above.

3.7.2   NON-LINEAR REGRESSION

Non-linear regression (also called *curve-fitting*) differs from above only in that the form of the equation that relates the dependent and input variables is not linear. It may be polynomial or even exponential. Complex algorithms exist to solve specific non-linear regression problems. However, often, the problem can be reduced to linear regression by applying some transformation.

For example, if the form of the regression equation is:

$$y = Ae^{Bx}$$

then, by taking the logarithm on both sides, we obtain:

$$\ln y = \ln A + Bx$$

This equation can now be solved using normal linear regression techniques using $\ln y$ and x as the dependent and input variables respectively.

3.7.3   DATA MINING AND MACHINE LEARNING APPROACHES

While the above methods for linear and non-linear regression are primarily obtained from Statistics, several data mining and machine learning approaches have also been developed. Many of these do not even assume a specific form of a regression equation. Instead, they work by adapting existing classification approaches.

One approach is to treat small ranges of the dependent numeric variable as classes and then apply classification approaches directly. Some classification approaches are well-suited for this. One example is *regression trees*, which are like decision trees except that instead of a class label at the leaf, we store the average value of the dependent variable for the training records that reach that leaf.

Neural network models such as backpropagation networks are also often used for regression. In fact, it is easy to see the connection between the regression equation for linear regression and the equation of a perceptron. Both seem to be doing essentially the same thing!

SUMMARY

Classification techniques are used to classify data records into a single class among a set of predefined classes. They work by constructing a model of a training dataset consisting of records with known class labels. These techniques have been studied extensively in Machine Learning and have numerous applications ranging from *spam e-mail* detection, credit-card fraud detection, speech recognition and computer vision.

Various classification algorithms have been designed including decision tree algorithms, Naïve Bayes, Bayesian Belief networks, nearest neighbour schemes and neural networks. Classifiers are evaluated by measuring their accuracy on a test dataset. Other performance metrics such as speed of classification or memory used are not so crucial, but still desirable.

One issue to beware of is that classifiers may learn too many nuances from the training data that are not useful later – a phenomenon known as over-fitting. Classifiers also need to be robust to handle missing data in the input, or noisy and inconsistent data. Classifiers can be combined simply by treating them as citizens in a democracy and allowing them to vote for the correct class.

EXERCISES

Test Your Understanding

1. Describe the basic notions of classification, training dataset, test dataset, and accuracy to a non-technical friend or relative.

2. Provide two example applications of classification.

3. What are precision and recall? How do they differ from accuracy?

4. Why is cross-validation useful in evaluating a classifier?

5. In what ways can a classifier handle missing data?

6. (a) The probability of cancer in a population is 1%. A test (test 1) for cancer identifies cancer patients with a probability of 50% and identifies non-cancer patients with a probability of 99.5%.

Given that a patient has tested positive, what is the probability that he actually has cancer? Also, calculate the entropy of the population and the information gain obtained by using this test.

(b) There is another test (test 2) that identifies cancer patients with a probability of 70% and non-cancer patients with a probability of 75%. Out of test 1 and test 2, which one will the ID3 algorithm select first for splitting the population?

7. Briefly describe the Naïve Bayes and *k*-NN approaches to classification.

8. A perceptron has three inputs I1, I2 and I3 and an output value OUT. The weights for the inputs are 0.3, 0.2, and 0.1 and the threshold is 0.5.

Considering the inputs as I1 = 1.5, I2 = 2, I3 = 1, what is the output of the perceptron?

Projects

1. Implement one of the classification algorithms discussed in this chapter and evaluate its accuracy, precision, and recall on any dataset.

    [The UCI KDD Archive at http://kdd.ics.uci.edu/ is an excellent source of datasets to test data mining algorithms.]

2. Implement a software tool to maintain a repository of classification algorithms, metrics, and datasets.

The software should automatically evaluate all the available metrics for each algorithm on each dataset present in its repository. The results of the evaluations should be stored on disk for future use.

This tool would be highly useful to anyone wanting to build new classification algorithms.

Improve Your Research Skills

1. Will any decision tree algorithms discussed work well for classifying *e-mails* into *spam* and *non-spam*? Why? If the answer is no, how can they be improved? What other strategies (other than decision trees) would be good for this task?

2. Design and analyze an algorithm to classify webpages into a Yahoo!-like directory hierarchy (e.g. Arts, Art History, Artists, Business, Computers, etc.). Use the existing Yahoo! directory as training data.

3. Given a record X, the Naïve Bayes classifier selects the class C for which $P(C/X)$ is maximum. This is intuitive because X has occurred and given this, state the class which has the maximum probability.

    However, intuition also works in another way; the *maximum likelihood estimation*

technique demands that the best estimate for the class of a sample record is the one that maximizes the likelihood of an occurrence of that record. Hence, select the class for which $P(X/C)$ is maximum.

Explain the contrast between the two approaches and resolve the conflict. Which approach is correct?

4. A random forest is a set of decision trees built from independent random samples of the training data. At classification time, all decision trees are used and the class with maximum 'votes' is chosen.

Why would a random forest perform better than a single decision tree built from the entire training data, and under what circumstances would it perform better? Be precise in your answer.

Improve the Field

1. Integrate the ideas from various classifiers to design a grand classifier that has the best features of the other classifiers.

2. Design a methodology whereby a classifier interacts with the user to build a classification model. The interaction should be as minimal as possible.

As an example, the interaction can be used to resolve the contradictions inherent in the training data, or to ask the user to label some unlabelled records. This is useful because typically, the amount of labelled data available is small, whereas the amount of unlabelled data is huge.

CHAPTER 4

CLUSTERING

Birds of a feather flock together.

INTRODUCTION

Every branch of knowledge depends on the division of its concepts into separate categories. For example, biologists have developed a taxonomy to categorize all the living things into kingdom, phylum, class, order, family, genus, and species. Music is categorized into various genres—*carnatic, hindustani, jazz, rock, bass, pop, new age*, etc. Directories on the World Wide Web such as Yahoo! categorize webpages based on their subject matter into various categories such as business, computers, etc.

In all the above examples, the objects within a category are considerably similar when compared to the objects across categories. While humans are adept at categorizing objects, the task of clustering in data mining is to automatically come up with such a categorization. Clustering is the task of organizing data into groups (known as clusters) such that the data objects that are similar to (or close to) each other are put in the same cluster. There is no one correct basis of clustering—there could be many different ways to categorize data objects. Clustering schemes are evaluated based on the similarity of objects within each cluster and the dissimilarity of objects across clusters.

To a beginner, clustering is often confused with classification. The two, however, are significantly different. Classification is a form of supervised learning, where the class labels of some training samples are given—these samples are used as examples to supervise the learning of a classification model. On the other hand, clustering is a form of unsupervised learning in which no class labels are provided. Instead, data records need to be grouped based on how similar they are to other records.

Clustering is often the first data mining task applied on a given collection of data and is used to explore if any underlying patterns exist in the data. The presence of dense well-separated clusters indicates that there are structure and patterns to be explored in the data. Examples of clustering tasks include dividing the stars in the sky into constellations, dividing a large group of people into small teams, and segmenting customers into small groups for additional analysis in marketing activities.

4.1   BASIC PROBLEM DEFINITION

A cluster is a collection of data objects that are similar to each other and dissimilar to the data objects in other clusters. The following illustration will help to grasp the abstract definitions provided later.

Illustration 4.1 Table 4.1 shows data related to students, their native state, and their marks in various subjects.

Table 4.1   Data of students

Roll No.	Name	Gender	State	Maths	Physics	Chemistry	English	Social Science
200101001	Govind	M	AP	94	89	75	62	57
200101002	Ramakanth	M	MP	72	65	67	80	85
200101003	Karuna	F	AP	95	92	77	65	60
...	...	...	...	...	...	...	...	...

In this table, it is clear that Govind and Karuna have obtained very similar marks in all the subjects. They can, therefore, be put as parts of the same cluster. In contrast, the marks obtained by Ramakanth are very different. Therefore, he needs to be part of a different cluster. In this manner, all the students can be grouped into a few clusters. This grouping can be very useful for several purposes such as career counselling, forming tutorial groups where different groups are taught differently, and even for future employers to know which group to target.

Instance   An instance is an object that is represented by a vector of numeric or categorical attributes.

The input data model for clustering consists of instances (also known as samples, cases, objects, or records) where each instance is defined by a number of attributes (also known as features or variables), which could be numeric (such as marks in various subjects) or categorical (such as gender and state). It may be recalled that in Chapter 3, the input data model for classification also consisted of such instances. The difference is that the instances here are not labelled.

In order to determine whether two data objects are similar to each other, clustering strategies use the notion of a distance function. Such a function takes two objects as input and returns a positive real number representing the distance between the two objects—the smaller the distance, the more similar the two objects are to each other.

Distance Function A distance function d is a mapping from every pair of instances (x, y) to real numbers such that,

1. $d(x, y) \geq 0$
2. $d(x, x) = 0$
3. $d(x, y) = d(y, x)$
4. $d(x, y) < d(x, z) + d(z, y)$

The first three properties are obvious. The fourth property is known as the *triangle inequality*. Several popular distance functions are available that satisfy these properties and one of them needs to be chosen for each clustering problem based on the application domain. Functions satisfying all four properties are also referred to as metrics. In some applications, distance measures are designed that do not follow the triangle inequality. Strictly speaking, such functions are not distance metrics, however, they are still useful for clustering.

Clustering Given a set of n instances $x_1,\ldots, x_n$ represented by vectors $v_1,\ldots,v_n$, and a distance function d, the clustering problem is to determine a function f such that $f(x_i) = j$, where j is a (small) natural number corresponding to a cluster. The function f is to be designed with the objective that, instances in the same cluster must be closer to each other (with respect to d) than instances across clusters.

For many practical applications, it is either very difficult or even impossible to design clustering algorithms that achieve the objective stated in the definition. Instead, algorithms are usually designed to satisfy the objective as much as possible. This means that there may be instances that are put as parts of the same cluster, but some of these are actually closer to instances in other clusters. This also means that there is usually no single correct answer for a clustering task.

4.2   CLUSTERING: APPLICATIONS

There are numerous potential applications of clustering analysis. Some of these applications are listed below, under two broad categories.

4.2.1   TARGETTING SIMILAR PEOPLE OR OBJECTS

Student tutorial groups   Consider students completing their tenth class exams. It is theoretically possible to analyze the performance of each student in various subjects and then provide specific training which will benefit that student. Although this kind of focussed training is very effective, it is clearly infeasible due to the size of faculty and resources required. However, by dividing the students into groups based on their exam scores, entire groups can be targeted differently.

Each group of students can be characterized by the fact that they may be good in some subjects, average in some others, and bad in the remaining. Specific tutorial classes or other learning material can be designed to train these students in the subjects in which they are weak. They can also be given special advanced lectures and study material to help them advance rapidly in the subjects in which they are good.

Hobby groups   Several popular chatting engines on the World Wide Web collect details regarding the hobbies and interests of their customers. By clustering the customers based on their shared interests, it is possible to identify people who might become very good friends. These hobby groups can be used as a starting point for other applications such as matchmaking or recommendation engines.

Health support groups   Health expert systems are software programs that are used to diagnose the condition of patients by enquiring about their symptoms. Patients could be asked to list the symptoms of their condition or disease. For most well-known diseases, the expert system usually has no trouble in finding the right diagnosis. However, for some conditions, the expert system may not have any diagnosis to provide.

Nevertheless, for all the conditions, these expert systems can be used to enable people, sharing similar symptoms, to communicate with each other. Most patients find comfort and obtain a sense of well-being when they communicate with fellow patients. This is especially useful when the underlying condition or trauma is due to psychological reasons.

Customer groups for marketing   It is useful for any company to find clusters of their customers based on characteristics such as age group, gender, occupation, etc. Such a segmentation of customers is invaluable for several reasons as given below:

- It can help in finding a suitable sample of people for surveys regarding their products—each cluster needs to be represented in the sample.

- The problems/suggestions of each group of customers might be unique.

- It can help decide on how to advertise their products based on the feedback given by each customer group.

Clustering e-mail   E-mail is one of the most pervasive applications of computers. People or organizations, who receive hundreds of e-mail messages, will definitely find utility in a program that can automatically categorize their e-mail messages into different groups. If e-mail messages are previously categorized (such as *spam* or *non-spam*), then this becomes a classification task. However, the groups are often not known in advance and therefore, a clustering algorithm is needed here.

4.2.2   Deciding on the Locations for an Activity

Exam centres   The addresses of the applicants for an exam can be utilized to form a map of their geographical locations. These locations can then be clustered into groups and suitable exam centres for each group can be decided. This would reduce the overall effort and the cost of travel for the numerous applicants for that exam.

Locations for a business chain   In order to decide locations for setting up a supermarket chain, Automatic Teller Machines (ATM), etc., it is necessary to identify densely populated regions of prospective customers. By surveying a sizeable sample of prospective customers and determining their geographical locations, it becomes possible to cluster these locations. The places to set up the supermarkets or ATMs can then be divided appropriately in these clusters.

Planning a political strategy   A political party may be weak (inactive) in some constituencies of the state or country and strong (highly active) in the others. By clustering each category of constituency (weak or strong) separately, it becomes possible to identify the entire regions that are either weak or strong. With this information, a politician could decide to form new centres of activity in the weak regions and distribute these centres appropriately. It may also be useful to consider shifting some centres from the strong regions to the weak ones.

Alternatively, if the party is by and large not very strong, the politician may decide to concentrate the strength of a party in one particular region.

4.3   MEASUREMENT OF SIMILARITY

Clustering algorithms rely on the ability to determine whether two data objects are similar to each other. For this they use the notion of a distance function (Section 4.1) where this function takes two objects as input and returns a positive real number representing the distance between the two objects—the smaller the distance, the more similar the two objects are to each other.

Several popular distance functions are available and one of these needs to be chosen for each clustering problem depending on the data types in that specific application. Some of these functions strictly follow the criteria listed in under the definition for distance function (Section 4.1) and are referred to as metrics. Other functions are not designed so strictly due to practical reasons and may not follow some of the criteria listed in that definition.

The distance function is chosen based on the type of attributes used to describe an instance in a clustering problem. The attributes may be categorical or numerical. Each of these has its own accepted ways of measuring distance. Here the distance functions, used for instances that consist of the same types of attributes, are described. Section 4.3.1 will deal with the possibilities of measuring distance when instances consist of more than one type of attributes.

It is to be noted that what follows should be treated only as generic guidelines for deciding what distance function to use. Ultimately, the nuances of specific applications should be taken into account before making the final decision.

4.3.1   NOMINAL (CATEGORICAL) VARIABLES

Categorical variables are also known as nominal variables. The values for a nominal variable are names or strings that come from a (small) set of possible names. For practical storage and processing purposes, the names may be numbers. However, normal processing of numeric variables such as addition and comparisons, such as 'less than', do not make sense. They are only useful for comparison of equality and inequality. Examples of nominal variables include gender, race, country, the make of a car, etc.

Consider two instances x and y, which consist of n nominal attributes. Then, the distance between x and y can be measured using the following function:

$$d(x, y) = (n - m)/n$$

where m is the number of matches, i.e. the number of attributes for which both x and y have the same value.

Weights   In some applications, certain attributes may be more important than the others in determining distance. As an example, in deciding whether two people are similar, it may be more important to consider whether they are from the same state rather than having the same name. To take care of this, it is possible to add different weights to different attributes. The distance computation then becomes

$$d(x, y) = 1 - (\Sigma w_i / W)$$

where w_i are the weights of the attributes whose values match the values in x and y, and W is the sum of the weights of all the attributes.

Binary variables   A binary variable is a special type of nominal variable that has only two possible values. Normally, gender, marital status, experimental results (success, failure), presence of a word in a document, etc. are represented as binary variables. In some applications it may be significant if two instances share one of the values of a binary variable but not the other. This is shown in the following example.

Example 4.1   Consider the task of measuring the distance between two text documents x and y. Here, each possible word is treated as a binary variable that is either present or absent in a particular document. Since there are many possible words, it is generally insignificant if any particular word is absent in both the documents. However, if a word is present in both the documents, it is considered significant for the purpose of distance computation.

It follows that higher weights are specified for the variables that are present in both the documents and lesser weights are specified for the variables that are absent in both the documents.

Note that the requirement in Example 4.1 is different from the solution discussed earlier where the weights were static—they were decided once and for all, for each variable. Here, the weight of a variable has to be changed depending on whether or not, the two instances share the same value of the weight. One way to do this is to use the *Jaccard coefficient*:

$$d(x, y) = (n - m)/(n - s)$$

where m is the number of the binary variables whose values match in x and y, s is the number of the binary variables whose values are 'absent' in both x and y, and n is the number of attributes.

The above situation may also arise in some applications with non-binary nominal variables– it may be necessary to give different weights to different attributes depending on the values they take in specific instances. For such applications, the solution is to treat a nominal variable v, which can take p different values, as p binary variables. These binary variables are set to 1 if the corresponding value of v is found in the current instance and or else, to 0.

4.3.2 NUMERIC VARIABLES

Consider two instances x and y that consist of n numeric attributes. The instances can be represented as vectors of the values of these attributes as $(x_1, x_2, x_3,..., x_n)$ and $(y_1, y_2, y_3,..., y_n)$. The distance between x and y will be determined as

$$d(x, y) = (|x_1 - y_1|^q + |x_2 - y_2|^q + ... + |x_n - y_n|^q)^{1/q}$$

where q is a positive integer.

This is known as the *Minkowski* distance. The most common forms of this function is when $q = 1$ (in which case it is known as the *manhattan* distance) and $q = 2$ (in which case it is known as the *euclidean* distance). When q becomes infinite the distance computed is known as the *chebychev* distance. As for nominal variables, weights can be applied on each attribute to signify how important it is. In this case, the computation is

$$d(x, y) = \left(w_i |x_1 - y_1|^q + w_2 |x_2 - y_2|^q + ... + w_k |x_n - y_n|^q \right)^{1/q}$$

where w_i is the weight of the ith dimension.

Ordinal variables

Ordinal variables are numeric attributes that are intended to represent the rank order of some measured entities. They have all the properties of nominal variables–they can be compared with respect to equality. In addition, they can be compared using 'less than', 'greater than', etc.

Examples of ordinal variables include the rank orders obtained in most competitions. These ranks can be used to determine if a person is better or worse than another, but not by how much. Two people may differ very slightly in their performance, but their ranks may be very different due to an intense competition. Hence, it is meaningless to add or subtract two ranks. Equal differences in rank values do not represent equal intervals.

Consider two instances x and y that consist of k ordinal variables. The range of these k variables may be different—some of them may have only a few ranks, while some may have many ranks. If the Minkowski distance function is applied directly, the result will heavily depend on the range of these variables. Therefore, before applying the Minkowski distance function, it is necessary to first standardize these variables.

If x has a rank r_i for an ordinal variable v whose maximum rank is M, then the standardized value of v is computed as

$$z_i = (r_i - 1)/(M - 1)$$

These standardized values are always in the range $(0, 1)$ and therefore do not have the drawback mentioned above. Hence, they can be used in the computation of the Minkowski distance and its variants.

Interval and ratio-scaled variables

Interval-scaled variables are the numeric attributes that satisfy all the criteria of the ordinal variables (that is comparisons of 'less than', 'equals', etc. are meaningful) and, in addition, have the property of equal distances between the values representing equal intervals. As a result, operations such as addition and subtraction become meaningful. However, the ratios between the values are not meaningful. Hence, multiplication and division cannot be carried out directly. However, the ratio of differences between the values is meaningful. An example of an interval-scaled variable is the date of an event.

Ratio-scaled variables are numeric attributes that satisfy all the criteria of interval-scaled variables, and in addition also have meaningful ratios between their values. Examples of the ratio-scaled variables are weight, height, length, mass, etc. of objects.

Both interval and ratio-scaled variables can be measured in different units. For example, height can be measured in inches, feet, cm, etc. Clearly, from the above formula of the Minkowski distance, different distances will be computed depending on the unit used. This is undesirable. To avoid this, it is necessary to first standardize these variables before using the Minkowski distance functions. One way to do this is to apply the following two step procedure on each variable v:

1. First, calculate the mean absolute deviation, m,

$$m = (|v_1 - \mu| + |v_2 - \mu| + \ldots + |v_n - \mu|)/N$$

where $v_1, v_2, \ldots, v_n$ are the values of attribute v that actually occur in the data and μ is their mean.

2. Calculate the standardized measurement, or *z-score*,

$$z_i = (v_1 - \mu)/m$$

This *z-score* is devoid of units and can be used to compute the Minkowski distance and its variants.

Cosine similarity

The cosine similarity measures the opposite of distance (unlike the previous functions which were distance functions)–its value is high when the two input instances are very similar to each other. Given two instances whose attribute values are given by the vectors $x = (x_1, x_2, x_3,..., x_n)$ and $y = (y_1, y_2, y_3,..., y_n)$, their cosine similarity is defined as

$$x \cdot y/|x||y|$$

where

$$x \cdot y = (x_1 y_1 + x_2 y_2 + ... + x_n y_n)$$

and

$$|x| = \sqrt{(x_1^2 + x_2^2 + ... + x_n^2)}$$

This similarity measure represents the cosine of the angle between the vectors x and y. It is very popular in determining the similarity between text documents. Recent research suggests that both cosine similarity and euclidean distance measures yield similar results when the number of variables is high. One advantage of using cosine similarity is that the distances are naturally normalized to be in the range (0, 1).

4.3.3 INSTANCES WITH MIXED TYPES

The above subsections described the guidelines to compute the distance between two instances that have several attributes of the same type. We now move on to the computation of distance when instances are described by attributes of different types. The following procedure shows one way to design a good distance function for this mixed case:

1. Standardize the variables according to the previous subsections.

2. Further standardize the variables so that their values are within a common range. To standardize the value v_i of a variable v, whose range is (min$_1$, max$_1$), to a range of (min$_2$, max$_2$), compute

$$min_2 + (v_i - min_1)(max_2 - min_2)/(max_1 - min_1)$$

3. Separate out the mixture—group all the variables of each type together, and find the distances for each group separately. Utilize appropriate weights to represent the significance or importance of each component in the distance computation.

4. Finally, compute the resultant distance which will be the weighted average of the individual distances.

4.4 EVALUATION OF CLUSTERING ALGORITHMS

The primary metric of evaluation of clustering algorithms is the quality of the clusters they produce, i.e. the extent to which they satisfy the clustering objective stated in Section 4.1. According to this objective, instances in the same cluster must be closer to each other than to instances across clusters.

Often, the quality of clustering algorithms is evaluated subjectively. Each algorithm is run over several test datasets for which the natural clusters are previously known. This is possible if the datasets consist of familiar objects. For example, we would know the correct clustering for a dataset of animals, based on biological classification into species, etc. Alternatively, the dataset may consist of only two or three numeric attributes. In that case, the instances can be plotted in a two- or three-dimensional space and the clusters can be identified visually.

Sections 4.4.1–4.4.3 describe techniques for the objective evaluation of the quality of clustering algorithms. This is followed by other metrics for the evaluation of clustering algorithms.

4.4.1 SQUARED ERROR CRITERION

Instances in a cluster should be closer to the centre of that cluster than to the centre of any other cluster. One way to define the centre of a cluster is to use the mean of that cluster, which is calculated as the average along each attribute of all the points in that cluster.

Cluster Mean   If there are N data points in a cluster represented by tuples of the form $(x_{i1}, x_{i2},..., x_{in})$ for $i = 1...N$, then its mean is defined as

$$\text{mean} = (\Sigma x_{i1}/N,\ \Sigma x_{i2}/N,...,\ \Sigma x_{in}/N)$$

One may also use the median or mode to represent the centre of a cluster. The use of mode for defining cluster centres is especially appropriate when the data consists of categorical attributes.

If some point x is erroneously placed in a wrong cluster C_i, then the distance between x and the centre of C_i (which is $d(x, C_i)$ is going to be larger than the distance if x was placed in its correct cluster. Thus, this distance can be considered as an error that needs to be minimized over all the possible choices of C_i.

In statistics, the square of the error is normally taken as the function to be minimized because, in some applications, the error could take both positive and negative values. Thus, the square of the sum of distances of all the points from their cluster centres needs to be minimized.

This squared error criterion is expressed as

$$E = \sum_{i=1}^{N} \sum_{x \in C} d(x, \bar{x}_i)^2$$

where d is the distance function and $\bar{x}_i$ is the centre of the cluster C_i. The algorithm that finds clusters in such a way that the above sum is minimized would be a good clustering algorithm.

4.4.2 ABSOLUTE ERROR CRITERION

The squared error criterion has one significant drawback, it is heavily affected by the presence of outliers (data points with extreme values) in the dataset. The distance of an outlier point from its cluster centre will be quite large. The square of this distance will be even larger.

To avoid the above drawback, squaring the distances of points from their cluster centres can be avoided. The resulting measure is known as the absolute error criterion. It is expressed as

$$E = \sum_{i=1}^{N} \sum_{x \in C} d(x, \bar{x}_i)$$

where d is the distance function (which should always return positive values) and $\bar{x}_i$ is the centre of the cluster C_i. This measure of the clustering quality is relatively immune to the presence of outliers.

4.4.3 DISTANCE BETWEEN CLUSTERS

For a good clustering algorithm, the distances between its clusters will be large. To determine the distances between the clusters, several approaches exist. Given below are some of the widely used approaches.

Minimum distance   This is the distance between the closest pair of points (x, y) where x belongs to one cluster and y belongs to the other.

Maximum distance   This is the distance between the farthest pair of points (x, y) where x belongs to one cluster and y belongs to the other.

Average distance   This is the average of the distances between every pair of points (x, y) where x belongs to one cluster and y belongs to the other.

Mean distance   This is the distance between the means of the two clusters.

4.4.4 OTHER PERFORMANCE METRICS

While cluster quality is the most important performance metric, clustering algorithms should also perform well according to the following metrics:

Clustering time   This is the amount of time required by the algorithm to find clusters. In several exploratory applications, clustering needs to be done online and in real time. Hence, it is imperative that the clustering time is as small as possible.

Main memory usage   The amount of main memory required during clustering is not critical, but should be within practical limits so that it can work on current machines.

Scalability   It is important that the clustering algorithm is scalable to handle datasets that contain a huge number of instances and/or attributes.

In addition to the above performance metrics, it is desirable that a clustering algorithm has the following features:

Handle noise/outliers   Most applications have noisy data containing data points that do not really belong to any cluster. Such a point could arise because of the errors or missing values in data. It could also be because of an extreme instance (outlier) that really does not lie within any cluster.

Data-order independence   Some clustering strategies may be sensitive to the order in which the input records are presented to them and produce different clusters depending on this order. This is undesirable.

Arbitrary-shaped clusters Many clustering algorithms produce clusters whose shape is constrained in some way. For example, they may only produce spherical or convex clusters. This is undesirable. If arbitrary shaped clusters exist in the data, the algorithm should find them.

4.5 CLASSIFICATION OF CLUSTERING ALGORITHMS

Clustering algorithms are classified into different categories based on the overall techniques they use and also the kind of clusters they produce. This is useful because when given a clustering problem in a new application domain, the focus can be on a particular category of algorithm, if the kinds of clusters desired are known. Following are the major categories of clustering algorithms:

Partitioning methods These algorithms partition the input data instances into *disjoint spherical clusters*. They are useful in applications where each cluster represents a prototype, and other instances in the cluster are similar to this prototype.

Hierarchical methods In these methods, clusters which are very similar to each other are grouped into larger clusters. These larger clusters may further be grouped into still larger clusters, etc. In essence, a hierarchy of clusters is produced.

Density-based methods In these methods, clusters are 'grown' starting with some data points and then including the other neighbouring points as long as the neighbourhood is sufficiently 'dense'. These methods can find clusters of arbitrary shape and are useful in applications where such a feature is desired.

Grid-based methods In these methods, the space of instances is divided into a grid structure. Clustering techniques are then applied using cells of the grid as the basic units instead of individual data points. This has the advantage of improving the processing time significantly.

Other methods for clustering have been proposed in machine learning and other areas outside the field of data mining. These methods make use of various concepts such as wavelets, neural networks, genetic algorithms, gradient descent, etc. These techniques work like 'black boxes' that are hard to interpret. The clusters produced are, therefore, hard to explain. This is not desirable of data mining techniques, whose main purpose is to produce patterns that are understandable by humans. Due to this reason such algorithms have not been covered in this book.

Sections 4.6–4.9 describe the different clustering algorithms belonging to each of the categories mentioned above. In all these cases, it is assumed that a distance function d is available to compute the distance between data instances.

4.6 PARTITIONING METHODS

These algorithms partition the input data instances into disjoint spherical clusters. They are useful in applications where each cluster represents a prototype, and other instances in the cluster are similar to this prototype.

Partitioning methods require as input k, the number of clusters to produce. This severely limits the applicability of these methods. In most exploratory studies, the number of clusters may not be previously known. In order to know the number of clusters, it may be necessary to first run another kind of a clustering algorithm (such as a hierarchical algorithm) that does not require k as input.

4.6.1 OVERALL STRATEGY

Partitioning methods follow an iterative strategy as shown in the pseudo-code of Fig. 4.1 and explained as follows:

Partitioning Cluster (Data D, int k)

1. select k prototypes t_1, t_2...t_k, from D
2. **for** $i = 1,..., k$: initialize cluster $C_i = \{t_i\}$
3. **repeat:**
4.   **for each** point p in D:
5.   let t_j be the prototype that minimizes $d(t, p)$
6.   put p in cluster C_j
7. $quality$ = ClusteringQuality (C_1, C_2...C_k)
8.   Re-compute prototypes
9. **until** $quality$ does not change

Fig. 4.1 Clustering using partitioning

A partitioning algorithm starts by selecting k prototypes or representative data points for each cluster (lines 1, 2 of Fig. 4.1). The selection of prototypes is changed at each iteration in a manner that improves the overall *clustering quality* (line 8). Once the prototypes are selected, each data point is put in the cluster whose prototype it resembles the most (lines 4–6). In line 5, the function d represents the distance function used. These iterations continue until the clustering quality does not improve any further (lines 7, 9). In some implementations, the algorithm stops after a fixed maximum number of iterations.

To handle huge datasets, the above basic strategy is applied on small samples of the dataset and the result is used for clustering the entire dataset. Specific partitioning algorithms differ in the details of the above strategy such as how to select the initial k prototypes; how to define the quality of clustering; how to re-compute the prototypes in each iteration; how to utilize sampling for huge datasets.

4.6.2   THE K-MEANS ALGORITHM

By far, the most popular clustering algorithm used in scientific and industrial applications is the k-means algorithm, which is a partitioning algorithm. Its popularity stems from its simplicity and its firm foundation in statistics.

The Algorithm

In its normal version, the k-means algorithm works only for datasets that consist of numeric attributes. It takes k, the number of desired clusters, and the data points as input and produces k clusters as output. The functioning of the algorithm follows the pseudo-code for the general partitioning strategy given in Fig. 4.1. The details that characterize the algorithm are as follows:

1. First, it selects the initial k prototypes arbitrarily.
2. The squared error criterion in Section 4.4.1 is used to determine the clustering quality.
3. In each iteration, the prototype of each cluster is re-computed to be the *cluster mean* as defined in Section 4.4.1.
4. The basic version of k-means does not include any sampling techniques to scale to huge databases.

Illustration 4.2 Consider the task of clustering people into two clusters based on their heights and weights given in Table 4.2.

Table 4.2 Data for k-means example

Id	Name	Height (in)	Weight (kg)
x_1	Ram	64	60
x_2	Shyam	60	61
x_3	Gita	59	70
x_4	Mohan	68	71

Since we want two clusters, $k = 2$. When plotted on a graph, the data looks as shown in Fig. 4.2(a).

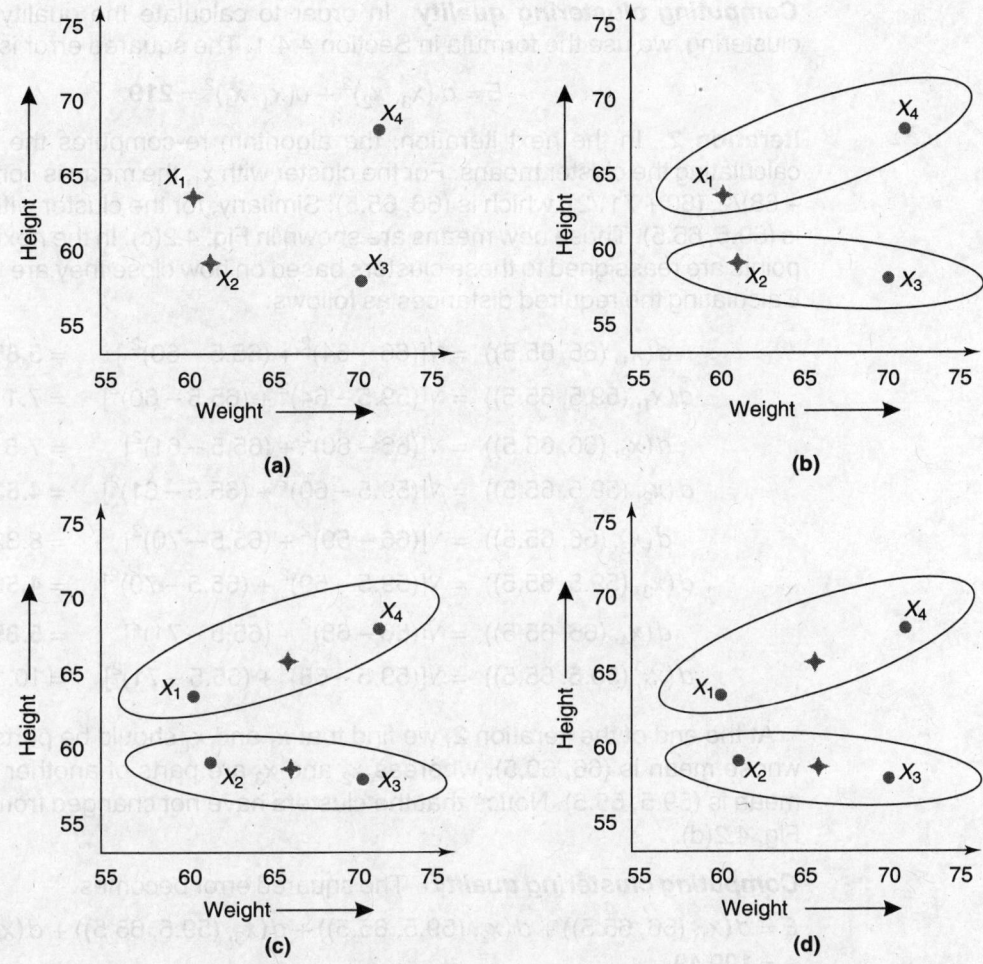

Fig 4.2 *k*-means illustrated

Iteration 1 Suppose the *k*-means algorithm initially selects points x_1 and x_2 as the cluster means [represented as diamonds in Fig. 4.2(a)]. In the next step (lines 4–6 of Fig. 4.1), the algorithm decides which clusters the remaining points (i.e., points x_3 and x_4) should fall into. This decision is based on how close they are to the prototypes. Calculating the euclidean distance, we obtain

$$d(x_3, x_1) = \sqrt{[(59 - 64)^2 + (70 - 60)^2]} = 11.18$$

$$d(x_3, x_2) = \sqrt{[(59 - 60)^2 + (70 - 61)^2]} = \mathbf{9.06}$$

$$d(x_4, x_1) = \sqrt{[(68 - 64)^2 + (71 - 60)^2]} = \mathbf{11.7}$$

$$d(x_4, x_2) = \sqrt{[(68 - 60)^2 + (71 - 61)^2]} = 12.81$$

Clearly, x_3 is closer to x_2 than x_1. Hence, it should belong to the cluster for which x_2 is a prototype. Similarly, x_4 should belong to the cluster for which x_1 is a prototype. These cluster assignments are marked in Fig. 4.2(b).

Computing clustering quality   In order to calculate the quality of the above clustering, we use the formula in Section 4.4.1. The squared error is obtained as:

$$E = d(x_3, x_2)^2 + d(x_4, x_1)^2 = \mathbf{219}$$

Iteration 2   In the next iteration, the algorithm re-computes the prototypes by calculating the cluster means. For the cluster with x_1, the mean is computed as $((64 + 68)/2, (60 + 71)/2)$, which is $(66, 65.5)$. Similarly, for the cluster with x_2, the mean is $(59.5, 65.5)$. These new means are shown in Fig. 4.2(c). In the next step, the data points are reassigned to these clusters based on how close they are to their means. Calculating the required distances as follows:

$$d(x_1, (66, 65.5)) = \sqrt{[(66-64)^2 + (65.5-60)^2]} \quad = \mathbf{5.85}$$
$$d(x_1, (59.5, 65.5)) = \sqrt{[(59.5-64)^2 + (65.5-60)^2]} \quad = 7.1$$
$$d(x_2, (66, 65.5)) = \sqrt{[(66-60)^2 + (65.5-61)^2]} \quad = 7.5$$
$$d(x_2, (59.5, 65.5)) = \sqrt{[(59.5-60)^2 + (65.5-61)^2]} \quad = \mathbf{4.53}$$
$$d(x_3, (66, 65.5)) = \sqrt{[(66-59)^2 + (65.5-70)^2]} \quad = 8.32$$
$$d(x_3, (59.5, 65.5)) = \sqrt{[(59.5-59)^2 + (65.5-70)^2]} \quad = \mathbf{4.53}$$
$$d(x_4, (66, 65.5)) = \sqrt{[(66-68)^2 + (65.5-71)^2]} \quad = \mathbf{5.85}$$
$$d(x_4, (59.5, 65.5)) = \sqrt{[(59.5-68)^2 + (65.5-71)^2]} \quad = 10.12$$

At the end of the iteration 2, we find that x_1 and x_4 should be parts of the cluster whose mean is $(66, 60.5)$, whereas x_2 and x_3 are parts of another cluster whose mean is $(59.5, 65.5)$. Notice that the clusters have not changed from Fig. 4.2(b) to Fig. 4.2(d).

Computing clustering quality   The squared error becomes

$$E = d(x_1, (66, 65.5)) + d(x_2, (59.5, 65.5)) + d(x_3, (59.5, 65.5)) + d(x_4, (66.5, 65.5))$$
$$= \mathbf{109.49}$$

Clearly, the squared error is much smaller now than after it was iteration 1. Although the original clusters have not changed at all, the means have been re-computed and hence, the squared error has changed. Further iterations will not yield any improvements in this case.

Analysis   In each iteration, the k-means algorithm computes the distances of each point from each of the prototypes. If there are n points and t iterations, then the complexity of the algorithm is $O(nkt)$. Thus, the algorithm is linearly scalable with respect to the data size.

Although the k-means algorithm is popular due to its simplicity and efficiency, it has drawbacks as follows:

Sensitive to bad initial prototypes   Illustration 4.2 demonstrates this defect. Visually, the most appropriate clustering in Fig. 4.2(a) is when points 1 and 2 are put in the same cluster and points 3 and 4 are in the other cluster. However, in Illustration 4.2, due to a bad initial selection of prototypes, this result is not obtained.

Prototypes are not actual instances   In this case, the computed cluster mean is unlikely to correspond to an actual instance in the dataset; in some applications this is not acceptable. For example, if the task is to categorize people based on several features and to also select a representative person from each cluster, then it is desirable that the selected prototypes are actual persons in the dataset.

Sensitive to outliers   The k-means algorithm is known to be sensitive to the presence of outliers (points with extreme values). This is because the mean of a population can be affected by the presence of points with extreme (either too large or too small) values.

4.6.3   PAM ALGORITHM

The PAM (Partitioning Around Medoids) algorithm alleviates the defects of the k-means algorithm at the expense of computational time. It ensures that the prototype of each cluster is an actual instance in the dataset. The prototypes in PAM are also known as *medoids*, to differentiate them from cluster means, which need not be actual data instances.

PAM is actually one among other algorithms that use the strategy of working with medoids–prototypes that are actual data instances. As a group, such algorithms are known as k-medoids algorithms.

The Algorithm

Similar to the k-means algorithm, PAM only works for datasets that consist of numeric attributes. It takes k, the number of desired clusters, and the data points as input and produces k clusters as output. The functioning of the algorithm follows the pseudo-code for the general partitioning strategy given in Fig. 4.1. The details that characterize the algorithm are as follows:

1. First, it selects the initial k prototypes arbitrarily.
2. The absolute error criterion in Section 4.4.2 is used to determine clustering quality.
3. In each iteration, the prototype of each cluster is reassigned to an actual data point that minimizes the absolute error criterion.
4. PAM does not include any sampling techniques to scale to huge databases.

Illustration 4.3 Consider the task of clustering people into two clusters based on their heights and weights given in Table 4.2. Since we want two clusters, $k = 2$. When plotted on a graph, the data looks as shown in Fig. 4.3(a).

Iteration 1 Suppose the PAM algorithm initially selects points x_1 and x_2 as the cluster means [represented as diamonds in Fig. 4.3(a)]. In the next step (lines 4–6 in Fig. 4.1), the algorithm decides which clusters the remaining points (i.e., points x_3 and x_4) should fall into. This decision is based on how close they are to the prototypes. Calculating the euclidean distance, we obtain:

$$d(x_3, x_1) = \sqrt{[(59 - 64)^2 + (70 - 60)^2]} = 11.18$$

$$d(x_3, x_2) = \sqrt{[(59 - 60)^2 + (70 - 61)^2]} = \mathbf{9.06}$$

$$d(x_4, x_1) = \sqrt{[(68 - 64)^2 + (71 - 60)^2]} = \mathbf{11.7}$$

$$d(x_4, x_2) = \sqrt{[(68 - 60)^2 + (71 - 61)^2]} = 12.81$$

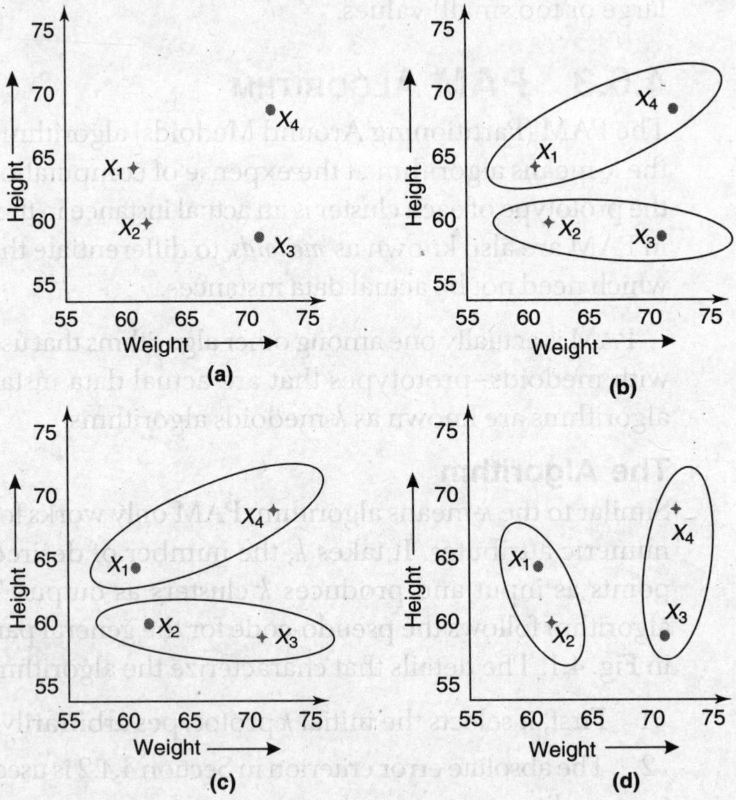

Fig. 4.3 PAM illustrated

Clearly, x_3 is closer to x_2 than x_1. Hence, it should belong to the cluster for which x_2 is a prototype. Similarly, x_4 should belong to the cluster for which x_1 is a prototype. These cluster assignments are marked in Fig. 4.3(b). So far, the algorithm is proceeding exactly as the k-means algorithm.

Computing clustering quality In order to calculate the quality of the above clustering, we use the formula in Section 4.4.2. The absolute error is obtained as

$$E = d(x_3, x_2) + d(x_4, x_1) = 20.76$$

Iteration 2 In the next iteration, the algorithm selects new medoids in place of the existing medoids. Either x_3 or x_4 can be selected in place of x_1 or x_2. For each of these four cases, a new clustering and its corresponding quality need to be computed. Next, the new clustering that has the best quality (i.e., minimum absolute error) should be selected.

Consider the case where x_4 is selected in place of x_1. The new medoids are shown in Fig. 4.3(c). In the next step, the data points are reassigned to new clusters based on how close they are to the medoids. Calculating the required distances

$$d(x_1, x_2) = \sqrt{[(60 - 64)^2 + (61 - 60)^2]} = 4.123$$
$$d(x_1, x_4) = \sqrt{[(68 - 64)^2 + (71 - 60)^2]} = 11.7$$
$$d(x_3, x_2) = \sqrt{[(59 - 60)^2 + (70 - 61)^2]} = 9.06$$
$$d(x_3, x_4) = \sqrt{[(59 - 68)^2 + (70 - 71)^2]} = 9.05$$

Therefore, at the end of the iteration 2, it is established that x_1 and x_2 should be parts of the same cluster, whereas x_3 and x_4 will be parts of another cluster. The new clustering is shown in Fig. 4.3(d).

Computing clustering quality The absolute error becomes

$$E = d(x_1, x_2) + d(x_3, x_4) = 13.17$$

The above procedure is repeated for each of the other three cases (of replacing x_1 or x_2 with x or x). The case, in which there is least error, is selected. If this minimum error is less than the error during iteration 1, then the corresponding change in medoids is enforced and the next iteration is started. For the current illustration, all the four cases will result in the same new clustering.

Clearly, the error (13.17) in the new clustering is much smaller than the error in the old clustering after iteration 1. The original clusters have changed to be more acceptable. Therefore, at the end of iteration 2, the new choice of medoids is retained. If the new error, at the end of iteration 2, had become worse, then the choice of medoids would have been undone and the previous selection at the beginning of iteration 1 would have been retained.

Analysis The PAM algorithm is much more time-consuming than the *k*-means algorithm as shown in Theorem 4.1.

**Theorem 4.1
(PAM
Complexity)** The time-complexity of PAM is $O(k(n - k)^2)$ where n is the number of data points, k is the desired number of clusters, and t is the number of iterations in PAM.

Proof   In each iteration, the PAM algorithm computes the distances of each point from each of the medoids. This does not incur any extra cost than the k-means algorithm (where there were means instead of medoids).

However, for the selection of new medoids, there are multiple possible cases and for each case, the remaining points need to be reallocated to the new medoids. If there are n points, then there are $k(n-k)$ ways of selecting new medoids and the remaining $(n-k)$ non-medoid points need to be reallocated to the medoid points.

Consequently, the complexity of each iteration is $O(k(n-k)^2)$. Hence, the theorem follows.

In spite of the non-linear time complexity of PAM, it is considered as an enhancement over k-means because as seen in Illustration 4.3, it is not sensitive to a bad initial selection of prototypes. Further, its prototypes are actual data instances. Finally, it is not so sensitive to the presence of outliers due to two reasons: (1) it does not depend on cluster means (which are sensitive to outliers); (2) it uses the absolute error criterion instead of the squared error criterion.

4.7   HIERARCHICAL METHODS

In these methods, clusters which are very similar to each other are grouped into larger clusters. These larger clusters may further be grouped into still larger clusters, etc. In essence, a hierarchy or tree of clusters is produced. This can be pictorially represented by a dendogram as shown in Fig. 4.4.

Example 4.2   Figure 4.4 shows the hierarchical clusters and their dendogram representation for the following data:

$$x_1 = (6, 8); \; x_2 = (5, 7) \; x_3 = (8, 4); \; x_4 = (11, 10); \; x_5 = (12, 8)$$

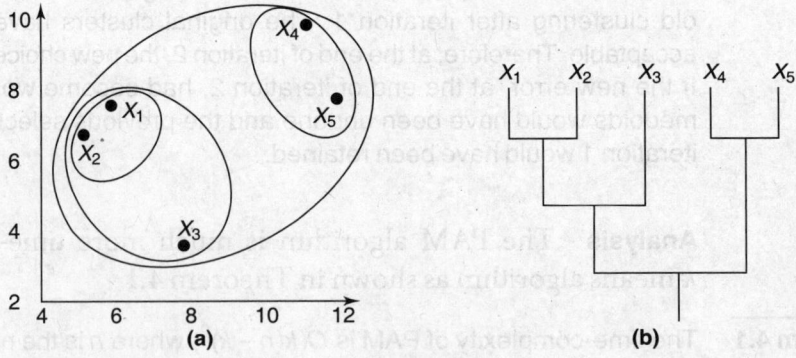

Fig. 4.4   (a) Hierarchical clusters; (b) Dendogram

It is clear from Fig. 4.4(a) that natural clusters exist at many different levels. Depending on the application, x_3 may (or may not) be put in the cluster containing x_1 and x_2.

These clusterings correspond to different levels of the dendogram shown in Fig. 4.4(b). A hierarchical clustering algorithm would output the entire dendogram. In contrast, other algorithms would be constrained to output clusters at some specific level. This would be unnatural and the resulting clustering would not reveal the inherent patterns in the data.

4.7.1 OVERALL APPROACHES TO HIERARCHICAL CLUSTERING

Hierarchical algorithms may be designed to construct dendograms either top-down or bottom-up. These correspond to the following two basic approaches to hierarchical clustering.

Agglomerative Approach

Agglomerative clustering algorithms start with all the data objects in separate clusters and then merge 'nearby' clusters until a single cluster is formed that contains all the objects. This corresponds to starting at the top of the dendogram in Fig. 4.4(b) and generating the rest of the tree. The pseudo-code for such a procedure is shown in Fig. 4.5 and described below.

AgglomerativeCluster (Data D):
1. $N = \varnothing$ # *dendogram being constructed*
2. **for each** point p in D:
3.   **initialize** cluster $C_i = \{p\}$
4. $N = N \cup C_i$
5. **Repeat:**
6. (C_i, C_j) = *closest pair of unmerged clusters in N*
7. C_k = *merge*(C_i, C_j)
8. $N = N \cup C_k$
9. **until** *no unmerged clusters exist in N*

Fig. 4.5 Agglomerative hierarchical clustering

The algorithm first initializes each data object (or point) to be in its own cluster and the current dendogram to contain all these clusters (lines 1–4 in Fig. 4.5). Then, in each iteration, it merges the closest pair of clusters (lines 6, 7) and inserts the resulting cluster into the dendogram (line 8). Specific agglomerative clustering algorithms differ in how they define the closeness between the clusters, as required in step 6. Different approaches for this are discussed in Section 4.7.2.

Divisive Approach

Divisive hierarchical clustering algorithms do the reverse of agglomerative algorithms. They start with all the data objects in a single cluster and then divide the cluster into sub-clusters repeatedly until each object is in its own cluster. This corresponds to starting at the bottom of the dendogram in Fig. 4.4(b) and working upwards to generate the rest of the tree. The pseudo-code for such a procedure is shown in Fig. 4.6 and described below.

The divisive clustering algorithm starts with a cluster containing all the data objects (known as points) in the input dataset D (line 1 in Fig. 4.6). Then, in each iteration, it selects the cluster with largest diameter (line 4)–the diameter of a cluster is the distance between its most distant points. This selected cluster is then split into two parts using the split function shown at the bottom of the figure.

DivisiveCluster (Data D):

1. C = cluster containing all points in D
2. $N = \{C\}$ # dendogram being constructed
3. **repeat:**
4. C_i = leaf node in N with largest diameter
5. $(C_j, C_k) = split(C_i)$
6.   **Insert** C_j, C_k **in N as children of** C_i
7. **until** all leaf nodes in N contain only a single point

split (**Cluster** C_i):

1. p = point in C_i that is most distant from other points in C_i
2. C_j = set of points in C_i that are closer to p than to C_i
3. $C_k = C_i - C_j$
4. **return** (C_j, C_k)

Fig. 4.6   Divisive hierarchical clustering

The split function finds the point p in the cluster, which is furthest from all the other points in the cluster (line 1 of the split function). This distance is usually calculated as the average distance of each point to all the other points in the cluster. The points in the cluster are then split into two groups based on whether they are closer to the most distant point p, or to the old cluster (lines 2, 3). Specific divisive clustering algorithms may differ in how they define the closeness between a point and a cluster, as required in this step.

Note that while splitting the points into two groups, an algorithm may dynamically decide to allocate a point p_i to the group that it is closer to. In this case, the division will depend on the order in which the points are enumerated.

4.7.2 LINKAGE METRICS

In both agglomerative and divisive approaches, it is necessary to be able to determine distances between the clusters. To do this, different approaches such as minimum distance, maximum distance, and average distance (Section 4.4.3) can be used. These metrics, used to compute the distance between clusters, are also known as linkage metrics. The minimum, maximum, and average distances between the clusters are also known as *single-link*, *complete-link*, and *average-link* metrics, respectively.

Single link methods have a disadvantage known as the 'chaining effect'—a few points that form a bridge between two clusters will cause them to be merged into one cluster. Average link clustering methods may cause the elongated clusters to split. Complete link methods usually produce more compact clusters than the single-link methods.

Computation of Linkage Metrics

Computation of linkage metrics is time-consuming and thus, the hierarchical methods based on these metrics have non-linear time complexity (at least $O(N^2)$ where N is the number of points in the given dataset).

For an efficient computation of linkage metrics, the data is usually represented by an $N \times N$ matrix of distances between the data points—the actual points are not required. Such a representation is known as a *connectivity matrix* or a *dissimilarity matrix*. Since the distance between two points or clusters is symmetric (i.e., $d(C_i, C_j) = d(C_j, C_i)$), the matrix can be represented as a triangular matrix.

For large data-set sizes, it may be infeasible to store the entire connectivity matrix in the main memory. In such cases, the matrix is made sparse by storing only the distances of the nearest neighbours of each data point. The resulting sparse matrix can then be represented by a *connectivity graph* in the main memory.

During the algorithm execution, for each cluster, a priority queue of the distances to other clusters (or its nearest neighbours) is maintained. When clusters are merged or split, it is necessary to re-compute the distances between the existing clusters and the newly formed clusters. This is done efficiently

using the Lance-Williams updating formula published in 1967 by G. Lance
and W. Williams in the *Computer Journal*. The general form of this formula to
compute a linkage metric of a merged cluster $C_i \cup C_j$, from a cluster C, is
given as

$$d(C_i \cup C_j, C_k) = a(|C_i|)\, d(C_i, C_k) + a(|C_j|)\, d(C_j, C_k) + bd(C_i, C_j)$$
$$+ c|\, d(C_i, C_k) - d(C_j, C_k)|$$

where a, b, and c are the coefficients that depend on the specific linkage metric
being used. For the single link method, the values of these coefficients are
$a = 0.5$, $b = 0$, and $c = -0.5$; for the complete link method, the values are:
$a = 0.5$, $b = 0$, and $c = 0.5$.

With the above approach, any general agglomerative linkage-metric-based
algorithm requires $O(N^2 \log N)$ time. Further improvements have been made
in special cases. As an example, the single-link clustering has been shown to
be reducible to the computation of the minimal spanning tree (which requires
$O(N^2)$ time) of the connectivity graph in a 1982 publication by A. Yao in the
SIAM Journal on Computing.

Illustration 4.4 Given below are the steps of an agglomerative single link algorithm for the dataset
used in Example 4.2 and shown in Fig. 4.4.

As shown in steps 1–4 in Fig. 4.5, an agglomerative algorithm starts with each
data point in its own cluster. Let $C_1, \ldots, C_5$ be the clusters corresponding to the given
data points $x_1, \ldots, x_5$. Next, the description of each iteration in steps 5–9 in Fig. 4.5
are given as follows.

Iteration 1 First, the distances of each cluster from all the other clusters are
computed and these distances (sorted in ascending order) are maintained in a priority
queue. Since the clusters, at present, contain only single data points each, the
inter-cluster distance is the same as the inter-point distance. Following priority queues
are obtained for each cluster:

C_1: $(C_2, 1.41)$, $(C_3, 4.47)$, $(C_4, 5.38)$, $(C_5, 6)$
C_2: $(C_1, 1.41)$, $(C_3, 4.24)$, $(C_4, 6.71)$, $(C_5, 7.07)$
C_3: $(C_2, 4.24)$, $(C_1, 4.47)$, $(C_5, 5.65)$, $(C_4, 6.71)$
C_4: $(C_5, 2.23)$, $(C_1, 5.38)$, $(C_3, 6.71)$, $(C_2, 6.71)$
C_5: $(C_4, 2.23)$, $(C_3, 5.65)$, $(C_1, 6)$, $(C_2, 7.07)$

The LHS of each line above (left of the colon) is a cluster and the RHS is the list
of other clusters sorted by their distances, in ascending order, from the cluster on
the LHS.

Next, the two clusters that are closest to each other need to be picked. For doing
this, it is only necessary to look at the first entries of each of the above lists and

determine the smallest distance among these. Clearly, the smallest distance is between C_1 and C_2, which occurs in the first and second rows. Hence, clusters C_1 and C_2 are merged to form a new cluster, which is labelled as C_6.

Next, the distances between C_6 and the other clusters have to be determined. For this, the Lance–Williams updating formula (with the coefficients for single link methods) is used. Thus, the priority queue of distances from C_6 to other clusters is computed as

$$C_6: (C_3, 4.24), (C_4, 5.38), (C_5, 6)$$

Iteration 2 In iteration 2, the closest pair of clusters will need to be determined. Again, only the first entry in each of the priority queues of the unmerged clusters needs to be looked at. This time, C_4 and C_5 are found to be the closest pair. Hence, these clusters are merged to form a new cluster, which is labelled as C_7. Again, using the Lance–Williams updating formula, the priority queue for the new cluster C_7 is computed as

$$C_7: (C_6, 5.38), (C_3, 5.65)$$

Iteration 3 In iteration 3, to determine the closest pair of clusters, as before, consider the first entry in each of the priority queues of the unmerged clusters. This time, C_3 and C_6 are found to be the closest pair. Hence, these clusters are merged to form a new cluster, which is labeled as C_8. Again, using the Lance–Williams updating formula, the priority queue for the new cluster C_8 is computed as

$$C_8: (C_7, 5.38)$$

Iteration 4 Finally, in iteration 4, two clusters C_7 and C_8 are left, which are merged to form a single cluster.

Analysis Hierarchical algorithms, based on linkage metrics, are time-consuming as they have quadratic time complexity as illustrated in the following theorem for the agglomerative case.

Theorem 4.2 (Complexity) The time complexity of agglomerative linkage based algorithms is $O(n^2)$ where n is the number of data points.

Proof As seen in Illustration 4.4, there will be $n-1$ iterations for any dataset with n points. In the first iteration, the distances of each point, from every other point, need to be computed. This requires $O(n^2)$ computations following which, in iteration i, there will be $(n-i)$ unmerged clusters. The Lance–Williams updating formula, therefore, needs to be applied $(n-i-1)$ times. Adding this, for iterations from $i=2$ to $(n-1)$, it is observed that $O(n^2)$ computations are required for all these computations. Therefore, the overall complexity is $O(n^2)$.

In addition to the quadratic time complexity, hierarchical methods based on linkage metrics also have the deficiency of not handling non-spherical clusters well. As an example, in the dataset represented in Fig. 4.7, the *C*-shaped cluster would not be identified as a single separate cluster during any iteration of a linkage-metric-based algorithm. This is because the top and bottom portions of the *C*-shaped cluster are likely to first be merged with the other cluster at the centre, because of its proximity.

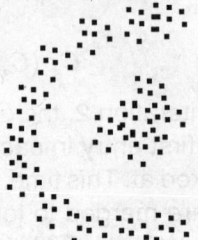

Fig. 4.7 Illustration of problem with non-spherical clusters

Another drawback with linkage-metric-based hierarchical methods occurs because they follow a greedy strategy to decide which clusters to merge (agglomerative) or where to split an existing cluster (divisive). Merging or splitting of clusters is irreversible. This could result in sub-optimal solutions.

4.7.3 BIRCH ALGORITHM

BIRCH (Balanced Iterative Reducing and Clustering using Hierarchies) is the first hierarchical algorithm that is designed to be scalable for very large datasets. It operates in two phases. During the first phase, it forms a hierarchical clustering. This clustering is known as a *clustering feature tree* (or just CF-tree). For many applications, the clustering obtained at the end of the first phase is reasonably sufficient. However, BIRCH recommends a second phase for further refinement in which the leaf level clusters obtained at the end of the first phase are re-clustered using any other standard clustering strategy.

For each cluster in the CF-tree built during the first phase, the algorithm maintains a vector of summary information known as a *clustering feature* (CF). If $x_1, x_2, \ldots, x_n$ are the points in a cluster (which themselves are vectors of attribute values), then its CF is given as $<n, \Sigma x_i, \Sigma x_i^2>$. The CF gives very useful summary information about a cluster; using the CF, it is possible to calculate the size, mean, and variance within a cluster.

BIRCH uses the CF to compute the diameter *M* of a cluster

$$M = \sqrt{\frac{1}{n(n-1)} \sum_{i=1}^{n} \sum_{j=1}^{n} (x_i - x_j)^2}$$

While forming the CF-tree, if the diameter of any leaf-level cluster exceeds a user-given threshold T, the cluster is split into two. This is done in a manner similar to the splitting of a node in a B+ tree, and would involve creating or updating the interior nodes that are the ancestors of the leaf being split. The algorithm also takes the branching factor B of interior nodes as an input parameter.

The pseudo-code of the algorithm as explained above is shown in Fig. 4.8.

```
BIRCH (Data D, B, T):
# Phase 1
1. N = { {} }      # initial CF tree with an empty leaf node
2. for each point p in D:
3.       m = leaf node in N that is closest to p
4.       add p to m
5.       Compute diameter M of m
6.       If M > T:
7.             Split(m)   # may require splitting of ancestors of m

# Phase 2
8. Apply another clustering algorithm to cluster the leaves of N
```

Fig. 4.8 BIRCH algorithm
$\langle 5, (42, 37), (390, 293) \rangle$

Illustration 4.5 Here the clustering features will be illustrated for the dataset used in Example 4.2 and shown in Fig. 4.4. If the CF of a cluster, containing a set X of data points, is denoted as $CF(X)$, then

$$CF(\{x_3\}) = \langle 1, (8, 4), (8^2, 4^2) \rangle = \langle 1, (8, 4), (64, 16) \rangle$$

$$CF(\{x_1, x_2\}) = \langle 2, (6 + 5, 8 + 7), (6^2 + 5^2, 8^2 + 7^2) \rangle = \langle 2, (11, 15),(61, 113) \rangle$$

$$CF(\{x_4, x_5\}) = \langle 2, (11 + 12, 10 + 8), (11^2 + 12^2, 10^2 + 8^2) \rangle = \langle 2, (23,18), (265, 164) \rangle$$

When the clusters are merged, the clustering features of the new interior level clusters can be easily calculated as

$$CF(\{x_1, x_2, x_3\}) = CF(\{x_1, x_2\}) + CF(\{x_3\}) = \langle 3, (19, 19), (125,129) \rangle$$

$$CF(\{x_1, x_2, x_3, x_4, x_5\}) = CF(\{x_1, x_2, x_3\}) + CF(\{x_4, x_5\}) =$$

Analysis The BIRCH algorithm is very scalable with respect to the number of records in a dataset. The complexity of the phase 1 algorithm is clearly linear with respect to the dataset size. Further, it alleviates the drawback of linkage-metric-based algorithms, which cannot undo the splitting or merging of nodes. However, one drawback still remains–BIRCH is useful for detecting only spherical clusters.

4.8   DENSITY-BASED METHODS

In density-based methods, clusters are grown by starting with some data points and then including other neighbouring points as long as the neighbourhood is sufficiently dense. These methods can find clusters of arbitrary shape and are useful in the applications where such a feature is desired. As an example, when applied to datasets such as the one shown in Fig. 4.7, these algorithms will output two desired clusters that are visible.

4.8.1   DBSCAN ALGORITHM

The DBSCAN (Density-Based Spatial Clustering of Applications with Noise) algorithm discovers clusters as contiguous dense regions in the instance space. Before describing the algorithm, it is first necessary to make the notion of a 'dense region' precise.

Dense Region Definition

Given below is the definition of the intuitive notion of the neighbourhood of a point, as this must contain enough points to qualify as a dense region.

Neighbourhood   The neighbourhood of a data point p consists of all the data points q such that $d(p, q) \leq \varepsilon$, where ε is a user-given parameter and d is the distance metric.

Core Point   A data point is a core point if its neighbourhood contains at least μ data points, where m is a user-given parameter.

Intuitively, the implication of this definition is that the neighbourhood of a core point is a dense region.

Directly Density-reachable   All the data points that are within the neighbourhood of a core point are said to be directly density-reachable from it.

Note that if p is directly density-reachable from a point q, then it is not necessary that q is directly density-reachable from p because p may not be a core point.

Density-reachable   A data point p is said to be density-reachable from a core point q if there exists a sequence of data points $p_1, p_2, p_3, \ldots, p_n$, such that $p_1 = p$ and $p_n = q$, and p_i is directly density-reachable from p_{i+1}, for i in $1, \ldots, n$.

Density-connected All the data points that are density-reachable from a core point are said to be density-connected to each other.

Density-based Cluster A maximal set of mutually density-connected data points constitutes a density-based cluster.

This definition finally captures the intuitive notion of a contiguous dense region, i.e. a maximal set of mutually density-connected data points. Here the adjective maximal is used, if not, a portion of a contiguous dense region (that is also contiguous) will qualify as a cluster.

The Algorithm

The pseudo-code for DBSCAN is shown in Fig. 4.9, and described below.

The DBSCAN algorithm operates by searching the dataset for core points by examining the density of the neighbourhood of each data point (steps 1–4 in Fig. 4.9). If a spatial index is available, then the *neighbourhood( )* function can be implemented efficiently. Or else, for each data point, the list of distances to the other points needs to be computed and sorted initially (as in the first iteration of Illustration 4.4). Step 2 in the pseudo-code is to ensure that the *neighbourhood( )* function is called only once for each point.

DBSCAN (Data D, ε, μ):

1. **for each** point p in D:
2.   **if** p has not been processed earlier:
3. n = neighbourhood(p, ε)
4.   if $|n| \geq \mu$:   # *p is a core point*
5. $C = \{p\} \cup n$ # *start a new cluster C*
6.   Expand(C, n, ε, μ)

expand (Cluster C, n, ε, μ):

1. **for each** point q in n:
2. m = neighbourhood(q, ε)
3.   if $|m| \geq \mu$:   # *q is a core point*
4. $C = C \cup m$
5.   Expand(C, m, ε, μ)

Fig. 4.9 The DBSCAN algorithm

Once a core point p is identified, the algorithm initializes a cluster C that consists of p and all the data points in the neighbourhood of p (step 5). Next, the algorithm calls the *expand* function that checks recursively for all data points that are density-reachable from p and adds them to C. In the actual implementation, the tail recursion in this function can be replaced by a more efficient iterative loop.

The DBSCAN algorithm deviates from the above pseudo-code in one aspect—during execution, it may turn out that some (non-core) point is density-reachable from two or more clusters. DBSCAN then assigns that point to the cluster discovered first.

Illustration 4.6 Figure 4.10(a) shows DBSCAN in execution on a small portion of a dataset.

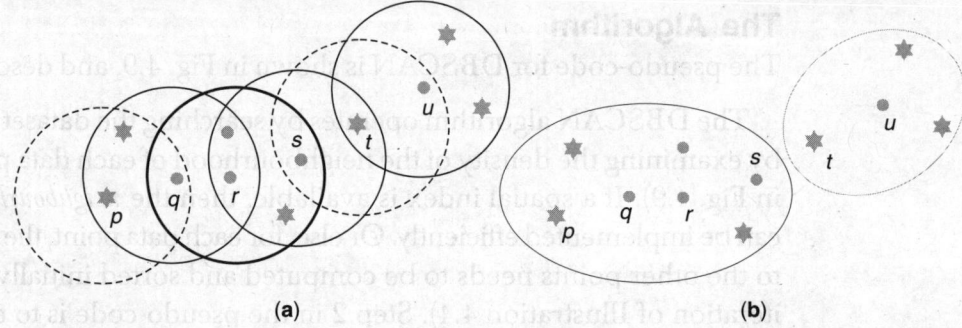

(a)   (b)

Fig. 4.10   (a) DBSCAN in execution with $\mu = 3$; (b) Final clusters obtained

Here μ (the minimum number of data points needed to form a core point) is set as 3. The core points are shown as dots whereas, the non-core points are shown as stars. Figure 4.10(b) shows the final clusters obtained for the same portion of the dataset.

To see how DBSCAN might have operated on the dataset shown in Fig. 4.10(a), suppose that the data points are ordered on disk in such a manner that DBSCAN first comes across point p. It retrieves the neighbourhood of p (shown as a dashed circle) and recognizes that it contains only two data points. Since $\mu = 3$, p is not a core point.

The next data point is retrieved from the dataset. Suppose that the point is μ. Its neighbourhood is retrieved (shown as a regular circle) and it contains four points. It is a core point. Hence, a cluster C_1 is created containing these four points in addition to μ.

Next, these four points in the neighbourhood of μ are checked for whether they are core points or not. In this case, none of them are core points, so the algorithm proceeds to the next data point on disk. Let us suppose that it is q. Its neighbourhood is retrieved (shown as a regular circle) and it contains four points. It is therefore, a core point. Hence, a cluster C_2 is created containing these four points in addition to q.

Next, these four points in the neighbourhood of q are checked for whether they are core points or not. If they are core points (for example, r), then the algorithm adds the data points in their neighbourhood to C_2. This way the cluster C_2 is grown and s

is also added to C_2. The algorithm would also attempt to add t to C_2. But since t is already in C_1, this fails and t is retained in C.

Analysis   It is clear from the pseudo-code shown in Fig. 4.9 that the *neighbourhood* ( ) function is called only once for each data point. If a spatial index is available, this function can be executed in *log n* time where *n* is the number of data points. Hence, the complexity of the algorithm becomes $O(n \log n)$. Or else, for each data point, the list of distances to the other points needs to be computed and sorted initially (as in the first iteration of Illustration 4.4). This requires n^2 computations, and so the complexity becomes $O(n^2)$.

OPTICS: An enhancement to DBSCAN

Clusters in real-life datasets may have varying densities. This means that the ε- (or μ-) value needs to be selected differently for each cluster. OPTICS is an algorithm that achieves this end. Rather than taking a fixed ε-value from the user, it takes ε_{max} as input and in essence produces multiple clusterings—as though DBSCAN is called with all the possible values of ε that are less than or equal to ε_{max}.

The main idea is as follows: If DBSCAN is to produce two clusterings for two different user-given values of ε, then the pseudo-code in Fig. 4.9 can be modified to process both the ε-values simultaneously. The only changes required will be in providing the ε-values to the calls of the *neighbourhood*( ) function.

At this time, instead of making two different calls to the *neighbourhood*( ) function, this function can be modified to take both ε-values and return two different answer-sets. Notice now, that the answer-set to the smaller of the ε-values will be a subset of the answer-set to the bigger ε-value. Therefore, this can be implemented easily because the function can operate as though it is given the bigger ε-values as input, but the returned answer-set is sorted so that its first part contains the answer-set to the smaller ε-value.

The above idea can be generalized to process not just two different ε-values, but all the possible ε-values below some user-given ε_{max}. The *neighbourhood*( ) function only has to sort its answer-set of data points by their distance from the respective core point.

The resulting OPTICS algorithm makes use of the above intelligent strategy and has the same time complexity as DBSCAN. Effectively it stores, for every data point, its neighbourhood consisting of data points sorted by distance. It makes use of this information at run-time to provide the user with the flexibility of selecting any ε-value (not exceeding ε_{max}) and shows the resulting clusters interactively.

4.9   GRID-BASED METHODS

In grid-based methods, the space of instances is divided into a grid structure. Clustering techniques are then applied using the cells of the grid, instead of individual data points, as the basic units. This has the advantage of improving the processing time significantly.

4.9.1   CLIQUE ALGORITHM

One of the algorithms that use a grid-based technique is CLIQUE (CLustering In QUEst). It has been designed to specifically handle datasets with a large number of dimensions. A high-level pseudo-code for the algorithm is shown in Fig. 4.11, and described below.

The algorithm first partitions the data space into a grid. This is done by partitioning each dimension into equal intervals known as units (lines 1 and 2 in Fig. 4.11). It then identifies dense units (line 3)—a unit is dense if the fraction of the data points in it is more than a user-given parameter.

```
CLIQUE (Data D):
# Phase 1: Find dense units
1. for each dimension d in D:
2.         Partition d into equal intervals (known as units)
3.         Identify dense units
4. k = 2
5. while (1):
6.       for each combination of k dimensions d₁, d₂,...,dₖ:
7.             for each intersection i of dense units along the k dimensions
8.                   if i is dense:
9.                        Mark i as a dense unit
10.                  if no units marked as dense, break from while(1) loop.
11.      k = k + 1

# Phase 2: Find Clusters
12. Identify clusters as maximal sets of connected dense units
```

Fig. 4.11   The CLIQUE algorithm

Once the dense units along single dimensions are found, the algorithm attempts to find the dense units along two dimensions. The intuition for this is based on heuristic followed by frequent itemset mining algorithms—if a high-dimensional unit is dense, then all the corresponding units in lower dimensions must also be frequent. This results in the 'Apriori-like' k-pass algorithm (of lines 4–11).

After the dense units along all dimensions are found, the algorithm proceeds to find the maximal sets of connected dense units, i.e. clusters, in a straightforward manner.

Illustration 4.7 If there are two dimensions A and B in the dataset with integer values between 1 and 100, then the algorithm would divide this data space into equal sized intervals. Suppose that the two dimensions are divided into ten equal-sized intervals each.

Consider the cell (or unit) defined by the interval ($30 < A \leq 40$ and $50 < B \leq 60$). If this cell is to be dense (for this, assume that it needs to have at least ten data points), then the single-dimensional cells represented by ($30 < A \leq 40$) and ($50 < B \leq 60$) must have at least ten data points. Hence, the Apriori-property follows for this problem.

Analysis The CLIQUE algorithm is very scalable with respect to the number of records in a dataset because it is grid based. It operates on cells (or units) instead of individual data points. In addition, it is also scalable with respect to the number of dimensions in a dataset because it uses the Apriori-property effectively. One drawback is that if the size of the cell is inappropriately set to a very high value, too much of approximation will take place and the correct clusters will not be found.

4.10 OUTLIER DETECTION

Outlier detection is a natural extension of data mining techniques. While data mining is the extraction of general patterns or trends in a dataset, outlier detection is the discovery of data objects that deviate significantly from such general patterns or trends. Such data objects that deviate significantly from other data objects in a dataset are known as outliers.

Finding data objects that are significantly different from other objects is an important activity. By standing out from the crowd, outliers could represent objects that are in some way, much better or much worse than the general trend. They may represent objects that need to be dealt with in some special manner. It is also possible that they represent an erroneously-entered data or even noise.

Some applications of outlier detection are as follows:

Fraud detection   Frauds in credit card transactions, bank loan applications, or telecommunication usage could be detected as outliers since they represent instances that deviate from the normal trend.

Network-intrusion detection   The behaviour of a malicious user who gains access into a network will be significantly different from that of an average user and this can be detected by analyzing various system log files.

Data cleaning   Data cleaning is a part of pre-processing data in preparation for further data analysis. It requires the highlighting of records that deviate significantly from the others as these may have been wrongly entered into the dataset.

Stock market analysis   Determining deviations in the usual trends in stock prices is of utmost interest to investors.

Several approaches exist to detect outliers which are discussed below.

4.10.1   DISTRIBUTION-BASED METHODS

Distribution-based methods were proposed during the earlier works on outlier detection and they are mostly applicable to datasets that have a single variable (univariate). In these methods, a statistical distribution that best fits the data is selected, and outliers are those data objects that deviate significantly from this distribution. Discordancy tests found in the standard statistics textbooks are used to determine if a data object deviates significantly from the selected distribution or not.

These methods have significant drawbacks that limit their applicability.

- They are mostly applicable to datasets having a single variable.
- They require that the dataset follow some standard statistical distribution.
- They may require computationally-intensive methods to determine the parameters of the selected statistical distribution before the actual outlier detection begins.

Once the distribution has been fully specified, however, the outlier detection can be done in linear time.

4.10.2   CLUSTERING-BASED METHODS

The clustering methods studied in this chapter naturally find outliers. Clusters of very small size are usually treated as containing only outliers. However, this approach for outlier detection has been sometimes criticized in the research literature because of two reasons as follows:

- The main objective of clustering techniques is to detect clusters and not outliers. Therefore, they may not be optimized for detecting outliers.
- Clustering techniques do not start with a precise definition of what an outlier should be. Therefore, the definition of outliers in these methods is implicit and hard to infer.

The first criticism above is to be reconsidered. With the current and ever-improving speeds of modern clustering techniques, they can no longer be considered as inferior to the specialized outlier detection techniques—they often have the same or sometimes better time complexity.

4.10.3 DISTANCE-BASED METHODS

These methods, unlike clustering-based methods, begin with a precise definition of what an outlier should be—an object p in a dataset D is a distance-based outlier if not more than a fraction b of the objects are in the neighbourhood of p. Here, b is a user-given value and neighbourhood is defined as in the definition given in Section 4.8.1.

These methods usually rely on a multi-dimensional index, which is used to retrieve the neighbourhood of each object to see if it contains sufficient points. If there are insufficient points, the object is flagged as an outlier. More efficient techniques use grid-based techniques to work on a cell-by-cell basis rather than a point-by-point basis.

The major drawback of these methods is that the outlier definition is based on a single global value of the user-given parameters. If the dataset has both dense and sparse regions, this can lead to problems. As an example, if a neighbourhood is specified to be small, then some sparse clusters will be erroneously flagged as outliers. On the other hand, if the neighbourhood is specified to be large, then some outliers will not be detected.

4.10.4 DENSITY-BASED METHODS

Density-based methods were invented to overcome the drawback of distance-based methods discussed in the previous subsection. They use similar ideas as in density-based clustering algorithms and compute what is known as the *local outlier factor* (LOF) of each data object.

This LOF is an indicator of the degree of 'outlier-ness' of an object. For the objects deep within clusters, the LOF is equal to 1, whereas for objects farther away from clusters, the LOF becomes larger than 1. Finally, data objects with high LOF are flagged as outliers.

The formalization of LOF is as follows:

---

k-distance   The k-distance of an object p, k_dist(p), is its distance from its kth nearest neighbour.

---

k-distance neighbourhood   The k-distance neighbourhood, N(p), of an object p is the set of objects q such that $d(p, q) \leq k\_dist(p)$.

Reachability Distance   The reachability distance of an object p with respect to an object q is defined as reach_dist(p, q) = max{k_dist(q), d(p, q)}.

Local Reachability Density   The local reachability density of an object p is given as

$$lrd\,(p) = \frac{|N(p)|}{\sum\limits_{q \in N(p)} reach\_dist\,(p, q)}$$

for a given neighbourhood threshold k.

It can be observed that for points in the interior of a cluster, the above formula will retrieve a value of 1, whereas for the points far away from clusters, it will retrieve approximately the (inverse of the) distance of the point to the nearest cluster.

Finally, with the above definitions in place, the LOF of a data point is defined below.

Local Outlier Factor   The local outlier factor, LOF(p), of an object p is given as

$$LOF\,(p) = \frac{\sum\limits_{q \in N(p)} \dfrac{lrd(q)}{lrd(p)}}{|N(p)|}$$

for a given neighbourhood threshold k.

As before, it can be seen that for the points in the interior of a cluster, the above formula will retrieve a value of 1, whereas for points far away from clusters, it will retrieve higher values. One drawback with the density-based methods is that they require a parameter k (to define k-distance) and the quality of results is sensitive to the selection of this parameter.

SUMMARY

Clustering is the task of organizing data into groups (known as clusters) such that the data objects that are similar to (or close to) each other are put in the same cluster. Clustering is often the first data mining task applied on a given collection of data and is used to explore the possibility of any underlying patterns existing in the data.

There are numerous potential applications for clustering analysis. Some of these are applications such as finding groups of people who share common properties or interests (student tutorial groups, hobby groups, groups for focused marketing activity, etc.) and for deciding the locations for an activity (such as setting up a business chain).

Clustering algorithms depend on the specification of a similarity or distance function between data objects. The distance function to be used depends on the application domain and on the data type (numerical or categorical) of the data objects.

Several algorithms are available for clustering. The main strategies used include partitioning-based strategies, where the data objects are partitioned into disjoint clusters; hierarchical-based strategies, where a hierarchy of clusters is obtained; density-based strategies that yield arbitrarily-shaped dense clusters; and grid-based methods, where the data space is divided into cells and processing is carried out using the cells rather than individual points, for better efficiency.

Finally, the discovery of outliers—objects that significantly deviate from the general trend seen in the rest of the data. These are useful for applications such as fraud detection and data cleaning.

EXERCISES

Test Your Understanding

1. Define the problem of clustering. How does it differ from classification?

2. Give two example applications of clustering that you have come across in your day-to-day life.

3. Consider the task of clustering students given their (roll no., name, age, gender, and marks in Maths, Physics, Chemistry, and English). Design a distance function for this data.

4. Consider the data shown in Table 4.2. Assume that all the records belong to one cluster. What is the mean of this cluster? What is the squared error criterion for this clustering? What is the absolute error criterion for this clustering?

5. Show the iferation steps for the *k*-means algorithm (for $k = 2$) on the data given in the following table.

x	2	1	3	3
y	3	5	3	6

6. Repeat problem 5 for the PAM algorithm and an agglomerative single-link algorithm.

7. Illustrate how for a constant μ-value, density-based clusters with reference to a higher density (i.e., a lower value for the neighbourhood radius) are completely contained in density-connected sets obtained with reference to a lower density.

8. Cluster the following eight points into three groups where the distance function is Euclidean.

   Use the k-means algorithm assuming that the initial cluster centres are A_1, B_1, C_1. Show the results at each iteration.

   $A_1(2, 10)$, $A_2(2, 5)$, $A_3(8, 4)$, $B_1(5, 8)$, $B_2(7, 5)$, $B_3(6, 4)$, $C_1(1, 2)$, $C_2(4, 9)$.

Project

1. Implement any of the clustering algorithms discussed and visually show the clusters formed if the number of dimensions is less than four.

Improve Your Research Skills

1. How would you represent a webpage as a vector of numeric and categorical attributes? What attributes would you use? Once you finalize on the attributes, design a distance function for your objects.

2. Each student in a university lists food items and ranks them on a scale of 1 to 10 (1 = likes, 10 = dislikes). Assuming that k messes can be set up in the campus, how best would you split the students into k groups?

   Next, assume that you are not given k and instead, need to recommend a reasonable number of messes to set up in the campus, how best would you do this?

Improve the Field

1. Rather than coming up with a totally automatic way of clustering data objects, how can user-interaction be effectively utilized to improve the clustering results? Note that the user-interaction should be as minimal as possible, but is allowed.

2. How can we automatically cluster incoming e-mail messages into different categories? Assign appropriate names to these categories.

3. Data entered in check boxes, radio buttons and drop-down lists is machine-friendly—it has a structure that a program can use. In contrast, a paragraph of textual data entered in text boxes is not machine-friendly—the textual data is unstructured.

   Write a program that can automatically categorize all the textual responses of users so that the resulting clusters (or hierarchy of clusters) can be used to design a more structured Graphical User Interface (GUI) design.

4. Are there any problems in attempting to categorize all human knowledge (at least what is available digitally, or on the web) into a good hierarchy of clusters? Will the result be useful? If not, what can be done to make it useful?

CHAPTER 5

PATTERN DISCOVERY IN REAL-WORLD DATA

In theory, there is no difference between theory and practice. But, in practice, there is.
—JAN L.A. VAN DE SNEPSCHEUT

INTRODUCTION

The basic data mining tasks of discovering frequent patterns, classification, and clustering were introduced in the previous chapters. Recall that each of these mining tasks has specific requirements regarding the structure of its input data. For instance, frequent itemset mining requires *transactional data* as input – this data is in the form of records, each of which contains a small number of items drawn from a finite set. Conversely, both classification and clustering require their input data to be in the form of records defined by a number of numeric or categorical attributes.

In practice, data in the real world is not always organized in the required manner for a specific mining task. Instead, it must be transformed into the required format. Sometimes, even when data is available in the required format, it may need to be restructured in different ways to bring out *implicit* patterns that may not be otherwise visible.

In this chapter, we look at different models in which real-world data is organized and see how pattern discovery techniques may be applied to each of them. In particular, we will study the data mining techniques applicable to the following data models:

(a) Relational data
(b) Transactional data
(c) Multi-dimensional data

(d) Distributed data

(e) Spatial data

(f) Multimedia data

(g) Data streams

(h) Time-series data

(i) Text data

(j) Web data

Further, each data model may suggest specific kinds of patterns that are unique to that model. Discovering such patterns may require modifications to the standard techniques seen in earlier chapters, or may even require totally new kinds of techniques.

5.1 RELATIONAL DATA

The relational data model is by far the most popular structured form in which real-world data is organized. Its popularity stems from the fact that it is simple to conceptualize, efficient to implement, and has a strong foundation in set theory and predicate logic.

5.1.1 THE DATA MODEL

Conceptually, all relational data is stored in the form of *tables* consisting of rows (also called *tuples* or *records*) and columns (also called *attributes* or *fields*). An RDBMS (Relational Database Management System) is an implementation of the relational data model to store, retrieve, and manipulate data. Typically, a *relational database* consists of multiple related tables (also called *relations*). Due to the popularity of RDBMS, the term *database* usually means *relational database* and the prefix is omitted.

Each attribute in a table has a fixed domain from which its values can be drawn. The domain of all attributes in a table is called as the *schema* of the table. It is specified at the time of creation of the table. The relational model insists that every table should have a *key* – this is a set of attributes which uniquely identify a given row. A table may have more than one key, in which case, one of them will be designated by the user as a *primary key*.

The following example will help clarify these relational data model concepts.

Example 5.1   The data pertaining to students in a class can be organized in the form of a table as shown in Fig. 5.1.

Roll No	Name	Gender	State	Maths	Physics	Chemistry	English	Social
200101001	Govind	M	AP	94	89	75	62	57
200101002	Ramakanth	M	MP	72	65	67	80	85
200101003	Karuna	F	AP	95	92	77	65	60
...		...	...	...	...	...	...	...

Fig. 5.1   A table storing student data

In an RDBMS, the schema of the above table might be specified as:

students (*roll_no*: integer, *name*: string, *gender*: boolean, *state*: string, *maths*: integer, *physics*: integer, *chemistry*: integer, *english*: integer, *social*: integer)

In this table, *roll_no* can be used to uniquely identify a given row. Hence it is a key for the table. No other keys exist for the table, since there may be more than one student with the same name, gender, state, and marks – although this is definitely rare. Since *roll_no* is the only key, it must be designated as the *primary key* for this table.

5.1.2 PATTERN DISCOVERY IN RELATIONAL DATABASES

In order to discover patterns in a relational database, a user has four choices:

(a) Manually explore the database by using a query language like SQL. This would be tedious and error-prone.

(b) Implement OLAP (Online Analytical Processing) queries and data mining algorithms using facilities provided by the RDBMS package.

(c) Transfer the relational data to a separate data warehouse or data mining package and use that package to discover patterns.

(d) Alternatively, some modern RDBMS packages allow the user to perform OLAP and data mining queries on relational databases directly, instead of first transferring them to another package.

We explain these choices in more detail below.

Using SQL

SQL (Structured Query Language) is the standard language used to retrieve and manipulate data in a relational database. It can be used to retrieve specific rows and columns from a single table or a combination (*join*) of tables. The retrieved rows can be *sorted* along specified columns, or *grouped* according to the values of a column. Further, the retrieved rows or groups of rows can be processed to compute *aggregates*, such as average, sum, max, min, count, etc. along specified columns.

Using SQL, a user can manually discover patterns by writing commands to sort and aggregate the data in various ways. This way, the user obtains several statistics and thereby gets a 'feel' of the trends and patterns in the data. After obtaining some statistics, the user may get some 'hunches' and these can in turn be verified by doing further analysis. The disadvantage of this technique is that it is tedious and error-prone – some or many patterns may be missed depending on the skill of the user.

Implementing OLAP and data mining algorithms in RDBMS

The second strategy for pattern discovery from relational databases is to implement OLAP and mining algorithms using facilities provided by modern RDBMS packages. Popular RDBMS packages allow users to implement arbitrary code that accesses relational data using several mechanisms as discussed hereunder:

Language extensions Most popular languages, such as C/C++, Pascal, Python, Perl, etc. have extensions that enable them to embed SQL statements into their code. In compiled languages, such as C and Pascal, certain preprocessors are used to convert the SQL statements into appropriate language code that can be compiled later. Interpreted languages such as Python and Perl use a cursor interface (described below) to execute SQL statements.

SQL cursor interfaces An SQL cursor interface is a mechanism that is implemented by all (SQL99-compliant) RDBMS vendors. It allows the execution of arbitrary SQL statements and to retrieve the resulting rows one-by-one. Interpreted languages such as Python and Perl provide wrappers around cursor interfaces to execute SQL statements.

Stored procedures Some RDBMS vendors provide the capability to implement stored procedures in their package. In a stored procedure, a user can write procedural code (consisting of variables, conditional statements, loops, etc.). The syntax differs from vendor to vendor, although some common features exist.

User-defined functions User-defined functions can be thought of as a special class of stored procedures that return values.

Any of the above mechanisms may be used to implement an OLAP query or a data mining algorithm that accesses relational data. The disadvantage of this technique is that it requires the user to be an expert at implementing data mining algorithms. This is not the case with most end-users, who are usually domain-experts in some other field of study.

Transferring data to another software

In this approach, the relational data is first transferred to another data warehousing or mining software in the format that is required by that software. Pattern discovery can then be carried out using this software.

In a study by S. Sarawagi *et al*, published in SIGMOD-1998, it was shown that this approach, where the data is taken out of a relational database and then mined separately, was the fastest of all. The other mechanisms discussed in the previous subsection did not perform as well due to the overheads involved in accessing data stored inside a relational database.

The disadvantage of this technique is the overhead involved in transferring the data to another software. This would especially be a problem if the data involved is huge.

Tightly-coupled vendor implementations

Some modern RDBMS packages allow the user to perform OLAP and data mining queries directly on relational databases, instead of first transferring them to another package. These implementations are usually very efficient since they directly access the underlying data, without going through several layers of indirection.

In order to use these implementations, the user needs to identify the *roles* played by different parts of the available data. The implementations provide special commands that enable the user to do this. For example, to execute OLAP queries, the user needs to perform the following steps:

(a) Identify specific columns of the relational data as the data warehouse *dimensions*.

(b) Define the *dimension hierarchies*. Commands are provided to create hierarchies over dimensions by marking other columns as being in specific levels of these hierarchies.

(c) Create a table for each warehouse *measure*.

(d) Create a *cube-object*, which consists of one or more measures accessed using a common set of dimensions.

Once the cube-object is created, the user can execute OLAP queries over it. The execution of data mining algorithms follows a similar sequence of steps as that of OLAP queries. Basically, the user needs to identify the roles played by different columns. For example, to execute a classification algorithm, the user needs to identify which column contains the class labels.

In addition, the underlying software provides commands for the user to *preprocess* the data by applying techniques such as normalization and binning. Such preprocessing is required for most mining techniques. For example, frequent itemset mining requires all columns to be binary attributes.

This technique of tightly-coupled vendor implementations is the most promising amongst the four choices for pattern discovery in relational databases. It does not have the overhead of transferring data to another software, while at the same time, it has the promise of efficiency.

5.2 TRANSACTIONAL DATA

Transactional data consists of records, each of which contains a set of *items*. Examples include customers buying sets of items from a supermarket, or users submitting sets of words as queries to a search engine. Transactional data is also referred to as *market-basket data* as it was originally used to model sets of items purchased by customers of any business enterprise. Each such set of items is called a *transaction* or *record*.

5.2.1   THE DATA MODEL

Conceptually, transactional data simply consists of records, each of which contains a set of items as shown in Fig. 5.2. This data model was discussed in Chapter 2 and is reproduced below for convenience.

Transaction ID	Items Sold
1	tomato, potato, onion
2	tomato, potato, brinjal, pumpkin
3	tomato, potato, onion, chilly
4	lemon, tamarind, chilly

Fig. 5.2   Sample market-basket dataset

In most applications, such data is either stored in text files or in relational databases. Packaging the data in a form suitable for pattern discovery may itself require a lot of fore-thought and effort. To store the data in a relational database, it needs to be normalized as shown in Fig. 5.3 for the sample data in Fig. 5.2.

TID	Items Sold
1	tomato
1	potato
1	onion
2	tomato
2	potato
2	brinjal
2	pumpkin
3	tomato
3	potato
3	onion
3	chilly
4	lemon
4	tamarind
4	chilly

Fig. 5.3   Normalized (relational) representation of transactional data

Irrespective of the original data format, mining algorithms typically expect transactional data to adhere to one of the four logical formats as outlined below. If the original dataset is not already in the required format, it needs to be converted before such mining algorithms can be applied.

Horizontal list format

This is the most common input format for transactional data. For the sample dataset in Fig. 5.2, the horizontal list format is shown in Fig. 5.4. The data consists of records or transactions – each record has a unique id, referred to

TID	Items Sold
1	tomato, potato, onion
2	tomato, potato, brinjal, pumpkin
3	tomato, potato, onion, chilly
4	lemon, tamarind, chilly

Fig. 5.4   Horizontal list format

as a *TID*. The items in the record are listed one after the other. Most algorithms expect that the items are listed in some consistent order for all records. For example, if tomato occurs before potato in some record, then in all records containing tomato and potato, tomato should occur before potato.

Horizontal vector format

In this logical format, each record is represented by a vector of bits of length m, where m is the number of distinct items in the dataset. The kth bit is set to 1 if the kth item is present in the record, and 0 if it is absent. For the sample dataset in Fig. 5.2, the horizontal vector format is shown in Fig. 5.5.

TID	tomato	potato	onion	brinjal	pumpkin	chilly	lemon	tamarind
1	1	1	1	0	0	0	0	0
2	1	1	0	1	1	0	0	0
3	1	1	1	0	0	1	0	0
4	0	0	0	0	0	1	1	1

Fig. 5.5 Horizontal vector format

Vertical list format

The vertical list format is shown in Fig. 5.6 for the sample dataset in Fig. 5.2. In this format, we store the list of TIDs of records containing each item – this is also referred to as the *tidlist* of that item. More generally, the *tidlist* of an itemset is defined as:

> **Tidlist** The tidlist of an itemset X is the list of TIDs of records that contain X as a subset.

The *tidlist* of an itemset can be computed by intersecting the tidlists of items contained in it.

tomato	potato	onion	brinjal	pumpkin	chilly	lemon	tamarind
1	1	1	2	2	3	4	4
2	2	3			4		
3	3						

Fig. 5.6 Vertical list format

Vertical vector format

In this format, we store a vector of bits of length n for each item, where n is the number of records in the database. For a given item x, the corresponding vector has its kth bit set to 1 if the kth record contains x. Otherwise, the bit is set to 0. These vectors are called *tid-vectors*. Like in the previous vertical list format, it is possible to define the *tid-vector* of an itemset as below.

Tid-vector   The tid-vector of an itemset X is a vector of bits of length n, where n is the number of records in the database, and the kth bit set to 1 if the kth record contains X, and 0 otherwise.

The *tid-vector* of an itemset can be efficiently computed by doing a bit-wise AND operation on the *tid-vectors* of items contained in it. The vertical vector format is shown below in Fig. 5.7 for the sample dataset in Fig. 5.2.

tomato	potato	onion	brinjal	pumpkin	chilly	lemon	tamarind
1	1	1	0	0	0	0	0
1	1	0	1	1	0	0	0
1	1	1	0	0	1	0	0
0	0	0	0	0	1	1	1

Fig. 5.7   Vertical vector format

Comparison of formats

While the horizontal list is the most widely used format for input to pattern discovery algorithms, the other formats are also useful. Some algorithms convert the dataset or a part of it from one format to another, as and when required. Conversion is efficient and is usually done 'on-the-fly' for parts of the dataset without storing multiple formats on disk.

The horizontal vector format is used when it is necessary to check for the presence of items in records very often. In this format, this checking operation can be done in constant time. The vertical list format is useful to efficiently determine the count of items and itemsets. The count of an item or itemset is simply the length of its *tidlist*. The *tidlist* of an itemset can be computed as the intersection of the *tidlists* of its items. This is a simple operation for which efficient algorithms can be easily designed. For the vertical vector format, this is even more efficient because the bit-wise AND operation required for it can be carried out efficiently in hardware.

Pattern discovery in transactional data

The transactional data model naturally yields frequent itemsets and related patterns as described in Chapter 2. In fact, any data must first be converted to the transactional data model either explicitly or implicitly, before frequent patterns can be mined from it.

Besides frequent itemsets, transactional data is also suitable for clustering and classification (if a *class* column is defined). This is possible because, if we observe the horizontal vector format of data storage (see Fig. 5.5), it corresponds neatly to a relational model – we see a table where the rows are of fixed length and the columns are binary attributes. Therefore, all the pattern discovery techniques that can be applied on relational databases are also applicable to transactional databases.

We will next review briefly the kinds of patterns that can be discovered from transactional databases. For additional details, refer the previous chapters, especially Chapter 2.

Frequent itemsets

A set of items is said to be frequent if the fraction of times it occurs as a subset in transactions is at least equal to *minsup*, a user-given threshold. Discovering such frequent itemsets is useful, as it conveys the amount of correlation between items in a transactional dataset. The fact that two items are correlated, or the amount of the correlation between them, might have been previously unknown to the user. Discovering such relationships therefore opens up new knowledge and can help in decision-making.

Association rules

If X and Y are disjoint sets of items, an association rule is a rule of the form $X \rightarrow Y$, indicating that in the presence of X, we can expect the presence of Y. A confidence factor can be computed for the rule, which is the fraction of those transactions that contain X, which also contain Y. Interesting association rules can be computed easily, after frequent itemsets have been mined.

Implication rules

Association rules are misleading. Even if a rule $X \rightarrow Y$ has a high confidence factor, it does not mean that the presence of X is a good indication of the presence of Y. It is possible that the *absence* of X may be an even better indicator of the presence of Y. The only reason that $X \rightarrow Y$ has a high confidence factor may be because Y has high support.

Implication rules handle this drawback as they are based on *conviction* rather than confidence. A rule $X \rightarrow Y$ has a high *conviction* factor only if the presence of X has a better correlation (than the absence of X) with the presence of Y.

Quantitative and categorical rules

The basic frequent itemset mining problem has been defined in terms of items, which are binary attributes – that is, an item is either present in a record or absent. Most real-world data has richer attribute types. Attributes in relational database tables can be *quantitative* (e.g. age, income) or *categorical* (e.g. postal code, day of the week). From the transactional database perspective, the model is enhanced in the following way: Each transaction consists of a set of items, where each item has an associated quantitative or categorical value.

The basic strategy to mine rules from such data is to first *convert* these quantitative and categorical attributes into binary attributes and then apply standard frequent itemset mining algorithms. For quantitative attributes, this is accomplished by dividing the possible values of each attribute into *ranges* and the treating each range as a binary attribute – either the value of the attribute for a given record lies within the range or not. For categorical attributes, a binary attribute is created for each possible value of the attribute, indicating whether that value is present in a given record or not.

Hierarchical rules

In many applications, *is-a hierarchies* (or ontologies) over the items is available. A familiar example of an ontology is the biological classification tree that classifies the entire animal and plant kingdom into classes and sub-classes. An ontology is a tree structure where each node indicates a concept and the children of that node indicate specific instances of that concept. Hierarchical rules are association rules where the LHS (Left Hand Side) or RHS (Right Hand Side) may include not just specific items, but may also correspond to internal nodes of an *is-a hierarchy*.

Cyclic/periodic rules

Cyclic or periodic rules are association rules that display regular cyclic variation over time. For instance, if we compute association rules over the monthly sales data of a store, we may observe seasonal variation where certain rules are true at approximately the same month each year – this may be due to the occurrence of certain festivals. An example rule of this kind could be:

Month = August, Place = Hyderabad → Turmeric, Wood-apple

This rule indicates that in August and at Hyderabad, people frequently purchase turmeric and wood-apples, perhaps due to the Vinayaka Chavithi festival. Discovering such rules and their periodicities may reveal interesting information that can be used for prediction and decision-making.

The basic approach to mining periodic rules is to modify each data record in a preprocessing phase to include date and time related attributes at various levels of granularity, such as 'month', 'year', 'day of week', 'day of month', 'week of month', etc. Following this, any standard frequent itemset mining algorithm can be applied.

Sequential rules

While association rule mining is applied on records containing *sets* of items, sequential rule mining is applied when the records contain *sequences* of items. Examples include customers buying items on consecutive visits to a store, or users visiting a sequence of Web pages. Frequent sequences of Web page visits could be used to decide if new links should be provided on some Web pages, pointing to other pages frequently visited after them. Section 11 of Chapter 2 shows how standard frequent itemset mining concepts can be used to mine sequential rules as well.

Classification and clustering

In many classification problems, the input data objects can be represented as sets of *binary* features – wherein, a feature is either present or absent for a given object. In such cases, the input data objects of each class constitute a transactional dataset and can be mined for frequent itemsets. The frequent itemsets so obtained can be considered a good summary of the features of that class. This is valuable for classification – given a new object to classify, we can verify if its features match significantly with the frequent features of a particular class. If so, the new object can be assigned the label of that class. Several new classification approaches have been proposed recently with this idea and have shown good results.

Similarly, in many clustering problems, the input data objects can be represented as sets of *binary* features. Frequent itemset mining provides a good starting point for developing clustering algorithms on such data.

5.3 MULTI-DIMENSIONAL DATA

The multi-dimensional data model is used in *data warehouses*. A data warehouse is a repository of data that is *integrated* from multiple data sources, each of which pertains to some aspect of the day-to-day operations of an enterprise. These data sources may be *volatile* – i.e. their accumulated data may be removed periodically. However, the data warehouse is relatively *non-volatile* and accumulates data over several years (*time-variant*).

5.3.1 THE DATA MODEL

Data in a data warehouse is organized in terms of *measures* and *dimensions.* Users are interested in studying how the measures (typically some quantitative data such as the total sales of products in an enterprise) are related to the dimensions (such as product, store location, and year). It is the user's job to initially specify which attributes of the original data are measures and which are dimensions. The data warehouse is then structured in terms of these *subjects* – i.e. measures and dimensions, so as to facilitate user exploration.

The data is conceptually organized as a multi-dimensional array, where each dimension of the array corresponds to a dimension of the warehouse and the values stored in each cell of the array correspond to the measures of the warehouse. This way of organizing data is referred to as a *multi-dimensional model* and the data repository is said to be *subject-oriented.*

Concept hierarchies could be defined over each dimension. For example, product hierarchies could be defined in terms of the specific model (e.g. parker pen model 75), or of a product type (e.g. all pens), or product category (e.g. all stationary). The term *granularity* defines the hierarchy level at which a dimension is specified – more granularity means more detail.

Specialized storage structures may be used to store and index multi-dimensional data. However, multi-dimensional data is often stored in plain relational databases – a central *fact* table is used to store the bulk of the data. Each row in this table contains the values of each measure for different values of the dimensions. There may be other tables to describe the attributes and hierarchies of each dimension.

5.3.2 PATTERN DISCOVERY IN MULTI-DIMENSIONAL DATA

As mentioned above, the multi-dimensional data model is used in *data warehouses.* It supports pattern discovery by means of user-interaction through OLAP queries – these queries enable the user to visualize different *views* of the data warehouse. Typical OLAP queries include the following:

Selection of dimensions to explore The data warehouse may contain several dimensions. Yet, it is only possible to visualize a few (about three or four) dimensions at a time. Thus, it is necessary for the user to specify which dimensions are to be explored at any point in time.

Roll-up and drill-down The user may want to view data at any level of granularity with reference to the concept hierarchies defined over dimensions.

The user can interactively ask to *roll-up* to a less-detailed level or *drill-down* to a more-detailed level.

Slice and dice   The user may specify an interest in only particular values of specific dimensions. For example, the sales measure should be totalled for the years 2003 and 2005 only. Computing such views is called as a *slice and dice* operation.

By exploring all of these views, the owner obtains a good understanding of the overall data in the enterprise. As mentioned, the data may actually reside in a relational database; but if it is structured in the form of measures and dimensions and supports the above OLAP queries, then it is referred to as multi-dimensional data.

The fact that multi-dimensional data can be stored in relational tables means that all the pattern discovery techniques that can be applied on relational databases can also be applied here. This includes all the well-known data mining techniques of frequent pattern mining, classification, regression, clustering, etc. To do this, the user needs to identify what role is played by each dimension or measure – for example whether it is a class attribute or not, for classification. Some data preprocessing may also be needed – for example all the dimensions and measures will need to be converted to binary attributes if frequent itemset mining is to be applied.

5.4 DISTRIBUTED DATA

With the advances of technology over the years, datasets have been growing rapidly in size and complexity. Many of these datasets are geographically distributed across multiple sites. For example, the sales records of hundreds of chain stores of a large enterprise are stored at different locations. To mine such large and distributed datasets, one option is to collect and integrate the data from these multiple sites into one common repository – this is the approach taken by data warehousing, and was the topic of the previous section. An alternative is to devise new algorithms that can mine patterns or run OLAP queries at each site separately and then somehow combine the results so obtained.

5.4.1 THE DATA MODEL

In the distributed data model, different portions of the dataset reside in different locations or sites. In addition, there is a *central server* from which the mining operation or OLAP query is initiated. The central server is usually one of the sites in which data resides. However, it could be a different site altogether.

The central server has access to the data residing at different locations through a network. However, it is inefficient to transfer large amounts of data through the network. Thus, the main design principle of distributed algorithms is to split the overall mining task into small parts that can be executed separately at different sites. This execution will yield *local patterns* at each site.

The size of the local patterns at each site is typically much smaller than the total data residing at that site and so, it can be transmitted easily through the network to the central server. The central server collects the local patterns at each site and uses that to compute the global patterns.

When the network bandwidth is high, large amounts of data transfer becomes feasible. However, even in such cases, the above strategy is worthwhile, as it can reduce the overall response time by making use of the parallel-processing power of multiple machines. In fact, even if the data is originally resident on a central server, it may be beneficial to transfer parts of the data to multiple sites to make use of their parallel-processing power.

5.4.2 PATTERN DISCOVERY IN DISTRIBUTED DATA

The task of combining local patterns at different sites into a set of global patterns is not as easy as it may seem. The results of some kinds of queries cannot be easily or automatically combined, as shown in the following subsection.

Patterns as aggregates

Aggregates are statistics that are computed from a data collection. Examples include maximum, minimum, average, total, etc. of attributes in the dataset. Although the traditional notion of an aggregate includes only these kinds of statistics, in our context, we can view *every* kind of pattern as an aggregate that is computed from the data.

This view of patterns is useful because research in statistics has identified three kinds of aggregate functions – *distributive, algebraic,* and *holistic.* This division is based on how easy it is to *incrementally* compute the aggregate function. These are illustrated in the following example.

Example 5.2   Consider a supermarket chain with 100 locations all over the country. Each location stores its local sales data. The owner of the supermarket chain wishes to compute the following aggregates across all locations:

(a) The maximum number of items that a customer buys at a time,

(b) The average number of items that a customer buys at a time, and

(c) The median number of items that a customer buys at a time.

For the first aggregate, it is required to compute the maximum number of items that a customer buys at a time across all supermarket locations. To do this, it is sufficient if each location computes its local maximum and sends that information to a central server. This central machine can then output the global maximum across all locations.

For the second aggregate, it is required to compute the average number of items that a customer buys at a time across all supermarket locations. We cannot directly follow the same approach as above. If each location sends its local average only to the central server, this cannot be used to compute the global average. Instead, each location needs to send two pieces of information: (i) the total number of items bought by all customers at that location, and (ii) the total number of customers at that location. The central server can then compute the global totals and use that to find the required average.

For the third aggregate, it is well-known in the statistics community that the above approach will fail. The global median cannot be computed by knowing just the local medians at each location. Typically, the entire local data needs to be transferred to the central server for the global median to be computed.

The first kind of aggregate function discussed above (e.g. *maximum*), where the aggregate can be computed easily is referred to as *distributive*. The second kind (e.g. *average*) that can be computed by transferring information of a constant size is referred to as *algebraic*. The third kind (e.g. *median*) is referred to as *holistic*.

The above example shows that some aggregates cannot be computed easily in a distributed fashion. For some tasks, such as mining the WWW (World-Wide Web), it may not even be feasible to collect and integrate all the data into a single repository. Luckily, most data mining tasks can be reduced to the computation of distributive or algebraic aggregate functions.

We describe below how the major data mining tasks can be performed on distributed data. These descriptions are only to illustrate the feasibility of mining distributed data. The research literature contains other highly optimized algorithms for distributed data mining.

Frequent itemset mining   In frequent itemset mining, the data residing at different sites can be treated as *partitions* and the Partition algorithm (Section 2.6.5 of Chapter 2) can be applied. This algorithm merely needs the local frequent itemsets from each partition and not the entire data. It combines these local frequent itemsets to form a global candidate set that is verified over each partition for being frequent.

Classification   For classification, the principles of *bagging* and *boosting* (Section 3.5 of Chapter 3) can be applied as follows. A classification model can be learnt at each site and each classifier obtained can be used to classify a new unlabeled record. In other words, each classifier casts a *vote* for which class the unlabeled record belongs to; and the votes are combined according to the principles of bagging or boosting.

Clustering   If frequent itemset based techniques are used for clustering, they are easily applicable on distributed data as described above. The *k*-means algorithm is also easily parallelizable. In this algorithm, we need to maintain a copy of the current (global) cluster centres at each site. Then, in each iteration, we assign the data points at each site to the cluster centre to which it is closest. Computing new cluster centres requires us to compute the cluster *mean*, which is an algebraic aggregate function (like *average* in Example 5.2).

5.5 SPATIAL DATA

Spatial data is any kind of data where the *location in space* of objects holds importance. It includes geographic maps, medical images of the human body, engineering drawings, architectural drawings, etc. It is estimated that the bulk of data in the real world has some spatial component. It is thus important to be able to deal with spatial data in a specialized manner for pattern discovery.

5.5.1 THE DATA MODEL

A spatial database is a database that has *spatial data types* (i.e. points, lines, and regions) in its data model and query language. In addition, it supports spatial predicates (e.g. near, adjacent, inside, etc.) in selection and join queries. It uses a spatial index to enable efficient access to required spatial objects for answering queries.

Spatial data types

Spatial database systems support three primitive spatial data types from which more complex data types can be built. The primitive types are:

Points   Each point is a point in two or three dimensions, typically represented with x, y, and z coordinates. For maps, it could be represented in terms of latitude and longitude.

Lines   These are polylines – sequences of connected straight line segments. They are used to represent paths such as roads or bridges, or connections such as electric wires. Internally, they are represented as sequences of points.

Regions   These are spatial objects that have an area. A region may have a hole in it, or may consist of several disjoint pieces. These are used to represent countries, states, etc. Internally, regions are represented using polygons, which are again represented as sequences of points.

Spatial predicates

Spatial objects may be compared with each other in many ways by means of predicates. There are three classes of spatial predicates:

Topological   These are relationships that do not change with topological transformations, such as translation, scaling, rotation, etc. Examples include *adjacent*, *inside*, and *disjoint*.

Direction   These are relationships that depend on direction, such as *above*, *below*, *left_of*, etc.

Metric   These are relationships that depend on distance, such as *distance* ≤ 10 km.

The most fundamental of these predicates are the topological ones. Research in spatial databases has concluded that there are five primitive topological predicates: *touch*, *in*, *cross*, *overlap*, and *disjoint*.

Spatial queries

Fundamental spatial queries include selection and join queries where spatial predicates are involved.

Example 5.3   Illustrative queries for spatial *selection* include:

(a) List all the cities in India.
(b) List all the blood vessels that pass through the stomach.

Illustrative queries for spatial *join* include:

(a) Get the list of all cities and the states to which they belong.
(b) Get the list of all ATMs that are near petrol bunks.

In order to answer such queries efficiently, a spatial index is built. Spatial indices enable efficient retrieval of spatial objects that lie within a given bounding rectangle. This allows most queries to be answered efficiently without retrieving *all* objects, which would otherwise have been necessary.

5.5.2   PATTERN DISCOVERY IN SPATIAL DATA

For pattern discovery purposes, after some initial preprocessing, spatial databases can be dealt with in the same way as relational databases.

The initial preprocessing augments each table that contains spatial data types with additional attributes. These attributes are derived from the *properties* of the spatial data types (such as length, area, etc.) or from the *predicates* that are satisfied by the spatial data types (such as being *near* an ATM, *in* a city, *adjacent to* a lake, etc.). Note that the augmentation of new attributes need not be done physically on disk. Rather, it can be done logically, on-the-fly, as each record is read from the disk.

There could be a large (potentially infinite) number of predicates. However, for practical purposes, it will suffice to only consider predicates that are satisfied by objects that are *close to* the object of interest. This strategy is based on the 'first law of geography', which states that: *Everything is related to everything else, but near things are more related than distant things.*

With the augmented database, it becomes possible to discover interesting patterns by using the same techniques that are applicable to relational databases. Illustrative patterns that could be discovered include:

Location prediction   We can predict where some species of organisms will reside by studying known locations of elements of those species. For example, we might discover a rule like: red-winged blackbirds live in humid and cold wetlands.

Spatial outliers   These are spatial objects that are significantly different from their neighbourhoods, though they may not be significantly different from the entire population. For example, a brand new building in an old area of a city is a spatial outlier.

OLAP queries are particularly applicable for spatial data because there are implicit concept-hierarchies present – a colony is *in* a city, which is *in* a state and *in* a country, etc. Thus, it becomes possible to roll-up and drill-down along a spatial attribute.

5.6   DATA STREAMS

A data stream is a continuous flow of data records into a computer system. Examples of data streams include web-logs, streaming stock prices, computer network traffic, phone conversations, ATM transactions, and sensor data. Typically, the records flowing in a stream are too many and they arrive too fast. Pattern discovery from such data streams is thus a challenging task.

5.6.1   THE DATA MODEL

Conceptually, a data stream consists of a sequence of records. Each record may either consist of a combination of numeric and categorical attributes (like in a relational database table), or it may consist of a set of items (like in a transactional database). What makes data streams different is that the records are *transient* – they simply arrive at the data processing system and get processed.

Synopsis   As there are too many records in a stream, the data processing system cannot store all of them. It can store only a small *running summary* of the records. Such a summary is called a *synopsis* or a *sketch*. Pattern discovery must be made by using this synopsis only – one does not have the luxury of making multiple passes over the data records. The design of stream mining algorithms therefore boils down to the design of the synopsis – what kind of summary of the records should be stored?

Approximate results   An immediate question that comes to mind is – Can *all* kinds of patterns be mined from just small running summaries of the data stream? The answer in general is *no*. However, most kinds of patterns (including those we have studied so far in this book) can be mined *approximately* from the small running summaries. By 'approximately', we mean that some existing patterns may not be discovered, some discovered patterns may be spurious, and the numeric parameters computed for some discovered patterns (such as support for frequent itemsets) may be offset by a small error.

Fortunately, the approximation is usually very good and is acceptable in most real-life situations. Typically, accuracy guarantees will be made in terms of a pair of user-specified parameters, ε and ∂, meaning that the error in approximation (of any computed numeric parameter) is within a factor of ε with probability ∂. The space and time complexity of the pattern discovery algorithm will consequently depend on ε and ∂.

It is surprising that it is actually possible to get such good results by making just a single quick pass over the streaming data. In fact, the overall idea of computing approximate results in a single quick pass is so useful that it is tempting to apply it even in the non-streaming scenario, where there is a *huge* resident database available on disk.

Continuous queries   In the context of data streams, it is common to have *continuous* queries – queries that execute continuously whenever the data is updated. For example, the user may be interested in keeping track of the running totals (or maximum, minimum, etc.) of numeric columns. Queries can also be pattern discovery tasks – the user may be interested in keeping track of frequent itemsets (or clusters, classification models, etc.) as and when they are updated by fresh data.

The concept of continuous queries is intimately related to that of *incremental pattern discovery* (see Section 1.7.2 of Chapter 1). Algorithms that have been devised for incremental pattern discovery may be directly used if the user is interested in keeping track of the corresponding patterns. However, this is possible only if the incremental algorithms do not have to access the entire data stream. Alternatively, the algorithms developed in the data stream literature for processing continuous queries can be of use in incremental pattern discovery if approximate results are tolerable.

Recent patterns   In many applications, the *recent* records in a data stream may be of more importance than the older records. It may be that the patterns and trends in the older data get outdated or old-fashioned. While some weight must still be given to patterns that persist with time, it is usually more important to find recent 'emerging' patterns as they may represent new opportunities that need changes in business strategy.

If recent records are of more importance in an application, the user may be interested in finding patterns, not over the entire data stream, but over the last week, month, year, or last few months. This requirement is quite demanding as it requires additional storage and processing time. Moreover, the design of algorithms becomes complex as it is not clear what data needs to be stored in the synopsis to enable user-queries to be computed over *any* time window.

Modern stream mining algorithms overcome the above difficulties using very elegant schemes by storing very little additional data in the synopsis. The size of the synopsis required is usually logarithmic or poly-logarithmic (i.e. $O((\log n)^k)$) in the size of the data stream. The design of such synopses is discussed further in Section 7.1.2.

Kinds of synoposes

The design of what information to store in the synopsis depends on the kind of patterns that analysts may want to discover. Nevertheless, a synopsis can be designed in a generic manner, such that it will be useful for a wide variety of pattern-types. In this subsection, we describe such generic designs of synopses. The idea of a synopsis is not new. Two techniques – random sampling and histograms have been widely used in database systems to represent summaries of data. These techniques are also useful for data streams.

Random samples   In this technique, a small set of records is selected at random from the data stream. The selected records must constitute a *random sample* of the data in the stream – i.e. every record in the stream must have an equal chance of being in the sample. Query processing or pattern discovery can then be done on the sample instead of the entire data stream. This results in reasonably accurate results for most pattern discovery tasks.

Selecting a random sample from a data stream is a tricky task because the size of the stream is not known beforehand. Algorithms that are capable of extracting random samples when the size of the dataset is unknown are called *reservoir sampling* algorithms.

The basic idea behind reservoir algorithms is to select a sample (called the *reservoir*) of *size*[3] n from which a random sample of size n can be generated. The first step of any such algorithm is to put the first n records of the dataset into the reservoir. The rest of the records are then processed sequentially, during which some of them are selected for insertion into the reservoir.

Reservoir algorithms generally maintain a *running random sample* containing a subset of the reservoir. When a new record is added to the reservoir, it replaces one of the records in the running random sample. An example of a reservoir algorithm is to select (for insertion into the reservoir) the tth record with a probability of (n/t) and to select the record to be replaced at random.

Histograms   A histogram is an approximate representation of the frequency distribution of an attribute in a dataset. The domain of the attribute is partitioned into buckets and the frequency of each bucket (i.e. number of records having their attribute value in that bucket) is stored in the histogram.

Histogram techniques differ in the manner in which they partition the attribute domain into buckets. Typical strategies include forming buckets that have the same *width* (i.e. the range of values in the bucket) or the same *depth* (i.e. the number of records that fall in the bucket). A more accurate, although more complicated, approach is to use *V-Optimal* histograms where the frequency variance within each bucket is minimized.

Pattern discovery can be done by using the histograms of the attributes in the data stream as a synopsis. This is possible because most pattern discovery tasks only require knowing the distribution of the data, and not the actual data records per se. The results are reasonably accurate for most pattern discovery tasks. Unlike sampling, here, special algorithms need to be devised to perform pattern discovery tasks on the histogram synopsis. We also need algorithms that can incrementally update histograms as new data arrives into the data stream.

Sliding windows   In this approach, the synopsis is a sliding window – i.e. the w most recent records seen so far in the stream, where w is the window size. Query processing or pattern discovery can be done on the sliding window instead of the entire data stream. This approach is useful when only the recent records are of importance to the task in hand.

The above model is an extreme case. Typically, even older records carry some useful information although the recent records are of more importance. To alleviate this, the synopsis should contain some other summary information about the older records (such as a sample or histogram) along with the sliding window.

Wavelets   A wavelet transform is a function that can be applied on a sequence of real numbers X to yield a different sequence of numbers X'. An inverse wavelet transform can then be applied on X' to get back X. The advantage of wavelet transforms is that the transformed sequence X' can be approximated by a very sparse sequence in which only the elements of X' whose value is more than a threshold are retained; all other elements are set to zero.

This means that a large (high information) sequence can be represented approximately by a much smaller (low information) transformed sequence, which is its wavelet. All operations that need to be carried out on the large sequence can in principle be carried out on its wavelet. Hence, a wavelet can be used as a *synopsis* of the original sequence.

In the data stream scenario, the synopsis consists of wavelets computed for each attribute in the dataset. The sequence of attribute values present in the data stream is given as input to a wavelet transform. Algorithms exist to compute wavelets incrementally as the stream grows. Special algorithms need to be devised to perform pattern discovery tasks on the wavelet synopsis.

Snapshots and time frames

To cater to the requirement of mining *recent* patterns as outlined in Section 5.6.1, modern stream mining algorithms maintain *snapshots* of information in their synopsis. The information in these snapshots may consist of the values of certain parameters, statistics, aggregates, or patterns that are obtained from the data stream at various points in time.

The set of the points in time at which the snapshots are stored is referred to as the *time frame*. The snapshots are *not* taken at regular intervals since that would require the size of the synopsis to be linear with respect to the stream size. Instead, the time frame is *tilted* with more snapshots being stored at recent points in time. It should be designed in such a way that it requires the synopsis size to be no more than poly-logarithmic (i.e. $O((\log n)^h)$) with respect to the stream size.

Examples of popular tilted time frame designs are given hereunder.

Natural tilted time frame   In this design, the snapshots are stored at different points in the natural or calendar time-scale. For example, snapshots are stored every 15 minutes for the last hour, every hour for the last 24 hours, every day for the last month, every month for the last year, and so on. With such a time frame, user-queries can be computed for the last hour with the precision of 15 minutes, for the last day with the precision of an hour, and so on.

Logarithmic tilted time frame   In this design, the snapshots are stored at different points in a logarithmic time-scale. For example, snapshots are stored at the last hour, last two hours, last four hours, last eight hours, and so on.

Pyramidal tilted time frame   In this design, snapshots are classified into different 'orders' which can vary from 1 to $\log(n)$, where n is the stream size. Snapshots are stored whenever the stream size is divisible by a^i, where a is a fixed integer greater than 1 and i is the snapshot 'order'. At any given time, only the last $a + 1$ snapshots of each order are stored. If a snapshot can be classified into more than 1 order, it is given the maximum possible order.

It is clear that each of these time frame models gives more importance to the recent records in the data stream than to the older records.

5.6.2   PATTERN DISCOVERY IN DATA STREAMS

The simplest way of discovering patterns in data streams is to use a random sample or sliding window as the synopsis and then perform regular pattern discovery algorithms on the synopsis. This will usually yield sufficiently accurate results. Alternatively, like in the case of distributed data, patterns can be treated as aggregates and algorithms can be developed that take advantage of this fact.

Data stream patterns as aggregates

For pattern discovery in data streams, we can follow the same strategy as for distributed data by treating patterns as *aggregates* (see Section 5.2.1). In short, the result of any pattern discovery task can be treated as an aggregate that needs to be updated as the data stream grows.

It is easy to see (as illustrated in Example 5.4 below) that distributive and algebraic aggregates can be computed easily in data streams. For each distributive or algebraic aggregate, a small amount of information needs to be maintained in the synopsis. Holistic aggregates are not so easy to handle; however, as discussed in Section 5.2.1, the major data mining tasks can be reduced to the computation of distributive or algebraic aggregate functions.

Example 5.4   In analysing stock market data, an analyst wishes to compute the following:

(a) The *maximum* number of shares that an investor buys at a time,

(b) The *average* number of shares that an investor buys at a time, and

(c) The *median* number of shares that an investor buys at a time.

The analyst is analysing real stock market data as it arrives – it is not a static store of data, but a live data stream.

For the first aggregate, it is required to compute the maximum number of shares that an investor buys at a time. This is a distributive aggregate and is thus easy to handle. All we need to do is to store the current maximum at each point of time in the synopsis. When a new data record arrives with larger number of shares than the maximum, the synopsis is updated to reflect this.

For the second aggregate, it is required to compute the average number of shares that an investor buys at a time. This is an algebraic aggregate and we cannot directly follow the same approach as above. Instead, we need to maintain two pieces of information in the synopsis: (i) the total number of shares bought, and (ii) the total number of records. We can compute the required average using these two pieces of information.

For the third aggregate, it is well-known in the statistics community that the above approach will fail. It is a holistic aggregate. We cannot maintain just the current median and a few other pieces of information and update it as new data arrives. Typically, the entire data needs to be stored for the median to be re-computed as new data arrives.

Most pattern discovery tasks can be reduced to the computation of distributive or algebraic aggregate functions. The same techniques described for distributed data, where we treated patterns as aggregates, can be applied (with some modifications) in the data stream scenario. We describe below how the major data mining tasks can be performed on data streams. These descriptions are only to illustrate the feasibility of mining data streams. The research literature contains other highly optimized algorithms for pattern discovery in data streams.

Frequent itemset mining   The data coming into a data stream can be conceptually imagined to be coming in bunches at a time rather than individually. These bunches can be considered as *partitions* and the first pass of the Partition algorithm (Section 2.6.5 of Chapter 2) can be applied.

The first pass of this algorithm merely computes the local frequent itemsets of each partition and does not need the entire data. At the end of this pass, it combines these local frequent itemsets to form a global candidate set. It is well-known that an itemset that is infrequent in every partition must be infrequent overall (see Section 2.6.5 of Chapter 2).

Now, if a candidate is frequent in r partitions, its count is added in all these partitions and stored with the candidate in the global candidate set, along with the total size of these r partitions. Define *partial support* of a candidate as its stored count divided by the total size of the partitions in which it is frequent.

It is easy to see that the partial support of any candidate is a good estimate of its actual support in the entire database. This is because it represents the support in those partitions where it is frequent. The calculation of the error in this estimation is left to the reader as an exercise. We can thus treat the partial support of any candidate as its actual support and avoid the second pass of the Partition algorithm!

Classification   For classification, the principles of *bagging* and *boosting* (Section 3.4.5 of Chapter 3) can be applied as follows. A classification model can be learnt for each bunch of records coming into the stream. Each classifier obtained can be used to classify a new unlabeled record. In other words, each classifier casts a *vote* for which class the unlabeled record belongs to; and the votes are combined according to the principles of bagging or boosting. As the number of classifiers gets large, we can remove those classifiers that do not perform well.

Clustering   Most clustering algorithms are not easily applicable in the data stream scenario as they implicitly require multiple passes over the data. However, if frequent itemset based techniques are used for clustering, they are easily applicable on data streams as described above. Alternatively, techniques like Birch (Section 4.7.3 of Chapter 4), which are designed to work well even with a single pass are directly applicable on data streams.

5.7 TIME-SERIES DATA

A time-series is a set of measurements taken at different points in time. Examples include the measurement of stock prices, weather parameters, health parameters of patients (such as blood pressure, temperature, etc.), health parameters of a mechanical system (such as load, stress, temperature, etc.), and so on.

In fact, the process of measuring is a fundamental human activity. The famous statement, *Measure what is measurable, and make measurable what is not so,* by the scientist Galileo Galilei, indicates the pervasiveness of this activity. Moreover, measuring is usually not a one-time activity, but repetitive. This means that a large amount of data exists in the form of time-series. It is thus important to discover patterns from such data.

5.7.1 THE DATA MODEL

Conceptually, a time-series consists of a set of pairs $\{<t_1,v_1>,<t_2,v_2>,...,<t_n,v_n>\}$, where each t_i indicates a time instant and v_i indicates the values of some measurement. Usually, the instants in time when measurements are made are well-defined, at regular intervals such as every second, or hour, or day, etc. In such a case, it is sufficient to represent the time-series as just an ordered list of values $<v_1, v_2,..., v_n>$.

A time-series is usually represented graphically with the x-axis denoting time and the y-axis denoting the measured values. In this format, it is easy for humans to look for trends and patterns.

One may generalize the above data model in various ways:

Complex measurements   In some applications, a measurement may involve more than one value—for example, to measure the state of a patient, we may have to measure several parameters. We can continue with the above data model and represent this data as several time-series – one for each parameter. However, the relationship between different parameters may be lost by doing this.

Data stream   A data stream is a continuous flow of data records into a computer system. As each record originates at some time-instant, a data stream may be considered as a time-series. The only difference is that in a data stream, only a synopsis of the records will be stored.

Sequence databases   A sequence database is an ordered list of records. We have seen that a time-series can often be represented as an ordered list of values. Thus, a sequence database is a generalization of a time-series. The difference is that in a sequence database, there may not be a concrete notion of time associated with the values.

While the above generalizations of time-series are interesting and useful, the most common notion of a time-series involves just a simple ordered list of measurements. The reason is that such data is very common and pervasive in many applications – it is thus a very important case that merits individual attention.

5.7.2   PATTERN DISCOVERY IN TIME-SERIES

There are three major pattern discovery tasks associated with time-series: (i) trend analysis, (ii) prediction, and (iii) similarity search. We will look at each of these below:

Trend analysis

When plotted on a graph, it is easy for a human to visualize trends in a time-series. Because of the large amount of time-series data available in some applications, it is desirable for such trends to be detected automatically. There are four major components in trend analysis:

Long-term trends   These describe the overall movement of the time-series when seen from a macroscopic or long-term viewpoint – we are usually not interested in the minor ups and downs in the time-series. To detect such trends, one may replace each measurement by the average of 'nearby' measurements. The average may be computed as a weighted average where more weight is given to the value being replaced.

Cycles   These describe the cyclic or repetitive behaviour of a time-series. To detect if there is a cycle of length k, one may use the concept of correlation from statistics, to determine if there is any correlation in the measurements between times (t_i and t_{i+k}) and the measurements between (t_{i+k+1} and t_{i+2k}), for every i.

Seasonal movements   These describe how the values in the time-series are affected by season. For example, the daily sales of some commodities may be more during certain festivals. While seasonal movements are usually cyclic, in principle, they need not be. For instance, a festival day in some years may be declared as a working day.

Outliers   These are values in the time-series that are different from the norm. They may include noise or random events. Sometimes, they may be associated with rare but significant events.

It is instructive to apply Newton's laws of motion to the study of time-series. In this concept, we theorize that the time-series is *stationary* – that is, *all* measurements will always have the same value, unless there is an external factor that affects them. This is akin to the first law of motion which states that: 'All bodies will have a constant velocity unless acted upon by an external force.'

Thus, any deviation from the expected values must be explained separately. In the context of time-series, we use the concept of an *index* – such as a *seasonal* or *cyclic index* to explain the deviations that occur. For example, in the sale of crackers (fire works), the seasonal index of the Deepavali (or Diwali) festival could be 2000. This indicates that during this festival, the sale of crackers is expected to go up by 2000%.

After all known indexes are accounted for, one may still observe significant variations in the time-series values. This is an indication that one must do further study to discover additional factors which affect the time-series.

Prediction

Prediction or forecasting is perhaps the primary purpose of analysing a time-series. There are different ways to perform prediction. Here are two of them:

Curve-fitting   The simplest is perhaps to use the statistical technique of curve-fitting (or regression). Unfortunately, this does not work well enough, usually because of errors and noise in practical time-series datasets. This may be addressed by smoothing the time-series in the manner described above in long-term trend analysis. Another drawback is that these techniques require the *form* of the curve to be known – that is, whether it is linear, exponential, etc.

Auto-regression   In this technique, we assume that each measurement is a linear combination of some k preceding measurements, where k is a parameter. The coefficients of the equation (called autoregressive parameters) can be computed from the data by forming k equations and solving them. The same equation can then be applied to predict future values.

Similarity search

In several applications, it is important to be able to compute the similarity between two sequences. For example, it may help in clustering companies based on how their stock price changes over time. A slightly different but related problem is to find all *sub-sequences* of a sequence that are similar to a user-given query sequence.

The above problem is general to all sequence databases. It makes sense to focus specifically on time-series because the notion of similarity depends on the nature of the data and the application.

For time-series, two sequences may be considered similar even if their lengths are not equal – each sequence may have some missing values and some extra outlier values. They may also not have the same baselines – that is the instances of time when measurements were made may differ in the two series.

Techniques for similarity search therefore work on the following principle: In order to determine if two sequences X and Y are similar, determine how many transformations are required to convert one sequence to the other. Transformations can be operations, such as adding a value, deleting a value, scaling a value, etc. The number of required transformations defines the similarity (or distance) between X and Y.

Once the definition of similarity is agreed upon, there is still an additional problem of *efficiently* retrieving all similar sequences or sub-sequences to a given query sequence. To achieve this, one may use multidimensional index structures such as *R-trees* or variations thereof.

5.8   TEXT AND WEB DATA

Data that is stored in a structured form, such as in relational databases, is like the tip of an iceberg. A gigantic amount of data is stored as unstructured or semi-structured text. Examples include books, newspaper articles, research papers, e-mail messages, Web pages, and XML documents. Retrieving patterns from such sources is the subject matter of text mining.

5.8.1   THE DATA MODEL

The specific format of text documents varies depending on the author and the tools used to create them. Conceptually, the data model consists of a large number of text documents, each of which is a sequence of characters drawn from some alphabet. Often, there is some structure implicit in the documents in that they have titles, sections, paragraphs, etc. In some cases, such as Web pages, the structure may be machine-readable, with explicit tags being used to mark the structure.

Links

Web mining is usually treated separately from text mining because of the presence of links between Web pages. The link structure of Web pages may hold a lot of information that is not explicitly mentioned in the main text of the documents. However, the structure of links is not specific to only Web pages. For instance, research papers contain citations to other related research papers. E-mail messages are generally written in reply to other messages.

Even general text documents may cite other sources; however, identifying such citations automatically may be difficult. Alternatively, a good hierarchical clustering algorithm for text documents may be able to identify related documents – this can be used to construct pseudo-links between closely related documents.

Bag-of-words model

It may seem that a full simulation of the human mind is necessary to write programs that make sense from text and Web documents. Luckily, this is not the case. Many seemingly intelligent programs can be written that are based on simple statistics applied in the right manner.

For many pattern discovery tasks, each document is treated simply as a bag of words – that is, the set of all words appearing in that document. Sometimes, this information is augmented with the frequency of the words in that document. These ways of modelling documents are usually quite effective for most tasks.

Vector-space model

In this model, the *dimensions* of the vector-space consist of all the words present in all the documents in the collection. This is a very high-dimensional space. Each document is then represented as a vector in this space containing the frequency of all the words in that document.

For example, if the dimensions are ('and', 'the', 'machine', 'learning'), then a document may be represented as $(2, 3, 2, 0)$ – the numbers indicate the frequency of the corresponding words in that document.

The advantage of the vector-space model is that it is possible to use mathematical techniques developed in linear algebra to solve problems. This can be done in theory, and in actual practice the bag-of-words model may be used, so as to avoid representing large vectors.

Stop-words and stemming

The set of *all* words in all documents is a large number to deal with. Most text and Web mining tasks apply some preprocessing in order to reduce the number of dimensions.

One such preprocessing task involves the removal of words that do not have much value to the process of pattern discovery. Words such as 'and' and 'the' are very frequent and their presence or absence should not really influence the outcome of mining. Such words are called *stop-words*. Lists of stop-words are widely available and are used to remove their presence in documents before processing them further.

A second task is to find the stems of words. Documents may contain a word in many different forms. For example, 'learn' may be present as 'learn', 'learning', 'learnable', 'learned', etc. In all forms, the concept of learning is present and it is this concept that is important – not the form. To handle this situation, *stemming* is done: all the different forms of each word are converted to its root form by removing suffixes and/or prefixes. Standard stemmers, which handle the task well, are widely available.

Term frequency-inverse document frequency (TF-IDF)

TF-IDF is another widely used technique to further reduce the number of dimensions. It has the added advantage that it provides the *relative importance* of words (dimensions) in each document and in the entire document collection. It also generalizes upon the stop-word removal technique.

The basic idea is that the relative importance of a term in a document is directly proportional to the frequency of that term in that document (referred to as the term-frequency or TF). However, if that term is also frequent in several other documents, then its relative importance in the original document is reduced. Thus, its relative importance is inversely proportional to the number of documents that contain it (referred to as the inverse document frequency or IDF).

The precise formulae used to compute the TF-IDF values differ slightly according to implementation. Care is taken to avoid improper division by zero and to normalize the values to a logarithmic space. Typical formulas for TF-IDF computation are as follows:

$$TF(d,t) = \begin{cases} 0 & \text{if } freq\,(d,t) = 0 \\ 1 + \log\,(1 + \log(\,freq(d,t))) & \text{otherwise} \end{cases}$$

$$IDF(t) = \log \frac{1 + |d|}{|d_t|}$$

$$TFIDF(d,t) = TF(d,t) \times IDF(t)$$

These TF-IDF values are computed for every term. Only terms that have a TF-IDF value more than some threshold are considered worthy of inclusion into the vector-space model. Other terms are neglected. This greatly reduces the number of dimensions that one must deal with.

5.8.2   PATTERN DISCOVERY IN TEXT AND WEB DATA

A wide variety of pattern discovery tasks are applicable on text and Web data. These include standard tasks, such as frequent itemset mining, classification, clustering, and summarization. However, there are also some tasks that are unique to this kind of data. These include text and Web search, mining themes and hot-topics, and document understanding.

We do not include Weblog mining here as Weblogs are *structured* relational-type data storing details of when each Web page was accessed by which user. However, it is possible that Weblogs can be used to enhance the above-mentioned tasks for pattern discovery in Web data.

Search

In this task, the user typically gives a set of keywords as a query and the required output is the set of documents that contain all those keywords. Put in this manner, the problem of search is straightforward – it does not involve any pattern discovery.

However, there are problems with treating search as such a simple problem:

Too many results   Usually, the number of documents that match a user's query is huge. This is especially so, on large document collections such as the Web. To solve this problem, we need a way to rank and/or organize the results. This way, the user can choose to see only the category of results of interest.

Efficiency   When the database contains a huge number of documents (such as the Web), finding documents that match a query may involve retrieving and processing enormous amounts of data. To solve this problem, we need an effective way to organize documents such that only the relevant documents for a query need to be retrieved and processed.

First, we look at approaches to solve the 'too many results' problem and then move on to the 'efficiency' problem.

Ranking documents based on text-content   Documents that match a user-given query may be ranked based on how well they match the query. Several heuristics are used. For example, if the keywords of the query are present in the title, beginning or conclusion of the document, they are likely to be important to the document. The relative frequency or TF-IDF score of the keywords in the document is also an indication of its relevance to the query.

Ranking documents based on link-structure   The success of search on the WWW relies on the idea that a large amount of useful information is present in the link-structure of the Web.

The core idea is that if a Web page has a large number of links that point towards it, then it is likely to be an 'important' page. Further, a Web page may be considered even more important if it is linked from a large number of 'important' pages. The results of a search query can then be ranked based on their importance.

The above idea led to an algorithm called PageRank that was developed at Stanford University by two students, Larry Page and Sergey Brin, who later moved on to start the company *Google*.

PageRank is an iterative algorithm. Initially, it assigns an equal importance (or *page-rank*) to all documents. Then, in each iteration, it refines this value using the following formula:

$$rank(x) = \sum_y \frac{rank(y)}{|links(y)|}$$

where y is the set of pages that link to x and $|links(y)|$ is the number of links in page y.

Mathematically, the page-ranks represent a probability distribution of the likelihood that a person randomly clicking on links will arrive at a particular page. The success of the PageRank algorithm in ranking search results is history.

Clustering search results   Some modern Web search engines such as *clusty.com* also cluster search results to make it easier for users to navigate through the huge number of search results. This is worthwhile because the search results may comprise of different topics that are all important. Within each topic, PageRank may be used again to rank the results.

Indexing text and web documents   All the above approaches handle the 'too many results'problem of information retrieval. The second problem mentioned above, namely the 'efficiency' problem is also related. Each of the above techniques requires efficient ways to organize and retrieve document data. This requires innovative data structures and indexes designed for this purpose.

The most widely used index structure for these tasks is the *inverted index*. The concept is simple and like most simple concepts, it is also very effective. An inverted index consists of a *document table* (where for each document, the list of terms it contains is given), and a *term table* (where for each term, the list of documents containing it is given).

To find the list of terms in a document, we only need to consult the document table. Conversely, to find the list of documents that contain a given term, we only need to consult the term table. To obtain the results of a search query, we can simply find the document lists for each term in the query and compute their intersection.

Frequent patterns

In the bag-of-words model, each document is treated as a *set* of words or terms (i.e. short phrases). Similarly, each query can be treated as a set of words or terms. Thus, we can treat these datasets as transactional databases and mine frequent itemsets. Documents and queries can also be treated as *sequences* of words and terms. We can then mine frequent sequences rather than frequent itemsets.

For many kinds of analysis, the frequent patterns discovered from a document database can be used instead of the original database. The frequent patterns can be treated as dimensions in the vector-space model of documents. They can also be used as features in the context of document classification or clustering.

The frequent patterns discovered from a query database can be used to characterize queries. Query patterns can be used to form *user profiles* indicating the different interests of users. This can be used in a variety of ways. The user profiles can be an additional factor used in ranking query results. Users can be clustered based on their profiles. Users can be recommended documents based on what other users with similar profiles are interested in. They can be used to help the user to refine a search query by inserting additional terms into the query.

Classification

Classification of documents into predefined classes is an important task with a wide range of applications, limited only by one's imagination. Here are some examples:

(a) Detecting spam emails is a classic application of text classification.

(b) Online directories are available at sites such as *yahoo.com* to categorize Web pages into different topics, such as 'business', 'computers', etc. Building classifiers that can automatically recognize the categories into which a new Web page should go is thus an important problem.

(c) Another application is to categorize emails sent to the help-desk of some company to decide which department the email should go to.

Because documents are semi-structured, the process of classification may seem to be different from that in structured relational databases. However, all that is required is to *extract features* from documents and store the features in a structured way – the problem then becomes identical to normal classification.

Standard features extracted from documents include the set of keywords or key-phrases in the document, the authors of the document, the date of creation, the size, etc. Frequent patterns mined from documents may also be used as features. Recent research has found this approach to be quite successful.

Once the features are decided upon, almost any classification technique will work well – usually it is the features that are important. However, some classification techniques are more popular for document databases. These include Naïve Bayes, support vector machines, entropy based approaches, and nearest neighbour classification.

Clustering

Most applications that benefit from document classification are also candidates for document clustering. This is because clustering is useful to initially decide what the classes should be. For example, before we classify Web pages into a Yahoo-type directory hierarchy, we must first decide what is the directory hierarchy.

As may be expected, hierarchical clustering algorithms are the most suitable for such applications. One peculiar issue with respect to document clustering is that typically a document may belong to more than one cluster. This is an important aspect to note while designing document clustering algorithms.

Like in classification, a structured database of features must be extracted before applying clustering algorithms. The same features mentioned for classification can be used for clustering as well. These include the set of keywords or key-phrases in the document, the authors of the document, the date of creation, the size, etc. Again, frequent patterns mined from documents may also be used as features profitably.

The similarity measure used for document clustering is usually *cosine similarity*. For two documents, d_1 and d_2, the cosine similarity is given as:

$$similarity\,(d_1,\, d_2) = \frac{d_1 \cdot d_2}{|d_1|\,|d_2|}$$

Summarization

If you read one new book everyday for 100 years, you would be able to read 36,500 books. But there are millions of published books available. And that does not include other kinds of documents, Web pages, etc. There is so much information available in the form of text and Web documents that it is impossible for humans to digest.

This is where the area of automatic document summarization comes in. The summary extracted is typically for human consumption. A lot of ongoing research is being done in this area. An annual international contest is held (http://duc.nist.gov) to evaluate systems for automatic summarization.

Luckily, it turns out that it is possible to achieve quite a good summarization without actually understanding the document. This can be done by extracting selected sentences verbatim from the document and putting them one after the other – usually in the same order in which they appear in the document.

The task is then reduced to the selection of sentences from a document. Several heuristics are used, such as the position of the sentence in the document, whether a new keyword or key-phrase is introduced in that sentence, etc.

Theme evolution and hot-topic mining

Analysing the *themes* of documents is an interesting and recent research topic. This may be reduced to document clustering because documents in the same cluster would be expected to have a common theme. An additional issue is to identify the *name* of the theme. If clustering is based on keywords and key-phrases, these could be used to name the themes.

Once the themes are identified, the next interesting step is to study how the themes of a document collection evolve over time. This is useful in the context of newspaper articles and research papers. In the former, it is interesting to see how news stories emerge and fade away. In the latter, it is interesting to see how research areas emerge and fade away.

It is vitally important to know what are the current topics of interest in a community, and what topics are likely to emerge tomorrow. Such topics that have a dominant presence in the literature are said to be *hot-topics*. Identifying such topics automatically may have seemed to be magic yesterday. However, in the context of the above, it is clear that it is possible by analysing a document collection and collecting simple statistics about themes.

Document understanding

In all the techniques of document mining discussed above, we have only assumed statistical analysis of the documents. There was no requirement of actually *understanding* the documents written in natural language. However, there is a lot of ongoing research in Computational Linguistics and Natural Language Processing that could greatly enhance the current statistical techniques.

Wordnet is a popular freely-available semantic lexicon for the English language. A *semantic lexicon* is a dictionary of words labelled with semantic classes. It can be used to infer properties about words that have not been previously encountered in the document database.

Simply put, Wordnet can be used to retrieve all the synonyms (words of the same meaning) and categories of a given word. This can be used very effectively. For example, some document may be talking about elephants. The word 'animal' however may not appear very frequently in the document. Using Wordnet, we can find out that elephants are a category of animals and use this information to update statistical information about animals in general.

Computational linguistics is concerned with not just the semantics of words, but also with the semantics of sentences. Parsers that are available for various languages can parse sentences and form parse trees identifying noun phrases, verb phrases, etc. Such structures can be used to identify meaning from documents. From a data mining point of view, such meanings can simply be added to the set of *features* of a document.

Finally, data mining techniques can be used in computational linguistics. Several problems in computational linguistics involve classification. Examples include deciding the precise meaning of ambiguous words, deciding the part-of-speech of a word, etc. Since the corpus of text documents available for computer linguistics study is usually very large, data mining techniques of classification are very appropriate.

5.9   MULTIMEDIA DATA

Multimedia refers to a source of information that incorporates one or more of the following media: images, audio, and video. We can also have text in multimedia, but text mining is a separate domain that was dealt with in the previous section. With the advent of technology such as digital cameras and multimedia systems, it has become easy to generate and store large volumes of multimedia data. It is therefore of specific interest to focus on issues in the pattern discovery of multimedia data separately.

5.9.1   THE DATA MODEL

The data model for multimedia document mining is similar to that of text or Web data. Conceptually, there is a collection of documents containing images, audio, or video. In most applications, the document collection is homogenous in that it contains only image files, only audio files, or only video files. However, for some applications the collection may be heterogeneous, containing a mixture of file types.

Further, the multimedia files may be *tagged* with textual information such as the author, the date of creation, and topic categories to which each file belongs. Sometimes, the multimedia data may be embedded in a Web document, in which case there may be a lot of text that describes the context of the multimedia data.

From a data mining perspective, important *features* must be extracted from multimedia documents and stored in a structured manner. Each multimedia document is then just a set of numeric or categorical features and all the usual mining tasks, such as frequent itemset mining, classification, and clustering are possible.

Additionally, audio and video data may be modelled as *time-series* data because the audio samples and video frames are collected at definite instances in time. Thus, in some applications, it may be of useful to mine interesting sub-sequences of an audio or video sequence.

5.9.2   PATTERN DISCOVERY IN MULTIMEDIA DATA

A multimedia document collection is qualitatively similar to a text document collection. Text, audio, and video documents can all be thought of as sequences. New features can be extracted from all these document types. These features can be used to define a bag-of-words type model or a vector-space model. It follows that all the pattern discovery tasks that were studied for text and Web data are also applicable for audio and video data.

Further, since audio and video data are also time-series, it follows that all the pattern discovery tasks discussed for time-series are applicable. Hence, the variety of pattern discovery tasks applicable on multimedia data is immense. Most of them are in active research and so, we will discuss only a few of the relatively well-studied tasks here.

Multimedia search

In this task, the user typically gives an example multimedia document (image, audio, or video) as a query and the required output is the set of documents that are *similar* to the query. If the multimedia documents are tagged with textual information, then the search process is reasonably straightforward, utilizing the techniques of text-based search. Otherwise, the quality of the search depends on the multimedia features that have been extracted from the documents.

The (dis)similarity between two multimedia documents is typically computed using a weighted Euclidean distance function. The intuition is that some features are more important and hence given more *weight* than others. For two documents, d_1 and d_2, the distance is given as:

$$distance\,(d_1,\,d_2) = \sum_{i=1}^{D} w_i\,(X_{i1} - X_{i2})$$

where w_i is the weight of feature i, and X_{ij} is the value of feature i in document j.

Usually, the weights that describe the relative importance of different features are unknown beforehand. Instead, they are learnt from the user's responses to whether the search results are relevant or not.

Classification

Multimedia document classification involves the classification of multimedia documents into predefined classes. For example, the class attribute could be the topic of an image, audio or video document, the singer of a song, the main actor in a movie, etc. It is interesting to study how standard classification approaches work for such tasks when example training data is given.

For video data such as that coming from a television channel, there are interesting applications of classification: To identify whether a particular *shot* (i.e. a consecutive sequence of similar frames) is a television advertisement, a movie, a newscast, or a serial. Such tasks are possible to a large extent using only statistical analysis of features, such as the audio volume, number of colours on screen or their histogram, how quickly shots are changing, etc.

Clustering

Clustering of multimedia documents is also a topic under active research. It is useful in organizing multimedia documents automatically into a directory hierarchy. Like for text data, hierarchical clustering algorithms would be most suitable for such applications. Again, it is important to note that a document may belong to more than one cluster.

Identifying *shots* (i.e. consecutive sequences of similar frames) in a video can be modelled as a clustering problem, as it involves grouping together of similar frames.

SUMMARY

Classical data mining techniques require their input data to adhere to a certain format. However, data in the real world may be organized in many different ways – corresponding to some structured or unstructured data model. Each data model lends itself to the discovery of certain kinds of patterns. In this chapter, we have seen how pattern discovery technologies may be applied on different data models including: (a) Relational data, (b) Transactional data, (c) Multi-dimensional data, (d) Distributed data, (e) Spatial data, (f) Data streams, (g) Time-series data, (h) Text data, (i) Web data, and (j) Multimedia data.

A common theme is that all these kinds of data can be explored using standard mining and warehousing techniques. Once it has been decided that some mining tasks are applicable, the specific algorithm used is typically not so important – much more important is the set of features that are extracted for that data for use in pattern discovery.

EXERCISES

Test your understanding

1. What are the pattern discovery tasks applicable on each of the 10 types of data discussed in the chapter? Discuss.

2. Give examples of distributive, algebraic, and holistic aggregate functions. Is frequent itemset mining distributive, algebraic, or holistic? Which of these function types can be incrementally computed?

3. What are the primitive spatial data-types? Why are they called primitive?

4. Describe three popular synopsis techniques for data streams.

5. What is a logarithmic tilted time frame in the context of data streams?

6. Smoothen the following time-series by replacing each value by the average of that value and its succeeding three values: 3 7 2 9 15 17 18 15 9 9 9 9. Plot the results graphically. Why is this smoothing operation useful?

7. Are there any outliers in the time-series data given in the previous question? If so, how will you find them automatically?

8. Describe two techniques by which the next value in the time-series data of Question 6 can be predicted.

9. Consider three Web pages that mutually link each other. Now add a fourth Web page that does not link to any other, but all the previous three Web pages linked to it.

   Now apply three iterations of the PageRank algorithm starting with the rank of all documents as equal to 1. What are the final ranks of the Web pages?

10. What is the distance/similarity measure generally used for text documents? What is the measure generally used for multimedia documents?

11. Describe some applications of classification and clustering for multimedia documents.

Project

1. Search for stemmers and stop-word removal programs on the Web. Collect 10 text documents and apply the stemmer and stop-word removal program on them. Then write a program to compute the TF-IDF measure of all the remaining words in the 10 documents.

2. Implement a Naïve Bayes classifier to classify spam and non-spam (also called *ham*) emails. Standard datasets for spam emails are available on the Web.

Improve your research skills

1. Do a literature survey on pattern discovery techniques on any of the data types discussed in this chapter and write a survey paper.

2. For each type of data discussed in this chapter, define a relational schema for that data. For this schema, describe what happens when each pattern discovery task (that is applicable on relational data) is applied.

Improve the field

1. For each type of data discussed in this chapter, define a multi-dimensional schema for that data. Implement a system to store, query, and visualize a data cube on this schema.

2. Implement a pattern discovery system for a specific domain, such as banking, health, law, education, etc. Identify the data available. Identify the pattern discovery tasks that can be applied.

   Transform or enhance the data if required for pattern discovery. Come up with a working and usable system.

3. Integrate the pattern discovery on different data types into a common framework.

DATA WAREHOUSING: THE DATA MODEL

Keep your world organized, and you will see what others don't.
—KRIST NOVOSELIC

INTRODUCTION

In Chapter 1, we introduced data warehousing and provided several motivating scenarios where it is useful. We also described the conceptual model of data warehousing, also called as the *multi-dimensional model*. Finally, we provided a user's viewpoint and described the kinds of queries that are possible.

In this chapter, we first recapitulate and expand on the above topics. Next, we look in depth into the overall data model used in data warehousing – at all the layers: conceptual, logical, and physical. In the next chapter, we will study how user queries may be efficiently processed on the data model described in this chapter.

6.1 FUNDAMENTALS

Data warehousing is a technology that allows us to gather, store, and present data in a form suitable for human exploration. The typical scenario is where there are multiple data sources at different physical locations in an enterprise (such as different branches of a supermarket, or different colleges under a university, or different departments in a college). The data in these different sources may be in different formats and may be erroneous to an extent. The task of data warehousing is to integrate data from these different locations into a common repository and provide an interface for an analyst to explore the integrated data.

The amount of data in such a data warehouse is naturally huge – typically in the gigabyte to terabyte range. Data warehouse analysts are not interested in looking at all the records in the data, but are more involved in detecting patterns and trends that could support decision-making of the enterprise. Thus, the kind of queries that the analyst is likely to pose would involve aggregating the data in various ways in order to understand its statistical properties. Data warehouses have inbuilt tools called OLAP (On-Line Analytical Processing) that enable the analyst to ask such queries and visualize their results using different kinds of diagrams, charts, and graphs.

6.1.1   Why Not Use a Database?

The traditional way to store and retrieve data is to use a database management system (DBMS). These systems are often referred to as Online Transaction Processing Systems (OLTP). Software applications designed to automate day-to-day operations in an enterprise use a DBMS to store and retrieve relevant data. It enables the computerization of an enterprise that would otherwise have maintained the same data manually in books/registers.

While some components of a DBMS may be useful for pattern discovery tasks, much more functionality is often required. Following are the key differences between a typical DBMS usage and the requirements of a data warehouse:

Query Complexity   DBMSs are designed to efficiently and reliably process simple insert/delete/edit/retrieve operations. The corresponding queries require accessing only a few records. On the other hand, for pattern discovery, the queries posed are much more complex, requiring aggregations in multiple dimensions. These queries need to access the entire data, often making multiple scans over it.

Current versus Historical Data   A DBMS typically needs to store only the current data required for operational purposes. For example, if data is being stored for maintaining financial accounts, the data is not required beyond one financial year. On the other hand, for pattern discovery, we need to store the entire historical data.

Storage and Processing Complexity   To maintain historical data, data warehouses need the capacity to store significantly more data (often in 100's of gigabytes) than a DBMS (typically, a few gigabytes at most). A corollary is that the processing of such data is much more complex as well (due to the data size and query complexity).

Table 6.1 summarizes the differences between a traditional DBMS and data warehouses.

Table 6.1 DBMS Vs Data Warehouses

DBMS	Data Warehouse (based on OLAP)
1. Supports day-to-day operations.	1. Supports information analysis.
2. Transaction update is critical.	2. Mostly retrievals, less updates.
3. Heavy concurrency.	3. Light concurrency.
4. Normalized design is essential.	4. Normalized design is appropriate.
5. Each transaction accesses only small amount of data.	5. Most analysis targets large amounts of data.
6. Focus on present.	6. Focus on past, present, and future.
7. Use of atomic data.	7. Use of aggregate data.
8. Changing, incomplete data.	8. Static, historic data.

There are two existing approaches to handle the above complexity. One of the approaches called ROLAP (or Relational OLAP) enhances DBMS technology to handle the above requirements. The other approach called MOLAP (or Multidimensional OLAP) uses a different storage mechanism optimized for data warehousing. These topics will be discussed in more detail later in the chapter.

6.1.2 NEED FOR DATA WAREHOUSING

Traditionally, decision support systems are used to obtain information from a limited amount of data to support decision-making. However, such decision support systems have difficulty dealing with complex, multiple data sources that are typically found in large organizations. A rapid growth of online (transactional) data is being generated by the organizations and the widespread use of databases across the organizations necessitates the development of techniques for efficiently integrating and storing huge amounts of data, extracting useful knowledge and for facilitating database access.

Data warehousing is emerging as a key technology for enterprises that wish to improve their data analysis, decision support activities, and the automatic extraction of knowledge from data. Data warehousing embraces technology and industrial practice to systematically integrate data from multiple distributed data sources and to use that data in annotated and aggregated form to support business decision-making.

A data warehouse is a special kind of database that is intended for deep analysis and strategic planning. Distinct from day-to-day operational databases or online transaction processing systems (OLTPs) that capture transactional data, for example point-of-sales data, a data warehouse combines disparate data sources, possibly including external sources such as census data, to provide a centralized view for decision support data. The aggregated data provide the consolidated and summary data that facilitates high-level business analysis. Furthermore, data warehouses can be used in concert with online analytical processing (OLAP) and data mining tools to discover trends and unknown patterns within the detail data.

Example: Banking Scenario

The top management of a bank, in order to face the competition and to survive in the market, is concerned with the following: (a) increase in the profit levels, (b) characteristics of profitable customers, (c) the profitable areas to deploy funds efficiently to earn good returns. To answer these issues, they need the tools to take strategic decisions, which help in improving the above mentioned analytical issues.

Data warehouse is one of the solutions to tackle the situations, which can tap the data, understand customers better, and make informed decisions with greater speed and accuracy. Taking advantage of information collected by a bank — assets, liabilities, customer profiles data, etc. has required dedicated staff and enormous amounts of processing time to create the queries and analyse the data. This method consumes bank's resources, but didn't produce results quickly, which meant the decision makers had to work with outdated information.

The speed of bank's business today requires decision makers to have up-to-the-minute information and solutions that shorten the span between knowledge and action. The data warehouse solution helps the decision makers to quickly discern trends, patterns, and relationships that represent important new opportunities and then use that intelligence to alter course in hours and minutes, rather than weeks or months. It further helps to understand customers more clearly, target customer segments more accurately, develop the products, features, and services that customers value.

Data warehouse requires high quality of information that can be derived from high-quality data sources.

6.1.3 ARCHITECTURE OF A DATA WAREHOUSE

A data warehouse system consists of many components. The overall architecture is shown in Figure 6.1 and the different components are described below.

Data sources

A data warehouse is a repository of data that is integrated from multiple data sources, which may be present in different geographical regions. For example, these data sources may correspond to different branches of a supermarket, or different colleges under a university, or different departments in a college. Most likely, the data in these sources is constantly updated, and these updates must be reflected in the data warehouse.

Extract transform load (ETL) tools

Mechanisms need to be put in place to ensure periodic *extraction* of fresh data from the data sources. *Data cleaning* is a part of extraction, where erroneous and duplicate data is identified and corrected. After the data is extracted, it needs to be *transformed* to match the schema and format of the data warehouse. For this, several rules need to be defined to specify how exactly the schema and format of the original data are to be transformed to match the final schema and format. The transformed data must then be actually *loaded* into the data warehouse.

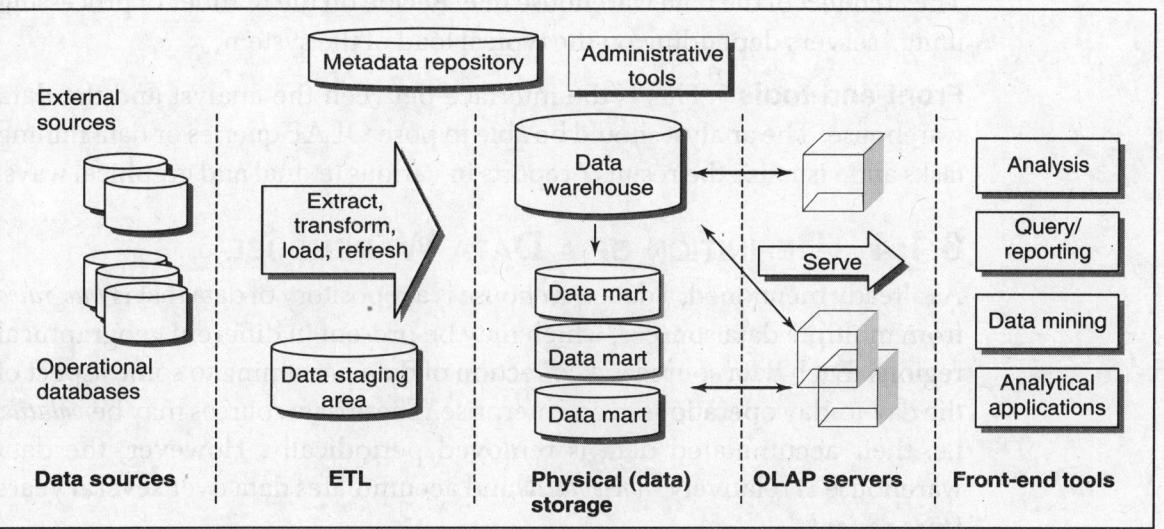

Fig. 6.1   Data warehouse architechture

Metadata repository and administrative tools   The data warehouse administrator manages the entire system by using these tools. The metadata repository contains the schema of the warehouse and the administrative tools can be used to monitor / control various aspects of the data warehouse. These include the data sources, the scripts for data transformation, preprocessing, etc.

Data marts   A data mart is a *subset* of what would be in a data warehouse of an enterprise. It may consist of data related to a single department, division, or geographical location. Data marts may be implemented because they are much cheaper than building an entire data warehouse. They can be used as 'proof-of-concept' to demonstrate the utility of data warehousing to the upper-level management in an organization. Once the management is convinced and decides to go for a complete data warehouse, the individual data marts become part of it and must be integrated (using ETL tools).

Physical storage   Due to the huge amount of data, the warehouse may be distributed onto multiple servers. In such a case, the metadata is usually replicated on each server. Alternatively, if the data warehouse simply consists of independent data marts, each server may contain the data pertaining to one data mart.

OLAP servers   These servers receive OLAP queries or data mining requests from front-end tools and process them by accessing data in the physical storage. The architect of the data warehouse may decide on the number of processing units / servers depending on the typical load of the system.

Front-end tools   This is the interface between the analyst and the data warehouse. The analyst should be able to pose OLAP queries or data mining tasks and visualize the results / reports in various textual and graphical ways.

6.1.4   DEFINITION OF A DATA WAREHOUSE

As already mentioned, a data warehouse is a repository of data that is *integrated* from multiple data sources, which may be present in different geographical regions. Each data source is a collection of data pertaining to some aspect of the day-to-day operations in an enterprise. These data sources may be *volatile*, i.e. their accumulated data is removed periodically. However, the data warehouse is relatively *non-volatile* and accumulates data over several years (*time-variant*).

Data warehouse users are analysts who explore data in search of useful patterns. They study how certain attributes of data elements (called *measures*) are related to other attributes of data elements (called *dimensions*). It is the user's job to initially specify which attributes of the original data to treat as measures and which to treat as dimensions. The data warehouse is then structured in terms of these *subjects*, i.e. measures and dimensions, so as to facilitate user exploration.

The data is conceptually organized as a multi-dimensional array, where each dimension of the array corresponds to a dimension of the warehouse and the values stored in each cell correspond to the measures of the warehouse.

This way of organizing data is referred to as a *multi-dimensional model* and the data repository is said to be *subject-oriented*.

The above description of a data warehouse is summed up in the following definition, originally proposed in 1990 by W.H.Inmon (known as the founder of data warehousing):

Data Warehouse   A data warehouse is a subject-oriented, integrated, time-variant, and non-volatile collection of data to support the decision-making process of an enterprise.

Moreover, data warehouses are expected to be huge in size (often in terabytes) because they accumulate data of an entire enterprise over several years.

Example 6.1   The owner of a supermarket chain is interested in studying what factors affect the sales of items. There are three broad classes of problems to be solved in order for the owner to make this study:

Data integration   Each supermarket location maintains its own data. This data needs to be collected and stored in a central repository for analysis. This is not a one-time task. As the data in each location changes, the central repository needs to be kept updated. Integration may be tiresome due to various reasons: (i) different locations may use different codes for the same product, (ii) The same product is sold with different prices at different locations, etc.

Data cleaning   The use of bar-code technology has made it possible for operators to enter data with hardly any errors. But errors and inconsistencies occasionally creep in. For example, when a new product is introduced in the supermarket, its code may not be registered in the data entry program. So whenever the product is sold, the operator manually enters its code and price.

Aggregation   Finally, the data stored at each location is very detailed – it contains the sales of items in each transaction. The supermarket owner is not interested in such fine-grained data, but instead wants to obtain a general 'birds-eye-view' of the data looking for anything that might necessitate new policies. The data needs to be aggregated (e.g. averaged or totaled) for this purpose. Common aggregation operators include average, total, count, max, and min.

6.1.5   THE MULTI-DIMENSIONAL MODEL

The data is conceptually organized as a multi-dimensional array, where each dimension of the array corresponds to a dimension of the warehouse and the values stored in each cell correspond to the measures of the warehouse. This way of organizing data is referred to as a *multidimensional model.*

Example 6.2   The owner of the supermarket in Example 6.1 suspects that the supermarket location and product category are the factors that affect the sales of items. Further, the overall sales seem to be changing year-by-year. Pondering in this manner, the owner decides that for the multidimensional model, the measure should be total sales and the dimensions should be supermarket location, product category, and year.

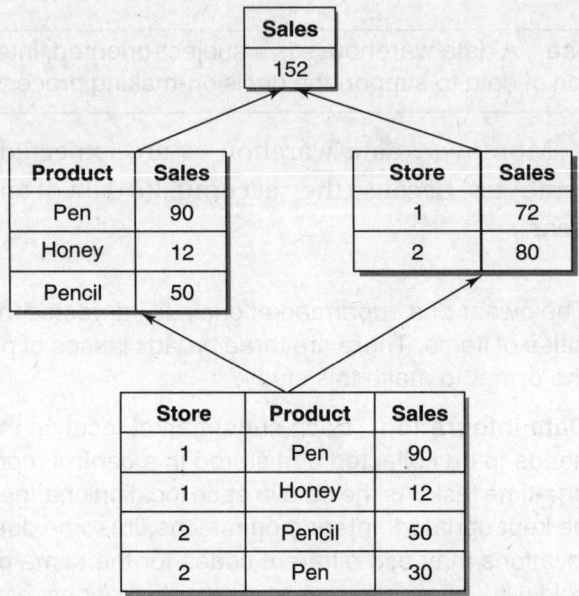

Sales
152

Product	Sales
Pen	90
Honey	12
Pencil	50

Store	Sales
1	72
2	80

Store	Product	Sales
1	Pen	90
1	Honey	12
2	Pencil	50
2	Pen	30

Fig. 6.2   Some views of the sales data

Once the data warehouse has been built, the owner proceeds to explore several *views* of the data. Some possible views are shown in Figure 6.2. Here, the dimension *store* represents the specific supermarket location and the dimension *product* represents the product category. *Sales* is the measure and represents the total number of sales.

In the bottom view, the total sales for each store and each product are given; whereas in the top view, the total sales over all stores and products are given. In the middle views, sales are aggregated over the *store* and *product* dimensions, respectively. Note that several views including the most detailed view (which is sales totaled separately over stores, products, and years) have not been shown in this figure.

6.1.6   QUERY TYPES: OLAP AND CUBES

Starting from the most detailed view, a warehouse analyst could explore any view by using OLAP (on-line analytical processing) operations. While seeing a particular view, the analyst may be interested in seeing other neighbouring views, more details, and may request for a more detailed view – this operation is called as *drilling down*. Alternatively, the owner may be interested in further aggregating along some dimension – this operation is called *rolling up*.

Example 6.3   Using the supermarket situation of Examples 6.1 and 6.2, we illustrate the above concepts as follows:

The owner (analyst) may be looking at the Product × Sales view (see Figure 6.1 and may want to know the overall sales figure irrespective of product (i.e. the top-most view in the figure), or may want to see a breakup based on sales of products in different stores (i.e. the bottom-most view in the figure).

Concept hierarchies could be defined over each dimension. For example, product categories could be defined in terms of the specific model (e.g. parker pen model 75), or of item type (e.g. all pens), or item category (e.g. all stationary). The term *granularity* defines the hierarchy level at which a dimension is specified – more granularity means more detail. The owner may want to view the data at any level of granularity and may interactively ask to *roll-up* to a lower level of granularity or *drill-down* to a higher level.

The analyst may also specify an interest in only particular values of specific dimensions. For example, the sales tables should show total sales of items for the years 2003 and 2005 *only*. Computing such views is called as a *slice and dice* operation. By exploring all of these views, the owner obtains a good understanding of the overall working of the supermarket chain.

Example 6.4   A university director is interested in studying how the number of publications of students is related to their grades in various subjects and their first language. One view for this example is shown in Figure 6.3.

Course	Grade	Language	Papers
Math	A	English	10
Math	B	English	2
C++	A	Hindi	3
C++	A	English	5

Fig. 6.3   A view for the publications example

Here, *course* represents the subject taken by students, *grade* is their grade in that subject, *language* represents their first language and *papers* represents the total number of publications of all these students. For example, the first row represents that 10 publications were written by students who scored an 'A' grade in mathematics and whose first-language is English.

Example 6.5   A music director in Bollywood is interested in studying the musical tastes of people. He hires a programmer to write plugins for popular digital media players to maintain a log that keeps track of how long and how often people listen to specific songs.

He collects this log information at various locations and integrates it into one warehouse. By analysing this warehouse, he obtains an idea of the features of music and the artistes involved that make specific songs popular.

Note: This exercise can be carried out in a small scale by any music enthusiast by using his own data of listening patterns – data warehousing is not only for the rich and famous! Rather, any sufficiently large collection of data should be probed for its potential in containing interesting patterns.

Example 6.6   An organization wants a web application that downloads data from the Indian Railways website and keeps track of the number of available vacant seats in trains going to different destinations. Here, the measure is the number of available seats and the dimensions could be the class of the coach (AC-2 tier, sleeper, etc.), the destination, the type of train (express, passenger, etc.), and so on. By exploring this warehouse, users could detect patterns such as 'express trains traveling from Chennai to New Delhi typically have more vacancies in sleeper class than the AC classes.'

Traditionally, data warehousing has been described in terms of business applications; however, as seen from the given examples, the concepts are applicable in more general scenarios. Notice that in most of these examples, each record (even in the most detailed view) is actually the aggregated sum over several records in the original data sources. Hence, trying to compute views in a naïve manner directly from the original data would consume too much time.

Further, recall that the original data may be scattered in several locations, in different formats, constantly updated, partly inaccurate and incomplete. The technical challenge in data warehousing is to overcome these hurdles and enable the user to have interactive response time in obtaining multidimensional views.

6.2   DATA WAREHOUSE DATA CHARACTERISTICS

The four terms, namely *subject-oriented, integrated, time-variant, and non-volatile* in the Inmon's definition are commonly referred as data warehouse data characteristics. Following is the brief explanation of these terms.

6.2.1   SUBJECT-ORIENTED DATA

Data is organized according to subject instead of application.

Example 6.7 Consider a bank that uses a data warehouse. It can organize the data by subjects, such as customer, product, vendor, and activity; instead of by different applications, such as loans, savings, and bankcards. The information provided by the data, which is organized based on application is not fulfilling the requirement of present banking system that is facing stringent competition.

To find the most loyal customer group to the bank, it cannot depend on the information provided with the application-oriented data. Because applications like savings, bankcards, loans do not give the required information for analysis, as they are developed only for transaction processing. So there is a need to collate data for a particular analytical need of the decision makers.

For finding a loyal customer group to the bank, some of the loans data, savings data, etc. should be consolidated under a single entity called, "Subject", viz. "Customer". Since the 'Customer' subject area organizes data for analytical purposes, it facilitates the decision makers to find the answers to the queries like 'What is the potential customer base for the bank?'

The operational databases are designed around application, such as investment in government securities, CDs, CPs, etc. while ideally data warehouse data are organised around major subjects, such as capital market information, money market information, forex market information, etc. Table 6.2 distinguishes the application orientation with subject orientation in the banking scenario.

Table 6.2 Subject-orientated Data

Application Orientation	Subject Orientation
Loans	Customer
Savings	Product
Credit Card	Vendor
Trust	Activity

Unlike application-oriented data, the data organized by subject can obtain the information necessary for decision support processing. So, the data in a data warehouse is organized in an optimized way such that it can provide answers to questions coming from diverse functional areas within an organization.

6.2.2 Integrated Data

A data warehouse is usually constructed by integrating multiple, heterogeneous sources, such as relational databases, flat files, and OLTP files. When data resides in many separate applications in the operational environment, the encoding of data is often inconsistent. When data are moved from operational environment into the data warehouse, they assume a consistent coding convention.

Integration can take place in various dimensions like consistent naming conventions, consistent measurement of variables, consistent encoding structures, consistent physical attributes of data, etc. In a data warehouse system, integration is done at data staging level (as part of ETL) without changing the operational application systems.

Example 6.8   Consider the Credit System that uses a numeric 7-digit code for A/C type, the Recovery System code consists of 9 alphanumeric, and the Borrower Details System uses 4 alphabets and 4 numerics. To create a useful subject area, the source data must be integrated. There is no need to change the coding in these systems, but there must be some mechanism to modify the data coming into the data warehouse and assign a common coding scheme.

Some integrity problems are:

- The same name can be spelled out differently. Examples: John, Jhon, Jahn, Jhan.
- There are multiple ways to denote a company name, e.g. Logic Software Private Limited, LSPL, Logic Software Pvt. Ltd.
- Places renamed, e.g. Bombay to Mumbai, Madras to Chennai, etc.
- Different account numbers generated by different applications for the same customer.
- Required fields left blank.
- Invalid product codes collected at point of sale.

So, data integration requires a well-organized effort to define and standardize all data that is captured from multiple and diverse sources with diverse formats. Though this integration process is time consuming, once accomplished, it provides a single unified view of the organization.

6.2.3 TIME-VARIANT DATA

Data are stored in a data warehouse to provide historical perspective. Every key structure in the data warehouse contains, implicitly or explicitly, an element of time.

Data warehouse data represent the flow of data through time (Figure 6.4). A data warehouse generally stores data that is 5-10 years old, to be used for comparisons, trends, and forecasting.

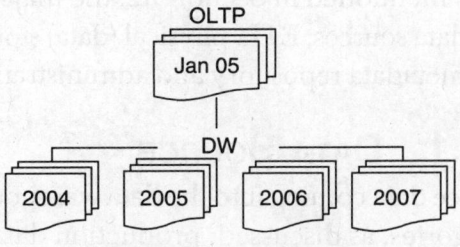

Fig. 6.4   Time variant

6.2.4   NON-VOLATILE DATA

Data that has been written into a data warehouse system once is not to be overwritten but extended. That is, the data are not updated or edited in any way once they enter the data warehouse, but are only loaded, refreshed and accessed for queries.

Unlike operational databases, ware-houses primarily support reporting, not data capture. The most frequent operation on a data warehouse is data querying, rather than inserting, deleting, and updating (Fig. 6.5).

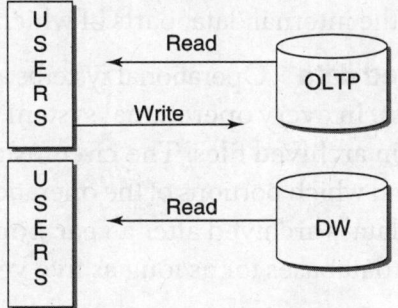

Fig. 6.5   Non-valatile

6.3   DATA WAREHOUSE COMPONENTS

The structure that brings all the components of a data warehouse together is known as the data warehouse *architecture*. In a data warehouse, architecture includes a number of factors. Primarily, it includes the integrated data that is the centerpiece. The architecture includes everything that is needed to prepare the data and store it. On the other hand, it also includes all the means for delivering information from the data warehouse. The architecture is further composed of the rules, procedures, and functions that enable the data warehouse to work and fulfill the business requirements.

As mentioned in Section 7.2, the major components in a data warehouse are: data sources, ETL, physical (data) storage, OLAP servers, front-end tools, and metadata repository and administrative tools.

6.3.1 DATA SOURCE

Source data coming into the data warehouse may be grouped into four broad categories, as discussed: production data, internal data, archived data, and external data.

Production data   This category of data comes from various operational systems of the enterprise. Based on the information requirements in the data warehouse, choose segments of data from the different operational systems. While dealing with this data, we come across many variations in the data formats. Also notice that the data resides on different hardware platforms. Further, the data is supported by different database systems and operating systems. This is data from many vertical applications.

Internal data   In every organization, users keep their 'private' spreadsheets, documents, customer profiles, and sometimes even departmental databases. This is the internal data, parts of which could be useful in a data warehouse.

Archived data   Operational systems are primarily intended to run the current business. In every operational system, the old data is periodically taken and stored in archived files. The circumstances in the organization dictate how often and which portions of the operational databases are archived for storage. Some data is archived after a year. Sometimes, data is left in the operational system databases for as long as five years.

External data   Most executives depend on data from external sources for a high percentage of the information they use. They use: (i) statistics relating to their industry produced by external agencies, (ii) market share data of competitors, (iii) standard values of financial indicators for their business to check on their performance, (iv) census information for customer demographics, (v) geographical data for various region-wise analysis, etc.

6.3.2 PHYSICAL DATA STORAGE

The operational systems of an organization support the day-to-day operations. These are online transaction processing applications. The data repositories for the operational systems typically contain only the current data. Also, these data repositories contain the data structured in highly normalized formats for fast and efficient processing. In contrast, data repository for a data warehouse needs to keep large volumes of historical data for analysis and quick retrieval of information. Therefore, the data storage for the data warehouse is kept separate from the data storage for operational systems.

Most of the data warehouse solutions employ relational database management systems. Multidimensional database management systems are also employed in some solutions. Data extracted from the data warehouse storage is aggregated in many ways and the summary data is kept in the multidimensional databases.

6.3.3 FRONT-END TOOLS

There are different types of users who are in need of information from the data warehouse. The range is fairly comprehensive. The novice user comes to the data warehouse with no training and, therefore, needs make-up reports and preset queries.

The casual user needs information once in a while, not regularly. This type of user also needs prepackaged information.

The business analyst looks for ability to do complex analysis using the information in the data warehouse.

The power user wants to be able to navigate throughout the data warehouse, pick up interesting data, format his or her own queries, drill through the data layers, and create custom reports and *ad hoc* queries.

Data mining tools, analytical applications, and point solutions can also be employed in deep analysis as well as focused analysis for certain applications.

6.3.4 METADATA REPOSITORY AND ADMINISTRATIVE TOOLS

Metadata in a data warehouse is similar to the data dictionary (or the data catalog) in a database management system. In the data dictionary, the information is kept about the logical data structures, the information about the files and addresses, the information about the indexes, and so on.

The data dictionary contains data about the data in the database. Similarly, metadata component is the data about the data in the data warehouse. Metadata contains information about the creation, management, and usage of the data warehouse. It provides information about the data, such as what it means, how to access it, and when it was last updated. Metadata also provides information about reports, spreadsheets, and queries related to the data.

In a data warehouse environment, there are two types of metadata – *technical* and business. *Technical metadata* describes data elements as they exist in the source systems, the data warehouse and data marts, and the interim data staging areas. For example, technical metadata could include the technology definitions for operational data in DB2, Oracle, or SQL Server databases. Technical metadata also includes specifications on how the data is extracted, transformed, cleansed, and aggregated at each stage and the schedules for the data warehouse processes. This metadata is used by data warehouse administrators, power users, and the tools that drive the processes of the data warehouse.

In contrast, *business metadata* is used by business users and by decision support tools. The information is related to the technical metadata, but the presentation is very different. Business metadata provides a subject-oriented view of data. It describes data objects like databases, tables, and columns, as well as informational objects like queries, charts, and reports. The metadata also contains the business dimensions, hierarchies, and formulas needed by business users to simplify their query and data navigation, and support more in-depth analysis.

Like technical metadata, business metadata includes information about transformations, aggregations, and schedules. Usually, all business metadata is given in business terms rather than technology terms. Business metadata should provide business users all the information needed to understand, locate, and use the data in the data warehouse in a way that fits naturally with their data analysis tasks.

Because technical and business metadata are very distinct in content and use, separate metadata stores, sometimes called *metadata repositories*, are often used with each being optimized for its particular users. In addition, some data warehouse tools have their own metadata store for flexibility and performance. These repositories simplify the tasks of data warehouse administrators and business users, and enhance their productivity.

Administrative tools (or components) of the data warehouse architecture sits on top of all the other components. These components coordinate the services and activate within the data warehouse and control the data transformation and the data transfer into the data warehouse storage. These components interact with the metadata component to perform the management and control functions. As the metadata component contains information about the data warehouse itself, the metadata is the source of information for the administrative module. Various services handled by these components include monitoring the growth, periodically archiving data from the data warehouse and recovering from failures, governs data security and provides authorized access to the data warehouse. Moreover, administrative tools also provide management services.

A detailed description of ETL and OLAP is given in Section 6.5 and section 6.7 respectively.

6.4 APPROACHES TO BUILD DATA MARTS AND DATA WAREHOUSE

> **Data mart**   A data mart is a logical subset of a data warehouse, which is a highly focused set of information that is designed in the same way as data warehouse, but implemented to address the specific needs of a defined set of users.

Usually, a data mart is designed for the use of a department (such as sales and finance) or according to a particular functional area (such as customer relationship and profitability) of an organization.

Example 6.9   A manufacturing company can typically have a data mart for each of its departments, such as sales, marketing, accounting, and finance. One department looks at data summarized by the week; another looks at data summarized by the month. Some departments look at customers along the lines of geographical regions, others look at commercial and retail customers, and so forth. There are fundamentally different ways of looking at customers, products, and all the other aspects of the organization for each department.

Data marts fall into two broad categories: (a) *subset data marts* created from a parent data warehouse or parent data mart, (b) *incremental data marts* used as independent information resources or as data warehouse building blocks. These categories reflect the two approaches to data warehousing that have evolved *top-down* (subset) and *bottom-up* (incremental).

In *top-down approach,* an enterprise of hugess data warehouse is constructed and populated. Subset data marts are then created by taking portions of the enterprise data warehouse and creating information resources to serve specific user groups with homogenous characteristics or needs. The incremental *bottom-up approach* to data warehousing uses incremental data marts as the building blocks of the enterprise data warehouse. Individual incremental data marts are created and deployed. They are used to test and perfect the methodologies, processes, and tools used in the creation of the corporate information resources. As the data marts prove themselves to be valuable corporate resources, the organization can justify the time and the expense associated with the enterprise data warehouse.

Each strategy has its own set of merits and demerits with respect to the time of implementation, efforts required, etc. and each should only be used where appropriate.

An improved approach is having a mix of both top-down and bottom-up approaches. Here, the *logical architecture* of the data warehouse at the enterprise-wide level is developed first. Then the data marts are developed according to the requirements, whose design is guided by the enterprise-wide logical architecture developed in the beginning.

6.5 ETL

Three major functions need to be performed for getting the data ready. They are: extract the data, transform the data, and then load the data into the data warehouse storage (Fig. 6.6).

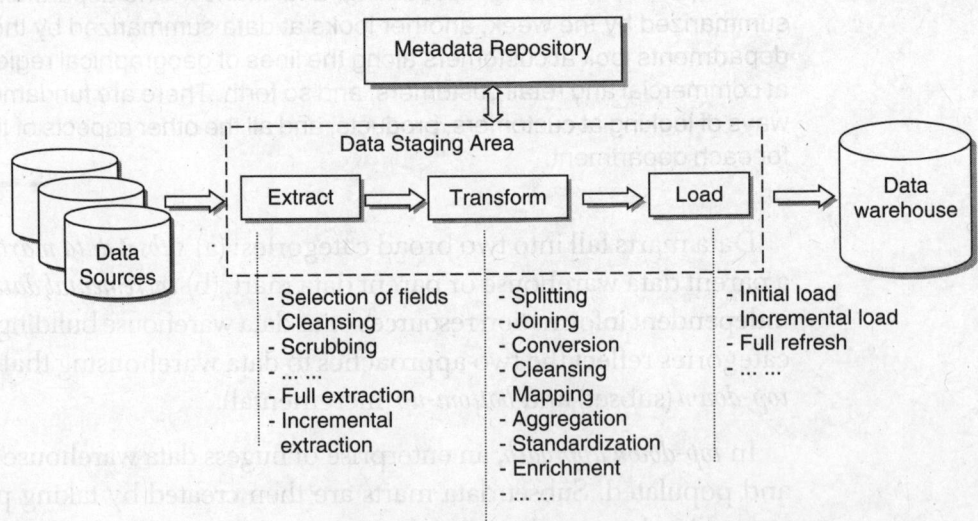

Fig. 6.6 The ETL process

After extraction of data from various operational systems and from external sources, the next step is to prepare the data for storing in the data warehouse.

The extracted data coming from several disparate sources needs to be changed, converted, and made ready in a format that is suitable to be stored for querying and analysis. These major functions of ETL usually take place in the data staging area.

Data staging area contains the data, software, and processes needed to cleanse, consolidate, and transform the data from their source system format to the data warehouse format. The extracted data undergoes the process of cleaning (merge, purge, and de-duplication) in order to be converted into useful information, which can be loaded into the data warehouse. Data staging area is located between data sources and data warehouse storage. (In practice, the ETL functions in the data staging area are carried out either in one server or multiple servers depending on the number of data sources, data size, cleaning efforts, time involved, etc. Sometimes, a few functions are handled in the data warehouse server itself.)

ETL tools are used to extract data from the source systems. This extracted data is transformed and loaded into the DW based on the business rules defined by the data model.

6.5.1 DATA EXTRACTION

This function identifies and extracts data from various relational databases and non-relational data sources. Features of data extraction are: moving data from multiple source environments, event-based change data capture, bulk data movement, support for concurrent processing of multiple source data streams, etc. Data extraction may become quite complex.

Data Extraction   Data extraction is a process of extracting data from source systems for future use in a data warehouse system.

Data extraction actually includes extracting data from the operational systems for the purpose of data warehousing. The extraction of data could be either from relational databases or from non-relational data sources or both. It is important to note that capturing the appropriate data from data sources (internal and external) to support required data analysis is must and complete. Otherwise, there is no way that a data warehouse will answer the analytical queries of users.

Example 6.10 The geographical data of an ATM (Automatic Teller Machine) are not extracted along with the ATM transaction details; one cannot perform analysis on area-wise profitability of the ATMs.

Table 6.3 shows a few important steps involved in extracting data from various data sources into the data warehouse.

Table 6.3 Steps of Extraction

Steps in Extraction	Description
1. Data retrieval – Consolidation	1. The merging of various data sets into a master data set (involves standardizing data types and fields)
2. Cleansing (or Scrubbing)	2. The cleaning of data to remove any inconsistencies or inaccuracies
3. Summarizing	3. The data resulting from the retrieval, consolidation, and scrubbing process must be summarized to obtain reasonable query response time
4. Updating the metadata repository	4. The repository should be kept up-to-date with any new data definitions; the meta data should be current and consistent

The following points are useful while data extraction:

- Identify the required fields from the source system.
- Provide detailed descriptions of the transformations to the fields.
- Identify triggering events that will result in extraction.

The extraction process determines the data which needs to be extracted from the source system, and bring the data into the data warehouse, especially to the data staging area. This process requires simple extraction and does not involve any complex functions like joins. The data extraction needs to be carried out at periodic intervals to keep the data warehouse up-to-date. This is mainly required for maintaining the data warehouse.

There are two kinds of extraction methods in data warehousing: full *extraction* and incremental extraction.

Full extraction

Each time, the complete data is extracted from source systems to the data staging area. After extraction, it needs an additional step of comparing with the previously extracted data to identify the changes. The advantages of this approach are:

- No need to keep track of changes at source systems since the last extraction point

- No additional information (or logic) such as time stamps is required at source systems

In this approach, the complete responsibility lies on the data warehouse system rather than the source system.

Incremental extraction

Incremental extraction is often referred to as *change data capture*. In this approach, the data that was changed from last successful extraction is only extracted from the data source. This requires time schedules or some triggering events to know about the next extraction due. That means an additional logic/ mechanism has to be provided at source systems. Here, the dependency on source systems is a major issue.

The next step of extracting data is the transformation.

6.5.2 DATA TRANSFORMATION

Data transformation process checks data for reliability, consistency and validity, and then transforms as required. It also provides facilities for defining complex transformation rules.

The data that need to be populated into a data warehouse is from multiple heterogeneous source systems, which may have different formats and conventions. Thus, there is a need to reconcile these data in appropriate unified format. This reconciliation and unification is carried out by the transformation step.

The transformation steps include the following:

- Identification of data elements that need to be loaded into the data warehouse.

- Identification of calculated and derived data values, which are computed using logical expressions.

- Aggregating the data based on the granularity requirements decided during data warehouse design for improving query performances.

- Cleaning the data.

- Defining transformation rules and data mapping criteria, and updation of metadata.

- Restructuring the data.

- Merging data fields from multiple sources into one entity.

- Standardizing data values, data types, and field lengths for the same data captured from various sources, and ensuring data integrity within the data warehouse.

- Manipulating the data into the warehouse format and structure.

- Purging the data elements that are not useful for loading into the data warehouse

- Enrichment of data by re-arranging and simplifying the individual fields such that the data warehouse is more useful to do analysis.

The transformation rules for data mapping from source database to target (data warehouse) database are done in various ways.

Example 6.11 A customer address filed in a source database can be mapped into six fields namely House Number, Street, City, State, Country and PIN Code into target database.

Commonly used transformation processes are: *union, normalization, aggregation, join, table lookup, filters, routing of data, enforcing keys, sequence generators, expression evaluation tasks, and Notifications*

In the transformation step, *surrogate keys* are created for each dimension record (see Section 6.6). These keys enable to keep away the dependency on the keys defined at source systems. Surrogate key generation ensures the referential integrity between the fact tables and dimension tables.

Data integration   The process of combining all related data from different sources based on source-to-target mapping is known as data integration.

Data Aggregation   The process of creating aggregates based on predefined procedures is known as data aggregation or data summarization.

In practice, several features of data extraction and data transformation overlap and also complement each other.

The transformation steps that are carried out during initial load should be followed for later loads as well.

6.5.3 DATA LOADING

After the data warehouse is designed and built and the data is in the desired format, the data is loaded into the data warehouse storage (database). This first time data load is referred to as *initial load*. Usually, the initial load moves large data, which takes time spread across many hours, say 8-10 hours. The time taken depends on how much history data is needed for effective analysis. Any changes to the source data needs to be extracted, transformed, and loaded with the incremental part.

There are three main approaches to load the data warehouse:

- Initial load – Loading all the data for the first time.
- Incremental load – Loading the incremental part of data from the last time load periodically.
- Full refresh – Deleting the contents completely and loading afresh with all the required data.

The various ways in which incremental load can be done are:

- Based on timestamp.
- Based on some FLAG column – pick up those rows which are marked 'Y'.

Database design should be standardized and tuned so as to avoid the unnecessary delay in loading process.

Full refresh approach is used rarely, usually, after loading trails made during testing and starting the data warehouse. Note that the indexes in the data warehouse database are created after the loading process (by initial load or full refresh) is completed.

Data needs to be cleaned before it is loaded into the data warehouse. So, data cleansing mostly takes place at both extraction and transformation phases. In the next section, we cover various reasons for poor data quality, and cleansing methods to clean them.

6.5.4 Data Cleansing

Data cleansing (also called data cleaning or scrubbing) is a major step in the data warehouse due to poor quality and too many formats of the data and their integration as well as subsequent aggregation.

Data cleansing   Data cleansing is a process that deals with detecting and removing errors and inconsistencies from the data to improve the data quality.

Data warehousing implements the process to access heterogeneous data sources; clean, filter, and transform the data; and store the data in a structure that is easy to access, understand, and use. The data is then used for query, reporting, and data analysis. As such, the access, use, technology, and performance requirements are completely different from those in a transaction-oriented operational environment. All these reasons result in poor quality of data in the data warehouse.

Usually, data extracted from operational systems contain a lot of errors because the data values from operational systems can be incorrect, inconsistent, unreadable, or incomplete. The data quality problem surfaces when the data are summarized or aggregated. Also, different notations and conventions are used in each department and there is an inconsistent usage of terms organization wide, thus creating some disparity between these departments. There are many problems that arise out of the poor quality in data.

There might be several reasons that lead to poor data quality in the warehouse. We list a few of them here.

Lack of validation routines

Many data entry errors can be prevented using validation routines that check data as it is entered into systems. Therefore, different types of validation routines are needed for different types of data sources.

Example 6.12   Sometimes in online data entry, when it is specified blank is not allowed, we can still get away from entering a valid value by simply pressing 'Space'. 'Space' is considered as a character and allowed to do that, but in effect there is only a blank, which is still invalid.

Valid, but incorrect

Even validation routines cannot catch some quality problems where the data represents a valid value i.e. the value, taken from the source is valid, but it is not a actual value. For example pin codes, telephone numbers, vehicle identification numbers, bank account numbers, and surnames. Though database integrity rules can catch some of these errors, it is really a mammoth task to avoid these types of errors, as it needs a complex strategy to deal with such errors.

Example 6.13   Name field should never contain three characters consecutively. Some users may want to play harm and just press on a character and enter an incorrect name. Similarly, names may not start with ZZZ.

Schema-level problems

These problems mainly arise due to mismatched syntax, formats, and structures at different source systems. The same data might be represented in different ways in various data sources. Moreover, several data entry errors are compounded when data from multiple source systems is integrated. There are mainly two kinds of conflicts: *naming conflict* and *structural conflicts.*

Naming conflicts arise due to: (i) homonyms – the same name is used for different elements, which results in inconsistency in the related schemas, and (ii) synonyms – different names are used for the same element. On the other hand, structural conflicts arise due to occurrence of same element in different formats and representations at different source system. Examples include different data types, different integrity constraints, and behavioural conflicts (such as variation in insertion and deletion policies).

Example 6.14 The name field can be entered in different ways depending on the notation followed by the data entry operator of the corresponding data source. The name 'Mohandas Karamchand Gandhi' can be entered as: M.K.Gandhi, Mohandas Karamchand Gandhi, and Gandhi Mohandas Karamchand. In Table 6.4, we can find some other trends in formats in some of the data fields.

Table 6.4 Different Formats for Representing Data

Field	Types of representations		
Name	*First-middle-last* (Initials) M.K.Gandhi	*Surname-first-last* Gandhi Mohandas Karamchand	*First-last-surname* Mohandas Karamchand Gandhi
Date	*dd/mm/yy* 28/03/79	*dd/mm/yyyy* 28/03/1979	*dd th month year* 28th march 1979
Gender	Male-female	m-f	1-0

Unexpected changes in source systems   Sometimes the changes are made in the structure of the data for some purpose and then the change is not reflected elsewhere; others using the data will be getting inconsistent status leading to inconsistencies. On the other hand, entering new types of information that was envisaged during the design of system also leads to confusion.

Lack of referential integrity checks   It is also true that target systems do not adequately check the integrity of data they are loading.

Example 6.15 Data warehouse administrators often turn off referential integrity when loading the data warehouse for performance reasons. If source administrators change or update tables, some integrity problems are created, which cannot be detected easily.

Poor system design Source or target systems that are poorly designed can create data errors. Some developers bypass many of the fundamental design and modeling principles, as they are in a hurry to complete the project. This leads to data integrity problems at a later date. Therefore, sufficient care has to be taken in the designing and modeling phases itself to minimize these errors.

Data conversion errors Data migration or conversion projects can generate defects, as well as extraction, transformation, and loading (ETL) tools that pull data from one system, make necessary transformations and load it into another system. Although systems integrators may convert databases, they often fail to migrate business processes that govern the use of data. Also, programmers may not take the time to understand source or target data models, and therefore they may inadvertently write codes that introduce errors. One change in a data migration program or system interface can generate errors in tens of thousands of records.

Data cleaning is mainly carried out at integration as well as at transformation steps. Cleaning may just be correction of misspellings, or may include resolution of conflicts between state codes and pin (or zip) codes in the source data, or may deal with providing default values for missing data elements, or elimination of duplicates when bringing in the same data from multiple source systems.

Cleansing methods

There are four basic methods for cleaning data: correct, filter, detect and report and prevent.

Correct This method is used to correct the data that is captured wrongly in the column/record values. It may involve the following:

- Misspelling errors. It needs updation of correct values for the existing incorrect value.

- Missing values. It needs replacing with real values.

Example 6.16 A default value can be used to replace a missing value. Other approach is to look at other databases to find a co-related value. Suppose salary for a person, who is a manager, is missing. Looking at the salaries of managers in the database can give a clue to the missing value. Another example is predicting the sales for a particular period based on history.

- Standardization. The data values specific to an industry can be modified with the standard codes.

Example 6.17 Fixing a standard for gender as 0 for male, 1 for female.

- De-duplication. This requires deletion of duplicate records. Sorting on a set of key attributes can be used to identify duplicates and then can be deleted.

Filter Filtering is used to eliminate duplicates, correct the missing values, and delete unwanted details. Care must be taken while filtering, as it may raise data integrity problems.

Detect and report Sometimes correcting data may not be cost-effective. In such cases, one can find the erroneous data and report it, rather than correcting them. However, the metadata needs to be updated with this information.

Example 6.18 Suppose address field of old customers are not available in a bank's database and most of them are not currently using their account, it is better not to update address for these customers.

Prevent Prevention involves educating data entry people, providing validation checks, enforcing integrity checks, update the metadata to ensure ETL process extracts correct data, etc.

It is fact that all the errors can not be eliminated with the help of automated tools, and sometimes, it is required human intervention to clean the data. Several procedures are available for handling some of the errors, such as missing values, schema integration and de-duplication. Below, we discuss two methods for detecting spelling errors and duplicate records.

Detecting spelling errors and duplicate records

Kukich (1992) described the N-gram sliding window procedure for detecting spelling errors. The steps are as follows:

(i) To check the words, consider an N-gram (N= 1, 2, 3.. letters) subsequence of strings from the words.

(ii) The N-grams obtained in Step 1 are looked up in an N-gram table to find the frequency, i.e. occurrence of N-grams in the rows.

(iii) If the word has highly infrequent N-grams or non-existent N-grams, then the word is probably a misspelling.

For example, in the word 'Pranav', the 2-gram are pr, ra, an, na and av. For a binary di-gram look-up index, create a 26×26 array of all two letter combinations of alphabets. Each array location has a 1 or a 0 indicating whether the di-gram occurs in any word or not.

To detect the duplicates, first construct a single associative array for the attribute using the N-grams as keys. The row identifiers represent the values for the associative array. Then, data pertaining to the word is scanned using these N-grams as keys. This array is looked up to find the rows in which the current N-gram occurs. If a word occurs in a large number of array elements where a second word occurs, then these two words are treated as duplicates. For example, if the word X occurs 10 times and the word Y occurs 8 times in the array, we can say that both X and Y are identical.

Sorted-neighborhood method

Hernandez and Stolfo (1995) described the Sorted-neighborhood method for eliminating duplicates (de-duplication). The steps involved in this approach are key creation, sorting, and merging.

(i) Scan the database and create a *key* by picking a portion from all the attributes.

(ii) Sort the database based on the key.

(iii) Scan the database by sliding a window of size w (Fig. 6.7) and compare the new record entering the window with the other records in the window. Merging of records is carried out using a set of (similarity) rules.

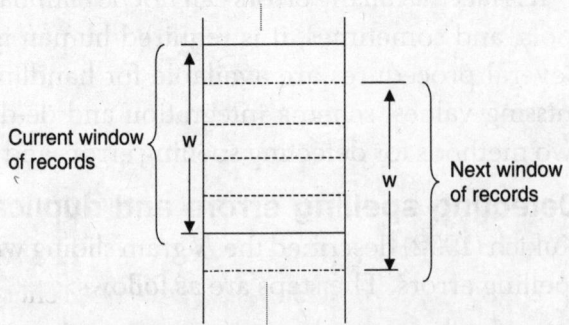

Fig. 6.7 Merging of records using sliding window

Typically, three characters from each attribute are considered to create a key. The rules can be defined based on the application. For example, if address of two students in a class and their surnames (or first name) are same and the given name (or last name) is slightly differing, we can say that both records are duplicates. To find the similarity, one can use *edit distance* and *soundex function.*

The above process may be repeated several times with different key values and window sizes to arrive at the duplicate records. The window size can vary from 2 to N, where N is the size of the data set.

In practice, a little bit human interpretation is required before actually deleting the duplicate records.

Overall, the metadata need to be updated to know the functions/operations during extraction, transformation, and load steps. This is required to query the metadata as well-obtaining useful information from the data warehouse.

The data warehouse database is a target data store for ETL. The data need to be stored in a structure that is easy to access, understand, and use. This database comprises fact tables and dimension tables, and its design aspects are covered in the next section.

6.6 Logical Data Modeling

Logical data modeling (or dimensional modeling) is the first step towards building the warehouse. Dimensional modeling is logical modeling design technique often used for data warehouses.

Dimensional models are used to overcome the performance issues for large queries in the data warehouse. Designing databases using dimensional modeling supports:

- Reporting, ad-hoc querying, performance dashboards, and business data analysis
- Faster access and better query performance on large data
- Ease of use

Dimensional modeling is different from entity-relation (ER) modeling, which is a widely used data modeling technique for DBMSs for transactional support. Table 6.5 illustrates the features of ER and dimensional models.

In practice, both ER modeling and dimensional modeling are used in designing data warehouse based on the architectural requirements. Several arguments by data warehouse researchers with respect to these two models exist. An interesting argument is that dimension modeling is a special form of ER modeling. However, dimensional modeling requires larger space than its relational modeling counterpart, i.e. ER model.

Table 6.5   ER Vs Dimensional Models

ER Model	**Dimensional Model**
1. Focuses on discrete business entities, their attributes, and their relationships.	1. Focus is on business processes and the entities that define them.
2. Normalized data models that minimize update anomalies. This is intended for read, write, insert, update, and delete operations.	2. Usually denormalized and intended for read-only access.
3. No explicit allowance for time.	3. Time-oriented.

6.6.1   Basics

Dimensional model is conceptually represented using *schemas* that are described by basic elements, such as facts, measures, attributes, dimensions, hierarchies and granularity.

- A *fact* is a focus of interest about a particular subject. Facts are used to store business information (*measures*) on which detailed analysis is carried out.

- *Measures* are continuous values (mostly numerical) that describe the fact from different points of view (e.g., each sale is measured by its revenue). Facts and measures are most often treated as synonyms.

- *Dimensions* determine the contextual background for the facts.

Example 6.19   The typical dimensions are customer, account, time, regions, etc. and typical facts (measures) are quantity, sales amount, etc.

- *Hierarchies* are made up of discrete dimension attributes linked by one-to-one relationships and determine how facts may be aggregated and selected significantly for the decision-making process.

Example 6.20   In a time dimension, the hierarchy could be

     Year → Quarter → Month → Day.

     Similarly, in a region dimension, the hierarchy could be

     Country → State → District → Mandal → Village.

- *Granularity* is related to fact table and it concerns about what detail level the fact table has. That is, granularity of a fact table represents the lowest level of information that will be stored in the fact table.
- Granularity is usually based on (i) which dimensions will be included, and (ii) the hierarchy of each dimension the information will be kept.
- Granularity determines storage volumes and the type of queries one can use with the data warehouse. However, the specification of granularity depends on the user's requirements and the availability of system resources.
- *Surrogate key*

The keys defined in the source systems are called *natural keys*, whereas the keys generated for data warehouse are called *surrogate keys*.

A surrogate key (also called *artificial key*) is a simple integer. As the data warehouse administrator assigns the first key the value 1, the next key the value 2, and so on. The keys themselves have no meaning. A surrogate key acts as a production key and is very useful in the data warehouse design.

Instead of natural keys, dimension tables and fact tables are joined based on surrogate keys in a data warehouse environment. Hence, during extraction of data from data sources, surrogate keys have to be generated systematically in place of incoming database keys.

Surrogate keys are added for each record (either dimension record or fact record) when they are loaded into data warehouse. In practice, surrogate keys are used only during modeling the data warehouse, however, for simplicity, in the following discussion, only natural keys are specified in the dimension and fact tables.

There are two types of tables in schema representation: (i) *dimension table*, and (ii) *fact table*.

Dimension table

Dimension table contains details pertaining to the dimension. The data in the dimension table is relatively static over time.

Dimension table is usually smaller in size when compared to fact table. It has a primary key and other attributes, which provide details about the dimension and also useful for querying.

Example 6.21 Table 6.6 shows an example branch dimension table

Table 6.6   Sample Branch Dimension

Branch_dimension	
Branch_ID	Primary key
Branch_name Branch_address Branch_Manager_Name Type_of_Branch	Other details

Fact table

Fact table contains transactional type information. The data in the fact table changes over time (for example, at each refresh instance).

There is a *foreign key* field in the fact table for each of the dimension tables. The fields containing the facts in the fact table are called *measures*. Though it is not a constraint, most of the times, the measures are numeric in nature. So, the fact table has three different kinds of fields:

- Keys
- Measures, and
- Own attributes, if any.

Example 6.22 Table 6.7 shows an example for account fact table.

Table 6.7   Sample Account Fact Table

Account_fact	
Account_ID Time_ID Customer_ID Region_ID Branch_ID	Keys
Balance_rupees Balance_dollars	Measures
Last_transaction_date *Ledger_folio_number*	Own attributes

Note that measures will become the contents of cube cells in OLAP (see Section 6.7).

Fact table is usually larger in size. At the lowest granular level, it may contain the transaction level details.

Generally, there are multiple dimension tables and one fact table in a data warehouse schema. The dimension tables are joined to fact tables using foreign key relationship. Thus, for each dimension table, there is an entry in the fact table as a foreign key. All these foreign keys constitute a composite primary key in the fact table. Hence, *null values* are not allowed in these fields.

The data in a fact table is accessed via dimension tables. Every record in the fact table is associated with one and only one member from each of the dimensions.

Dimensions can have hierarchies. Hierarchies specify aggregation levels, and hence, granularity of viewing the data. The hierarchy levels in a dimension table represent the relationship between different attributes within a dimension. The root of the hierarchy defines finest aggregation granularity, whereas other dimension attributes define progressively coarser granularities. A dimension can have multiple hierarchies and a hierarchy can have multiple paths.

Example 6.23   Time dimension exists in almost all schemas. Figure 6.8 illustrates different paths in hierarchy in the time dimension.

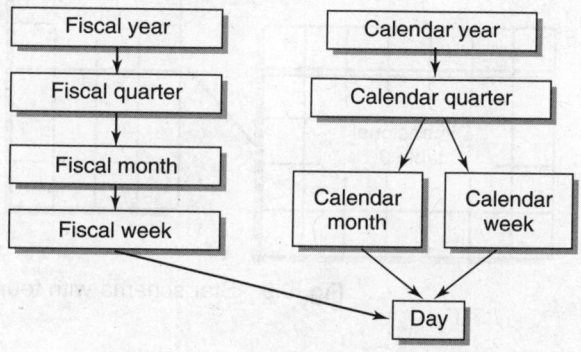

Fig. 6.8   Hierarchies in time dimension

Note that hierarchies present in dimension tables allow data aggregation at various levels of hierarchies, and thus provide roll-up or drill-down operations.

In a typical schema, the fact table has less number of attributes and more records, whereas dimension table has more number of attributes and less records.

6.6.2 SCHEMAS DESIGN IN DIMENSIONAL MODELING

There are mainly two types of schemas:

- Star schema
- Snowflake schema

There is also a third type of schema called *fact constellation*. All these schemas are used to model the multiple dimensions of the warehouse data.

Star schema

Star schema consists of one central fact table (for a subject area) and a set of dimensional tables directly connected to the fact table (Fig. 6.9). As shown in the figure, this schema looks like a star, and hence the name star schema. Each dimension in the schema is represented in a single table. Star schema put into practice the dimensional data structures by means of de-normalized dimensions.

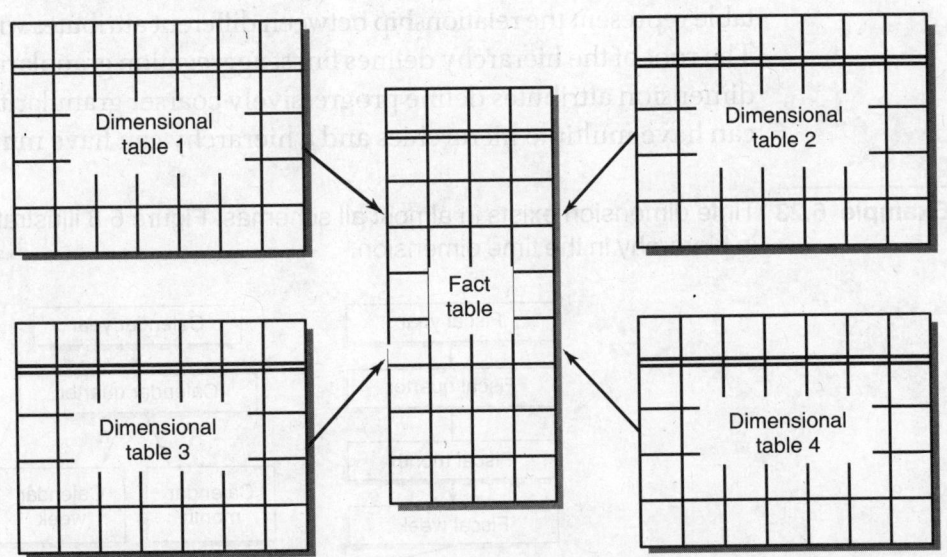

Fig. 6.9   Star schema with four dimensions

Example 6.24   Figure 6.10 shows star schema for loan subject. It has five dimension tables: Account, Customer, Loan, Time and City. The central fact table contains the primary keys of the five dimension tables and three measures, namely Total Loan Amount, Interest Paid, and Amount Paid.

The primary keys of fact table and dimension tables are shown as underlined. A query such as 'find the total agricultural loans given in the northern states during last five fiscal years' can be easily addressed using this schema.

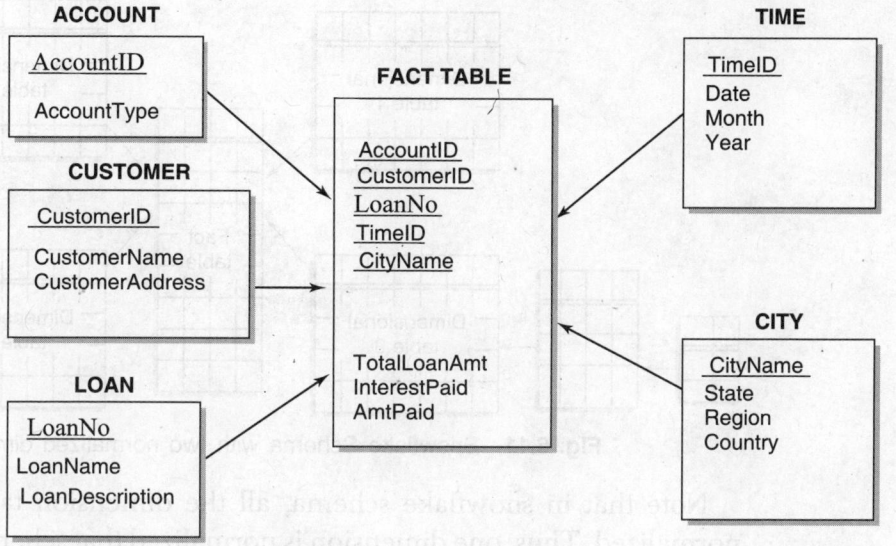

Fig. 6.10   Star schema for loans

The query first finds the desired dimensions and navigates along them towards the fact table to get the result. Note that join operations have to be performed among the dimension tables as well as fact table.

Advantage of star schema:

- Since the dimensional tables are in de-normalized form, accessing the data for a given query is fast.

Disadvantage of star schema:

- Dimension tables occupy more disk storage due to their de-normalized form.

Snowflake schema

Snowflake schema is a modification of star schema where some dimensional hierarchy is normalized into a set of smaller dimension tables, shaping like a snowflake. Unlike star schema where the dimensional tables are de-normalized, dimensional tables in snowflake schema are normalized. That is, a snowflake schema consists of one central fact table surrounded by (one or more) normalized dimensional tables (Fig. 6.11).

The main advantage of snowflake schema over star schema is that it requires less storage space due to normalizing one or more dimensions. Due to this normalization, more query performance will be reduced due to increase in the number of joins.

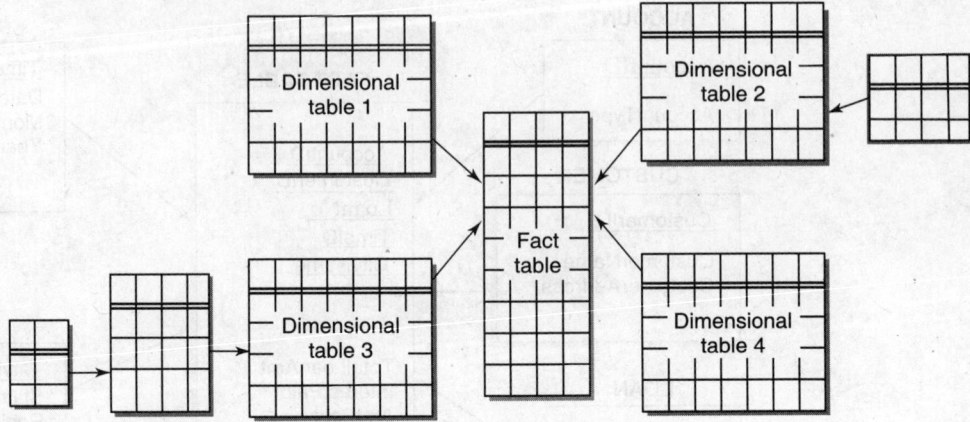

Fig. 6.11   Snowflake Schema with two normalized dimensions

Note that in snowflake schema, all the dimension tables need not be normalized. Thus, one dimension is normalized that schema is referred to as snowflake schema.

Example 6.25   Figure 6.12 shows a snowflake schema for a sample Deposit DW with one fact table and dimension tables representing Customer, Branch, Scheme, Transaction, and Time. Here, the dimensions CUSTOMER, TIME, and BRANCH are normalized.

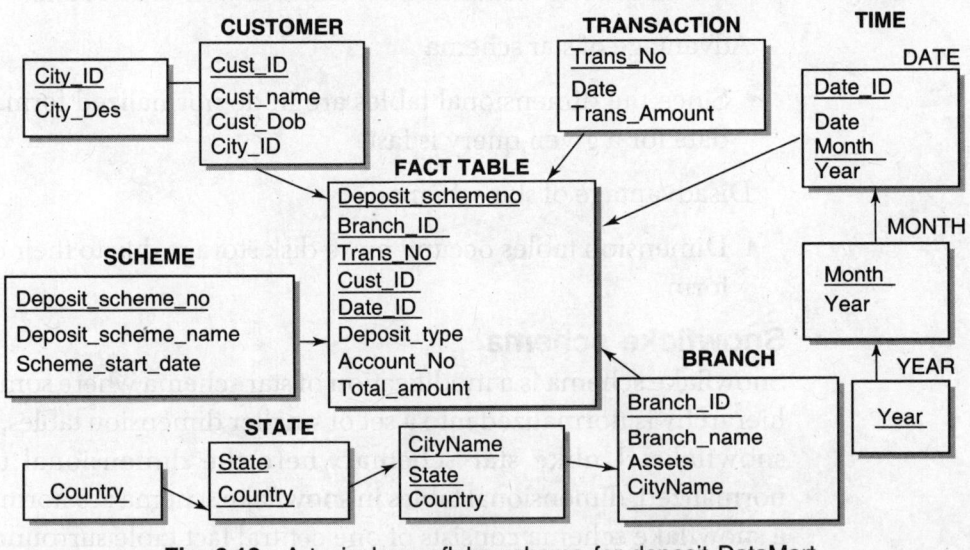

Fig. 6.12   A typical snowflake schema for deposit DataMart

The main advantage of snowflake schema over star schema is that it requires less storage space due to normalizing one or more dimensions. Due to this normalization, the query performance will be reduced due to increase in the number of joins.

Fact constellation

The *fact constellation* or *galaxy schema* has multiple fact tables that share dimensional tables, viewed as a set of stars.

Example 6.26 Figure 6.13 shows fact constellation with two fact tables sharing a common dimension CUSTOMER. This kind of schema is useful to extract information about the customers who have deposits and loans with a bank. Here, the CUSTOMER dimension is called conformed dimension.

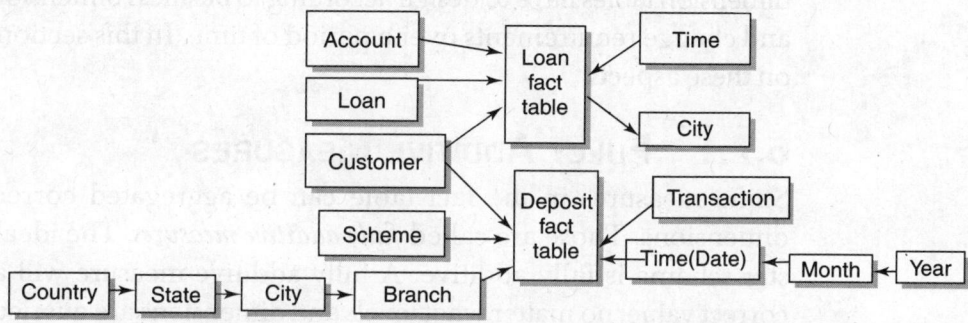

Fig. 6.13 An example schema for fact constellation

The above schema looks simple; however, for an organization, the schema for an enterprise-wide data warehouse would be very large and more complex (Fig. 6.14).

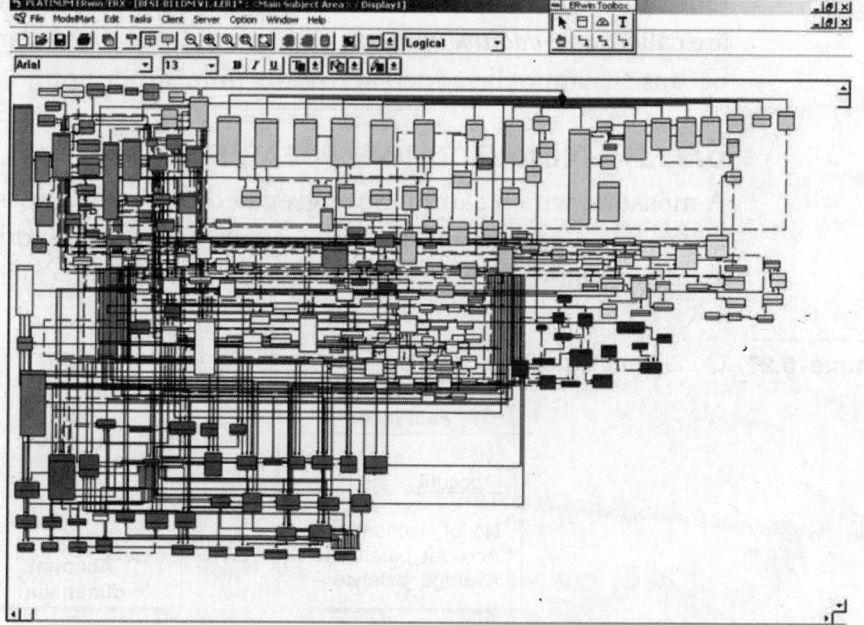

Fig. 6.14 A typical enterprise-wide data model for an organization

6.7 More on Dimensional Modeling

Once suitability of a schema for an organization is identified, the next step is to design schema, which mainly involves operations on facts and dimension attributes. Since most business applications require retrieving large size of rows rather than a single row and apply various aggregation operations, it is important to know various additive properties of facts in a fact table. Moreover, dimension tables have to design according to business dimensional hierarchies and change requirements over a period of time. In this section, we highlight on these aspects.

6.7.1 Fully Additive Measures

Some measures in the fact table can be aggregated correctly across all dimensions. Those are called *fully additive measures*. The ideal measure in a star schema is fully additive. A fully additive measure will aggregate to a correct value, no matter what levels and dimensions are queried. When cubes are created, the fully additive measures can be pre-aggregated, so that the most rapid OLAP navigation can be achieved.

6.7.2 Semi-Additive Measures

Some measures in the fact table can be aggregated correctly across some dimensions but cannot be added across at least one dimension. These measures are called *semi-additive measures*. For instance, account balance is semi-additive because it cannot be added across the time dimension.

6.7.3 Non-Additive Measures

A measure, which cannot be aggregated correctly across any dimension, is called a *non-additive measure*. The examples for non-additive measures are average values and many other values derived from calculations.

Example 6.27   Consider the partial schema shown in Fig 6.15. Here,

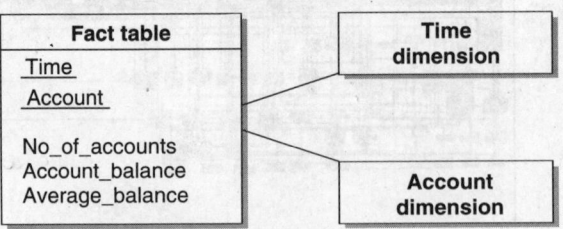

Fig. 6.15   Additive Measure

- No_of_Accounts is fully additive because we can aggregate over all dimensions.

- Account_Balance is semi-additive because we can aggregate over the Account dimension but it cannot be aggregated over the time dimension.

- Average_Balance per account is non-additive because there is no logical situation in which these numbers have any significance when added together.

6.7.4 FACT-LESS FACTS

Measures that do not have a value in the source data are called *fact-less facts*. A fact-less fact exists because the intersection of dimensions has meaning in itself. It always has a value of 1.

Example 6.28 The only fact in the fact table shown in Figure 6.16 is the count_of_ customer_ contacts. The value of this fact is 1 for every record in the fact table.

To implement fact-less facts,

- We can add a field to the fact table that is always filled with a value of 1.

- We can define the fact-less fact as the COUNT of any of the non-null fields in the fact table.

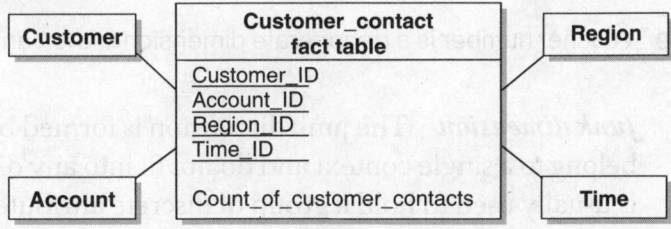

Fig. 6.16

6.7.5 DIMENSION TABLE CHARACTERISTICS

As seen previously, there are three kinds of fields in the dimension tables: *primary key field, hierarchy level fields,* and *attribute fields.* The dimensional tables provide different perspectives for the analyst to analyse the data.

Primary keys

The keys of the dimension tables are generally numerical. But the key values from the source system cannot be used as keys in a data warehouse. Instead, all key values should be generated automatically.

Hierarchy fields

For each level of the dimension's hierarchy, dimensional tables have a field. The names for these levels in the hierarchy are generally the field names.

Members of a level in a hierarchy   The data values in the hierarchy fields are the members of that particular level of the hierarchy.

Multiple hierarchies in one dimension table   In case if a dimension has more than one hierarchy, fields for levels of all hierarchies must be incorporated in the dimension table.

Attribute fields

Attribute fields give additional information regarding the members at one of the levels of the dimension's hierarchy.

Degenerate dimension   A degenerate dimension is a single field that is not an element of any dimension. It does not have its own dimension table, and can be included in the fact table when a fact table's grain represents transactional level data. A degenerate dimension is a field that should be in its own dimension, but is permitted to remain as a field in the fact table, because it is the only piece of information for that dimension.

Example 6.29   Voucher number is a degenerate dimension in the banking scenario.

Junk dimension   The junk dimension is formed by a set of fields that do not belong to a single context and do not fit into any dimension. Junk dimension is usually used to hold a group of discrete attributes.

A junk dimension naturally lacks hierarchy. All its fields are attributes. These attributes do not necessarily have some connection with each other.

Conformed dimension   In some cases, a dimensional table is used for more than one schema. This dimension is called the *conformed dimension*. Fact tables that share conformed dimensions can be joined together. Note that fact constellation schema uses conformed dimensions, which are shared by two or more schemas.

Slowly changing dimensions   Generally, data in dimension tables is static. However, sometimes the data values for a record vary over time. The dimensions in which the data varies over a period of time are called *slowly changing dimensions*.

There are three ways to incorporate the changes in dimension tables:

- Type 1: Original record is replaced by a new record. That is, the old record is lost.

- Type 2: New record is added into the dimension table, and hence there will be two records for the same information.

- Type 3: Original table structure is modified to reflect the change in the record.

Based on the design requirements, one of the above strategies is adapted.

Type 1 When a need arises to substitute the existing data with the new data, then this type of strategy is adopted. This strategy can produce faulty information when browsing historical data.

Appropriate in the following situations

- To correct an error that was previously made by altering the dimension record may still cause a problem, because there could be reports that have been prepared based on the previous condition of the data.

- We can change the field that has no effect on multidimensional analysis.

Not appropriate in the following situations

- It is not desirable to change the value of the field if its historical data is required in the analysis.

Example 6.30 Consider Table 6.8.

Table 6.8 Customer Dimension Table

S.No	Name	Sex	Address	Marital status
1	Ramesh	M	Hyderabad	M
2	Haritha	F	Delhi	U

If the name 'Ramesh' is entered as 'Rameh', we will change the Name attribute value after Type1 change (Table 6.9).

Table 6.9 Customer Dimension Table

S.No	Name	Sex	Address	Marital status
1	Ramesh	M	Hyderabad	M
2	Haritha	F	Delhi	U

Type 2   In Type 2 strategy, a new record is created for handling dimension change. This strategy preserves the accuracy of historical browsing, but makes it impossible to give a consistent view of data browsed across time.

The challenge here is in using this strategy to construct an accurate view of the past combined with the present. For example, if a new record is added to the customer table when a customer moves into the new income record, the user may be able to view the organization's interactions with that single customer across time. That is, the one customer appears theoretically as two customers.

Example 6.31   If the marital status of Haritha is changed from **U** to **M,** after Type 2 change, a new record is added for the customer Haritha (Table 6.10). Here, the flag attribute specifies the current active record after the change.

Table 6.10   Customer Dimension Table

S.No	Name	Sex	Address	Marital status	Flag
1	Ramesh	M	Hyderabad	M	Y
2	Haritha	F	Delhi	U	N
2a	Haritha	F	Delhi	M	Y

In practice, in addition to flag field, two more fields, namely effective from date and effective to date, are added to the dimensional table for Type2 change.

Type 3   In this strategy, dimension changes are handled by creating separate fields for the old and the new data. It is the most difficult strategy to implement because of the change in structure of the table, but useful in a few specialized situations. Type3 strategy maintains both the accuracy of historical browsing and the validity of browsing across the past and present. This strategy may become cumbersome in case there are regular changes to a dimension table.

Example 6.32   If the marital status of Haritha is changed from **U to M,** for Type 3 change, a new field 'New Marital Status' is added to the dimension table (Table 6.11).

Table 6.11   Customer Dimension Table

S.No	Name	Sex	City	Marital status	New marital status
1	Ramesh	M	Hyderabad	M	M
2	Haritha	F	Delhi	U	M

6.8 OLAP

A data warehouse is a repository from which data are gathered from internal and external sources. The storing of data is designed in such a way that it supports efficient analytical processing.

The traditional analytical tools are not enough to provide the intelligence required to make informed business decisions. Usually, the data can be best visualized when it is represented in two-dimensional tables. However, as the number of dimensions increases, it is very difficult to visualize as well as understand the data.

Example 6.33 Suppose we want to analyse the number of account types along different cities. We need to capture the details about account type, number of customers, and city. A simple data is shown in Table 6.12. To analyse such data, a two-dimensional table (for instance, spreadsheet) is useful.

Table 6.12 City-wise, Account-wise Customer Details

City/ Account Type	Hyderabad	Mumbai	Chennai	Kolkata
Savings Account	123	555	145	5001
Current Account	102	260	54	2010
Joint Account	20	89	32	245
Corporate Account	22	213	32	9450

Further, to add third dimension (for instance, time), the data can be represented as shown in Table 6.13 (alternatively, separate worksheet needs to considered for each dimension value in the spreadsheet) The situation becomes more tedious in the case of supporting four or more dimensions, and including several aggregate functions such as totals and subtotals.

Table 6.13 Year-wise, City-wise, Account-wise Customer Details

Year City/ Account Type	2006				2007			
	Hyderabad	Mumbai	Chennai	Kolkata	Hyderabad	Mumbai	Chennai	Kolkata
Savings A/c	123	555	145	5001	250	479	235	6233
Current A/c	102	260	54	2010	89	798	211	3875
Joint A/c	20	89	32	245	50	148	42	472
Corporate A/c	22	213	32	9450	55	641	89	14205

OLAP (*On-Line Analytical Processing*) is a standard data analysis technique for analysing large volumes of data. OLAP transforms raw data to reflect the real dimensions of the information as understood by the user, and provides users with a wide variety of interactive views of the information. It facilitates users in reporting, aggregating, trending, summarizing, averaging and graphing across multiple dimensions.

The OLAP term is coined by E.F. Codd in 1993. Codd defined OLAP as 'the dynamic synthesis, analysis, and consolidation of large volumes of multidimensional data'.

OLAP   According to OLAP Council, OLAP is a category of software technology that enables analysts, managers, and executives to gain insight into data through fast, consistent, interactive access to a wide variety of possible views of information that has been transformed from raw data to reflect the real dimensionality of the enterprise as understood by the user.

In simple terms, OLAP is a category of software tools that enable users to analyse different dimensions of multidimensional data stored in a data warehouse. For example, it provides time series and trend analysis views.

The principal component of OLAP is the *OLAP server*, which sits between a client and a data warehouse storage (database). The OLAP server understands how the data is organized in the database and has special operations for analysing the data.

Dimensional modeling provides a natural way of working with multidimensionality of warehouse data. The basic construct for multidimensional analysis is the OLAP cube (or data cube). OLAP technology organizes data in multidimensional tables called OLAP cubes and provides access to the data warehouse through and interactive Graphical User Interface (GUI). Note that, usually, the cube stores aggregated values for measures of a fact table. That is, the cells of cubes have pre-computed values, which helps to execute the query in a faster way.

6.8.1   OLAP CUBE

OLAP cube (or simply data cube) is the building block for OLAP analysis. The intersection of all dimensions of a cube is called a *cell*. Each axis of a cube represents a dimension and each cell represents values of measure(s) across all the dimensions.

The concept of dimensional modeling is the core of OLAP systems, which provide fast answers for queries that aggregate large amounts of detail data.

The dimensions, hierarchy in dimensions, and measures provide support in building OLAP cubes. That is, each cell in a cube contains a set of measure values.

Example 6.34 Figure 6.17 shows a data cube conceptualized from a star schema of a banks' warehouse. The cube cells contain the measure values (BalanceAmount or Interest), which are defined from combinations of dimension values.

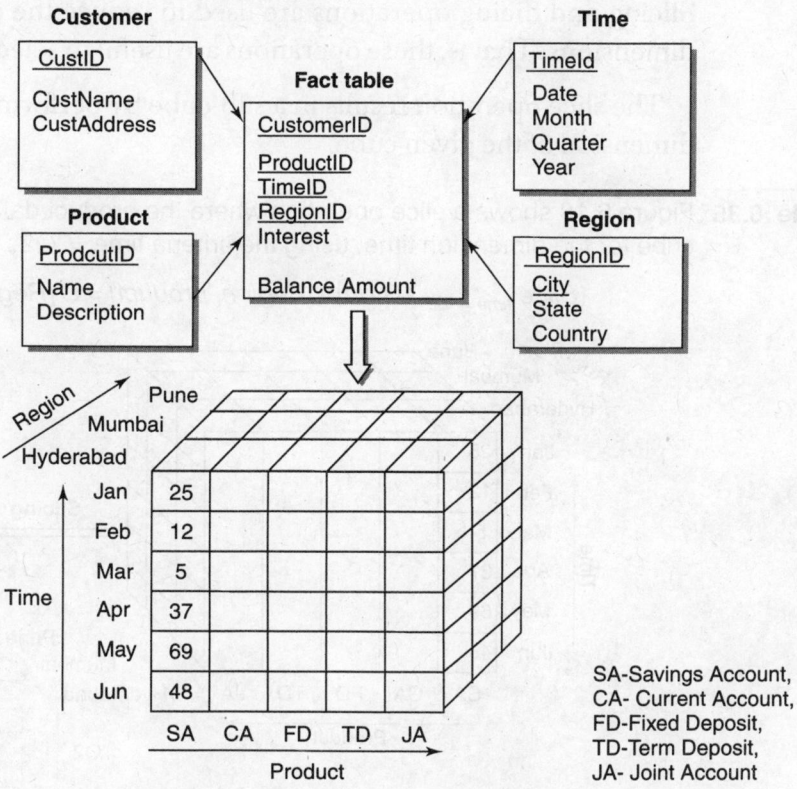

Fig. 6.17 Star schema and sample data cube

Note that several cubes can be conceptualized from a schema in order to visualize the data as per the analysis requirements. A cell can contain more than one measure value. For instance, both balance amount and interest values can be stored in one cell of the cube. Though normal cube contains three dimensions, the term *cube* in OLAP is commonly used for any number of dimensions.

6.8.2 OLAP OPERATIONS

The OLAP data is arranged into multiple dimensions and each dimension contains multiple levels of abstraction. Such an organization of data provides the users with the flexibility to view data from different perspectives. OLAP operations allow users for interactive query and analysis of the data.

There are several OLAP operations. The most basic OLAP operations are: slicing and dicing, roll-up, drill-down, drill-across, and pivoting (rotate the cube)

Slicing and dicing

Slicing and dicing operations are used to reduce the cube by one or more dimensions. That is, these operations are useful to select a subset of the cube.

The slice operation results in a sub-cube by performing a selection on *one* dimension of the given cube.

Example 6.35   Figure 6.18 shows a slice operation where the product data are selected from the cube for the dimension time, using the criteria time = 'Q2':

(*Slice* $_{time = 'Q2'}$ *C [Time, Region, product] = C [Region, Product]*)

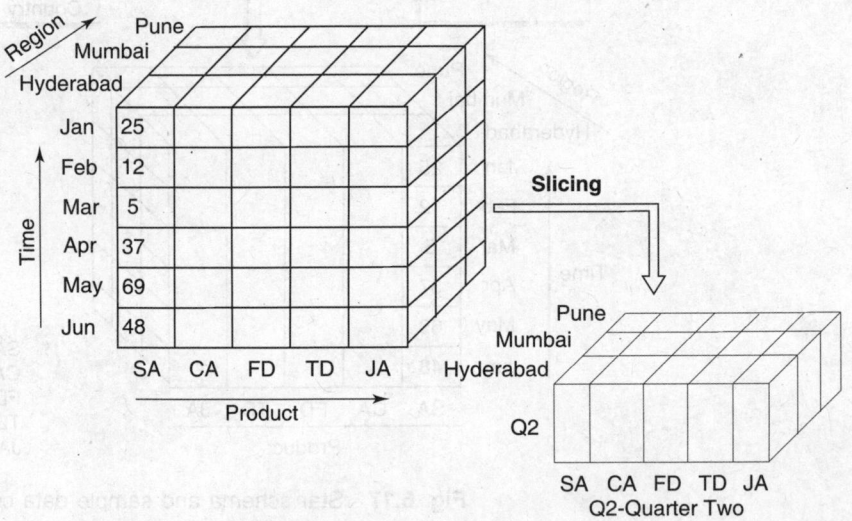

Fig. 6.18   Slicing operation

In the above example, the slicing has been done for time dimension for the second quarter. For simplicity, in the figure, after slicing, the time dimension is shown in terms of quarter. (This can be achieved by roll-up operation; we will explain this later).

Dicing is for selecting a smaller data cube and analyzing it from different perspectives. This operation results in a sub-cube by performing a selection on *two or more* dimensions.

Example 6.36 Figure 6.19 shows a dice operation on the cube based on the following selection criteria:

Dice [time = 'Q1' or 'Q2' and location = '"Mumbai" or "Pune" and product ≠ "JA"] C [Time, Region, product] = C [Time, Region, product]

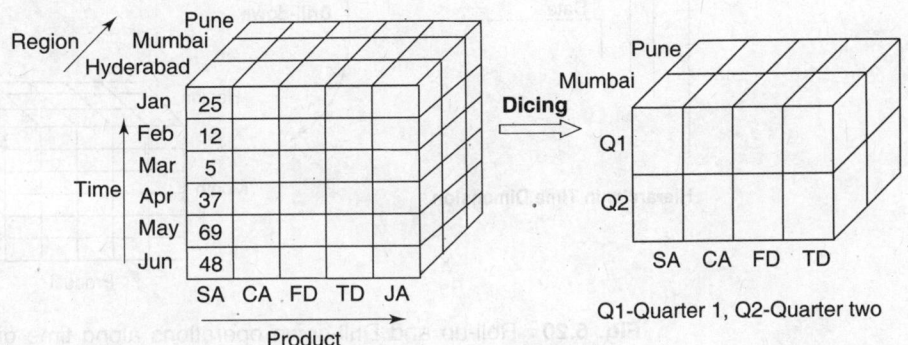

Fig. 6.19   Dicing operation

Here, *Time* and *Region* have truncated domains, such as {Q1, Q2} and {Mumbai, Pune}, respectively.

Roll-up and drill-down

Roll-up and drill-down operations are used for moving up and down along concept hierarchies. That is, these operations are useful to increase or decrease the level of aggregation.

Roll-up (or drill-up)   Roll-up performs aggregation on a data cube. Within the same hierarchy, this operation deals with rolling up from a detailed to an aggregated level.

Drill-down   Drill-down operation is useful for switching from an aggregated to a more detailed level within the same hierarchy. Basically, it is the reverse of roll-up operation. It navigates from detailed data to more detailed data.

Example 6.37 In Figure 6.20, the month-wise data is rolled up (aggregated) to quarter (roll-up operation). Here, the time dimension hierarchy is Year → Quarter → Month → Date. Similarly, the quarter-wise data can be drilled down to month-wise (drill-down operation).

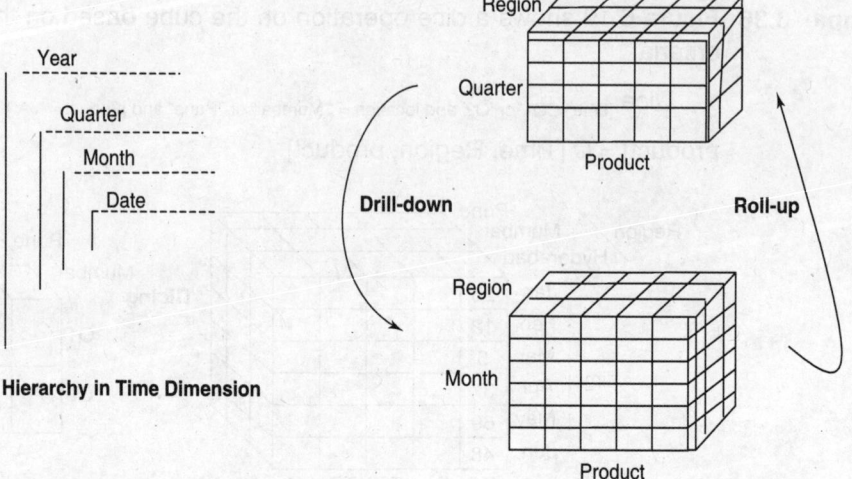

Fig. 6.20 Roll-up and Drill-down operations along time dimension

Drill-within

Drill-within operation used within the same dimension, when more than one hierarchy exists in that dimension. This operation switches from one hierarchy to another hierarchy in the same dimension.

Drill-across

Drill-across operation used for switching from a hierarchy in one dimension to a hierarchy in another cube's dimension (Fig. 6.21). Usually, drill across operation navigates across cubes using some common dimensions.

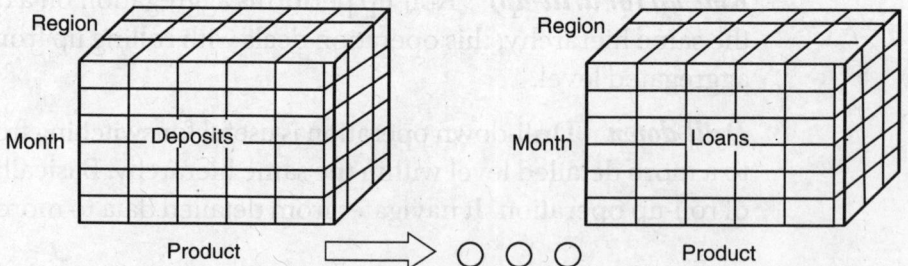

Fig. 6.21 Drill-across operations from deposits to loans

Pivot (rotate)

Pivot is a visualization operation. It rotates the data axes to provide an alternative presentation of the same data. Figure 6.22 shows the rotation of the cube. Rotating the axes in a 3-D cube or transforming a 3-D cube into a series of 2-D planes are the other examples.

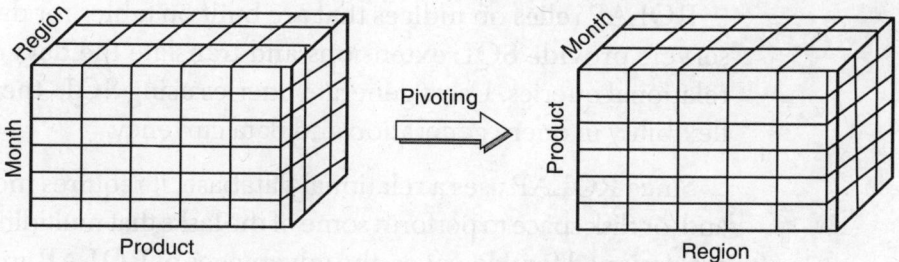

Fig. 6.22 Rotation operation

6.8.3 OLAP Server Architectures

A scalable infrastructure to support analysing massive transaction data continuously is needed to provide maximum flexibility for various OLAP operations, such as roll-up, drill down, drill-across, and pivoting. Selection of OLAP server architecture is mainly based on analyzing the data in multiple dimensions along with the support for indexing and data caching, and it reduces database access significantly.

There are two main categories of OLAP servers: Relational OLAP (ROLAP) and Multidimensional OLAP (MOLAP). The differences between the two are based on their storage structures, data processing capability, and data currency.

To build and query the system, relational databases are used in case of ROLAP and multi-dimensional structures such as arrays are used in case of MOLAP. A hybrid version of both the approaches are also used which are called Hybrid OLAP, or in short, HOLAP. A description of these servers is given below.

ROLAP

In ROLAP, data is aggregated and stored in relational (or extended relational) DBMSs, called relational OLAP servers. ROLAP performs dynamic multidimensional analysis of data that is stored in a relational database.

The features of ROLAP are:

- Store and manage warehouse data in relational DBMS or specialized relational DBMS.

- Maps operations on multidimensional data to standard relational operators.

- Requires OLAP middleware to support missing pieces.

ROLAP relies on indices that are built on tables for data access. ROLAP servers provide SQL extensions and translate the data cube operations to relational queries. Users generate queries using SQL, thereby offering more flexibility in query generation and data currency.

Since ROLAP uses a relational database, it requires more processing time and/or disk space to perform some of the tasks that multidimensional databases are designed for. However, the advantages of ROLAP architectures are: (i) it can be easily integrated with existing relational systems, (ii) data can be efficiently stored in the relational form than multidimensional structure, and (iii) it supports larger user groups and greater amounts of data and is often used when these capacities are crucial, such as in a large and complex department of an enterprise.

MOLAP

In MOLAP, data is stored in multidimensional databases. These are special-purpose servers that use non-relational specialized storage structures such as arrays. These storage structures help in implementing multidimensional data and operations directly to carry out multidimensional analysis.

The features of MOLAP are:

- Store and manage warehouse data in multi-dimensional DBMS (MDDBMS).
- Array-based storage structures.
- Direct access to array data structures.

MOLAP processes data that is already stored in a multidimensional array in which all possible combinations of data are reflected, each in a cell that can be accessed directly. For this reason, MOLAP is, for most uses, faster and more user-responsive than ROLAP. Moreover, MOLAP systems *pre-compute the results of complex operations* in order to increase the query performance. So, the data needs to be uploaded into a data cube periodically to maintain data currency.

HOLAP

HOLAP is a combination of ROLAP and MOLAP. It combines the greater data capacity of ROLAP with the superior processing capability of MOLAP.

HOLAP can use varying combinations of ROLAP and MOLAP technology. A simple way is to store the data in both RDBMS and MDDBMS, and use appropriate database that is best suited to the user queries. Another interesting approach is to store the data in RDBMS and store the aggregated data in MDDBMS. The features of this approach are:

- Storing detailed data in RDBMS

- Storing aggregated data in MDDBMS

- User access via MOLAP tools

Since, HOLAP offers the best features of both OLAP and ROLAP, HOLAP is increasingly preferred.

As seen above, cells of a cube contain pre-computed values. There is always a tradeoff between storage space, accessing cube data, and cube update time. Storing all possible combinations of GROUP-BYs occupies more space. On the other hand, building a cube with a few groupings (it is equivalent to creating a view that is materialized) and compute other values on-the-fly saves storage space as well as cube update time. *Materialized views* are covered in the next chapter.

6.8.4 FEATURES OF OLAP TOOLS

There are several OLAP tools that offer several features. The major features that define capabilities of the tools are as given below:

Summarization It refers to the *degree of aggregation* of information. This feature is measured based on the number of hierarchies, granularity of the data (level of detail), and the capability to swap between summarized and detailed levels.

Visualization It allows the users to create summary tables, charts, and graphs interactively. This feature depends on the users' requirements, occurrences of multidimensional tables, and the kind of analysis that needs to be carried out. Provision of what-if analysis is one of the most important criteria for OLAP analysis.

Navigation Roll-up and drill-down are most common operations in OLAP. Navigation feature allows roll-up and drill-down between levels of details. The capability of this feature can be assessed based on support for number of concurrent users.

Dimensionality It refers to the support for maximum number of dimensions, and the time for data refresh after re-definition.

Query Processing and Performance   It refers to extracting data from multidimensional databases by query engine and provides results in a more useful manner. Response time and query building capabilities are other factors that define performance.

6.9 STORAGE AND CHUNKS

In this section, we cover how the OLAP cubes are stored and optimized for faster query processing.

Complex queries and operations on large data require special storage structures and access methods. Aggregation is a predominant operation in OLAP applications. OLAP databases often need to summarize data at various levels of detail and on various combinations of attributes. This requires computing multiple related group-bys and aggregates in a faster and efficient way.

As seen in the previous section, fact data and aggregated data are stored in relational databases in case of ROLAP, and in multidimensional databases in case of MOLAP. The optimization process generally followed for relational databases can be extended for efficient storing of data cube in case of ROLAP. In case of MOLAP, a more efficient way of storing data needs to be evolved. One such approach is storing the array in multiple chunks.

Different operators are proposed by several researchers to support OLAP operations on relational databases. One such operator is *data cube* operator, introduced by Gray *et al.* in 1996. This operator, because of its wide applicability, is becoming a part of SQL standard for relational databases.

The *data cube* operator expands relational table to support aggregates in OLAP databases. It computes group-by aggregations over all possible subsets of the specified dimensions. The cube operator is based on a relationship of aggregate data using ALL value to denote the set over which each aggregation is computed.

Example 6.38   Consider an OLAP table Loans with four attributes loan_type, year, region, and loan_amount, that records the loan details by a bank. To find the total loan amount disbursed for each loan_type, for each year, for each region, for each loan_type-year combination, for each year-region combination, and so on, the collection of aggregate queries can be expressed using the cube operator as follows:

SELECT loan_type, year, region, SUM(loan_amount) as Amount

FROM LOANS

WHERE Loan_type in ('Agriculture', 'Education', 'Housing')

AND year BETWEEN 2001 AND 2007

GROUP BY CUBE loan_type, year, region;

CUBE BY is an extension of GROUP BY operator for multidimensional cubes. This operator generalizes all possible GROUP BYs (all possible combinations) on all attributes available. A CUBE BY with N grouping attributes will compute 2^N group-bys. Usually, a fact table is often very large and sparse. Hence, the size of a group-by is possibly close to the size of the fact table, and the size of a data cube increases exponentially after computation. Thus, the problem with CUBE BY operator is the cube size, both for computing and storing it. To compute a data cube for a table, special aggregation operators are required. Some of the approaches to do such tasks are:

- Initially compute a few aggregates, and then compute other aggregates from the available aggregates (e.g. Compute aggregations for loan_type as well as year, then compute aggregate loan_type_year from the two previously computed aggregates).
- Bring together related tuples using some grouping operations on the dimension attributes.

The commonly used optimization techniques for performing data cube operations are smallest-parent, cache-results, amortize-scans, share-sorts, and share partitions, and combination of sort-based and hash-based methods for computing single group-bys with these optimizations. These optimizations are often conflicting.

Several algorithms exist to combine them so as to reduce the total cost. The sort-based algorithm, called *Pipesort*, develops the best plan by reducing to a minimum weight matching problem on a bipartite graph. The hash-based algorithm, called *PipeHash*, develops the best plan by first creating the minimum spanning tree showing what group-by should be generated from what and then choosing a partitioning that takes into account memory availability. This algorithm gives a lot of improvement over straightforward methods.

Another approach to store a cube is based on *Quotient Cubes (QC)* defined by Lakshmanan, Pei, and Han (2002). In this approach, a cube is partitioned into sets of cells with similar behaviour, each set is associated with some semantic in the cube. Here, all tuples of a table are divided into equivalence classes, preserving roll-up/drill-down semantics. By this representation, only upper and lower bounds for equivalence class needs to be stored, rather than the whole table. Then, compute all inner cell values for each equivalence class. That is, the original table is transformed into a table with three attributes (upper bound, lower bound, and value of inner cells).

Quotient cubes are represented in a special data structure called QC-Trees. This representation provides optimal storage and allows fast query processing. Moreover, it facilitates cube maintenance operations such as update, insert, and delete nodes.

Below, we discuss the *dwarf algorithm* for efficient cube storage and fast querying it.

6.9.1 DWARF

Dwarf algorithm, proposed by Sismanis et al. (2002), describes a highly compressed tree-like structure for computing, storing, and querying data cubes. This algorithm is based on notion of coalescing tuples in the fact table. It solves the storage space problem by identifying prefix and suffix redundancies among cube tuples and factoring them out of the store.

In this approach, a cube is stored in a Dwarf cube (or compressed cube), which is in the form of a tree. Each cell of Dwarf tree node is associated with a tuple from the fact table. Initially, the tree is constructed from the fact table. The height of the tree equals to the number of dimensions (D). At each level k in the tree, all possible $d \in D(k) \cup ALL$ values are created. In case two node values are same, coalesce them. That is, after coalescing, nodes are aggregating different paths, and different multidimensional points. Answering a query starts from the root node and select the next node that was marked as query attribute.

Example 6.39 Figure 6.23 shows the tree (Dwarf cube) for the fact table for the data shown in Table 6.14. It is a full cube using the aggregate function sum. The nodes are numbered according to the order of their creation. Since the table has three dimensions (region, customer number, and loan type), the tree has three levels.

The root node contains a set of cells, each corresponds to a distinct value in that dimension and shown in the form [key, pointer]. The pointer of each cell points to the node below containing all the distinct values of the next dimension those are associated with the cell's key. For instance, the cell East of the root dominates the node containing the keys C2, C3. Each non-leaf node has a special ALL cell, holding a pointer and corresponding to all the values of the node.

A path from the root to a leaf such as ⟨East, C3, Car⟩ corresponds to an instance of the group-by region, customer, loan type and points to a cell [Car, 2] which stores the aggregate of that instance. Some of the cells in the path can be open using the ALL cell. For example, ⟨North, ALL, Car⟩ points to the cell [Car, 2], which corresponds to the sum of the loan amount taken by all customers for Car loan in North region. ALL cell in each node is shaded in Fig. 6.23.

Table 6.14   A Sample Table

Region	Customer Number	Loan type	Loan amount (in lakh)
East	C2	Home	30
East	C3	Car	4
North	C1	Car	2
North	C1	Home	45

At the leaf level, each cell is of the form [key, aggregate] and holds the aggregate of all tuples that match a path from the root to it. Each leaf node also has an ALL cell that stores the aggregates for all the cells in the entire node. ⟨ALL, ALL, ALL⟩ leads to the total Loan amount (group-by NONE).

As can be observed that the three paths ⟨North, C1, Car⟩, ⟨North, ALL, Car⟩, and ⟨ALL, C1, Car⟩, whose values are extracted from processing just the last tuple of the fact-table, all point to the same cell [Car, 45], which, if stored in different nodes, would introduce *suffix redundancies*. These nodes are *coalesced*. In Fig. 6.23 all nodes pointed by more than one pointer are coalesced nodes.

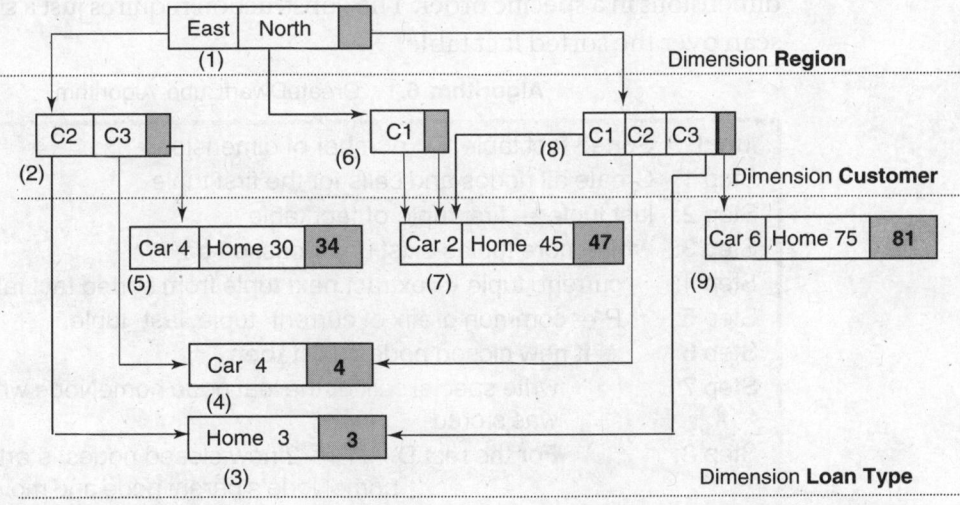

Fig. 6.23   Cube for Table 6.14

DWARF algorithm

Some points about Dwarf algorithm are:

- A node N_A is called *ancestor* of N iff N is a descendant node of N_A.

- During the construction of the Dwarf cube, a node N at level j of the Dwarf structure is *closed* if there does not exist an unprocessed tuple of the fact-table that contains a prefix equal to the primary leading prefix of N.

- An existing node of the Dwarf structure is considered as *open*, if it is not *closed*.

- The construction of a Dwarf cube is preceded by a single sort on the fact table using one of the cube's dimensions as the primary key, and collating the other dimensions in a specific order. The choice of the dimensions' ordering has an effect on the total size of the Dwarf Cube.

- Dimensions with higher cardinalities are more beneficial if they are placed on the higher levels of the Dwarf cube. This will cause the branching factor to decrease faster, and coalescing will happen in higher levels of the structure.

- The ordering used will be either user-specific or automatically chosen by the Dwarf after computing a few statistics related to dimensions.

CreateDwarfCube algorithm   The Dwarf construction algorithm *CreateDwarfCube* is presented in Algorithm 6.1. Initially, the fact table is sorted using one of the cube's dimensions as the primary key, and collating other dimensions in a specific order. The construction requires just a single sequential scan over the sorted fact table.

Algorithm 6.1   CreateDwarfCube Algorithm

Input:	Sorted fact table, D : number of dimensions
Step 1:	Create all nodes and cells for the first tuple
Step 2:	last tuple ← first tuple of fact table
Step 3:	**while** more tuples exist unprocessed **do**
Step 4:	current_tuple ← extract next tuple from sorted fact table
Step 5:	P ← common prefix of current_tuple, last_tuple
Step 6:	**if** new closed nodes exist **then**
Step 7:	write special cell for the leaf node homeNode where last_tuple was stored
Step 8:	For the rest D –	P	– 2 new closed nodes, starting from homeNode's parent node and moving bottom-up, create their ALL cells and call the SuffixCoalesce Algorithm
Step 9:	**end if**

(Contd.)

(*Contd.*)

Step 10:	Create necessary nodes and cells for current_tuple {D – I P I – 1 new nodes created}
Step 11:	last_tuple → current_tuple
Step 12:	**end while**
Step 13:	Write special cell for the leaf node homeNode where last_tuple was stored
Step 14:	For the other open nodes, starting from homeNode's parent node and moving bottom-up, create their ALL cells and call the SuffixCoalesce Algorithm

For the first tuple of the fact table, the corresponding nodes and cells are created on all levels of the Dwarf structure. During scanning the table, last tuple's common prefixes are read. Here, a common prefix of a Dwarf cube is the ancestor of the current node. Then, create the necessary cells to accommodate new key values as the algorithm progresses through the fact table. At each step of the algorithm, the common prefix *P* of the current and the previous tuple is computed.

Example 6.40 Consider Table 6.14 and Fig. 6.23. The nodes in the figure are numbered according to the order of their creation.

The first tuple ⟨East, C2, Home⟩ creates three nodes (Nodes 1, 2, and 3) for the three dimensions (Region, Customer, and Loan type) and inserts one cell to each node. Then, the second tuple ⟨East, C3, Car⟩ is read, which shares only the prefix East with the previous tuple. This means that cell C3 needs to be inserted to the same node as C2 (Node 2), and the node containing Home (Node 3) is now closed. The ALL cell for Node 3 is now created (the aggregation here is trivial, since only one cell exists in the node). The third tuple ⟨North, C1, Car⟩ is then read, which contains no common prefix with the second tuple.

Continuing in this way, finally, ALL cell for Node 4 is created and call SuffixCoalesce routine for Node 2 to create the sub-dwarf of the node's ALL cell.

Suffix coalescing *Suffix coalescing* creates the sub-dwarfs for the ALL *cell* of a node. It tries to identify *identical dwarfs* and coalesce their storage. Two or more dwarfs are *identical* if they are constructed by the same subset of the fact table's tuples. Prefix expansion would create a tree if it were not for suffix coalescing. The SuffixCoalesce algorithm is presented in Algorithm 6.2. It requires input as a set of Dwarfs (*inputDwarfs*) and merges them to construct the resulting dwarf. The algorithm makes use of CalculateAggregate function to compute the aggregates.

Algorithm 6.2 SuffixCoalesce Algorithm

Input:	inputDwarfs = set of Dwarfs
Step 1:	**If** only one dwarf in inputDwarfs **then**
Step 2:	return dwarf in inputDwarfs coalescing happens here
Step 3:	**end If**
Step 4:	**while** unprocessed cells exist in the top nodes of inputDwarfs **do**
Step 5:	find unprocessed key Key_{min} with minimum value in the top nodes of inputDwarfs
Step 6:	toMerge ← set of Cells of top nodes of inputDwarfs having keys with values equal to Key_{min}
Step 7:	**If** already in the last level of structure **then**
Step 8:	curAggr ← calculateAggregate(toMerge.aggregateValues)
Step 9:	write cell [Key_{min}, curAggr]
Step 10:	**else**
Step 11:	write cell [Key_{min}, SuffixCoalesce(toMerge.sub-dwarfs)]
Step 12:	**end If**
Step 13:	**end while**
Step 14:	Create the ALL cell for this node either by aggregation or by calling SuffixCoalesce
Step 15:	Return position in disk where resulting dwarf starts

SuffixCoalesce is a recursive algorithm that tries to detect at each stage whether some sub-dwarf of the resulting dwarf can be coalesced with some sub-dwarf of *inputDwarfs*. If there is just one dwarf in *inputDwarfs*, then coalescing happens immediately, since the result of merging one dwarf will obviously be the dwarf itself. The algorithm then repeatedly locates the cells *toMerge* in the top nodes of inputDwarfs with the smallest key Key_{min} which has not been processed yet. A cell in the resulting dwarf with the same key Key_{min} needs to be created, and its *content* (sub-dwarf or aggregateValues) will be produced by merging the *contents* of all the cells in the toMerge set. There are two cases:

- For leaf node, the function calculateAggregate is called to produce the aggregate values for the resulting cell.
- Otherwise, coalescing cannot happen at this level. Hence, call SuffixCoalesce recursively to create the dwarf of the current cell, and check if parts of the structure can be coalesced at one level lower.

At the end, the ALL cell for the resulting node is created, either by aggregating the values of the node's cells (if this is a leaf node) or by calling SuffixCoallesce, with the sub-dwarfs of the node's cells as input.

Example 6.41 Consider Fig. 6.23. Suppose Algorithm 6.1 calls SuffixCoalesce for creating the sub-dwarf of the ALL cell of Node 6. Since only one sub-dwarf exists in inputDwarfs (the one where C1 points to), immediate coalescing happens (case in Line 1) and the ALL cell points to Node 7, where C1 points to. Now, the sub-dwarf of the ALL cell for Node 1 must be created. The cell C1 will be added to the resulting node, and its sub-dwarf is created by recursively calling SuffixCoalesce, where the only inputDwarf is the one that has Node 7 as its top node. Therefore, coalescing will happen there.

Similarly, cells C2 and C3 will be added to the resulting node one by one, and coalescing will happen in the next level in the both cases, because just one of the inputDwarfs contains each of these keys. Then, the ALL cell for Node 8 must be created (Line 14). The key car is included in the nodes pointed by C1 and C3 (Nodes 7, 4), and since the leaf node reached, the aggregate value for the two cells is computed(Line 8).

6.9.2 CHUNKS

MOLAP structures allow storing the data values in fixed positions in an array based on the dimension values. Since, data warehouse tables are large; the data that is stored in array structures is fairly large to fit in a memory. To overcome this problem, large arrays are split into multiple *chunks* in such a way that each chunk fits in the memory during its processing.

Sarawagi and Stonebraker (1994) introduced chunking the array for large multidimensional arrays. Usually, a chunk will be of one disk block size in order to reduce the disk access (I/O), and hence result in higher query performance. Arrays are often sparse in MOLAP structures. In case of sparse arrays, compression techniques can be used to compress the chunks and thereby saving storage space.

Chunking Chunking is the process of dividing the array into chunks that are stored and accessed as a single unit.

A *chunk* represents a semantic subset of the cube. That means, a chunk is a sub-cube within a cube with the same dimensionality as the encompassing cube. Chunks are either fixed size or variable size. The semantics are drawn from the parent-child relationships along aggregation paths on each dimension. A chunk system designed for OLAP cube storage usually provides the following features (Nikos and Timos, 2002):

- Storage allocation: Stores chunks into blocks, each block corresponding to the bucket of underlying file system.

- Chunk addressing: A unique identifier must be assigned to each chunk such that a chunk must be made addressable from other modules. Moreover, this identifier provides an efficient access path to the corresponding chunk.

- Enumeration: Navigation from one chunk to the next chunk should be fast.

- Data point location addressing: A cell value in a Cube should be accessible by its location in the multi-dimensional multi-level space.

- Data sparseness management: Optimize the space for efficient storing of sparse data cubes.

- Maintenance: Provides support for workloads such as periodic incremental loads (in a batch form).

In case of HOLAP, one approach is that the data can be separated according to dense regions and sparse regions. The dense regions are stored in MOLAP approach for fast accessing, and the other regions in a ROLAP approach. Another approach is to store stream of fact data in relational table, and chunks of this table are stored in MOLAP structures.

SUMMARY

In contrast to application orientation of transactional processing systems (OLTPs), subject orientation feature of data warehouse enables storing analytic data that is processed for decision-support. Thus, this feature strikes off the data that will not be used for decision-support systems. Further, the data needs to be stored in such a way that it provides a single view of data at any point of time. It requires integration of data before entering the data warehouse and the challenging part here is having a common (or unified) format for the complete enterprise. The time variant feature ensures the data in the data warehouse is accurate over the whole data history. Lastly, the non-volatile feature keeps storing the data for a longer period and not changed, but refreshed periodically.

ETL part of data warehouse is responsible for extraction of data from heterogeneous data sources, their cleaning, customization, and loading into a data warehouse database. Data from data sources (typically relational databases, semi-structured or flat files) are extracted (complete data or incremental portion) by extraction routines, and transformed and cleaned (mostly in the data staging area) before being loaded to the data warehouse.

Dimensional modeling is a popular logical data modeling in data warehouse, as it provides better query performance on very large queries. The two basic models in dimensional modeling are star schema and snowflake schema. Star schema has a large central table known as fact table, and a set of smaller tables known as dimension tables, which are directly related to the fact table. Snowflake schema is similar to star schema except that one or more of the dimensions, which have hierarchies, are decomposed (normalized) into smaller tables.

OLAP servers enable a more sophisticated user interface to navigate the data warehouse. Moreover, the multidimensional structures allow users to do complex analysis on the data. OLAP operations make data analysis more effective and easy to use. The MOLAP architecture provides a direct multidimensional view of the data warehouse. On the other hand, the ROLAP architecture provides a multidimensional interface to relational data.

Efficient storage of data for both relational and multidimensional databases in terms of cubes and chunks respectively improves the OLAP query performance. A good amount of research is currently going on to have an OLAP system that answers for complex queries in constant-time or near-constant time.

EXERCISES

Test Your Understanding

1. How does data warehouse help in improving business of an organization

2. Prove that the four DW characteristics provide a better way of organizing the data for Decision Support Systems.

3. Explain the architecture of a data warehouse and explain its components.

4. Discuss various steps and approaches for Data cleansing.

5. Explain the star schema and the snowflake schema. How are they useful in handling *ad hoc* queries.

6. What are the different storage design structures of a cube? What are the differences between them?

7. Discuss various OLAP operations. Explain how query performance can be improved by cascading the operations.

8. Designing a data warehouse mainly depends on queries for which you want to get answers. Identify the most complex queries and develop a data warehouse for your university/organization.

Improve Your Research Skills

1. What are the shortcomings in ER Modeling for analytical applications? How do Dimension Modeling concepts enhance ER Modeling?

2. What is the effective way of modeling metadata in the data warehouse?

3. Do a comparative study on various ETL tools and OLAP tools.

4. Is it needed to have a separate data warehouse system in addition to the OLTP system to analyse data? Substantiate your answer and discuss the advantages and disadvantages.

5. Design an efficient algorithm to store a star schema with n dimension tables and a fact-table.

6. Study various cube storage for ROLAP, MOLAP, and HOLAP servers and perform a comparison.

Improve the Field

1. Aggregation is an important aspect in data warehousing. Come out with a strategy that decides possible aggregation level for a given set of data sources.

2. Design OLAP operations for processing top K queries.

3. Describe the computer architectures that are suitable for data warehousing databases.

DATA WAREHOUSING: QUERY PROCESSING

We find what we expect to find, and we receive what we ask for.
—ELVERT HUBBARD

INTRODUCTION

Data warehousing integrates data from multiple, possibly very large, distributed, heterogeneous databases and other information sources. Typically, data flows from one or more online transaction processing (OLTP) databases into a data warehouse at regular time intervals like monthly, weekly, or daily basis. The data is normally processed in a staging area before being added to the data warehouse. Data warehouses commonly range in size from thousands of gigabytes to tens of terabytes. OLAP provides to query the data warehouse to make faster and informed decisions as well as answer *ad hoc* queries.

Ad hoc query   An ad hoc query is a query that could be asked by a user at any point of time for any aspect on the data stored in a database.

The main purpose of a data warehouse is to provide response to the user queries and analyse the query results. Data warehouse is generally used to evaluate queries on aggregated data rather than looking at individual records. Usually, in a data warehousing environment, the queries are complex and *ad hoc*. Several queries are repetitively posed to data warehouse for certain applications such as trend analysis and forecasting. Queries on a data warehouse may access a very large data and may contain join operations involving large number of records. Moreover, aggregate (Group-by) and range queries are most common in data warehouse environment. Thus, query processing on a data warehouse takes significant amount of time. Note that the basic designing of data warehouse starts with identifying the queries that needs to be addressed by the warehouse.

Hence, one of the key (aspects) challenges is to reduce the query response time. The two approaches that deal with reducing query processing time are: (i) Materialized views and (ii) Indexing.

In traditional database systems, (logical) views are virtual in nature. That means, these views have only schema derived from table(s) and does not contain the data. A query on a view uses the logical schema; however, it is processed on underlying tables on which the view is created. Commonly, the views are associated with aggregation and joins. In data warehousing, special kind of views are used, which are known as *materialized views*. A view is said to be *materialized* when it is stored in the database. Since these views contain data (meaning materialized), they avoid accessing the original data source and, hence, increase the speed of query processing in a data warehouse. Materialized view concept allows storing pre-computed results as well as intermediate results that are accessed by the queries. On a sufficiently abstract level, a data warehouse can be seen as a set of materialized views over the data extracted from the distributed heterogeneous databases.

Indexing also helps in improving the efficiency of query processing. An index is a data structure defined for a table to provide quick access to data in response to queries. This technique is widely used in traditional database systems for performance tuning. These information systems (OLTP systems) are mainly used for read, write, and update operations. The queries on these systems are typically point queries and access only a few numbers of records. Many indexing techniques from sequential indexing to B-tree indexing have been adopted by the existing OLTP systems. On the other hand, data warehouses are used for read-only purpose and queries access large number of records. Hence, in data warehouses, special indexing techniques such as bitmap index and join indexes are needed for improving the performance.

This chapter provides an overview on materialized views and indexing, and discusses the problems with these concepts and approaches to overcome them.

Segmentation and clustering techniques are also used to improve the query performance. Segmentation is the process of storing data in different (logical) partitions on the disk. On the other hand, clustering technique stores related data in a particular segment. These two techniques are concerned with space allocation in different partitions to store the data for efficient query processing; however, details of these techniques are not covered in this chapter as the same apply to traditional database systems as well.

7.1 MATERIALIZED VIEWS

Usually, the fact tables contain large data. OLAP queries are typically aggregate queries on the large fact tables. Querying these large fact tables for required information takes a substantial amount of time. To improve query performance, one approach is to pre-compute the summaries required for a query and storing it in a table.

Example 7.1   Consider Sales-Data table (see Figure 6.2). A table can be created to contain the sums of sales by store and by product. The SQL statement on a base relation Sales-Data can be written as

> SELECT SUM(Sales)
>
> FROM *SALES-DATA*
>
> GROUP BY store, product;

In data warehouses, the above query is evaluated and stored (called materialized view), which avoids the repetitive execution of that query every time a user wants.

> CREATE MATERIALIZED VIEW Sum-Sales
>
> AS
>
> (SELECT SUM(Sales)
>
> FROM *SALES-DATA*
>
> GROUP BY store, product);

Next time onwards, whenever to compute the same query, it can be computed based on the materialized view Sum-Sales (which was computed and stored result) rather than computing afresh on the base relation as the case with virtual views.

The pre-computed summaries would typically be very small compared to the original source data. Since the query does not need to access the large data records and required only to retrieve data from the summary table, such a query can be processed using this table very quickly. These summaries are often called as *materialized views*. So, a materialized view is the pre-calculated (materialized) result of a query and the resulting view is stored in a table.

Materialized views are used when immediate response is needed and the query where the materialized view bases would take too long to produce a result.

In database literature, there are two kinds of views: *virtual views* and *materialized views* (see Fig. 7.1).

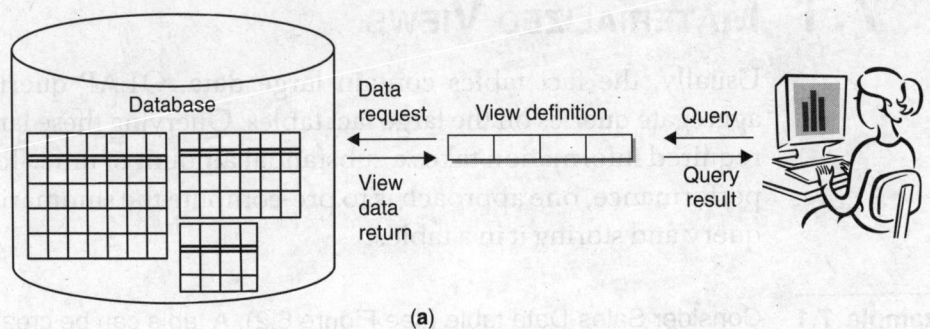

(a)

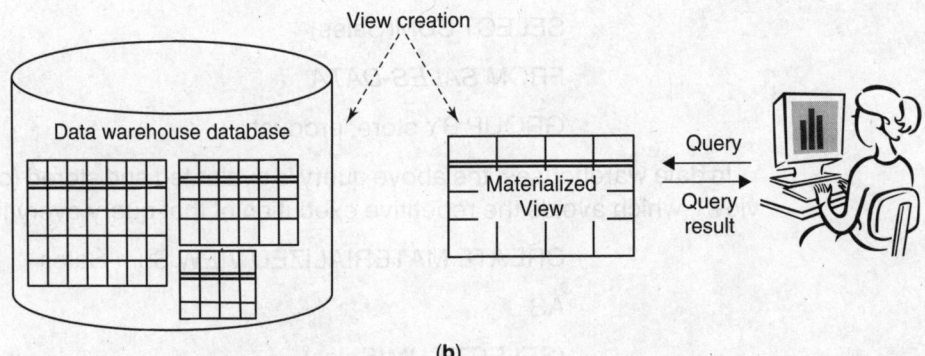

(b)

Fig. 7.1   (a) Virtual view   (b) Materialized view

Virtual view

- Virtual view is a derived relation that is defined in terms of base tables.

- The contents of virtual views are computed on-demand (when user wants to query), every time from scratch. This approach is often called *lazy approach.*

- These views do not contain the data.

- In response to queries on this kind of view, the queries are computed on the base relations.

Materialized view

- Materialized view contains data. That is, data (material) is stored in these views and, hence, the name materialized views.

- In response to queries on this kind of view, the queries are computed on the view itself as it has the required data.

- These views are used in data warehouses for faster query processing.

Virtual view approach is suitable when the data sources change frequently (insert/delete/update). However, materialized view approach is suitable when the data sources change infrequently. In data warehouse systems, for materialized views, the source data (data warehouse data) is referred to as *base relations* (or base data). Since, the focus of this chapter is on materialized views, referring views below means materialized views.

Materialized view A materialized view is a special kind of aggregate view that computes the result and stores the contents in that view.

Note that in the previous example, a view is created on a singe base relation. Usually, a materialized view can be created on several base relations using join operations. A query can also be answered using the combination of materialized view and base relation by joining them. Joins are very expensive in databases. Materialized views improve query execution speed by pre-computing expensive joins and aggregation operations prior to execution and storing the results in a table in the database.

It is interesting to note that the data warehouse itself can be considered as a set of materialized views, derived from the (internal and external) data sources.

Materialized views can increase the speed of queries execution that accesses a large number of records. Materialized views are important in data warehouses for fast retrieval of derived data regardless of the access paths and complexity of view definitions.

Materialized views have to be refreshed in order to update the data with the changes done at base relations. Basically, a materialized view can be refreshed immediately or deferred; it can be refreshed fully or, to a certain point, in time based on the application requirements.

The main advantage of materialized views is the improved performance in query processing. Calculating the results in advance for very complex queries will greatly reduce the load on the system, due to the following:

- Less physical reads – Less data is scanned when compared to scanning the base relations for a query.

- Less writes – No frequent computation of complex operations such as sorting and aggregating.

- Reduced CPU utilization – No need to compute Group-Bys and other functions on the data. This is because they are already computed and stored in the views.

- Faster response times – Queries using the summaries can be processed quickly, as opposed to the details.

The disadvantages of materialized views are:

- Requires additional storage space

- Needs update when there are changes to the base relations. This requires computation of the functions again.

Nowadays, storage units have become cheaper, providing extra storage for storing materialized views is reasonable at the cost of time to retrieve the query result. Moreover, data warehouses are read-intensive environment, updating materialized views is rarely done.

Materialized views are mainly used to pre-compute aggregates and joins. A materialized view can also be created to join two tables without aggregates. Here, expensive joins are pre-computed resulting in increased query execution performance. Sometimes, materialized views are defined over other existing materialized views. These views are known as nested materialized views.

Nested materialized view   A materialized view whose definition is based on another materialized view is referred to as nested materialized view.

A nested materialized view can also reference some base relations in addition to existing materialized views.

The creation of materialized views is transparent to application. That is, given a query to data warehouse, it can be executed either by using materialized views if views for such queries exist, or by using base relations in a normal way (where there is no materialized view exist for such queries). Thus, an application query can be processed irrespective of adding or dropping materialized view(s), except difference in the performance.

There are two major issues with materialized view: (i) materialized view selection and (ii) materialized view maintenance.

Materialized view selection is one of the many challenging issues in data warehouses. Here, the issue is how to select the views that are to be materialized from a given possible set of views so that it minimizes (or optimizes) the querying cost as well as view maintenance cost. There are different choices to materialize the views.

1. All materialized views

   Materialize all the views of the DW so that best query performance can be achieved at the highest cost of maintenance.

2. All virtual views

   Leave all views virtual; it will have the poorest performance but the lowest cost of maintenance.

3. Selected materialized views

   Materialize some views and leave others as virtual.

The most preferable choice is the third one and it turns out view selection problem. The three factors, namely query response time, maintenance cost, and storage space influence the performance of OLAP queries.

7.2 MATERIALIZED VIEWS SELECTION

Creating a materialized view for each query increases the performance. At the same time, these views occupy more space. There is always a trade off between the storage space and fast accessing. Effectively, in a data warehouse environment, it is very difficult to create a materialized view for each possible query due to constraints, such as available storage space, computation time, and maintenance cost. Hence, there is a need to select a set of materialized views for responding to queries posed to the data warehouse. This problem is referred to as *view selection problem*.

View selection problem Selection of (a set of) materialized views under some resource constraints that results in improved query processing is known as view selection problem.

Note that solving the above problem is NP-hard. The primary goal of selecting a set of views is to minimize the total query response time.

The view selection could be either static or dynamic. In the static case, the materialized views are created for the known queries, which are frequently submitted to the data warehouse. Usually, the materialized views will be placed based on their usage, that is, how frequent the data in these views are queried. In case a view is not accessed frequently, that view can be dropped. On the other hand, data warehouses support *ad hoc* queries. That means, there will be new queries posed to data warehouse by the users. Moreover, sometimes, the existing materialized views will be outdated due to changes in expectations (for example, trends) by the users. Thus, some materialized views need to be dropped and some more needs to be created based on the access patterns.

A simple strategy for view selection problem is to materialize the views which are frequently accessed by user queries. Another interesting strategy is to materialize the commonly shared views that are used for generating other views. Below, we discuss the *greedy approach* for selecting materialized views.

7.2.1 GREEDY ALGORITHM

OLAP queries are modeled by the data cube operator for multidimensional databases. Greedy algorithm described by Harinarayan, Rajaraman, and Ulman (1996) is based on the data cube where dimensions contain hierarchies. Group-bys are used to compute the aggregate functions, such as Sum, Min, and Max. These functions can also be computed using Group-by from the pre-computed result of another Group-by. This kind of relationship can be viewed as a *lattice*. Sometimes, this lattice structure is referred to as *hypercube lattice* structure because the aggregates are vertices of an *n*-dimensional cube.

A hypercube lattice of aggregate views possesses the following properties:

(a) A partial order '≤' exists between aggregate views in the lattice. For two aggregate views *u* and *v*; $v \leq u$ if and only if *v* can be answered using the results of *u* by itself.

(b) There is always a base view in the lattice. Every view is dependent on the base view. The base view is the database.

(c) There is a completely aggregated view referred to as 'ALL', which can be computed from any other view in the lattice.

In the lattice diagram, two nodes (views) *a* and *b* are connected with an edge if view *a* is dependent on view *b*. The higher view is used to precompute the lower view.

Example 7.2 In Fig. 7.2, the top view Product-Store (PS) is a base view; and bottom view is ALL. The edge between PS view and Product view means that PS can be used to compute

Product. In case the Product view is not materialized (not precomputed), then a query on P needs to be answered using the base view PS. For instance, to find product-wise sales, for each product sum of the sales across all stores for each product can be computed from PS to get the answer.

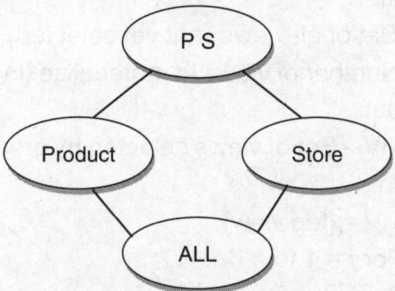

Fig. 7.2   Example lattice structure

The *greedy* algorithm uses the concept of a derivation graph (also known as *lattice*). Each node in the graph represents a view that needs to be materialized. These views are aggregated on certain dimensions that may have hierarchies.

In the greedy algorithm, top view is always materialized. This is because any query can be answered using this view.

The greedy algorithm starts materializing the top (root) view that all other views depend upon. The next view is selected based on the *benefit* yielded by materializing this view. This process is repeated till the desired number of views (specified as input) is selected for materializing. In this approach, new views are selected based on the *benefit* from the query efficiency of view materialization. The steps of this approach are:

1. Materialize the top view
2. Select additional views to materialize, one at a time, until the desired number of views are selected. At each step, select that unmaterialized view with the greatest benefit

In the first step, the approach always chooses the materialization of the view that can be used to derive any other view, that is, *top view*. Next, for each view in the graph that does not yet belong to the set of materialized views, the algorithm determines the total benefit of materializing this view. Among these analysed views, the algorithm selects the view, which maximizes the benefit and adds it to a materialized set. This second step is repeated until a desired number of materialized views are selected. Greedy approach provides optimal set of materialized view and it guarantees at least 3/4 optimal.

The greedy algorithm is given below.

Algorithm 7.1 Greedy approach for materialized view selection

Input:
V – Set of all views (not yet selected) in the lattice
K – Number of views to materialize (in addition to top view)
Output:
    MV – Set of views selected by greedy approach
Begin
    MV = {top view}
    For j = 1 to k do
    Begin
       Select a view $v \in V$ that is not in MV such that B(v, MV) is maximized
       MV = MV $\cup$ {v};
    End
    Output MV
End

Here, B(v, MV) is the benefit yielded by selecting view v relative to MV, which is computed based on some heuristic. This function is useful to find the cost of evaluating views. One simple heuristic to compute benefit is based on the cost corresponding to number of rows in a view from which another view is materialized.

Harinarayan, Rajaraman, and Ulman (1996) defined B(v, MV) as follows:

1. For each aggregate view $u \le v$, define the quantity B_u by

    (a) Let w be the least cost view in MV such that $u \le v$. (Since top view is always present, there must be at least one such view in MV).

    (b) If $\text{Cost}(v) > \text{Cost}(w)$ then $B_u = \text{Cost}(w) - \text{Cost}(v)$, else $B_u = 0$

2. Define B(v, MV) = sum of B_u over $u \le v$.

Thus, for each view u that is a descendant of v, it is checked whether computing u from v is cheaper than computing u from any other view in the set MV. If it is beneficial, then pre-compute v. Since any aggregate can be computed from the base relation, a least aggregate view w can always be found.

In the Greedy's approach, a simple way of cost computation is to find the number of records in a view used to answer a query. That is, the cost of answering a query is equal to the number of records retrieved to answer the query.

Example 7.3 Consider Fig. 7.3. The costs of views V_1, V_2, V_3 and V_4 are 100, 85, 55, and 15 respectively. Suppose we want to select three views. In greedy approach, the top view, i.e. V_1, is to be selected first. Here, MV = $\{V_1\}$

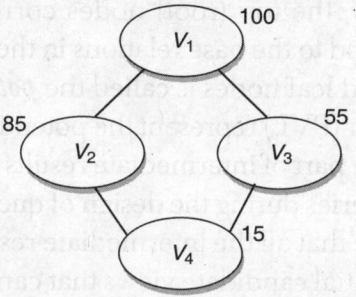

Fig. 7.3 Example lattice structure of views to be materialized

Selection of other two views is evaluated based on the V_1 view, whose cost is 100.

That is, selecting V_2 view for materialization, the cost is reduced by 15 (i.e., 100 − 85) for itself and for view V_4, which is below V_2 view. So, the benefit of materializing the V_2 view is (100 − 85) × 2 = 30.

Similarly, the benefit of materializing the view V_3 is (100 − 55) × 2 = 90; and the benefit of materializing the view V_4 is (100 − 15) × 1 = 85.

Since, the benefit of materializing view V_3 is higher than the other two views, V_3 is selected as second view for materialization. At this stage, MV = $\{V_1, V_3\}$.

Now, the benefit for V_2 and V_3 need to be recomputed such that they will be created either by V_1 or V_3.

For this example, the benefit of materializing V_2 remains same as 30, because V_2 can be derived from V_1 only. Since, V_4 can be materialized using V_3 (which is already selected in MV), the benefit of materializing V_4 is (55 − 15) × 1 = 40. Now, the benefit of V_4 is higher than benefit of V_2, so V_4 will be selected as third materialized view. So, finally MV = $\{V_1, V_3,$ and $V_4\}$.

Note that the greedy approach does not consider the maintenance cost. Unfortunately, if storage space is inadequate for containing all the views that are dependent on other views, then the greedy algorithm has the worst performance.

Another approach of selecting materialized views is to exploit *common sub-expressions* that exist in most of the queries. Yang, Karlapalem, and Li (1997) described the Multiple View-Processing Plan (MVPP) algorithm for selection of materialized views based on common sub-expression in queries.

7.2.2   MULTIPLE VIEW-PROCESSING PLAN (MVPP)

MVPP is a Directed Acyclic Graph (DAG). The MVPP graph represents query processing strategy for views. Figure 7.4 shows an example MVPP. In the DAG, the top (root) nodes correspond to queries and the leaf nodes correspond to the base relations in the warehouse. The layer between the top nodes and leaf nodes is called the *potential view layer*. Nodes in the potential view layer (PVL) represent the potential views that can be materialized. These nodes are part of intermediate results representing common sub-expressions in the queries during the design of queries execution plan. It can be seen from the figure that all the intermediate results (shown in small circles) in the PVL are potential candidate views that can be materialized.

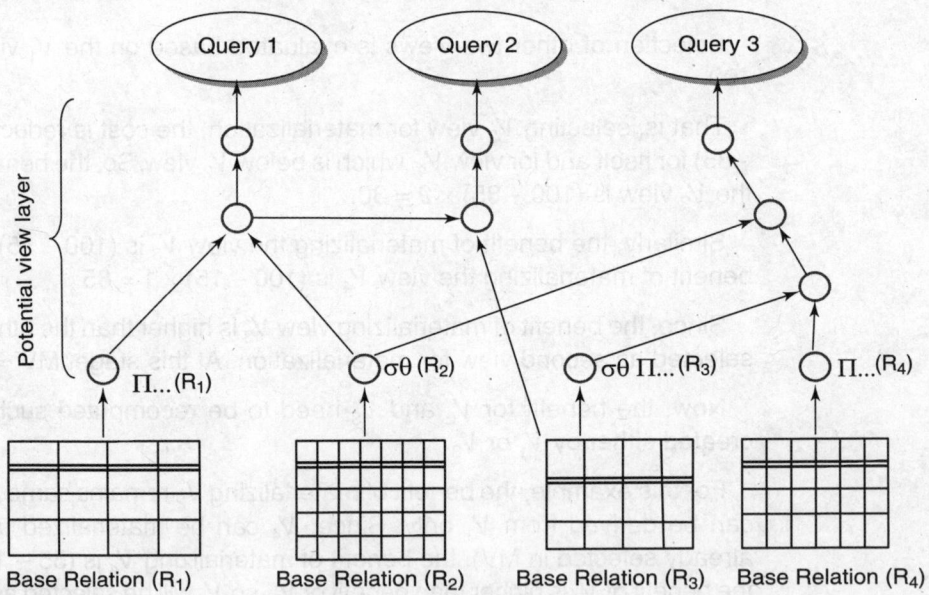

Fig. 7.4   An example MVPP

In the works of Yang, Karlapalem, and Li (1997), each node in the PVL is assigned with two costs, namely the query processing cost and the maintenance cost in order to select the materialized views. For a given MVPP, heuristic rules are used to find a set of nodes to be materialized so that the total cost is minimal. Note that there can be different MVPPs for the same set of queries depending upon the access characteristics of the application and physical data warehouse parameters.

7.3 MATERIALIZED VIEW MAINTENANCE AND CONSISTENCY

The views in the warehouse can become inconsistent when the underlying base relations change. So, materialized views need to be maintained in response to changes to the base relations in order to provide consistency in data warehouses.

> **Materialized view maintenance**   Materialized view maintenance is the process of keeping the contents of materialized views up-to-date with the changes in contents of underlying base relations.

7.3.1 REFRESHING MATERIALIZED VIEWS

Materialized views have to be refreshed (maintained) when its dependent base relations are updated to ensure the correctness of results to queries (see Fig. 7.5).

The strategy for refreshing materialized views could be:

- *Never*   Data is loaded into the views only at the beginning. This strategy is useful for static data only.

- *Immediately*   Refreshing immediately after update to the base relation(s). That is, re-compute the materialized view after each update. The same transaction that updates the base relation may refresh the materialized view.

- *Deferred*   Depending on the application requirements. For instance, once in a day, after last data load into the base relations.

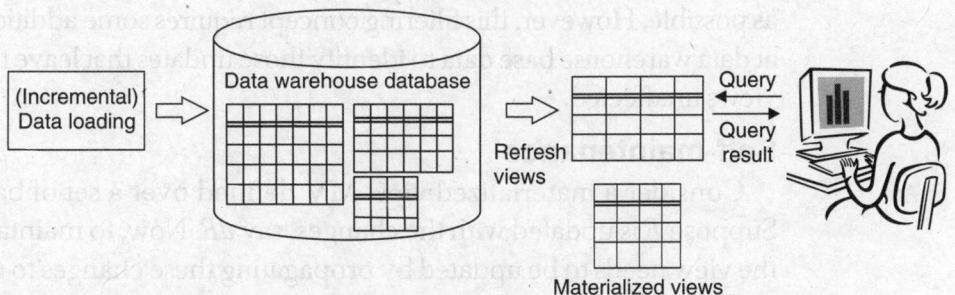

Fig. 7.5   Refresh materialized views

A refresh can be done in the following ways:

- Full refresh – complete refreshment, almost re-computing from scratch.
- Incremental refresh – refresh only the incremental part.

Full refresh

Complete refresh takes a lot of time, whereas differed refresh is fast a but needs some computation (for instance, storing information about update in a log table) to identify the new data. Updating the materialized view by full re-computation is often expensive.

Incremental refresh

Incrementally updating materialized views is a good solution. In incremental view maintenance strategy, the changes to base relations are used to compute the changes required to the materialized view and then updated accordingly. There are several approaches for maintaining materialized views incrementally. In incremental approaches, only those portions of the view that are affected by the changes in the relevant sources are updated. That is, a new view is computed from the existing view as and when there are changes in the base relations.

Update filtering

Usually, all the changes that have taken place at base relations may not require updating materialized views. If we find the changes that does not affect the updation of materialized views, they can be filtered instead of propagating them to the views.

Update filtering   Filtering those changes that guarantees no view updates and propagating other changes that requires view updates for view maintenance is known as update filtering.

The advantage of update filtering is that it reduces the maintenance time, thereby keeping consistency with respect to base relations changes as quickly as possible. However, this filtering concept requires some additional knowledge at data warehouse base data to identify those updates that leave the materialized views unaffected.

Self-maintenance

Consider a materialized view MV defined over a set of base relations R. Suppose R is updated with the changes, say dR. Now, to maintain consistency, the view needs to be updated by propagating these changes to the views. If the updated view can be computed using the MV and dR without depending on base relations, then the view is referred to as *self-maintainable*.

> **Self-maintenance**   A materialized view is said to be self-maintainable if it can be updated using only the view and the information related to update its underlying base relations, without access to the base relations.

Self-maintenance of materialized views usually needs some intermediate views to store additional information. That is, materialized views can be maintained without accessing the base relations by materializing and maintaining some additional views known as *auxiliary views*. Typically, the candidates for auxiliary views could be the intermediate results obtained during the generation of materialized views, because these intermediate results consist of several joins and aggregations on base relations to meet the execution of a query. This approach of creating auxiliary views is very useful when several queries have common sub-expressions.

Mohania *et al.* (2004) described an approach to derive auxiliary views based on the functional dependencies that hold on base relations, materialized views and the key participation of the base relations in the materialized view. This approach determines the optimal set of auxiliary relations to be materialized and, thus, reduces storage space and improves the efficiency of view maintenance.

The approach of materializing auxiliary relations saves on base data sources access, but it may require a large amount of data to be stored and maintained at the warehouse.

7.4 INDEXING

Materializing views is a good approach to improve the performance of query processing for predetermined queries. However, for *ad hoc* queries, the corresponding data may not be available in the materialized views and, hence, the system must look at the data warehouse database. This results in query performance degradation. Indexing is another alternate approach for improving query performance for predetermined as wells as *ad hoc* queries. Unlike materialized views, indexing does not require a large storage space. Further, detailed information can be queried using indexes. The same may not be the case with materialized views where summarized data are mostly stored.

In databases, indexing is used to quickly access the data in tables. In data warehouse environment, indexing allows accessing data with as few disk I/Os as possible, by accessing only selected records rather than accessing large number of records. That is, indexing provides localizing the data needed without looking through all the data. This improves the efficiency and performance of query processing.

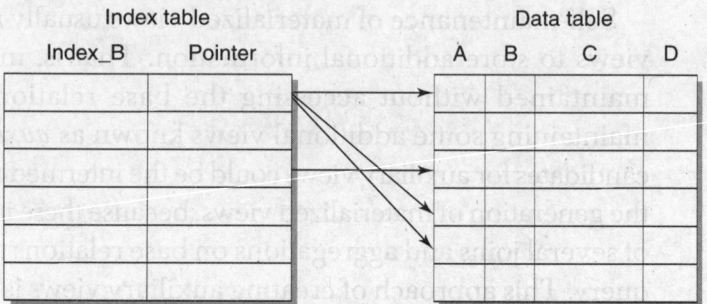

Fig. 7.6   Representing index on attribute B of data table

Index is a data structure associated with tables. Usually, an index is created either on a single attribute or multiple attributes of a table. Indexes provide a pointer to data to access it (Fig. 7.6). The two most commonly used indexing techniques in traditional database systems are B-Trees and hashing.

B-Tree   *B-Tree* (Balanced Tree) indexes maintain a list of primary keys. The indexing is also suitable for attributes that have high cardinality. These indexes are also known as *value-list indexes*. B-Tree is a tree-like structure with a root, internal nodes, and leaf nodes. The root and internal nodes point to the next level in the index, whereas the leaf nodes point to the physical data records. The structure of the B-Tree is shown in Fig. 7.7. A record can be searched by matching the primary key in the B-Tree, rather than searching the entire table. Once a matching node is found, the corresponding record is located directly using the pointer from the node to the record in the table.

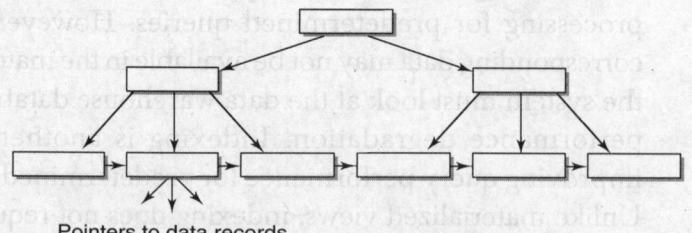

Pointers to data records

Fig. 7.7   An example of the B-Tree indexing

Example 7.4   Consider the table CUSTOMER table shown in Table 7.1. Figure 7.8 shows B-Tree indexing on Age attribute of Customer table. The leaf nodes point to the corresponding records in the CUSTOMER table.

Table 7.1 CUSTOMER Table

Cust_Id	Customer_Name	Age	Sex	Account_type	City
00027	Ravi Kumar	47	M	Savings	Delhi
00034	Prethi	28	F	Current	Hyderabad
00078	Arun	33	M	Current	Mumbai
00093	Vivek	51	M	Savings	Hyderabad
00072	Manoj	25	M	Current	Delhi
00035	Deepa	42	F	Savings	Mumbai
00095	Rani	30	F	Savings	Hyderabad
00036	Bhaskar	25	M	Current	Delhi

B-Tree indexing results in less data reads and increases efficiency in searching the record. In this scheme, the size of index is not dependent on the attribute cardinality. This scheme requires more I/O operations and page faults, as the records are fetched in the index key order rather than RIDs (Row Identifiers) order.

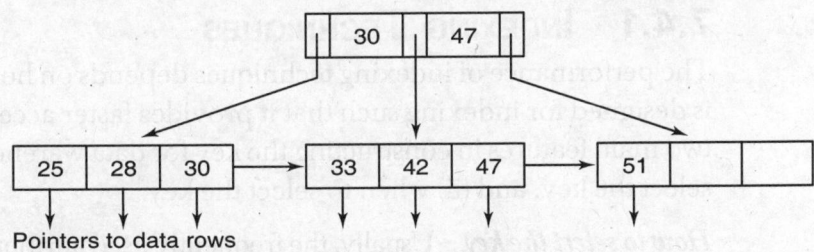

Fig. 7.8 The B-Tree indexing on age attribute of CUSTOMER table

Hashing   Hashing (or hashed indexes) technique finds the record in a table using a randomization function called *hash function*. This technique provides direct accessing the record using the hash value by computing the hash function using the primary key value of that record (Fig. 7.9).

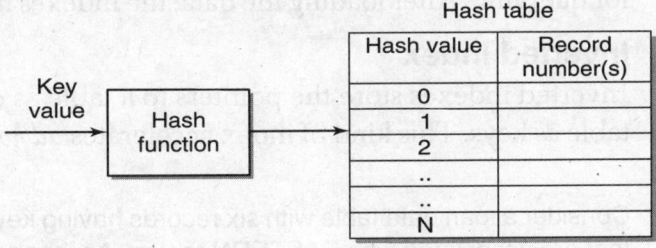

Fig. 7.9 Hashing

B-Tree hash indexing techniques are very efficient when you know exactly what you are looking for, however, they do not support *ad hoc* query requirements which are most common in data warehouses.

Example 7.5   Consider the following *ad hoc* queries

(i) Find top 20 valued customers, and

(ii) Which products give highest profit in the eastern region.

Such queries may require scanning the entire database and then computing the result. Moreover, the results may change for the same queries after a certain period of time.

These aspects suggest that more sophisticated indexing techniques are needed for data warehouses. Descriptions of indexing techniques sutiable for data warehouse environments are described below.

7.4.1   INDEXING TECHNIQUES

The performance of indexing techniques depends on how effectively the key is designed for indexing such that it provides faster accesses to the data. The two main features in constructing the key for data warehousing are: (i) how to select the key, and (ii) when to select the key.

How to select the key   Usually, the frequently used attributes for query retrieval are used for the choice of the key. Sometimes, retrieving the index itself satisfies the query results.

When to select the key   Indexing the data, when loading data into a data warehouse, degrades the performance of load. So, usually the indexes are created after the data is fully loaded into the warehouse database.

Typically, when data is being loaded into a data warehouse, it is not available for querying. After loading the data, the indexes need to be re-computed.

Inverted Index

Inverted indexes store the pointers to a table as data and the data from the table as keys. This kind of index accelerates *ad hoc* searches.

Example 7.6   Consider a loan data table with six records having key values as 10, 20, 30, 40, 50 that are associated with EASTERN region. An inverted index contains EASTERN with pointers to the records 10, 20, 30, 40, and 50.

Inverted indexes are helpful in searching the database based on the content, rather than key values (which are usually implemented as numbers). This facility enables the users to provide names instead of numbers while querying the database. Inverted indexes also support storing a lot of details. So, this indexing technique is useful to store more detailed data based on granularity requirements of an application. Finer granularity produces more detailed data.

Bitmap index

Bitmap indexing is widely used in designing data warehouses. It takes each unique value in the underlying table structure and represents the data as an array of bits (also called *bitmap vector* or simply *bitmap*). These bits are set to 1 or 0 depending on the existence of that value in a particular record.

Suppose a table has N rows and the indexing attribute has k distinct values. The bitmap indexing technique generates k bitmaps. In each bitmap, a bit is set to 1 if the attribute value in that record is present; otherwise it is set to 0. Thus, if the record j in the indexed attribute contains x, a bit j in a bitmap vector is set to 1 representing value x. In this indexing scheme, the length of the bitmap is equal to the cardinality of the indexed attribute(s).

Example 7.7 Consider the customer data shown in Table 7.1. Suppose a bitmap index is created on attribute 'Sex'. Since there are two distinct values 'M' and 'F' in the attribute, it contains two bit maps (B_M, B_F) as shown in the Figure 7.7 (a). Similarly, for the attribute 'City', the three bitmaps are shown in Figure 7.7(b).

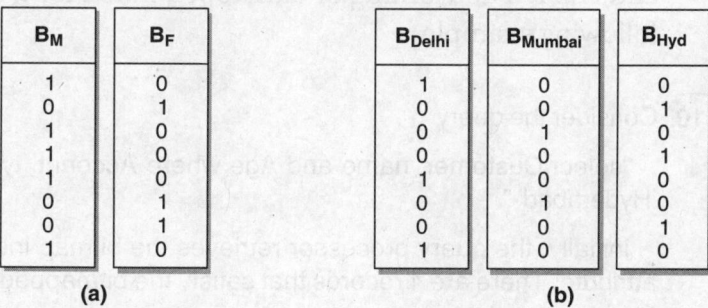

Fig. 7.10   Bitmaps for attributes (a) sex, and (b) City for the data given in Table 7.1

Example 7.8 Consider the attribute 'day-of-week'. For this attribute, there would be seven bitmap vectors, one for each day(Sunday to Saturday). The bitmap vector corresponding to Monday would have a 1 at position K if record K contains Monday in the day-of-week attribute.

Sometimes, in bitmap indexing, a series of bits are used to represent indexing. This is just another way of representing the bitmaps (concatenation of the bitmaps).

Example 7.9 Consider the data given in Table 7.1. The attribute 'Account_type' has two distinct account types, namely 'Savings' and 'Current', then two bits are needed for indexing the entire attribute. Savings account is represented as 01 and Current account is represented as 10. Similarly, for the attribute 'City', three bits are needed, 001 for Delhi, 010 for Mumbai, and 001 for Hyderabad (see Figure 7.11).

$B_{A/C\ Type}$	B_{City}
01	100
10	001
10	010
01	001
10	100
01	010
01	001
10	100

Fig. 7.11 Bitmaps for attributes account_type and city for Table 7.1

Bitmap indexing allows fast access to records based on the attribute values, by evaluating queries using bitwise logical operations, such as AND, OR, and NOT. The working of bitmapped index for a query is described in the following example.

Example 7.10 Consider the query

"select Customer_name and Age where Account_type is 'Savings' and City is 'Hyderabad'"

Initially, the query processor retrieves the bitmap indexes of the Account_type attribute. There are 4 records that satisfy the bitmapped index 01 for Account_type Savings.

Next, the processor retrieves the 3 records which satisfy the bitmap indexes for City Hyderabad. But there are only two records that satisfy the bitmap indexes for both Account_type Savings and City Hyderabad (Table 7.2).

Query processor evaluates the query by taking the bitmaps for Account_type = 'Savings' and City = 'Hyderabad' and performs a logical AND operation, resulting in two rows: <Vivek, 51> and <Rani, 30>.

Table 7.2 Query Processing Using Bitmapped Index

Account_type	City	Customer_Name	Age
→ 01	001	Ravi Kumar	47
10	→ 010	Prethi	28
10	100	Arun	33
→ 01	→ 010	Vivek	51
10	001	Manoj	25
→ 01	100	Deepa	42
→ 01	→ 010	Rani	30
10	001	Bhaskar	57

Bitmap indexing works well on different query types including range queries, join queries, and aggregation queries. It is an efficient indexing technique for low cardinality attributes (less number of distinct values) and offer significant speed. In case of high cardinality attributes, compressing techniques are mostly used. Different kind of encoding techniques, such as equality-encoded bitmap index, range encoded bitmap index, and 2-component bitmap indexes have evolved for reducing space and time requirements for fast query processing.

The advantages of Bitmap Index are:

- Very efficient for indexing on low cardinality attributes.

- Indexes can be grouped (using Boolean operations) before accessing the data.

- Occupies less space and easy to implement.

- Very efficient for aggregate queries, especially for scalar functions.

- Updating index values (such as adding new index values) is easy.

The disadvantages are:

- Less efficient for indexing on both high cardinality attributes and sparse data.

- Updating the indexing attributes is expensive. This is because of locking the bitmaps corresponding to updating records.

- Most commercial databases (such as Oracle, DB2, and Sybase) support implementation of these indexes.

Value-list index

Value-list index is an encoded scheme for bitmap indexes. This index scheme maintains two parts: Balanced Tree (B-Tree) structure and a mapping scheme that uses bitmaps. In value-list index, the bitmaps are attached to the leaf nodes of B-Tree and points to the records in the table. Note that in traditional value-list (B-tree) index, the leaf node of B-Tree contains a sequence of RIDs (Row Identifiers), each one corresponds to a distinct attribute value. Here, the RID specifies the disk position of the record. On the other hand, the value-list index for data warehouse uses bitmaps in place of RIDs. Bitmaps are more space-efficient than RID lists in a Value-List index (B-Tree).

The advantages of value-list index are:

- Very efficient for the queries that are known apriori.
- The space requirement is independent of the indexed attribute(s) cardinality.
- Individual records are locked during updation of indexed attributes and, hence, it is less expensive.

The disadvantages are:

- No *ad hoc* query support.
- Not suitable for low cardinality attribute(s).
- I/O operations are more for a large range of queries.
- Indexes cannot be grouped (unlike bitmap indexes) before accessing the data.

Projection index

Projection index is described by Neil and Quass (1997). A projection index on an attribute C in a table T consists of a stored sequence of attribute values from C in the same order as they appear in T (that is, RID order).

Projection index stores one value of C for every record and this scheme will not eliminate duplicates. Simply, the projection index on a column means a copy of a column of a table, in the same order as the table.

Example 7.11 The projection index for the attribute 'Age' of Table 7.1 is given below.

Index_Age   47, 28, 33, 51, 25, 42, 30, 25

The advantages of projection index are:

- Projection index on an attribute provides fast access to the values of that attribute without accessing the entire record and, thus, improving query performance.

- Querying on projection indexed attribute(s) reduces the query cost. The cost reduction will be more, especially for large records having more number of attributes.

The disadvantage is:

- Not efficient for the queries that require access to the attributes other than projection indexed attributes.

Note that for an index on attribute C, in the bitmap index, a 1 is placed in the corresponding bitmap vector for each row in the table, whereas in the projection index, the value in C is placed for each record in the index (see Figure 7.12).

Index_Age	B_{25}	B_{28}	B_{30}	B_{33}	B_{42}	B_{47}	B_{51}
47	0	0	0	0	0	1	0
28	0	1	0	0	0	0	0
33	0	0	0	1	0	0	0
51	0	0	0	0	0	0	1
25	1	0	0	0	0	0	0
42	0	0	0	0	1	0	0
30	0	0	1	0	0	0	0
25	1	0	0	0	0	0	0

Projection Index   Bitmap Index

Fig. 7.12 Projection index and bitmap index for the attribute 'Age' of Table 7.1

By using projection index and value-list index, some of the queries can be answered from a table without accessing the table itself.

Bit-sliced index

A bit-sliced index (BSI) is described by Neil and Quass (1997) and Chan and Ioannidis (1998). It is a set of projections of an attribute. Bit-sliced index takes an orthogonal bit-by-bit view of the same data. In this indexing scheme, if an attribute stores binary numbers, then slice their bits vertically. This can be thought of taking a projection index and slicing it into attributes of bits (Figure 7.13).

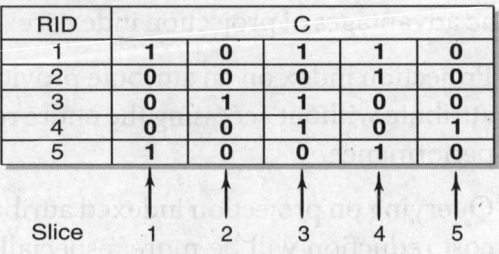

Fig. 7.13 Bit-sliced index

The advantages of bit-sliced index are:

- Uses space efficiently.
- Useful to compute aggregates by using simple base-2 arithmetic operations.
- Very efficient for large range queries.

The disadvantages are:

- Less efficient for equality queries.
- The index needs to be re-created whenever a new indexed value is added, especially when the addition runs out of bit.

Join index and star join index

Join indexes are useful when performing a query on two tables. A join index on a table involves an attribute value from different table through a commonly encountered join. That is, the join index maintains relationship between primary key and foreign key values.

In data warehouse, the data is stored in multi-dimensional form (see Chapter 6 for star schema or snow-flake schema). Using join indexing, dimensional data can be indexed to records in the fact table. They relate the values of a dimension of a star schema to rows in the fact table. The join index is created on primary keys of dimension tables and corresponding foreign keys of fact table. In a star schema (or snow-flake schema), a join index created on multiple tables is often called as *star join index*.

Bitmap join index

In bitmap join indexing, the join index is implemented as bitmaps. Multiple join indexing is carried out by performing a sequence of bitwise operations. This technique is very useful for reducing the space complexity for joining tables. The bitmap join index is such that the index creates from one table, which points the records in some other table.

Example 7.12 Consider a dimension table (Table 7.1) and a fact table (Table 7.3). Join index on attribute 'Account_type' between CUSTOMER and CUST_TRANS tables can be created as follows:

Table 7.3   CUST_FACT Table

CREATE BITMAP INDEX	Trans_Date	Cust_ID	Balance_Amount
Account_indx	01-01-2008	00027	22610
ON *CUST_FACT*	23-12-2007	00078	750
(CUSTOMER.Account_type)	05-12-2007	00093	1500
FROM *CUSTOMER*, *CUST_FACT*	14-01-2008	00072	1950
WHERE *CUSTOMER*.Cust_ID =	16-01-2008	00035	8000
Cust_TRANS.Cust_ID	08-12-2007	00095	50000

Execution of the following SQL query uses the created index on Account_type.

SELECT Time, Account_type, Balance_Amount
FROM *CUSTOMER*, CUST_FACT
WHERE *CUSTOMER*.Cust_ID = *CUST_FACT*.Cust_ID

Here, the join index on the Account_type attribute in the CUST_FACT table is built by using the Account_type attribute in the CUSTOMER table and the foreign key Cust_ID in the CUST_FACT table.

Note that CUST_FACT does not contain the Account_type attribute. The results for the above query along with the bitmapped index is shown in Table 7.4.

Table 7.4   Query Result Based on Join Bitmap Index

Time	Account_type	Amount	Bitmapped index for Account_type
01-01-2008	Savings	22610	01
23-12-2007	Current	750	10
05-12-2007	Savings	1500	01
14-01-2008	Current	1950	10
16-01-2008	Savings	8000	01
08-12-2007	Savings	50000	01

The advantages of bitmap join index, in addition to pure bitmap index, are:

- Very efficient for queries that involve joins, especially on the join indexed attributes.

- Supports star queries.

- Very efficient for OALP queries which are *ad hoc* in nature.

The disadvantage is:

- Query efficiency will depend on the order of indexed attribute values.

Clustered index

Clustered index is a kind of index that combines both index segment and data segment into one partition. This index is suitable for sequential indexes, bitmap indexes, and the leaf nodes of B-trees that contain address of the data. For instance, by the application of clustered index, the leaf nodes of B-Tree contain actual data partitions rather than addresses for the data rows. The advantage of clustered index is that it increases the speed of the queries by reducing the number of I/O's while reading data from the disk.

Further, clustered index improves the efficiency of group-by queries.

7.5 GENERAL QUERY EVALUATION

Consider the following relations:

LOAN (Loan_ID, Loan_Name, Category, Interest_Rate)
BRANCH (Branch_ID, Branch_Name, City, State)
LOANAPPROVED (Loan_ID, Branch_ID, Year, Start_Date,
End_Date, Loan_Amt)

The first attribute of each relation is a primary key for that relation. The Loan relation contains information about each loan being offered to customers. The Interest_Rate attribute contains the interest rate for a particular type of loan, such as housing, education, and car. The Branch relation contains the details of branches of the bank. The LoanApproved relation contains one tuple for every loan being sanctioned. The relations have the following characteristics.

- There are 100 loans in the loan relation, 10 of which are in the housing loan category.

- There are 100 branches in the branch relation, 10 of which are in the Delhi region.

- There are 10 years worth of loan duration LoanApproved relation, from 1997 through 2006.

- On an average, each branch sanctions each loan 20 times a year, resulting in 20,000 entries in the LoanApproved relation.

Table 7.5 shows different types of queries that are most commonly used in databases. The point queries and multipoint queries are most common in traditional database systems. However, in a data warehouse environment, most of the queries are of aggregate and range type queries, besides join type queries.

Table 7.5 Types of Queries

Type of Query	Example
Point query	SELECT Interest_Rate FROM *LOAN* WHERE Loan_ID = 36;
Multipoint query	SELECT Loan_Amt FROM *LOANAPPROVED* WHERE Branch_ID = 1952;
Aggregate query	SELECT Branch_ID, AVG(Loan_Amt) FROM *LOANAPPROVED* GROUP BY Branch_ID;
Range query	SELECT Loan_Amt FROM *LOANAPPROVED* WHERE Start_Date > "01/01/2004" and End_Date <= "31/12/2006";

7.5.1 AGGREGATE QUERY

The following example illustrates how a materialized aggregate view can be used to help in answering an aggregate query.

Suppose one wants to know how housing loans in the Delhi region have been going up or down during the last five years. This type of query, aggregating large amounts of data, is typical for a decision-support application.

Example 7.13 An aggregate SQL query to calculate the total year-wise housing loans in Delhi region by year-wise can be written as

```
SELECT Year, SUM(Loan_Amt)
FROM LOAN, BRANCH, LOANAPPROVED
WHERE LOAN.Branch_ID = BRANCH.Branch_ID
AND LOANAPPROVED.Loan_ID = LOAN.Loan_ID
AND LOANAPPROVED.Year >= 2002
AND LOAN.Category = "Housing"
AND BRANCH.State = "Delhi"
GROUP BY Year
```

Most of the OLAP queries over the cubes require aggregation of measures at some level. For 3 dimensions, there are $2^3 = 8$ granularities at which aggregation is computed. A granularity for aggregated values in the cube is referred to as a *subcube*. This is a region of the cube with smaller dimension. A cube can be represented as a set of subcubes. A d-dimensional cube has 2^d subcubes. Each subcube can be computed from the base data. Some subcubes can be directly computed from other subcubes.

An edge between two subcubes shows that one subcube can be computed from the other (see Figure 7.14). Edges are from finer to coarser granularity. The coarser granularity is specified by one attribute less than the finer one. The SQL notation for computing aggregations over cube dimensions involves several group-bys.

Figure 7.14 illustrates the expression tree corresponding to the query shown in Example 7.13. Here, each edge represents the number of tuples participated in the sub-query. The numbers shown in the figure are samples for easy understanding. We assume uniform selectivity of the selection conditions. The sizes of intermediate results are often a good predictor of query execution time, so we annotate the edge to compare the query trees before and after using the materialized view.

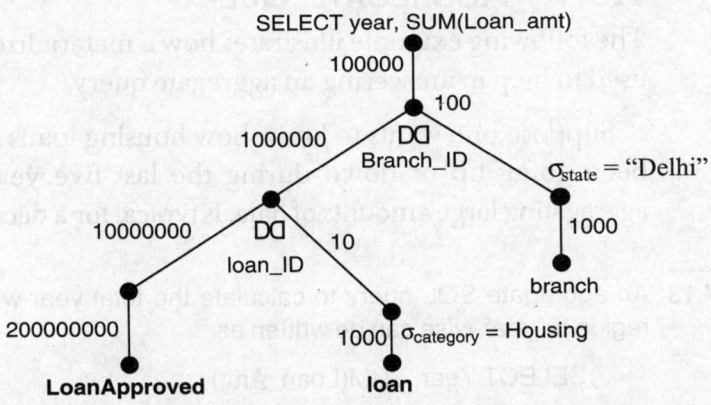

Fig. 7.14   Tree representation of the aggregate query evaluation

Single-attribute SUM aggregate queries can be evaluated using one of the following four plans (described by Neil and Quass in SIGMOD 1997):

1. Access the records directly from base table and compute the SUM.

    This plan does not worry about materialized views and indexes. However, it involves incurring more I/O cost and CPU cost for retrieving the related records and attribute values form buffer resident page.

2. Create a Projection index on the attribute and compute the SUM.

3. Create a Bitmap index on the attribute and compute the SUM.

4. Create a Bit-sliced index on the attribute and compute the SUM.

Thus, efficiency of single-attribute attributes depends on the indexing scheme that was implemented on the said attribute. Moreover, it also depends on the memory-resident of the required data for a particular query.

7.5.2 RANGE QUERY

Range partitioning maps data to partitions based on ranges of partition key values that are established for each partition. It is the most common type of partitioning and is often used with dates. For example, one might want to partition loan data into monthly partitions.

Range partitioning maps records to partitions based on ranges of attribute values. It is defined by the partitioning specification for a table or index in PARTITION BY RANGE(attribute_list) and by the partitioning specifications for each individual partition in VALUES LESS THAN(value_list). Here, attribute_list is an ordered list of columns that determines the partition to which a record or an index entry belongs. These attributes are called the *partitioning attributes*. The values in the partitioning attributes of a particular row constitute that record's partitioning key.

On the other hand, value_list is an ordered list of values for the attributes in the attribute_list. Only the clause VALUES LESS THAN (notation used in the case of Oracle database) is allowed. This clause specifies a non-inclusive upper bound for the partitions. All partitions, except the first, have an implicit low value specified by the VALUES LESS THAN literal on the previous partition. Any binary values of the partition key equal to or higher than this literal are added to the next higher partition. Keyword, MAXVALUE, represents a virtual infinite value that sorts higher than any other value for the data type, including the null value.

Example 7.14 A table, say LOANRANGE, that is range partitioned on a Start_Date field for processing range queries can be created as given below:

CREATE TABLE *LOANRANGE*

(Loan_ID NUMBER(5), Loan_Name VARCHAR2(30), Loan_Amt NUMBER(10), Start_Date DATE)

```
COMPRESS

PARTITION BY RANGE(Start_Date)

(PARTITION Sales_Jan2007 VALUES LESS
    THAN(TO_DATE('02/01/2007', 'DD/MM/YYYY')),

PARTITION Sales_Feb2007 VALUES LESS
    THAN(TO_DATE('03/01/2007', 'DD/MM/YYYY')),

PARTITION Sales_Mar2007 VALUES LESS
    THAN(TO_DATE('04/01/2007', 'DD/MM/YYYY')),

PARTITION Sales_Apr2007 VALUES LESS
    THAN(TO_DATE('05/01/2007', 'DD/MM/YYYY')));
```

Range queries can be evaluated using one of the following two plans (described by Neil and Quass in SIGMOD 1997):

1. Create the projection index on the attribute and evaluate the range predicate.

2. Create value-list index on the attribute and evaluate the range predicate.

Some queries involve both aggregate and range evaluation. These kinds of queries are known as *range-aggregate queries*.

Consider a query that finds the total loan amount for all the loan customers for top-10 cities. This query requires scanning all records and sorts the records accordingly and it is too expensive operation on a large database. The general approach to solve this kind of query is to make a guess on some attribute values. For instance, make a guess over the loan amount and then include all those values for loan amount which are less than the guessed loan amount. If the guess is correct, a single iteration is enough to fulfill the query; otherwise, try another guess until you meet the requirements.

In this approach, one should take care that the guess is not too small. One more approach to address this kind of queries efficiently is to materialize the cubes using R-Trees. The leaf nodes of the cube tree contain dimension attributes and aggregate value of measure attribute which are components of data cube records. In order to execute range aggregate queries, the aggregate function on the selected leaf nodes data will result in as output.

Example 7.15 The following table creates a table for performing a range query

        CREATE TABLE *LOANRANGE*

        (Loan_ID NUMBER(5), Loan_Name VARCHAR2(30), Loan_Amt NUMBER(10), Start_Date DATE)

        COMPRESS

        SELECT Year, SUM(Loan_Amt)

        PARTITION BY RANGE(Loan_Date)

        (PARTITION Sales_Jan2007 VALUES LESS THAN(TO_DATE('02/01/2007', 'DD/MM/YYYY')),

        PARTITION Sales_Feb2007 VALUES LESS THAN(TO_DATE('03/01/2007', 'DD/MM/YYYY')),

        PARTITION Sales_Mar2007 VALUES LESS THAN(TO_DATE('04/01/2007', 'DD/MM/YYYY')),

        PARTITION Sales_Apr2007 VALUES LESS THAN(TO_DATE('05/01/2007', 'DD/MM/YYYY')));

Another important aspect for improving query performance is online aggregation. Online aggregation is a strategy that helps the user to quickly analyse the results by providing intermediate results for an aggregate query being under processing and avoids the long waiting time for the query completion. The statistical techniques or sampling techniques play a major role in obtaining online aggregate query results.

SUMMARY

Data warehouse queries are usually complex and *ad hoc*. One of the challenges of data warehousing is to respond to the queries efficiently. Query processing can be accelerated by maintaining materialized views as well as indexes. To reduce the cost of executing aggregate queries, frequently accessed queries are often pre-computed and stored in a view. These views are called materialized views. Unlike traditional views, materialized views store the contents. The two problems with materialized views are: (i) view selection problem, and (ii) view maintenance problem.

A simple strategy for view selection problem is to materialize the views which are frequently accessed by user queries. Other strategy is to materialize the commonly shared views that are used for generating other views. Greedy algorithm and MVPP approach are described in this chapter for view selection problem.

When the data in the base relations change, the views in the warehouse can become inconsistent with the base relations. So, in order to provide consistency, materialized views need to be maintained in response to updates in the base relations of the data in views. There are two usually followed strategies: full refresh and incremental refresh. Recent works on view maintenance problem focuses on self-maintenance, where a materialized view update can be carried out using that view as well as the update transaction information without depending on underlying base relations.

Performance of queries, especially *ad hoc* queries, can be improved by providing indexes on frequently accessed columns. Bitmap indexes, join indexes, and projection indexes are most popular index implementations in data warehousing environments, and most commercial databases support these indexes. Several variations of these indexes including combinations of them are used in practice for efficient query processing. Selection of these indexes is based on the type of queries that are answered from a data warehouse. This chapter ends with a brief description on the general evaluation of different types of data warehouse queries.

EXERCISES

Test your understanding

1. How do materialized views improve the query performance? Mention the problems associated with these kind of views.

2. Deduce some heuristics to select the optimal number of materialized views.

3. Explain different approaches for view maintenance. What are the factors that have to be considered in view maintenance?

4. Compare and contrast the design indexing

schemes useful in data warehousing environment.

5. Which are the attributes suitable for bitmap indices? Characterize these attributes in terms of the cardinality of their domain of values and the type of queries on the attribute.

6. Explain the different types of queries and their efficient query processing in data warehousing.

Improve your research skills

1. Describe various solutions for View Selection and View Maintenance problems.

2. How would you determine the time to adopt new strategies for materialization and indexing?

3. There are several aggregate functions besides common aggregate functions, such as sum, max, min, avg, and count. List those classes of aggregate functions (such as distributive, algebraic, and holistic) and their significance in data warehouses.

4. Describe the most efficient index schemes for minimum, average, and count aggregate operations.

5. The problem with auxiliary views is that they also need to be maintained. Can you suggest an approach for self-maintenance of auxiliary views?

Improve the field

1. Propose mining algorithms for materialized view selection problem.

2. Explain how different indexing schemes are better suited in terms of storage and retrieval of data from data warehouses.

3. Index maintenance is also an important area in data warehousing, as the target data is large. Derive possible solutions for index maintenance.

CHAPTER 8

CASE STUDIES

Example isn't another way to teach, it's the only way to teach.
—ALBERT EINSTEIN

INTRODUCTION

Pattern discovery technologies, like most other computer science areas, are guided by the need to solve practical problems. Yet, most research papers in these areas focus on isolated algorithms rather than the development of complete systems. Ironically, it is well acknowledged that the core algorithms for pattern discovery are a very minor part (about 10%) of the entire effort of *knowledge discovery*.

In order to apply pattern discovery in real-world tasks, it is important to study the ideas and the working behind completed applications. Good case studies also inspire researchers, users, and the wider public (in case of socially beneficial applications), thus promoting the field as a whole. Moreover, they also aid in teaching, because examples are often easier to understand than abstract concepts.

Building complete applications requires computer scientists to interact closely with experts in other domains. It is imperative for computer scientists to immerse themselves and not to stay aloof, expecting domain experts to provide well-defined problem statements. This is a challenging but rewarding effort.

In this chapter, we describe five case studies that showcase the potential of pattern discovery technologies. These case studies cover a range of technologies from data warehousing, OLAP, and data mining. Case studies 1–3 are related to data warehousing and OLAP for the domains of telecom industry, fast-food industry, and banks, respectively. Case studies 4–5 are related to data mining. Case study 4 identifies customer churn (i.e. unsatisfied customers who leave) from banks. Finally, Case study 5 identifies intruders into a computer system.

8.1 STUDY 1: TELECOM CONTENT WAREHOUSE

This study describes the creation and working of a data warehouse for a telecom company. This data warehouse consolidates content from different channels – private, public, and operators.

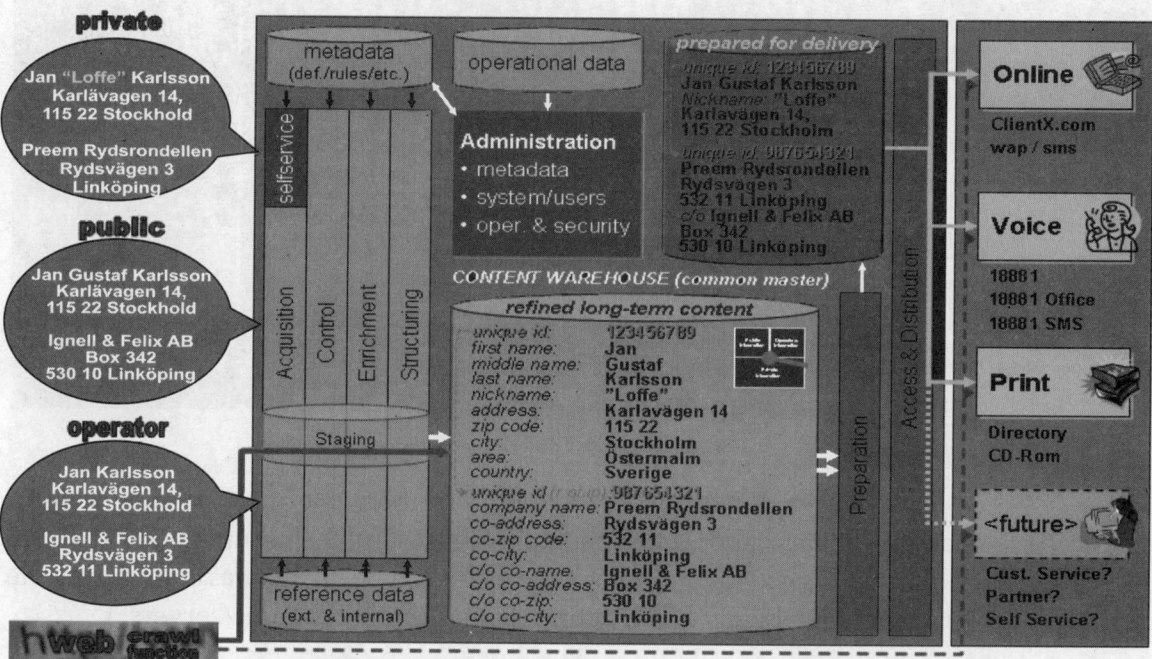

Fig. 8.1 Requirements for the case of basic content processing

8.1.1 SOLUTION ARCHITECTURE

Figure 8.2 shows the *Content Warehouse Framework* that depicts the key functions to be supported by a highly modular, component-based architecture. The project required extreme care to be taken in data cleansing and data integrity, before the transactions are loaded into the content data warehouse. Audit trail (control checks, $ checks, call duration checks) were to be implemented with utmost precision. The project team conceptualized a process framework for data quality management that comprised 3 major processes: viz. creation, maintenance, and delivery of data to the data warehouse. The Solution's conceptual architecture was designed to provide for data profiling in order to ensure uniformity of data acquisition; data quality was further enhanced with advanced cleaning techniques (noise removal, duplicate suppression, etc.).

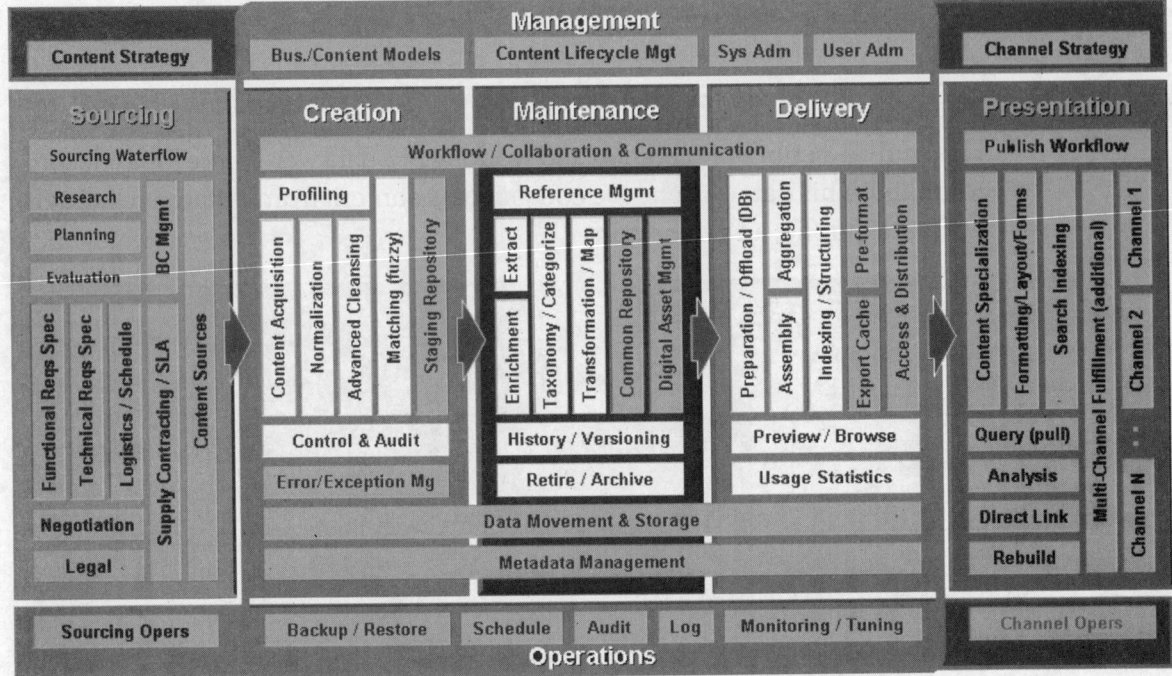

Fig. 8.2 Content Warehouse Framework

Data referencing or master data management was implemented so as to maintain linkage across information irrespective of their sources. Dimensional data was designed to capture change history (type 3); this was considering the huge backlog of daily ETL routines from different regions/servers.

The project sponsor also insisted on capturing data usage information from the new content data warehouse. To address this requirement, which served the purpose of rolling up ROI, the Solution Architecture provided for usage statistics data mart. This usage data mart captured details pertaining to user/user groups, type of information delivered (bulk load/report, etc.), subject area for which data was delivered, etc. This would facilitate analysis of various patterns in usage by different business units/functions within the telecom company and the most used features.

8.1.2 Technical Architecture

The technical architecture for the project is shown in Fig 8.3. The key consideration in technical architecture (extension of Solution Architecture) was to maintain parity in tools and provide for seamless integration of metadata across layers. Use of same set of tools across technical jobs ensured high level of data integrity. Four sets of ETL/Data Cleansing/OLAP tools were evaluated for comparison and the key consideration was the need to structure the tools within the same family of tools, so that metadata interfaces and operational integration are streamlined.

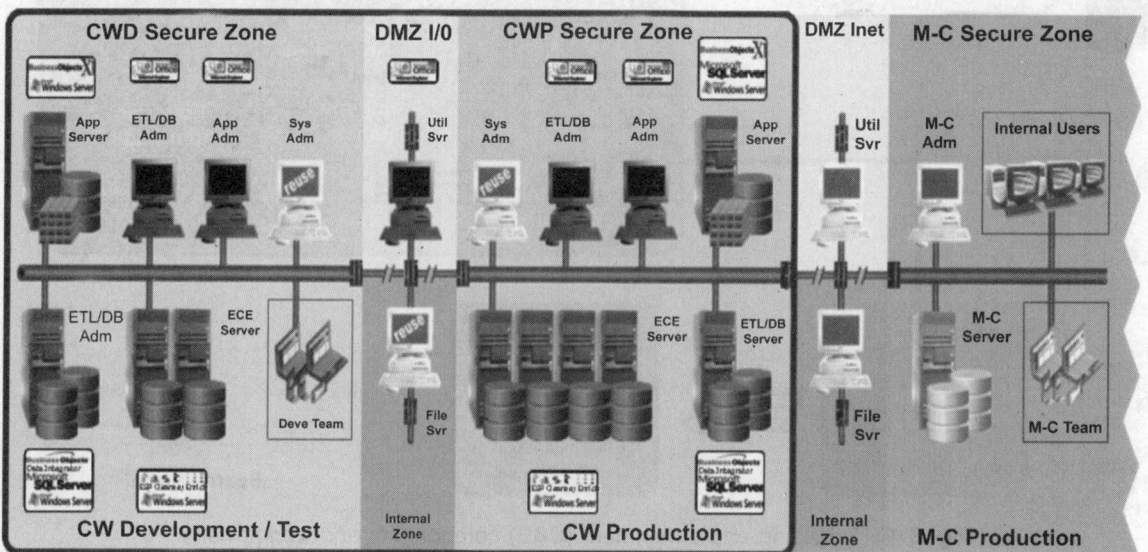

Fig. 8.3   Technical architecture

The key characteristics of the technical architecture are:

- High performance and availability, persistently reliable operations

- Easy integration with other systems, especially in regards to content capture and distribution

- Rich functionality, intuitive, GUI-based, and user-friendly tools

- Flexible handling of various content types and historical content over many years

- Cost efficient solution in regards to both development and maintenance

8.1.3   CONTENT CLEANSING AND ENRICHMENT

Data cleansing was a very critical and large component of the ETL processes; the cleansing engine fed the selective data elements through an external search portal; the rule engine for data cleansing was automated (Figure 8.4). Enterprise Search Platform (ESP) tool is used for data cleansing (data search).

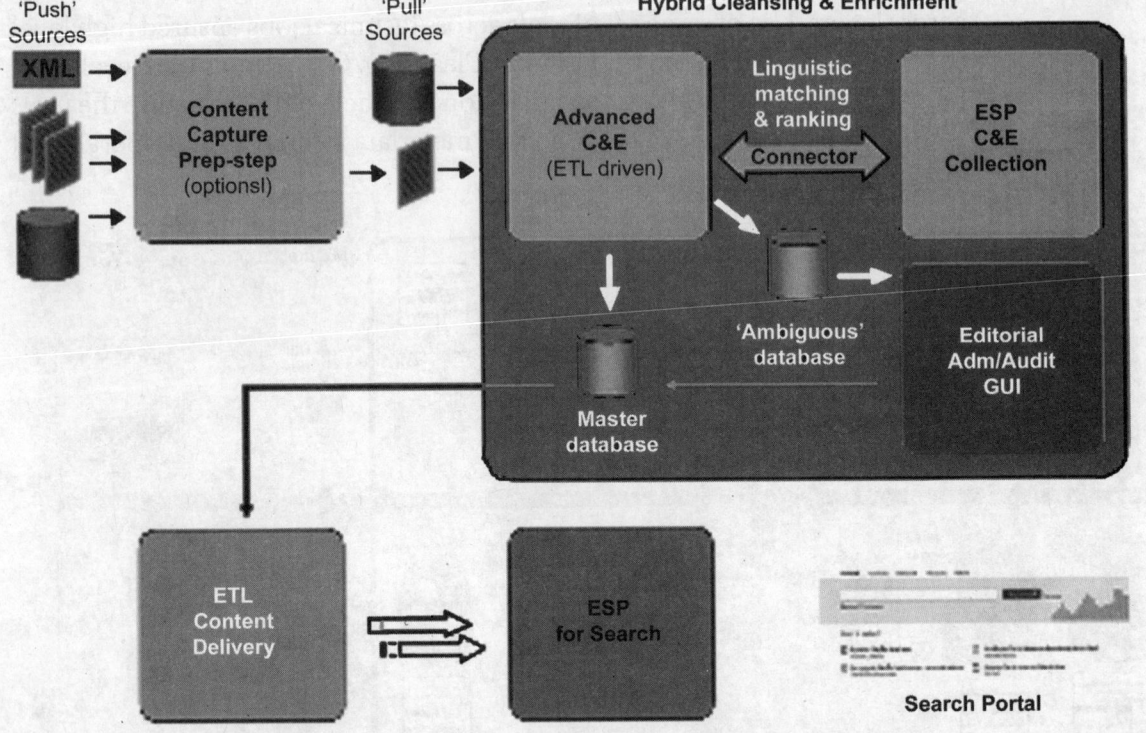

Fig. 8.4 Cleansing and enrichment (C&E) components and workflows

The key components of cleansing and enrichment engine are:

- Content capture prep-step – Fetching data from multiple sources and controlling the interaction.

- ETL tool: Advanced C&E engine – Runs the logic of the cleansing and enrichment process

- ETL-ESP Connector – Looks up to ESP for fuzzy matching and writes clean data back to ESP Content APIs

- ESP: C&E Collection – Linguistic data cleansing functionality (multiple algorithms) and contextual relevancy framework (scope-fields)

Content capture prep-step (Fig. 8.5) extends the ETL functionality on complex data acquisition to provide the following features:

- Connects to multiple file locations for file access

- Listens and triggers on new-file-event to push content or work on 'timer'

- Retries on intervals if the file is not present when expected

Data feed

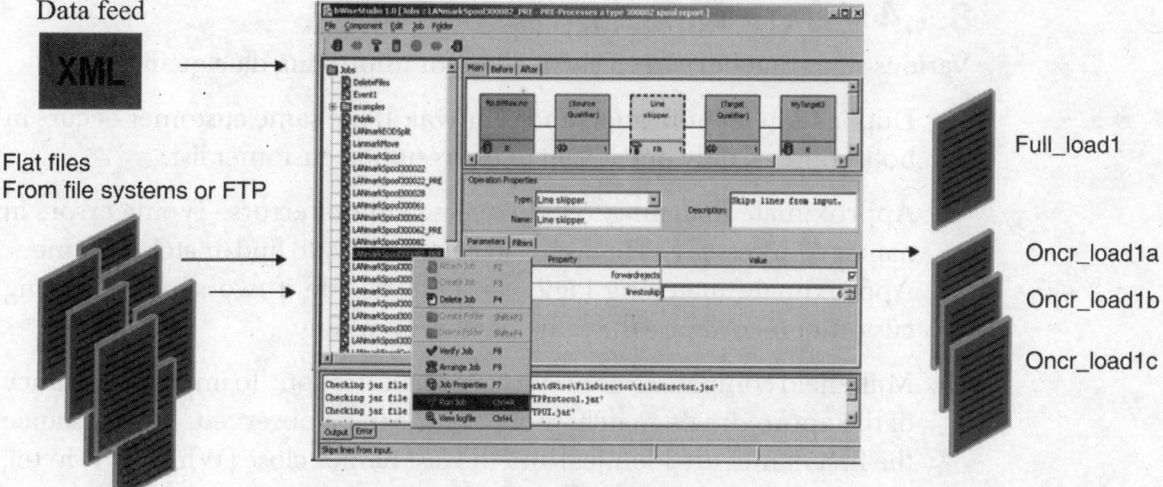

Flat files
From file systems or FTP

Full_load1

Oncr_load1a
Oncr_load1b
Oncr_load1c

Fig. 8.5 Content capture prep-step

- Supports incrementally changing file naming conventions
- Checking for file format compliance
- Logistics to check for duplicate file transmissions
- Guaranteeing one and only one delivery per file

The ETL-ESP connector builds a query string and sends it to ESP to read the results. The queries are of the type of dynamic/content-driven queries and dynamic rank-profile selection. The connector also prepares an N-Gram for matching and de-normalizes the top-N hits.

The Engine for Linguistic Matching and Contextual Scoping does free text search; identify fields that have been misused (such as first-name in surname field, etc); multi-field compare (such as If Name AND Address AND Gender match; then …); N-Gram matching for fuzzy or approximate match (N-Gram distance is computed based on how many N-Grams are common with respect to the total); Levinstein Edit Distance (how many changes must be done in order to make two strings identical/equal – for example, L(beWise,bWise) = 1, one remove 'e' operation) to ignore minor errors; phonetic search to match on vocal similarity; character-set normalization; scope search for better accuracy; support for proper-spelling dictionaries and support for Synonyms to cover known variants.

8.1.4   DATA QUALITY

Various steps that have been carried out for improving data quality are:

1. Duplication identification and removal: If the same customer occurs in both sources, only one is sent to the resulting customer list.

2. Approximate matching to help oversee minor errors: Typing errors in names or adresses will break a database's ability to find/match customers. Approximate matching logic can help decide if two similar–looking customer records are the same person/company.

3. Multi-field compare to ensure secure identification: To improve accuracy of the approximate match, more fields can be observed. If for instance the first names are identical and the last names close (White vs Whyte), an identical address-field can help decide.

4. Tunable relative importance of each field: When using multi–field compares, some fields (name fields) are considered more important than others (the zip code).

5. Spell checking and error correction included: Checking towards a 'thesaurus' of names, errors can be detected and corrected. When matching two close (similar looking) names, doubt situations can be determined by our 'correct names' list.

6. Private attributes from either source are merged to a super-set:

   If Source A contains the fields ID, Name, Address, Status AND

   Source B contains the fields ID, Name, Address, Zip THEN

   the result can contain ID, Name, Address, Status, Zip

Given below is the sample logic elements used for a cleansing process:

- N-Grams to score two strings on similarity
- Levinstein algorithms for 'edit distance'
  - Calculates the difference between strings (names), capable of overlooking minor errors.
  - James Miller = James K. Miller , Adrian = Ardian
- Phonetic match
  - Calculates an integer from the strings, and matches on 'sound-alikes'

- ▪ Christin = Kristin, Nygaard = Nygård, Schwupp = Svupp
- • 'Charset' normalization
  - ▪ Anérudd = Anerudd, Jürgen = Jurgen, etc. For multinational chars and name combinations
- • Scope fields
  - ▪ Finds the contextual relevancy in a scope, for example, 'Person' vs. 'Address'.
  - ▪ Dictionaries in Query pipeline to support 'proper spelling'

In this work, FAST data cleansing is used for data normalization. This toolset uses linguistic analysis to create a cleansed master data index, helping businesses more quickly develop accurate search and business intelligence solutions. Moreover, FAST data cleansing combines ETL technology for data extraction and integration with the linguistic analysis and fuzzy matching technology in FAST ESP to clean the data.

This study mainly focuses on describing the solution and technical architecture for building a data warehouse for a telecom company. The process of ETL carried out is also described in detail and listed are the various steps which are taken for the purpose of handling data quality issues.

8.2 STUDY 2: OLAP FOR THE FAST FOOD INDUSTRY

This case study describes the design and implementation of a data warehouse for a fast food company conducted by Exclusive Ore Inc. The fast food industry is highly competitive and a small change in operations can have a significant impact. The goal is to provide quick access to comprehensive information for both standard and on-demand reporting. This data warehouse provides strategic and tactical *decision support* to all levels of management are listed.

The data warehouse is implemented in Microsoft SQL Server 2000, and incorporates data from two principal sources:

- ▪ Daily sales information.
- ▪ Period based accounting information from the accounting database.

This data is automatically refreshed periodically (or on-demand if required) and is maintained historically over several years for comparative purposes.

Six OLAP cubes were created for reporting and analysis purposes, which are accessed through Excel. OLAP operations such as slicing and dicing are used to analyse the data by store, by company, by zone and area, by accounting year, quarter and period, and by brand and concept. The six cubes that were used to analyse the data are as given below:

1. PL Cube: Used to analyse Profit & Loss and Cash Flow data. Amounts can be viewed for any period, and can be compared across budgets.

2. BS Cube: Used to analyse the Balance Sheet data. Balances can be viewed for any period, and can be compared to the preceding period or the corresponding period in the prior year.

3. SalesMix Cube: Used to analyse daily sales of all menu items in all stores. This cube computes sales amounts, and counts costs and variance from list price.

4. SalesDayPart Cube: Used to analyse sales data in terms of amounts, and counts at 15 minute intervals.

5. SalesOps Cube: Used to analyse sales summary data by each store. Many amounts can be viewed optionally as variances, as a percent of sales, or summarized as week-to-date, period-to-date, year-to-date, or rolling 52-week amounts.

6. ReportCard Cube: Used to analyse the daily report card amounts. Some of these are also in the SalesOps cube. In addition, the Report Card contains speed-of-service and peak–hour information.

Analysis can also be carried out *across* cubes.

The data warehouse and the resulting OLAP cubes facilitate investigation along the corporate hierarchies, such as by operating company, by zone or area, or by brand or concept. This enables comparisons between concepts, say, or of all stores within a concept. Similarly, it is easy to do area-to-area comparisons, or zone-to-zone comparisons, or to view the performance of all stores within an area.

8.3 STUDY 3: PROTOTYPE CREDIT DATAMART FOR A BANK

Building a data warehousing and business intelligence system is a complex business and engineering effort. There are significant technical challenges to overcome in successfully deploying a data warehouse. Prototype datamart development is the first viable, full-functioned data warehouse and business intelligence platform to be offered at a price that will make data warehousing and business intelligence available to a broad set of organizations.

This case study is on developing a prototype for Credit Datamart for a bank in India. The datamart has been designed mainly to serve as a decision support system. The primary purpose of the datamart is to perform fast calculations with ease and do modeling over important business metrics.

The datamart will make the data available in a format, which is suitable for On-Line Analytical Processing using the dimensional modeling. The dimensional modeling provides for high query performance and user comprehension. A dimension may be thought of as major perspective, entity, and factor or as an important business metric. For example, in the credit datamart, the dimensions are Borrowers, Account Type, Time, Branch, Constitution, Caste, Area, Activity, etc.

In this case study, MS-SQL Toolkit is used for developing the prototype datamart. Data Transformation Services (DTS) of this toolkit provides the functionality to import, export, and transform data between Microsoft SQL Server and any OLE DB, ODBC, or text file format. Packages are the main objects of DTS. Each DTS package defines one or more tasks to be executed in a coordinated sequence. The DTS package can be created manually by using a language that supports OLE Automation, such as Microsoft Visual Basic, or interactively by using the DTS wizards or DTS designer. Microsoft SQL Server OLAP services is a new middle-tier server for online analytical processing (OLAP). The OLAP services server constructs multidimensional cubes of data for analysis and provides rapid client access to cube information. PivotTable Service, the included OLE DB compliant provider, is used by Microsoft Excel and applications from other vendors to retrieve multidimensional data from the server and present it to the user.

Users can query the cube data by just drag and drop the dimensions from the dimension pane to the cube grid. Any measure can be analysed with any dimension. This cube was very user-friendly and delivers key features of OLAP, such as slice and dice, drill-down, and multiple graphical views. MS-OLAP provides cube browser, an easy interface to analyse the cube. MS Excel 2000 was chosen as a front-end for the cube. Users can interactively change the Dimensions and Measures from his/her view for analysis and reporting. MS Excel 2000 provides pivot charts to represent the graphical view of OLAP data. These graphs will change automatically when the user changes Dimensions and Measures.

8.3.1 CREDIT DATAMART

Subject area identification is the initial task carried out to find OLAP entities. The following are the (sub-)subject areas identified. Each subject area has its own characteristics.

- **Borrower**
  Borrower category
  Borrower sub category
  Borrower relation
  Caste
  Community
  Constitution of borrower
- **Bank**
  Head office
  Regional office
  Branch office
- **Designation**
- **Guarantor**

- **Facility**
  Facility category
  Facility code
- **Purpose**
- **Sanction**
  Sanctioning authority
  Nature of sanction
- **Scheme**
- **Security**
  Security code
  Security nature
  Security value
- **Sector**
  Sector category
- **Interest Rate**

These subject area attributes are candidates for Dimensions. Numeric values, which are measurable, are candidates for Measures. There is a date field available in existing system database. This field was chosen as Time Dimension. Following are the selected Dimensions and Measures for the Credit Datamart:

Dimensions

Category	Interest	Branch Name	Facility
Loan No	Gender	Scheme	Time

Measures

Sanction Amount
Recovery Amount
Disburse Amount

The following two Dimensions have hierarchies.

Time

Year	Month
Quarter	Day

Branch

Region
Branch Name

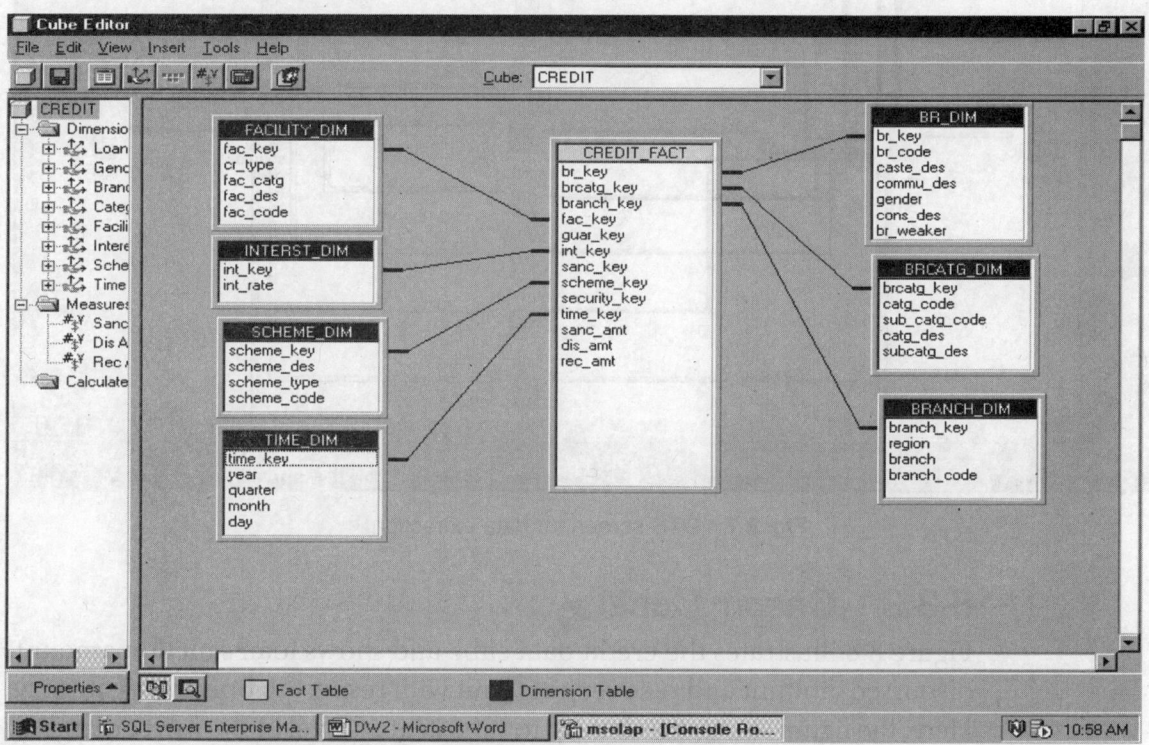

Fig. 8.6 Star schema for credit DataMart using MS-SQL

Using the above information, star schema was designed to facilitate multidimensional analysis. Transaction level granularity was chosen, because very less amount of transaction data is available for this prototype. Figure 8.6 represents a star schema for the Credit Datamart

8.3.2 PHYSICAL DATAMART DESIGN

Dimension and fact tables were created in MS-SQL Server 7.0. A DTS package was created in MS-SQL Server 7.0 DTS. This package was designed to transform data from source database to Dimension tables and Fact table. This package was scheduled to extract data from source system in periodic intervals. Figure 8.7 represents a DTS package for the Credit Datamart.

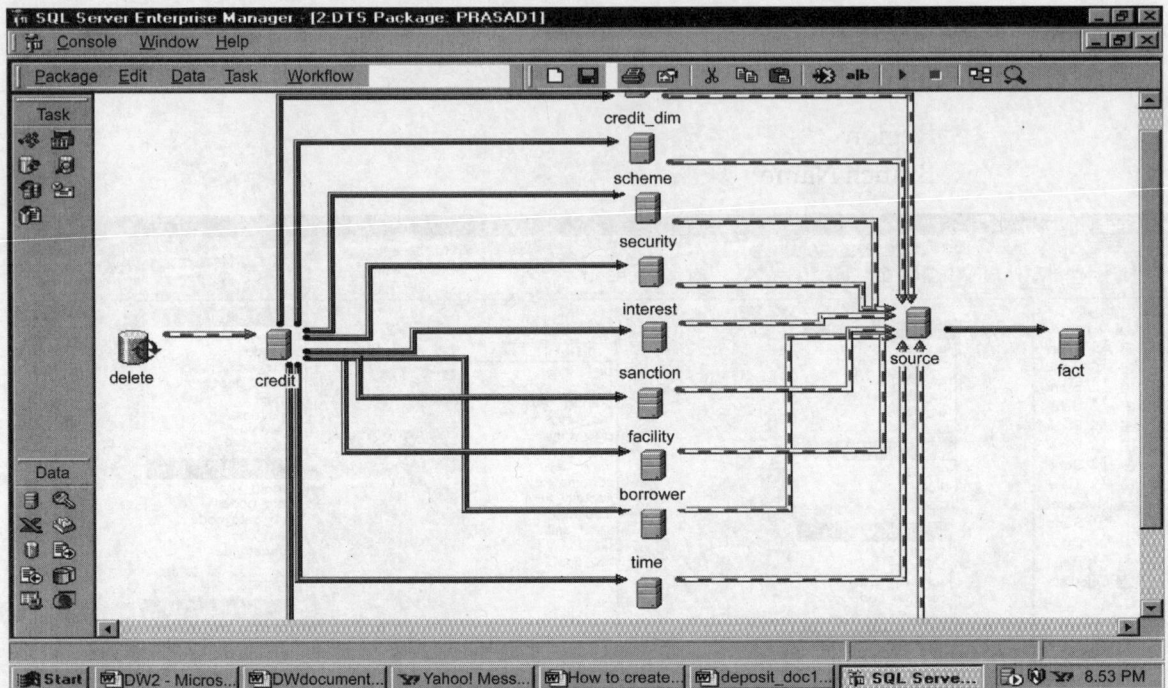

Fig. 8.7   DTS screen for data extraction

8.3.3   CREDIT CUBE

Figure 8.8 illustrates the credit data cube and shows loan sanction amount, disbursed amount and recovery amount with respect to borrower category. Here, the figure shows the data up to subcategory level of Borrower category. The user can refine his query by selecting one of the desired values from the combo boxes, which contain Dimension values. The + sign on the left of Dimension value indicates that it is a hierarchical Dimension. By clicking on the plus sign, the user can get the detailed data (drill-down) with respect to the category (for example, agriculture category).

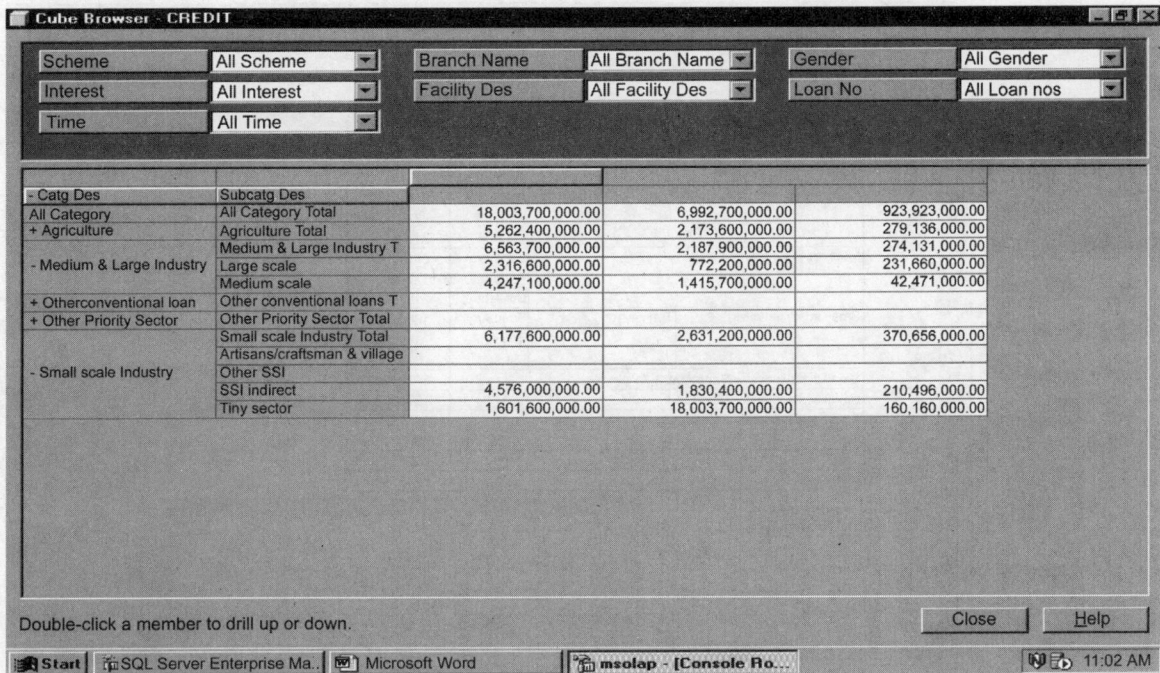

Fig. 8.8 Credit data cube

Figure 8.9 shows Credit cube data on MS Excel 2000 spreadsheet . MS Excel uses pivot table to browse OLAP data on Excel spreadsheet. The user can change his query by removing one or more Dimensions from spreadsheet layout. To remove a Dimension, the user has to drag the Dimension from spreadsheet layout and drop it on pivot table. To add a Dimension to the lay out, drag a Dimension from pivot table and drop it on the desired axis of the spreadsheet layout. To refine query, the user has to click on the down arrow of the desired dimension on the layout, select the Dimension value, and then click OK.

Figure 8.10 illustrates graphical representation of Fig. 8.9 data. Any changes in the data of this graph will reflect at the corresponding spreadsheet. To refine query, the user has to click on the down arrow of the desired dimension on the layout, select the Dimension value, and then click OK. To find percentage of one part of the above pie chart, place the cursor on the desired part, a tooltiptext will appear showing percentage of that part of data.

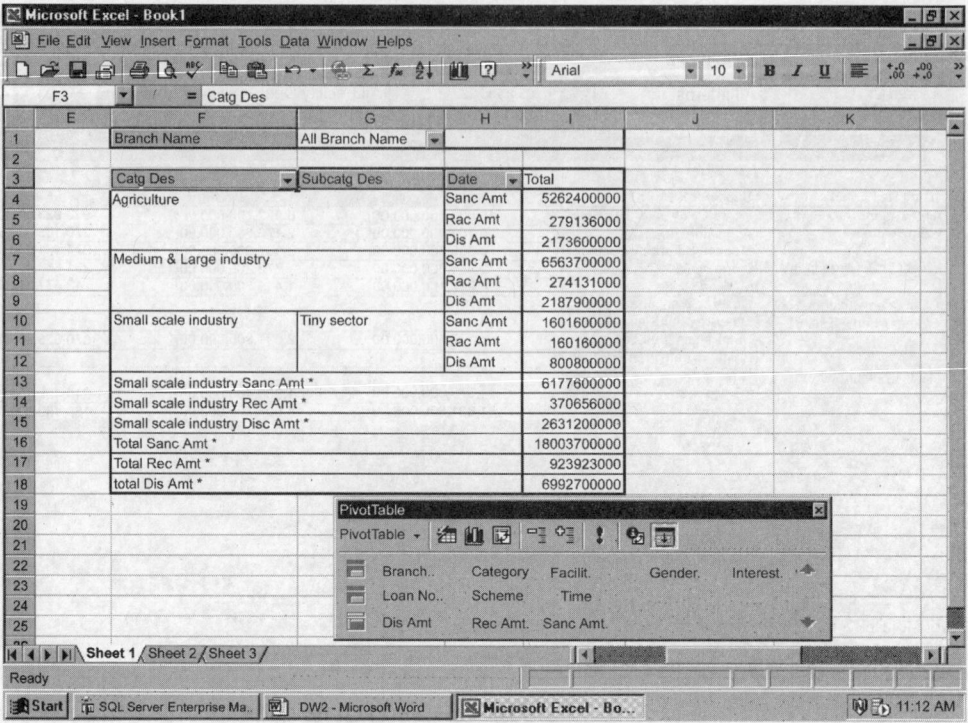

Fig. 8.9   Pivot tablet

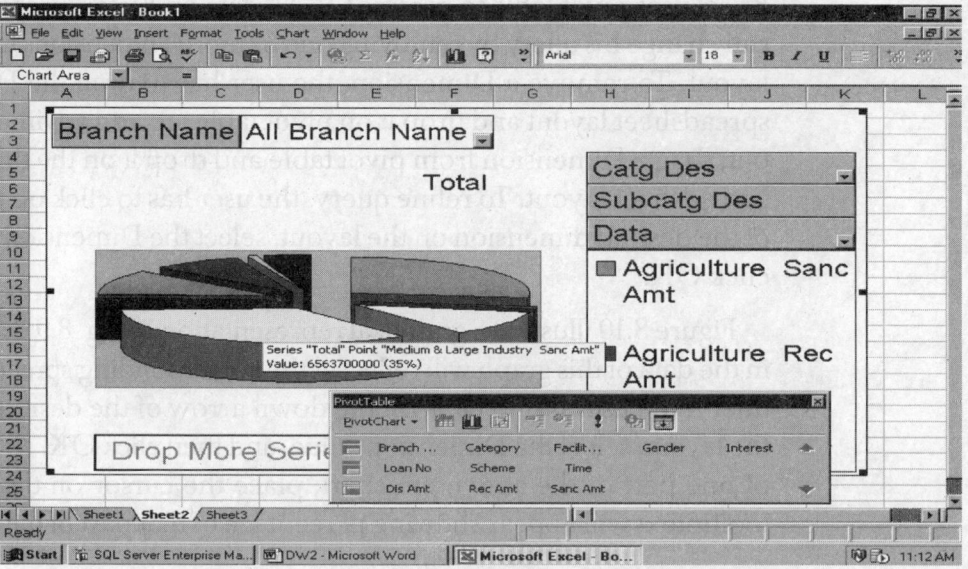

Fig. 8.10   Graphical representation of Fig. 8.9 data

Beginning with a description of importance of data warehouse for a bank, this Credit DataMart case study walked through the details of creating the target dimensional model, identifying facts and dimensions, designing and building the reports and drawing graphs. It can be noted that all of these steps tie back to the business requirements. The Datamart allows the user to do different kinds of statistical, financial analysis and also has a very sophisticated, inbuilt analytical tool which allows the user to do rigorous analysis online. Every point describes the practical steps in the context of the MS-SQL Server platform.

8.4 STUDY 4: CHURN MODELING FOR A BANK

One of the prominent concerns being faced by the banks is to retain the customers. This case study focuses on building a predictive data mining model to carry out the churn analysis.

High cost of customer acquisition and customer education requires companies to make large upfront investments on customers. However, due to easy access to information and a wide range of offerings, it is easier than ever before for customers to switch between service providers - be it in the area of banking, mortgages, telecom or insurance. Customer churn – the propensity of customers to cease doing business with a company in a given time period, has become a significant problem and is one of the prime challenges financial institutions worldwide are learning to face. Studies reveal that retaining a customer is much easier before the customer has slipped into active or passive attrition.

8.4.1 DATASET DESCRIPTION

The data pertaining to demographic and transactional (psycho graphic) details was collected from one of the banks in India which consisted of 19,000 customers' records. However, analysing bank databases for customer behaviour prediction is difficult due to the data being distributed over bank databases with multitude of dimensions. Hence, to conduct the study, four separate databases namely, 'general ledger (GL)', 'customer information (CUST)', 'transactional detail (TL)' and 'closed Account (CLOSE)' were considered. Data preprocessing and transformation steps were performed and 1086 customers' details were randomly sampled. The data set contained 23 attributes from which 7 attributes namely, gender, age, amount balance, transaction count, Bank duration, average monthly transaction, and status (Table 8.1) were used. The database of 1086 customers consisted of 704 active accounts (64.8% of the data set), 203 dormant accounts (18.6% of the data set), and 179 closed accounts (16.6% of the data set).

Table 8.1 Attribute description

Variables	Data Type/Range	Description
Gender_Code	0,1	0 if Female, 1 if Male.
Age	Integer	Account owner's age.
Amount_Balance	Real	The balance present in the account.
Transaction_Count	Integer	The total number of transactions by done the customer.
Bank_Duration	Real	The duration since the customer is associated with the bank.
Avg._monthly_Transaction	Real	The ratio of the transaction count and bank duration.
Status	0,1,2	0 if Active, 1 if Dormant, 2 if Closed.

8.4.2 MODELING

Churn model in this case study is based upon techniques used for classification, since the target variable is a discrete value. 'Status of the customer' field with three values, namely active, dormant, closed, is designated as the target variable. The database is divided into the learning data sample and test data sample in the ratio of 7:3 keeping the same proportion of target variable.

For this case study, CART decision tree is employed in order to build the churn model to help one identify the sub-segments of the customer base that is likely to churn away, providing a well-identified segment to target with retention programs. Figure 8.11 shows the schematic diagram of classification process for churn modeling. We used Gini concentration coefficients to summarize power curves of prediction.

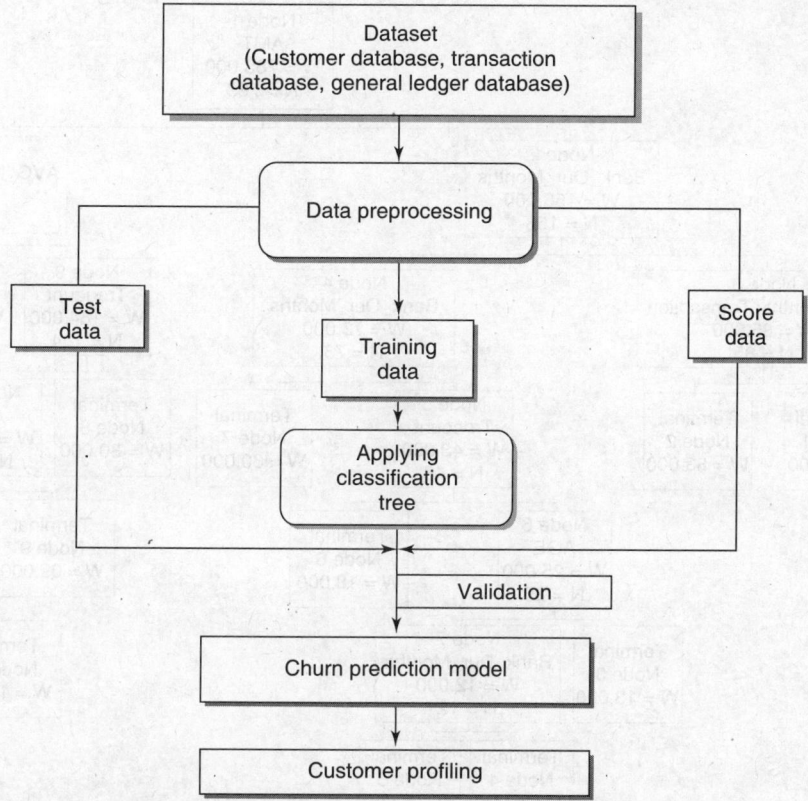

Fig. 8.11 Schematic diagram of churn modeling

Customer's status is taken as target variable while balance amount, average monthly transaction, duration since association with the bank: total transaction count, education, age and gender are the predictor variables. The resultant classification tree is displayed in Figure 8.12.

8.4.3 EXPERIMENTAL RESULTS

Table 8.2 displays the prediction success and the resultant confusion matrix for the training data set. The predictive validity of the model was performed on a hold out test sample of customers, which revealed that our model is competent and consistent on the majority of predictions. Model testing gave an estimate of model accuracy. The test operation accepts the name of the previously built model and data for testing the model. The test data with 324 records conforms to the logical data specification used for building the model. Table 8.3 displays the prediction success and the resultant confusion matrix for the training data set. The confusion matrix provides the basis for the coefficients for the churn management model.

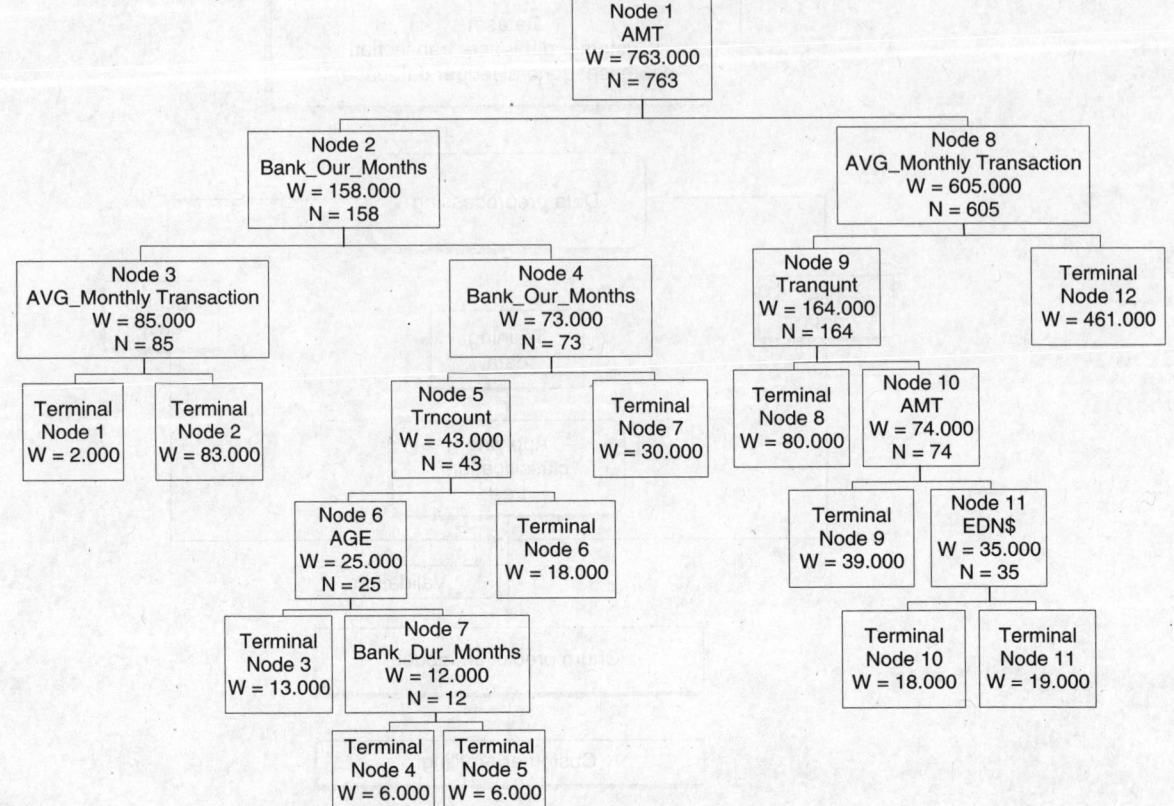

Fig. 8.12   Classification tree

Table 8.2   Prediction success and confusion matrix for learning data

Actual class	Total cases	Percent correct	Predicted class (0)	Predicted class (1)	Predicted class (2)
0	493	90.872	448	34	11
1	143	81.82	19	117	7
2	127	96.85	0	4	123

Table 8.3   Prediction success and confusion matrix for test data

Actual class	Total cases	Percent correct	Predicted class (0)	Predicted class (1)	Predicted class (2)
0	211	60.66	128	70	13
1	60	78.33	7	47	6
2	52	96.15	1	1	50

The relatively lower prediction success rate of active customers is because some of them exhibit the traits of dormant and churned customers, and it is these customers on which the bank has to employ churn prevention technique. After a model is built, model validation is employed to compute the accuracy of a model's predictions when the model is applied to a new data set. Scoring is done which is the application of a supervised learning model to data results in scores or predictions with an associated probability. When scoring was done on the classification model using the test data set, 70% accuracy was observed and also CART yielded 12 *if–then rules* of which seven have sufficient number of cases to be used as *rules of thumb*.

This case study demonstrates churn modeling in the context of Indian banking industry. In this study, behavioural profiles for defectors are identified using the if-then rules, which enable the bank to form an early warning system for churn prevention, considering that the customers exhibiting similar behaviour to defectors are also likely to churn. The study is based on predictive modeling using data mining to predict churn rate of personal banking customers.

8.5 STUDY 5: INTRUSION DETECTION USING kNN CLASSIFICATION

Intrusion detection is the process of monitoring and analysing the events occurring in a computer system in order to detect signs of security breaches. Data mining techniques are useful for intrusion detection.

8.5.1 ABOUT IDS

Intrusion Detection Systems (IDS) are classified mainly into two: (i) misuse-based, and (ii) anomaly-based. Misuse-based is also called signature-based. Misuse-based method uses specifically known patterns of unauthorized behaviour to predict and detect similar attempts. On the other hand, anomaly-based intrusion detection systems are designed to uncover abnormal patterns of behaviour. In this method, IDS establishes a baseline of normal usage patterns and anything that widely deviates from it gets flagged as a possible intrusion. This work mainly focuses on anomaly-based intrusion detection.

8.5.2   kNN CLASSIFICATION

Classification algorithms help in predicting future trends as well as extracting a model of important data classes. In this work, kNN classification algorithm is used to design a classifier for intrusion data. Here, each intrusion is considered as a sequence of system calls, and sequence information is extracted by selecting sub-sequences.

kNN classification algorithm does not make a classifier in advance. Whenever a new data sequence (or stream) comes, kNN finds the k near neighbours to new data sequence from training data set using some distance/similarity metric. These k samples are known as the k nearest neighbours of the new sample. The new sample is assigned the most common class of its k nearest neighbours. In the nearest neighbour model, choice of a suitable distance function and the value of the members of nearest neighbours (k) are very crucial.

8.5.3   SUB-SEQUENCES

Sub-sequences of fixed sizes: 1, 2, 3… are considered for this study. This fixed size sub-sequence is called the *window*. This window is slided over the traces of system calls to find the unique sub-sequences of fixed lengths over the whole dataset. A frequency count of each sub-sequence is recorded. For example, consider the sequence given below, which consists of the traces of system calls.

execve open mmap open mmap mmap mmap mmap mmap open mmap exit

| *execve open mmap open mmap mmap mmap mmap mmap open* |

Sliding window of size 3

Unique sub-sequences with their frequencies for the above sequence are computed as given below:

execve open mmap	1	*mmap open mmap*	2
open mmap open	1	*mmap mmap open*	1
open mmap mmap	1	*open mmp exit*	1
mmap mmap mmap	3		

These encoded frequencies for sub-sequences are useful in order to apply any vector-based distance/similarity measure.

8.5.4 DARPA 98 IDS DATASET

DARPA 98 IDS dataset consists of TCPDUMP and BSM audit data. The network traffic of an Air Force Local Area Network was simulated to collect TCPDUMP and BSM audit data. The audit logs contain seven weeks of training data and two weeks of testing data. There were 38 types of network-based attacks and several realistic intrusion (*abnormal*) scenarios conducted in the midst of *normal* background data. For experimental purpose, 605 unique processes were used as a training dataset, which were free from all types of attacks. Testing was conducted on 5285 normal processes. In order to test the detection capability, 55 intrusive sessions are incorporated into the test data.

8.5.5 DISTANCE/SIMILARITY MEASURES

Experiments are conducted on DARPA 98 IDS dataset with the following three distance/simlairty measures:

$$\text{Jaccard similarity: } S(X, Y) = \frac{|X \cap Y|}{|X \cup Y|}$$

where, X and Y are two distinct sets.

$$\text{Cosine similarity: } S(X, Y) = \frac{X \cdot Y}{|X| \, |Y|}$$

where, X and Y are two distinct vectors.

$$\text{Euclidean distance: } D(X, Y) = \left[\sum_{s=1}^{n} (X_s - Y_s)^2 \right]^{1.2}$$

where, X and Y are two vectors.

Here, all the normal data serves as the training dataset. In testing phase, whenever a new process P comes to the classifier, it looks for the presence of any new sub-sequence of size s. If a new sub-sequence is found, the new process is marked as abnormal. When there is no new sub-sequence in the new process P, calculate the similarity of new process with all the sessions. If similarity between any session in training set and new process is equal to 1, mark it as normal. In other case, pick the k highest values of similarity between new process P and training dataset. From this k maximum values, calculate the average similarity for k-nearest neighbours. If the average similarity value is greater than user defined theresheld value (t), mark the new proccss P as normal, else mark P as abnormal.

8.5.6   EXPERIMENTAL RESULTS

For kNN classification experiments, $k = 5$ was considered. Experiments are carried out, with the distance/similarity measure (Jaccard similarity measure, Cosine similarity measure, and Euclidean distance measure) at different subsequence lengths (sliding window size) $L = 1, 3, 5$. Here, $L = 1$ means that no sequential information is captured whereas, for $L \geq 1$ some amount of order information across elements of the data is preserved.

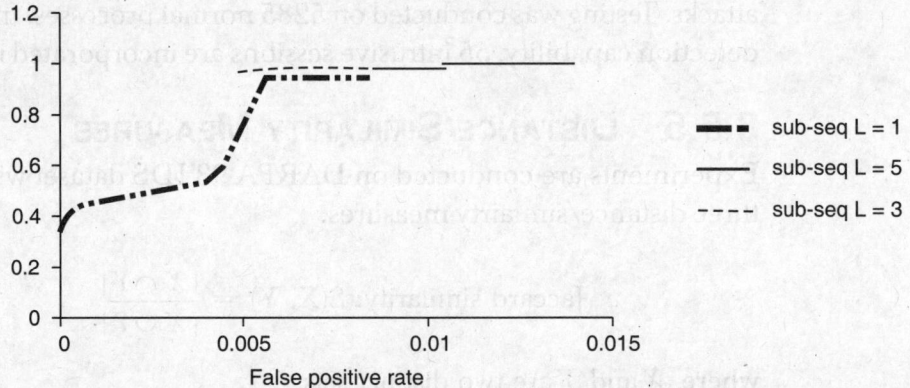

Fig. 8.13   ROC curve for Jaccard similarity metric using kNN classification of $k = 5$

Receiver Operating Characteristics (ROC) curves have drawn for comparing accuracy of a classifier for each distance metric used. The ROC curve is an interesting tool to analyse two-class problems and is very useful in situations where detection of rarely occurring event is done. ROC curve depicts the relationship between False Positive Rate (FPR) and Detection Rate (DR) at various threshold values. DR is the ratio of the number of intrusive sessions (abnormal) detected correctly to the total number of intrusive sessions.

The FPR is defined as the number of normal processes detected as abnormal, divided by the total number of normal processes. ROC curve gives an idea of the trade off between FPR and DR achieved by classifier. An ideal ROC curve would be parallel to FPR axis at DR equal to 1.

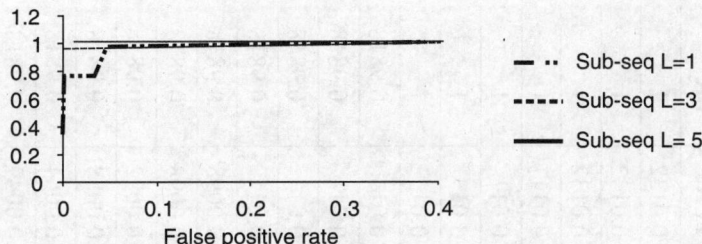

Fig. 8.14 ROC curve for cosine similarity using kNN classification for *k* = 5

Tables 8.4, 8.5, and 8.6 show the FPR and DR values at various thresholds for Jaccard, Cosine and Euclidean (for SL = 1, 2, 3, 4, and 5) respectively and Figures 8.13, 8.14, and 8.15 show the corresponding ROC curves for Jaccard, Cosine and Euclidean (for SL = 1, 2, and 3) respectively. It can be observed from figures that as the sliding window size increases from SL = 1 to SL = 5, high DR (close to ideal value of 1) is observed with all the distance/similarity metrics.

Rate of increase in false positive rate is less for Jaccard similarity measure (0.005-0.015) as compared to Cosine similarity and Euclidian distance (0.05-0.15) (0.1-0.4)

This case study exhibits the application of data mining techniques in the area of Intrusion Detection. In addition, this study describes the usefulness of utilizing subsequence information for kNN classification of sequential data in the context of Intrusion Detection.

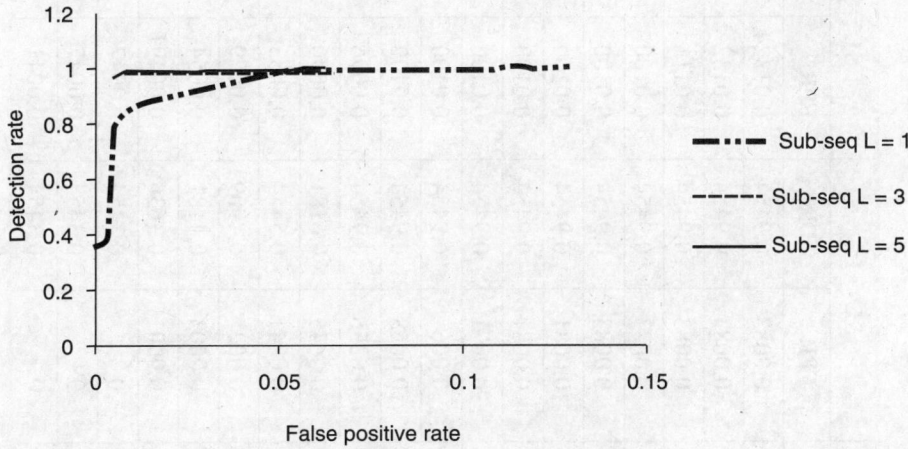

Fig 8.15 ROC curve for Euclidian distance metric kNN classification for *k* =5

Table 8.4   FPR vs DR for Jaccard similarity measure at $k = 5$

Th	SL = 1		SL = 2		SL = 3		SL = 4		SL = 5	
	FPR	DR	FPR	DR	FPR	DR	FPR	DR	FPR	DR
0.99	0.0083	0.9454	0.01324	0.9818	0.0132	1	0.0138	0.9818	0.0132	1
0.98	0.0083	0.9454	0.0132	0.9818	0.0132	1	0.0138	0.9818	0.0132	1
0.97	0.0083	0.9454	0.0111	0.9818	0.0132	1	0.0138	0.9818	0.0132	1
0.95	0.0083	0.9454	0.0100	0.9636	0.0111	1	0.0138	0.9818	0.0111	1
0.93	0.0083	0.9454	0.0100	0.9636	0.01	0.9818	0.0117	0.9818	0.01	1
0.9	0.0081	0.9454	0.0100	0.9636	0.01	0.9818	0.0102	0.9636	0.01	1
0.89	0.0081	0.9454	0.0100	0.9636	0.01	0.9818	0.0102	0.9636	0.01	1
0.88	0.0071	0.9454	0.0100	0.9636	0.01	0.9818	0.0102	0.9636	0.01	0.9818
0.87	0.006	0.9454	0.0100	0.9636	0.01	0.9818	0.0102	0.9636	0.01	0.9818
0.86	0.0058	0.9454	0.0100	0.9636	0.01	0.9818	0.0102	0.9636	0.01	0.9818
0.84	0.0056	0.9454	0.0096	0.9636	0.01	0.9818	0.0102	0.9636	0.01	0.9818
0.8	0.0045	0.6181	0.0090	0.9636	0.0098	0.9818	0.0100	0.9636	0.0098	0.9818
0.78	0.0041	0.5454	0.0083	0.9636	0.0098	0.9818	0.0100	0.9636	0.0098	0.9818
0.75	0.002	0.4909	0.0079	0.9636	0.0092	0.9818	0.0100	0.9636	0.0092	0.9818
0.7	0.0003	0.4181	0.0054	0.9454	0.0088	0.9818	0.0098	0.9636	0.0088	0.9818
0.65	0.0001	0.3636	0.00491	0.9272	0.0064	0.9818	0.0088	0.9636	0.0064	0.9818
0.6	0	0.3454	0.0047	0.9272	0.0049	0.9636	0.0079	0.9636	0.0049	0.9818
0.55	0	0.3454	0.0047	0.9272	0.0049	0.0636	0.0070	0.9636	0.0049	0.9818
0.52	0	0.3454	0.0041	0.9272	0.0049	0.9636	0.0068	0.9636	0.0049	0.9818

Table 8.5 FPR vs DR for cosine similarity measure at $k = 5$

Th	SL = 1		SL = 2		SL = 3		SL = 4		SL = 5	
	FPR	DR	FPR	DR	FPR	DR	FPR	DR	FPR	DR
0.99	0.051	0.963	0.079	0.981	0.129	1	0.480	1	0.364	1
0.98	0.010	0.945	0.053	0.963	0.125	0.981	0.457	0.981	0.326	1
0.97	0.003	0.909	0.038	0.963	0.097	0.981	0.441	0.981	0.325	1
0.95	0.002	0.818	0.022	0.963	0.084	0.981	0.237	0.963	0.319	1
0.93	0.002	0.818	0.019	0.963	0.047	0.981	0.049	0.963	0.098	1
0.90	0.0003	0.763	0.007	0.963	0.037	0.981	0.032	0.963	0.085	1
0.89	0.0003	0.763	0.007	0.963	0.037	0.981	0.025	0.963	0.055	1
0.88	0.0003	0.763	0.006	0.963	0.030	0.981	0.018	0.963	0.055	1
0.87	0	0.763	0.006	0.963	0.029	0.981	0.017	0.963	0.054	1
0.86	0	0.745	0.005	0.963	0.004	0.963	0.015	0.963	0.054	1
0.84	0	0.363	0.004	0.963	0.004	0.963	0.014	0.963	0.052	1
0.80	0	0.363	0.004	0.963	0.004	0.963	0.014	0.963	0.051	1
0.78	0	0.363	0.003	0.963	0.004	0.963	0.007	0.963	0.038	1
0.75	0	0.345	0.003	0.945	0.004	0.963	0.007	0.963	0.037	1
0.7	0	0.345	0.003	0.945	0.004	0.963	0.007	0.963	0.014	0.981

Table 8.6   FPR vs DR for Euclidean distance measure at $k = 5$

Th	SL = 1		SL = 2		SL = 3		SL = 4		SL = 5	
	FPR	DR	FPR	DR	FPR	DR	FPR	DR	FPR	DR
0.99	0.0052	0.7272	0.0087	0.9272	0.0089	0.98181	0.0107	0.9636	0.0121	0.9636
0.98	0.0026	0.3454	0.0066	0.9272	0.0073	0.9636	0.0094	0.9636	0.0111	0.9636
0.97	0.0026	0.3454	0.0056	0.9272	0.0064	0.9636	0.0085	0.9636	0.01021	0.9636
0.95	0.0017	0.3454	0.0056	0.9272	0.0064	0.9636	0.0085	0.9636	0.01021	0.9636
0.93	0.0015	0.3454	0.0055	0.9272	0.0064	0.9636	0.0083	0.9636	0.01021	0.9636
0.9	0.0015	0.3454	0.0055	0.9272	0.0062	0.96363	0.0083	0.9636	0.01021	0.9636
0.89	0.0015	0.3454	0.0055	0.9272	0.0062	0.96363	0.0083	0.9636	0.01002	0.9636
0.86	0.0015	0.3454	0.0055	0.9272	0.0062	0.96363	0.0083	0.9636	0.01002	0.9636
0.84	0.0002	0.3454	0.0042	0.9272	0.0049	0.96363	0.007	0.9636	0.00851	0.9636
0.8	0	0.3454	0.004	0.9272	0.0047	0.96363	0.0068	0.9636	0.00851	0.9636
0.78	0	0.3454	0.004	0.9272	0.0047	0.96363	0.0068	0.9636	0.00851	0.9636
0.75	0	0.3454	0.004	0.9272	0.0047	0.96363	0.0068	0.9636	0.00851	0.9636
0.7	0	0.3454	0.004	0.9272	0.0047	0.96363	0.0068	0.9636	0.00851	0.9636

SUMMARY

In this chapter, we described a number of case studies to showcase the potential of pattern discovery technologies. These case studies covered a range of technologies from data warehousing to OLAP and data mining. Case studies 1–3 were related to data warehousing and OLAP for the domains of telecom industry, fast food industry and banks, respectively. Case studies 4-5 were related to data mining. Case study 4 identified customer churn (i.e. unsatisfied customers who leave) from banks, while Case study 5 identified intruders into a computer system.

EXERCISES

1. For each of the case studies described in this chapter, describe a few potentially interesting patterns from a user's-viewpoint. Also, describe the kind of queries that the user would be interested in asking.

2. For each of the case studies described in this chapter, describe alternative technologies that could have been used and compare them with the technology described in this chapter.

3. Write a survey paper summarizing several case study[+] research papers on pattern discovery.

[+] Refer the Proceedings of the International Workshop on Data Mining Case Studies (www.dataminingcasestudies.com)

CURRENT TRENDS IN
PATTERN DISCOVERY

Don't follow a trend. Follow your heart.
—KRIST NOVOSELIC

INTRODUCTION

Pattern discovery is an exciting multi-disciplinary field that has attracted the attention of research, academia, and industry. The scope for high-impact problems and elegant solutions perpetuates the interest in this subject. Researchers have identified various kinds of patterns, such as classification/regression models, clusters, association rules, frequent sequences, time-series patterns, data cubes, etc. Among these different data mining tasks, frequent pattern mining, classification and clustering have received most attention from the data mining research community. This is perhaps justified by the fact that most other data mining tasks can be reduced to these three. Here are some examples of such reductions:

1. Association rules may be considered as merely another way to represent frequent itemsets.

2. Time-series are a special case of sequence databases and mining them reduces to mining frequent sequences.

3. Regression can be reduced to classification if the dependent attribute (i.e. the attribute whose values are to be estimated) is discretized into small ranges.

4. Outlier mining can be reduced to clustering, and then identifying data points that do not lie in any cluster.

In this context, the question naturally arises as to whether there is *really* anything more in data mining than frequent pattern mining, classification and clustering. This is an important question because if it is answered in the affirmative, then future research may rather focus on the aspects of data mining that are beyond these core tasks. On the other hand, if the question is answered in the negative, then we may well consider data mining as a 'closed problem' because of the availability of very efficient algorithms for these three core tasks.

The objective of this chapter is to discuss this high impact and provocative question, which is basically a disguised way of asking: Do any fundamental research issues remain to be solved in data mining?

9.1 TEN CHALLENGING PROBLEMS

The short answer to the question of whether fundamental research issues remain in pattern discovery is: Yes. Even though the core tasks of pattern discovery are well-solved, it only means that the available solutions can be used as tools to solve larger problems. A recent survey conducted by Qiang Yang and Xindong Wu identified ten challenging problems that remain to be solved satisfactorily. Below, we briefly describe them.

9.1.1 DEVELOPING A UNIFYING THEORY OF DATA MINING

The field of data mining has developed in an *ad hoc* manner by attempting to solve bits and pieces of the larger puzzle of finding interesting patterns. Researchers had identified different tasks, such as classification, clustering, frequent pattern mining, etc. However, there is no theory that unifies these approaches. A unifying theory can help to intelligibly answer questions like "Are there other interesting pattern types yet to be discovered?" It can thus provide a direction for future research.

A unifying theory can also help in developing pattern discovery systems that are more automated, requiring very little input from the analyst. It is possible to conceive a system that takes a database as input, studies its schema and distribution, and outputs all potentially interesting patterns (of all types).

9.1.2 SCALING UP FOR HIGH-DIMENSIONAL DATA AND HIGH-SPEED STREAMS

With increasing capacity of computer hardware systems and digital equipment, the amount of total data available is enormous. New applications are being conceived that make use of this data. Text and web data mining applications are modeled with millions of features. High-speed data streams such, as from network traffic, sensor networks, and RFID applications also pose a scalability problem. The records flowing in a stream are too many, and they arrive too fast. So, they cannot be stored. Any analysis must be done 'on the fly'.

9.1.3 MINING SEQUENCE AND TIME-SERIES DATA

Clustering, classification, and trend prediction in sequence and time-series data remains an open problem. Examples include stock-market data, weather parameters, health parameters of patients, and so on. In most applications, the time-series data is not self-contained – i.e. its trend cannot be predicted by analysing the available data only. For example, stock-market data may be influenced by external variables, such as news paper and television reports. Another problem is the presence of *noise* (i.e. inaccurate data values). Mining patterns from such data is a challenging problem.

9.1.4 MINING COMPLEX KNOWLEDGE FROM COMPLEX DATA

Real-world data is usually complex and is modeled as such. Pattern discovery from spatial, text, web, multimedia, and graph data has, started recently. One direction is to integrate all these different systems – it is possible to conceive a system that takes as input a database with complex types, studies its schema and distribution, and outputs all potentially interesting patterns (of all types). It is also desirable to automate the pattern discovery system to be able to suggest real-world decisions in the decision-making process, instead of merely outputting patterns.

9.1.5 MINING COMMUNITY AND SOCIAL NETWORKS

Social networking sites are among the most talked-about areas of content growth on the Internet. Some of the better known sites include friendster.com, myspace.com, facebook.com, and classmates.com. In these websites, individuals with similar personal and/or professional interests can create an online 'profile' and share information about those interests so that others can read about them. Knowing how to mine this wealth of information that people post about themselves (or what their friends post about them) can be a boon to online researchers needing to find out background information on people, or to help locate someone who has gone missing.

Such community information is not always available directly. Instead, it could be inferred from multiple sources, such as in websites, blogs, emails, and address books. For example, we can model the address books of people as a graph where nodes are people and a link is present to indicate the presence of an entry in the address book. By searching for cliques in this graph, it is possible to form communities of closely knit people. It is also possible to find a set of links that connect any two people.

9.1.6   Mining Distributed and Multi-agent Data

Mining data that is distributed on multiple geographically separated servers is not an easy problem as indicated in Section 5.4. This problem becomes much more difficult if the different sites contain data in different formats and schemas. An example is the data of people located in different banks along with the data related to their tax payments. Such multi-relational data mining is an important problem, since it reflects the kind of data available in real life.

Moreover, it is possible that the data is manipulated by *adversaries* in order to prevent some patterns from being detected, such as in email spam, intrusion detection, fraud detection, etc. To perform such *adversary data mining,* it would be necessary to combine data mining with game theory.

9.1.7   Data Mining for Biological and Environmental Problems

Bioinformatics deals with the application of computer science to genetics and related areas. Its main purpose is to understand the functioning of living organisms at the level of genes, and the way they regulate metabolism through the formation of necessary proteins. It has very important applications: (i) developing new medicines for dreaded diseases like cancer, and (ii) developing new crops or animals with desired characteristics, such as nutrition and strength. As with any other capable science, it can be used for negative purposes like the creation of biological weapons.

Bioinformatics is considered as one of the 'killer' applications of data mining. The available data related to genes, proteins, and metabolomes is enormously large. Most of this data is freely downloadable. Due to the size of the data, domain scientists depend heavily on data mining to extract potentially interesting patterns of interactions and relationships between genes, proteins, and their functions in metabolism. Laboratory experiments may then be done to validate the hypotheses suggested by data mining. The experiments are usually very expensive and so, it is important that the data mining algorithms are very accurate in their predictions.

Data mining may also be used to analyse large amounts of data related to environmental factors, such as local weather patterns and global climatic conditions. It can be used in various studies: the environmental effects of pollution of specific industries, the nature in which environmental factors influence each other, and the way they influence agricultural pests, droughts, hurricanes, volcanic eruptions, etc.

9.1.8   DATA MINING PROCESS RELATED PROBLEMS

In spite of the drive to automate as much as possible, pattern discovery is still quite an art and requires expert manual guidance. It requires data gathering, data cleaning, selecting features, selecting the data mining task, selecting the interesting results, and selecting the manner in which results are to be visualized. As mentioned in the beginning of the previous chapter, it is estimated that 90% of the total effort of pattern discovery is in data preprocessing (gathering, integrating, and cleaning).

It is therefore important that data mining is applied to automate these processes themselves. For example, classification algorithms can be used to identify erroneous portions of the data that may require cleaning. Reducing the cost of these processes will have a greater impact now than the development of better core data mining algorithms.

9.1.9   SECURITY, PRIVACY, AND DATA INTEGRITY

Organizations and individuals need to hide and protect their sensitive data. This is opposed to the nature of data mining, whose purpose is to extract implicit hidden patterns and information from data. Several issues arise due to this mismatch of technologies, as has been described in Chapter 1. These issues include:

1. How to discover patterns from data that has been made inaccurate to protect privacy?

2. How to modify data to ensure privacy and yet preserve inherent patterns?

3. How to modify data minimally to hide sensitive patterns?

4. Can discovered patterns be used to retrieve original data records?

The last question can be answered affirmatively for patterns that are too specific. For example, a pattern like 'men in ABC company who wear red hats also grow beards' would compromise privacy if there are only few men who wear red hats.

9.1.10 DEALING WITH NON-STATIC, UNBALANCED, AND COST-SENSITIVE DATA

Most existing data mining techniques assume that the underlying data distribution is static and does not change with time. Unfortunately, this is unlikely to hold true for most real-world datasets. In some cases, changes may be so rapid that by the time data mining analysis is carried out, the underlying patterns may have changed. New techniques are required to handle such cases.

Many existing techniques assume that the available data is balanced – i.e. all classes are equally likely. They also assume cost-sensitive data – i.e. the costs of misclassification are the same for both false positives and false negatives. These assumptions do not hold in many important applications, such as email spam detection and credit card fraud detection.

The number of spams and frauds will be only a small fraction of the whole data (hopefully!). Also, it is usually okay to have a few spam emails in your inbox; but it may be costly if some of your regular important emails are classified into your spam folder. For credit card operations, on the other hand, it may be very costly to allow even a single fraud. It is okay to suspect a normal operation as fraud and confirm the operation by asking the customer.

SUMMARY

This chapter described ten topics that deserve more attention from the research community. The identification of these topics was the outcome of a recent survey conducted by Qiang Yang and Xindong Wu. One more topic that deserves attention is the design of parameter-free algorithms. Most data mining algorithms have several parameters that must be set by the user. Selecting values for these parameters is currently a 'black-art' and techniques need to be developed to obtain them automatically. Algorithms need not be totally parameter-free—however, the designers must ensure that parameters make sense to the end-user, and thereby enhance the algorithm instead of being a burden.

We close this chapter and this book by commenting that pattern discovery is an essential component of any intelligent system. A perfect system for pattern discovery is an 'AI-Complete' problem. This term denotes that it reduces to the problem of designing a true and fully intelligent system – a problem that has eluded the best minds over the last century.

INDEX